SECOND EDITION

Prometheus: Up & Running
Infrastructure and Application
Performance Monitoring

Julien Pivotto and Brian Brazil

Beijing · Boston · Farnham · Sebastopol · Tokyo

Prometheus: Up & Running, Second Edition

by Julien Pivotto and Brian Brazil

Published by O'Reilly Media, Inc., 1005 Gravenstein Highway North, Sebastopol, CA 95472.

O'Reilly books may be purchased for educational, business, or sales promotional use. Online editions are also available for most titles (*http://oreilly.com*). For more information, contact our corporate/institutional sales department: 800-998-9938 or *corporate@oreilly.com*.

Acquisitions Editor: John Devins	**Indexer:** Ellen Troutman-Zaig
Development Editor: Rita Fernando	**Interior Designer:** David Futato
Production Editor: Ashley Stussy	**Cover Designer:** Karen Montgomery
Copyeditor: Kim Cofer	**Illustrator:** Kate Dullea
Proofreader: Sonia Saruba	

July 2018:	First Edition
April 2023:	Second Edition

Revision History for the Second Edition

2023-04-04:   First Release

See *http://oreilly.com/catalog/errata.csp?isbn=9781098131142* for release details.

978-1-098-13114-2

[LSI]

Table of Contents

Preface. xi

Part I.   Introduction

1. **What Is Prometheus?**. 3
  What Is Monitoring?   4
    A Brief and Incomplete History of Monitoring   6
    Categories of Monitoring   7
  Prometheus Architecture   11
    Client Libraries   12
    Exporters   13
    Service Discovery   14
    Scraping   14
    Storage   15
    Dashboards   15
    Recording Rules and Alerts   16
    Alert Management   16
    Long-Term Storage   17
  What Prometheus Is Not   17

2. **Getting Started with Prometheus**. 19
  Running Prometheus   19
  Using the Expression Browser   23
  Running the Node Exporter   27
  Alerting   31

Part II. Application Monitoring

3. Instrumentation. **41**
  A Simple Program   41
  The Counter   43
    Counting Exceptions   45
    Counting Size   47
  The Gauge   47
    Using Gauges   48
    Callbacks   50
  The Summary   50
  The Histogram   52
    Buckets   53
  Unit Testing Instrumentation   56
  Approaching Instrumentation   57
    What Should I Instrument?   57
    How Much Should I Instrument?   59
    What Should I Name My Metrics?   60

4. Exposition. **65**
  Python   66
    WSGI   66
    Twisted   67
    Multiprocess with Gunicorn   68
  Go   71
  Java   72
    HTTPServer   73
    Servlet   74
  Pushgateway   76
  Bridges   79
  Parsers   80
  Text Exposition Format   80
    Metric Types   81
    Labels   82
    Escaping   82
    Timestamps   82
    check metrics   83
  OpenMetrics   83
    Metric Types   84
    Labels   85
    Timestamps   85

5. Labels.. 87
What Are Labels?   87
Instrumentation and Target Labels   88
Instrumentation   88
   Metric   90
   Multiple Labels   90
   Child   91
Aggregating   93
Label Patterns   94
   Enum   94
   Info   96
When to Use Labels   98
   Cardinality   99

6. Dashboarding with Grafana............................. 103
Installation   104
Data Source   106
Dashboards and Panels   107
   Avoiding the Wall of Graphs   109
Time Series Panel   109
   Time Controls   111
Stat Panel   113
Table Panel   115
State Timeline Panel   117
Template Variables   118

Part III.   Infrastructure Monitoring

7. Node Exporter... 125
CPU Collector   126
Filesystem Collector   127
Diskstats Collector   128
Netdev Collector   129
Meminfo Collector   130
Hwmon Collector   130
Stat Collector   131
Uname Collector   132
OS Collector   132
Loadavg Collector   132
Pressure Collector   133
Textfile Collector   134

Using the Textfile Collector   135
Timestamps   137

8. Service Discovery. 139
Service Discovery Mechanisms   140
Static   141
File   142
HTTP   145
Consul   146
EC2   148
Relabeling   149
Choosing What to Scrape   150
Target Labels   153
How to Scrape   162
metric_relabel_configs   164
Label Clashes and honor_labels   166

9. Containers and Kubernetes. 169
cAdvisor   169
CPU   170
Memory   171
Labels   171
Kubernetes   172
Running in Kubernetes   172
Service Discovery   174
kube-state-metrics   184
Alternative Deployments   185

10. Common Exporters. 187
Consul   187
MySQLd   189
Grok Exporter   191
Blackbox   194
ICMP   195
TCP   199
HTTP   201
DNS   204
Prometheus Configuration   205

11. Working with Other Monitoring Systems. 209
Other Monitoring Systems   209
InfluxDB   211

StatsD   212

12. **Writing Exporters.** **215**
    Consul Telemetry   215
    Custom Collectors   219
      Labels   223
    Guidelines   224

Part IV.   PromQL

13. **Introduction to PromQL.** **229**
    Aggregation Basics   229
      Gauge   229
      Counter   231
      Summary   232
      Histogram   233
    Selectors   235
      Matchers   235
      Instant Vector   237
      Range Vector   238
      Subqueries   240
      Offset   241
      At Modifier   242
    HTTP API   242
      query   242
      query_range   245

14. **Aggregation Operators.** **249**
    Grouping   249
      without   250
      by   251
    Operators   252
      sum   252
      count   253
      avg   254
      group   255
      stddev and stdvar   255
      min and max   256
      topk and bottomk   256
      quantile   257
      count_values   258

15. Binary Operators. **261**

Working with Scalars   261
  Arithmetic Operators   261
  Trigonometric Operator   263
  Comparison Operators   263
Vector Matching   265
  One-to-One   266
  Many-to-One and group_left   268
  Many-to-Many and Logical Operators   271
Operator Precedence   275

16. Functions. **277**

Changing Type   277
  vector   278
  scalar   278
Math   279
  abs   279
  ln, log2, and log10   279
  exp   280
  sqrt   280
  ceil and floor   281
  round   281
  clamp, clamp_max, and clamp_min   281
  sgn   282
  Trigonometric Functions   282
Time and Date   283
  time   283
  minute, hour, day_of_week, day_of_month, day_of_year, days_in_month,
    month, and year   284
  timestamp   285
Labels   286
  label_replace   286
  label_join   286
Missing Series, absent, and absent_over_time   287
Sorting with sort and sort_desc   288
Histograms with histogram_quantile   288
Counters   289
  rate   289
  increase   291
  irate   291
  resets   292
Changing Gauges   293

changes 293
deriv 293
predict_linear 294
delta 294
idelta 294
holt_winters 295
Aggregation Over Time 295

17. **Recording Rules.** **297**
Using Recording Rules 297
When to Use Recording Rules 300
Reducing Cardinality 300
Composing Range Vector Functions 302
Rules for APIs 302
How Not to Use Rules 303
Naming of Recording Rules 304

Part V. Alerting

18. **Alerting.** **311**
Alerting Rules 312
for 314
Alert Labels 316
Annotations and Templates 318
What Are Good Alerts? 321
Configuring Alertmanagers in Prometheus 322
External Labels 323

19. **Alertmanager.** **325**
Notification Pipeline 325
Configuration File 326
Routing Tree 327
Receivers 334
Inhibitions 344
Alertmanager Web Interface 345

Part VI. Deployment

20. **Server-Side Security.** **351**
Security Features Provided by Prometheus 351

Enabling TLS   351
Advanced TLS Options   353
Enabling Basic Authentication   354

21. Putting It All Together.................................... 357
Planning a Rollout   357
Growing Prometheus   359
Going Global with Federation   360
Long-Term Storage   363
Running Prometheus   365
Hardware   365
Configuration Management   367
Networks and Authentication   368
Planning for Failure   370
Alertmanager Clustering   372
Meta- and Cross-Monitoring   373
Managing Performance   374
Detecting a Problem   375
Finding Expensive Metrics and Targets   375
Reducing Load   376
Horizontal Sharding   377
Managing Change   379
Getting Help   379

Index... 381

Preface

This book describes in detail how to use the Prometheus monitoring system to monitor, graph, and alert on the performance of your applications and infrastructure. This book is intended for application developers, system administrators, and everyone in between.

Expanding the Known

When it comes to monitoring, knowing that the systems you care about are turned on is important, but that's not where the real value is. The big wins are in understanding the performance of your systems.

By performance we don't only mean the response time of and CPU used by each request, but the broader meaning of performance. How many requests to the database are required for each customer order that is processed? Is it time to purchase higher throughput networking equipment? How many machines are your cache misses costing? Are enough of your users interacting with a complex feature in order to justify its continued existence?

These are the sorts of questions that a metrics-based monitoring system can help you answer, and beyond that help you dig into why the answer is what it is. We see monitoring as getting insight from throughout your system, from high-level overviews down to the nitty-gritty details that are useful for debugging. A full set of monitoring tools for debugging and analysis includes not only metrics, but also logs, traces, and profiling; but metrics should be your first port of call when you want to answer systems-level questions.

Prometheus encourages you to have instrumentation liberally spread across your systems, from applications all the way down to the bare metal. With instrumentation you can observe how all your subsystems and components are interacting, and convert unknowns into knowns.

The Evolution of Prometheus

As Prometheus has crossed the 10-year mark, this second edition brings new developments across all sections. Prometheus has continued to evolve and expand, offering even more options for scraping, storing, and querying data. This progress is a result of the dedicated community of users and contributors who use Prometheus across a wide and growing range of industries and applications.

The second edition of this book provides coverage of the many new PromQL functions, service discovery providers, and Alertmanager receivers that have been added since the first edition.

A new dedicated chapter covers server-side security features, such as TLS, that have been added to Prometheus and some of the exporters.

Conventions Used in This Book

The following typographical conventions are used in this book:

Italic
> Indicates new terms, URLs, email addresses, filenames, and file extensions.

`Constant width`
> Used for program listings, as well as within paragraphs to refer to program elements such as variable or function names, databases, data types, environment variables, statements, and keywords.

`Constant width bold`
> Shows commands or other text that should be typed literally by the user.

`Constant width italic`
> Shows text that should be replaced with user-supplied values or by values determined by context.

> This element signifies a tip or suggestion.

> This element signifies a general note.

This element indicates a warning or caution.

Using Code Examples

Supplemental material (code examples, configuration files, etc.) is available for download at *https://github.com/prometheus-up-and-running-2e/examples*.

If you have a technical question or a problem using the code examples, please send email to *bookquestions@oreilly.com*.

This book is here to help you get your job done. In general, if example code is offered with this book, you may use it in your programs and documentation. You do not need to contact us for permission unless you're reproducing a significant portion of the code. For example, writing a program that uses several chunks of code from this book does not require permission. Selling or distributing examples from O'Reilly books does require permission. Answering a question by citing this book and quoting example code does not require permission. Incorporating a significant amount of example code from this book into your product's documentation does require permission.

We appreciate, but generally do not require, attribution. An attribution usually includes the title, author, publisher, and ISBN. For example: "*Prometheus: Up & Running*, Second Edition by Julien Pivotto and Brian Brazil (O'Reilly). Copyright 2023 Julien Pivotto, 978-1-098-13114-2."

If you feel your use of code examples falls outside fair use or the permission given above, feel free to contact us at *permissions@oreilly.com*.

O'Reilly Online Learning

 For more than 40 years, *O'Reilly Media* has provided technology and business training, knowledge, and insight to help companies succeed.

Our unique network of experts and innovators share their knowledge and expertise through books, articles, and our online learning platform. O'Reilly's online learning platform gives you on-demand access to live training courses, in-depth learning paths, interactive coding environments, and a vast collection of text and video from O'Reilly and 200+ other publishers. For more information, visit *https://oreilly.com*.

How to Contact Us

Please address comments and questions concerning this book to the publisher:

O'Reilly Media, Inc.
1005 Gravenstein Highway North
Sebastopol, CA 95472
800-998-9938 (in the United States or Canada)
707-829-0515 (international or local)
707-829-0104 (fax)

We have a web page for this book, where we list errata, examples, and any additional information. You can access this page at *https://oreil.ly/prometheus-up-running-2e*.

Email *bookquestions@oreilly.com* to comment or ask technical questions about this book.

For news and information about our books and courses, visit *https://oreilly.com*.

Find us on LinkedIn: *https://linkedin.com/company/oreilly-media*

Follow us on Twitter: *https://twitter.com/oreillymedia*

Watch us on YouTube: *https://youtube.com/oreillymedia*

Acknowledgments

This book would not have been possible without all the work of the Prometheus team, and the hundreds of contributors to Prometheus and its ecosystem. A special thanks to Julius Volz, Richard Hartmann, Carl Bergquist, Andrew McMillan, and Greg Stark for providing feedback on initial drafts of the first revision of this book. Thanks to Brian Brazil, Bartłomiej Płotka, Carl Bergquist, TJ Hoplock, and Richard Hartmann for their feedback on the second edition.

PART I

Introduction

This section will introduce you to monitoring in general, and Prometheus more specifically.

In Chapter 1 you will learn about the many different meanings of monitoring and approaches to it, the metrics approach that Prometheus takes, and the architecture of Prometheus.

In Chapter 2 you will get your hands dirty running a simple Prometheus setup that scrapes machine metrics, evaluates queries, and sends alert notifications.

CHAPTER 1
What Is Prometheus?

Prometheus is an open source, metrics-based monitoring system. Of course, Prometheus is far from the only one of those out there, so what makes it notable?

Prometheus does one thing and it does it well. It has a simple yet powerful data model and a query language that lets you analyze how your applications and infrastructure are performing. It does not try to solve problems outside of the metrics space, leaving those to other more appropriate tools.

Since its beginnings with no more than a handful of developers working in Sound-Cloud in 2012, a community and ecosystem has grown around Prometheus. Prometheus is primarily written in Go and licensed under the Apache 2.0 license. There are hundreds of people who have contributed to the project itself, which is not controlled by any one company. It is always hard to tell how many users an open source project has, but we estimate that as of 2022, hundreds of thousands of organizations are using Prometheus in production. In 2016 the Prometheus project became the second member[1] of the Cloud Native Computing Foundation (CNCF).

For instrumenting your own code, there are client libraries in all the popular languages and runtimes, including Go, Java/JVM, C#/.Net, Python, Ruby, Node.js, Haskell, Erlang, and Rust. Many popular applications are already instrumented with Prometheus client libraries, like Kubernetes, Docker, Envoy, and Vault. For third-party software that exposes metrics in a non-Prometheus format, there are hundreds of integrations available. These are called exporters, and include HAProxy, MySQL, PostgreSQL, Redis, JMX, SNMP, Consul, and Kafka. A friend of Brian's even added support for monitoring Minecraft servers, as he cares a lot about his frames per second.

---

1 Kubernetes was the first member.

A simple text format[2] makes it easy to expose metrics to Prometheus. Other monitoring systems, both open source and commercial, have added support for this format. This allows all of these monitoring systems to focus more on core features, rather than each having to spend time duplicating effort to support every single piece of software a user like you may wish to monitor.

The data model identifies each time series not just with a name, but also with an unordered set of key-value pairs called labels. The PromQL query language allows aggregation across any of these labels, so you can analyze not just per process but also per datacenter and per service or by any other labels that you have defined. These can be graphed in dashboard systems such as Grafana (*https://oreil.ly/f5uMZ*) and Perses (*https://oreil.ly/YF-xW*).

Alerts can be defined using the exact same PromQL query language that you use for graphing. If you can graph it, you can alert on it. Labels make maintaining alerts easier, as you can create a single alert covering all possible label values. In some other monitoring systems you would have to individually create an alert per machine/application. Relatedly, service discovery can automatically determine what applications and machines should be scraped from sources such as Kubernetes, Consul, Amazon Elastic Compute Cloud (EC2), Azure, Google Compute Engine (GCE), and OpenStack.

For all these features and benefits, Prometheus is efficient and simple to run. A single Prometheus server can ingest millions of samples per second. It is a single, statically linked binary with a configuration file. All components of Prometheus can be run in containers, and they avoid doing anything fancy that would get in the way of configuration management tools. It is designed to be integrated into the infrastructure you already have and built on top of, not to be a management platform itself.

Now that you have an overview of what Prometheus is, let's step back for a minute and look at what is meant by "monitoring" in order to provide some context. Following that, we will look at what the main components of Prometheus are, and what Prometheus is not.

What Is Monitoring?

In secondary school, one of Brian's teachers told him that if you were to ask 10 economists what economics means, you'd get 11 answers. Monitoring has a similar lack of consensus as to what exactly it means. When he tells others what he does, people think his job entails everything from keeping an eye on temperature in factories, to

---

2 Next to the simple text format, a more standardized version, slightly different, called OpenMetrics has been created out of the Prometheus text format.

employee monitoring where he is the one to find out who is accessing Facebook during working hours, and even detecting intruders on networks.

Prometheus wasn't built to do any of those things.[3] It was built to aid software developers and administrators in the operation of production computer systems, such as the applications, tools, databases, and networks backing popular websites.

So what is monitoring in that context? Let's narrow this sort of operational monitoring of computer systems down to four things:

Alerting

Knowing when things are going wrong is usually the most important thing that you want monitoring for. You want the monitoring system to call in a human to take a look.

Debugging

Now that you have called in a human, they need to investigate to determine the root cause and ultimately resolve whatever the issue is.

Trending

Alerting and debugging usually happen on timescales on the order of minutes to hours. While less urgent, the ability to see how your systems are being used and changing over time is also useful. Trending can feed into design decisions and processes such as capacity planning.

Plumbing

When all you have is a hammer, everything starts to look like a nail. At the end of the day, all monitoring systems are data processing pipelines. Sometimes it is more convenient to appropriate part of your monitoring system for another purpose, rather than building a bespoke solution. This is not strictly monitoring, but it is common in practice so we like to include it.

Depending on who you talk to and their background, they may consider only some of these to be monitoring. This leads to many discussions about monitoring going around in circles, leaving everyone frustrated. To help you understand where others are coming from, we're going to look at a small bit of the history of monitoring.

---

3 Temperature monitoring of machines and datacenters is actually not uncommon. There are even a few users using Prometheus to track the weather for fun.

A Brief and Incomplete History of Monitoring

Monitoring has seen a shift toward tools including Prometheus in the past few years. For a long time, the dominant solution has been some combination of Nagios and Graphite or their variants.

When we say Nagios, we are including any software within the same broad family, such as Icinga, Zmon, and Sensu. They work primarily by regularly executing scripts called *checks*. If a check fails by returning a nonzero exit code, an alert is generated. Nagios was initially started by Ethan Galstad in 1996 as an MS-DOS application used to perform pings. It was first released as NetSaint in 1999, and renamed Nagios in 2002.

To talk about the history of Graphite, we need to go back to 1994. Tobias Oetiker created a Perl script that became Multi Router Traffic Grapher, or MRTG 1.0, in 1995. As the name indicates, it was mainly used for network monitoring via the Simple Network Management Protocol (SNMP). It could also obtain metrics by executing scripts.[4] The year 1997 brought big changes with a move of some code to C, and the creation of the Round Robin Database (RRD), which was used to store metric data. This brought notable performance improvements, and RRD was the basis for other tools, including Smokeping and Graphite.

Started in 2006, Graphite uses Whisper for metrics storage, which has a similar design to RRD. Graphite does not collect data itself, rather it is sent in by collection tools such as collectd and StatsD, which were created in 2005 and 2010, respectively.

The key takeaway here is that graphing and alerting were once completely separate concerns performed by different tools. You could write a check script to evaluate a query in Graphite and generate alerts on that basis, but most checks tended to be on unexpected states such as a process not running.

Another holdover from this era is the relatively manual approach to administering computer services. Services were deployed on individual machines and lovingly cared for by system administrators. Alerts that might potentially indicate a problem were jumped upon by devoted engineers. As cloud and cloud native technologies such as EC2, Docker, and Kubernetes have come to prominence, treating individual machines and services like pets with each getting individual attention does not scale. Rather, they tend to be looked at more as cattle and administered and monitored as a group. In the same way that the industry has moved from doing management by hand, to tools like Chef and Ansible, to now starting to use technologies like Kubernetes, monitoring also needs to make a similar transition. This means moving

---

4 Brian has fond memories of setting up MRTG in the early 2000s, writing scripts to report temperature and network usage on my home computers.

from checks on individual processes on individual machines to monitoring based on service health as a whole.

Moving to a more recent time, OpenTelemetry is born from two other open source projects, OpenCensus and OpenTracing. OTel[5] is a specification and a set of components that aim to offer built-in telemetry for projects. Its metrics component is compatible with Prometheus with the addition of the OpenTelemetry collector,[6] which is responsible for collecting and providing metrics to your Prometheus server.

You may have noticed that we didn't mention logging, tracing, and profiling. Historically, logs have been used as something that you use `tail`, `grep`, and `awk` on by hand. You might have had an analysis tool such as AWStats to produce reports hourly or daily. In more recent years, logs have also been used as a significant part of monitoring, such as with the Elasticsearch, Logstash, and Kibana (ELK) and OpenSearch stack. Tracing and profiling are generally done with their own software stack: Zipkin and Jaeger are made for tracing, while Parca and Pyroscope deal with continuous profiling.

Now that we have looked a bit at graphing and alerting, let's look at how metrics and logs fit into the landscape. Are there more categories of monitoring than those two?

Categories of Monitoring

At the end of the day, most monitoring is about the same thing: events. Events can be almost anything, including:

- Receiving an HTTP request
- Sending an HTTP 400 response
- Entering a function
- Reaching the `else` of an `if` statement
- Leaving a function
- A user logging in
- Writing data to disk
- Reading data from the network
- Requesting more memory from the kernel

---

5 OTel is an informal name for OpenTelemetry.

6 At the time of writing, developers at a Prometheus developer summit have decided that the Prometheus server will support the OTel protocol natively in the future, but there is no firm decision about when and how this will happen.

All events also have context. An HTTP request will have the IP address it is coming from and going to, the URL being requested, the cookies that are set, and the user who made the request. An HTTP response will have how long the response took, the HTTP status code, and the length of the response body. Events involving functions have the call stack of the functions above them, and whatever triggered this part of the stack, such as an HTTP request.

Having all the context for all the events would be great for debugging and understanding how your systems are performing in both technical and business terms, but that amount of data is not practical to process and store. Thus, we see roughly four ways to approach reducing that volume of data to something workable, namely profiling, tracing, logging, and metrics.

Profiling

Profiling takes the approach that you can't have all the context for all of the events all of the time, but you can have some of the context for limited periods of time.

Tcpdump is one example of a profiling tool. It allows you to record network traffic based on a specified filter. It's an essential debugging tool, but you can't really turn it on all the time as you will run out of disk space.

Debug builds of binaries that track profiling data are another example. They provide a plethora of useful information, but the performance impact of gathering all that information, such as timings of every function call, means that it is not generally practical to run it in production on an ongoing basis.

In the Linux kernel, enhanced Berkeley Packet Filters (eBPF) allow detailed profiling of kernel events from filesystem operations to network oddities. These provide access to a level of insight that was not generally available previously. eBPF comes with other advantages, such as portability and safety. We'd recommend reading Brendan Gregg's writings (*https://oreil.ly/n15mM*) on the subject.

Profiling is largely for tactical debugging. If it is being used on a longer-term basis, then the data volume must be cut down in order to fit into one of the other categories of monitoring, or you'd need to move to *continuous profiling*, which enables the collection over longer runs.

What's new with continuous profiling is that in order to cut down the data volume and keep a relatively low overhead, it reduces the profiling frequency. One of the emerging continuous profiling tools, the eBPF-based Parca (*https://parca.dev*) Agent, uses a 19Hz frequency.[7] As a consequence, it tries to get statistically significant data over minutes rather than seconds, while still providing the data required to

---

7 To be compared to Go runtime's 100Hz frequency or even 10,000Hz in Chromium.

understand how the CPU time is spent in an infrastructure, and helping to improve application efficiency where it's needed.

Tracing

Tracing doesn't typically look at all events, rather it takes some proportion of events such as one in a hundred that pass through some functions of interest. Tracing will note the functions in the stack trace of the points of interest, and often also how long each of these functions took to execute. From this you can get an idea of where your program is spending time and which code paths are most contributing to latency.

Rather than doing snapshots of stack traces at points of interest, some tracing systems trace and record timings of every function call below the function of interest. For example, one in a hundred user HTTP requests might be sampled, and for those requests you could see how much time was spent talking to backends such as databases and caches. This allows you to see how timings differ based on factors like cache hits versus cache misses.

Distributed tracing takes this a step further. It makes tracing work across processes by attaching unique IDs to requests that are passed from one process to another in remote procedure calls (RPCs) in addition to whether this request is one that should be traced. The traces from different processes and machines can be stitched back together based on the request ID. This is a vital tool for debugging distributed microservices architectures. Technologies in this space include OpenZipkin and Jaeger.

For tracing, it is the sampling that keeps the data volumes and instrumentation performance impact within reason.

Logging

Logging looks at a limited set of events and records some of the context for each of these events. For example, it may look at all incoming HTTP requests, or all outgoing database calls. To avoid consuming too many resources, as a rule of thumb you are limited to somewhere around a hundred fields per log entry. Beyond that, bandwidth and storage space tend to become a concern.

For example, for a server handling 1,000 requests per second, a log entry with 100 fields each taking 10 bytes works out as 1 megabyte per second. That's a nontrivial proportion of a 100 Mbit network card, and 84 GB of storage per day just for logging.

A big benefit of logging is that there is (usually) no sampling of events, so even though there is a limit on the number of fields, it is practical to determine how slow requests are affecting one particular user talking to one particular API endpoint.

Just as monitoring means different things to different people, logging also means different things depending on who you ask, which can cause confusion. Different types of logging have different uses, durability, and retention requirements. As we see it, there are four general and somewhat overlapping categories:

Transaction logs
> These are the critical business records that you must keep safe at all costs, likely forever. Anything touching on money or that is used for critical user-facing features tends to be in this category.

Request logs
> If you are tracking every HTTP request, or every database call, that's a request log. They may be processed in order to implement user facing features, or just for internal optimizations. You don't generally want to lose them, but it's not the end of the world if some of them go missing.

Application logs
> Not all logs are about requests; some are about the process itself. Startup messages, background maintenance tasks, and other process-level log lines are typical. These logs are often read directly by a human, so you should try to avoid having more than a few per minute in normal operations.

Debug logs
> Debug logs tend to be very detailed and thus expensive to create and store. They are often only used in very narrow debugging situations, and are trending toward profiling due to their data volume. Reliability and retention requirements tend to be low, and debug logs may not even leave the machine they are generated on.

Treating the differing types of logs all in the same way can put you in the worst of all worlds, where you have the data volume of debug logs combined with the extreme reliability requirements of transaction logs. Thus as your system grows, you should plan on splitting out the debug logs so that they can be handled separately.

Examples of logging systems include the ELK stack, OpenSearch, Grafana Loki, and Graylog.

Metrics

Metrics largely ignore context, instead tracking aggregations over time of different types of events. To keep resource usage sane, the amount of different numbers being tracked needs to be limited: 10,000 per process is a reasonable upper bound for you to keep in mind.

Examples of the sort of metrics you might have would be the number of times you received HTTP requests, how much time was spent handling requests, and how many requests are currently in progress. By excluding any information about context, the data volumes and processing required are kept reasonable.

That is not to say, though, that context is always ignored. For an HTTP request you could decide to have a metric for each URL path. But the 10,000 metric guideline has to be kept in mind, as each distinct path now counts as a metric. Using context such as a user's email address would be unwise, as they have an unbounded cardinality.[8]

You can use metrics to track the latency and data volumes handled by each of the subsystems in your applications, making it easier to determine the cause of a slowdown. Logs cannot record that many fields, but once you know which subsystem is to blame, logs can help you figure out which exact user requests are involved.

This is where the trade-off between logs and metrics becomes most apparent. Metrics allow you to collect information about events from all over your process, but with generally no more than one or two fields of context with bounded cardinality. Logs allow you to collect information about all of one type of event, but can only track a hundred fields of context with unbounded cardinality. Cardinality and the limits it places on metrics is important to understand, and we explore it in later chapters.

As a metrics-based monitoring system, Prometheus is designed to track overall system health, behavior, and performance rather than individual events. Put another way, Prometheus cares that there were 15 requests in the last minute that took 4 seconds to handle, resulted in 40 database calls, 17 cache hits, and 2 purchases by customers. The cost and code paths of the individual calls would be the concern of profiling or logging.

Now that you have an understanding of where Prometheus fits in the overall monitoring space, let's look at the various components of Prometheus.

Prometheus Architecture

Figure 1-1 shows the overall architecture of Prometheus. Prometheus discovers targets to scrape from service discovery. These can be your own instrumented applications or third-party applications you can scrape via an exporter. The scraped data is stored, and you can use it in dashboards using PromQL or send alerts to the Alertmanager, which will convert them into pages, emails, and other notifications.

---

8 Email addresses also tend to be personally identifiable information (PII), which bring with them compliance and privacy concerns that are best avoided in monitoring.

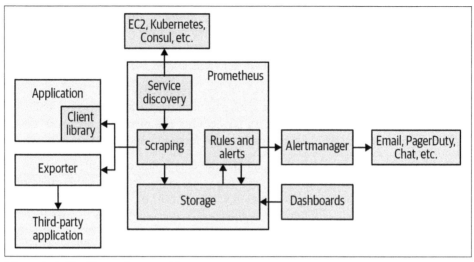

Figure 1-1. The Prometheus architecture

Client Libraries

Metrics do not typically magically spring forth from applications; someone has to add the instrumentation that produces them. This is where client libraries come in. With usually only two or three lines of code, you can both define a metric and add your desired instrumentation inline in code you control. This is referred to as direct instrumentation.

Client libraries are available for all the major languages and runtimes. The Prometheus project provides official client libraries in Go, Python, Java/JVM, Ruby, and Rust. There are also a variety of third-party client libraries, such as for C#/.Net, Node.js, Haskell, and Erlang.

Official Versus Unofficial

Don't be put off by integrations such as client libraries being unofficial or third party. With hundreds of applications and systems that you may wish to integrate with, it is not possible for the Prometheus project team to have the time and expertise to create and maintain them all. Thus the vast majority of integrations in the ecosystem are third party. In order to keep things reasonably consistent and working as you would expect, guidelines are available on how to write integrations.

Client libraries take care of all the nitty-gritty details such as thread safety, bookkeeping, and producing the Prometheus text and/or OpenMetrics exposition format in response to HTTP requests. As metrics-based monitoring does not track individual events, client library memory usage does not increase with the more events you have. Rather, memory is related to the number of metrics you have.

If one of the library dependencies of your application has Prometheus instrumentation, it will automatically be picked up. Thus by instrumenting a key library such as your RPC client, you can get instrumentation for it in all of your applications.

Some metrics, such as CPU usage and garbage collection statistics, are typically provided out of the box by client libraries, depending on the library and runtime environment.

Client libraries are not restricted to outputting metrics in the Prometheus and OpenMetrics text formats. Prometheus is an open ecosystem, and the same APIs used to feed the text format generation can be used to produce metrics in other formats or to feed into other instrumentation systems. Similarly, it is possible to take metrics from other instrumentation systems and plumb them into a Prometheus client library, if you haven't quite converted everything to Prometheus instrumentation yet.

Exporters

Not all code you run is code that you can control or even have access to, and thus adding direct instrumentation isn't really an option. For example, it is unlikely that operating system kernels will start outputting Prometheus-formatted metrics over HTTP anytime soon.

Such software often has some interface through which you can access metrics. This might be an ad hoc format requiring custom parsing and handling, such as is required for many Linux metrics, or a well-established standard such as SNMP.

An exporter is a piece of software that you deploy right beside the application you want to obtain metrics from. It takes in requests from Prometheus, gathers the required data from the application, transforms it into the correct format, and finally returns it in a response to Prometheus. You can think of an exporter as a small one-to-one proxy, converting data between the metrics interface of an application and the Prometheus exposition format.

Unlike the direct instrumentation you would use for code you control, exporters use a different style of instrumentation known as *custom collectors* or *ConstMetrics*.[9]

---

9 The term ConstMetric is colloquial, and comes from the Go client library's `MustNewConstMetric` function used to produce metrics by exporters written in Go.

The good news is that given the size of the Prometheus community, the exporter you need probably already exists and can be used with little effort on your part. If the exporter is missing a metric you are interested in, you can always send a pull request to improve it, making it better for the next person to use it.

Service Discovery

Once you have all your applications instrumented and your exporters running, Prometheus needs to know where they are. This is so Prometheus will know what to monitor, and be able to notice if something it is meant to be monitoring is not responding. With dynamic environments you cannot simply provide a list of applications and exporters once, as it will get out of date. This is where service discovery comes in.

You probably already have some database of your machines, applications, and what they do. It might be inside Chef's database, an inventory file for Ansible, based on tags on your EC2 instance, in labels and annotations in Kubernetes, or maybe just sitting in your documentation wiki.

Prometheus has integrations with many common service discovery mechanisms, such as Kubernetes, EC2, and Consul. There is also a generic integration for those whose setup is a little off the beaten path (see "File" on page 142 and "HTTP" on page 145).

This still leaves a problem, though. Just because Prometheus has a list of machines and services doesn't mean we know how they fit into your architecture. For example, you might be using the EC2 Name tag[10] to indicate what application runs on a machine, whereas others might use a tag called app.

As every organization does it slightly differently, Prometheus allows you to configure how metadata from service discovery is mapped to monitoring targets and their labels using *relabeling*.

Scraping

Service discovery and relabeling give us a list of targets to be monitored. Now Prometheus needs to fetch the metrics. Prometheus does this by sending an HTTP request called a *scrape*. The response to the scrape is parsed and ingested into storage. Several useful metrics are also added in, such as if the scrape succeeded and how long it took. Scrapes happen regularly; usually you would configure it to happen every 10 to 60 seconds for each target.

---

10 The EC2 Name tag is the display name of an EC2 instance in the EC2 web console.

Pull Versus Push

Prometheus is a pull-based system. It decides when and what to scrape, based on its configuration. There are also push-based systems, where the monitoring target decides if it is going to be monitored and how often.

There is vigorous debate online about the two designs, which often bears similarities to debates around Vim versus EMACS. Suffice to say both have pros and cons, and overall it doesn't matter much.

As a Prometheus user you should understand that pull is ingrained in the core of Prometheus, and attempting to make it do push instead is at best unwise.

Storage

Prometheus stores data locally in a custom database. Distributed systems are challenging to make reliable, so Prometheus does not attempt to do any form of clustering. In addition to reliability, this makes Prometheus easier to run.

Over the years, storage has gone through a number of redesigns, with the storage system in Prometheus 2.0 being the third iteration. The storage system can handle ingesting millions of samples per second, making it possible to monitor thousands of machines with a single Prometheus server. The compression algorithm used can achieve 1.3 bytes per sample on real-world data. An SSD is recommended, but not strictly required.

Dashboards

Prometheus has a number of HTTP APIs that allow you to both request raw data and evaluate PromQL queries. These can be used to produce graphs and dashboards. Out of the box, Prometheus provides the *expression browser*. It uses these APIs and is suitable for ad hoc querying and data exploration, but it is not a general dashboard system.

It is recommended that you use Grafana for dashboards. It has a wide variety of features, including official support for Prometheus as a data source. It can produce a wide variety of dashboards, such as the one in Figure 1-2. Grafana supports talking to multiple Prometheus servers, even within a single dashboard panel.

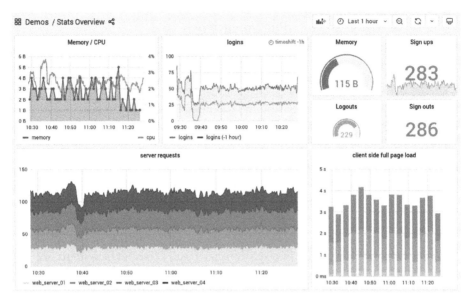

Figure 1-2. A Grafana dashboard (https://oreil.ly/ytkNa)

Recording Rules and Alerts

Although PromQL and the storage engine are powerful and efficient, aggregating metrics from thousands of machines on the fly every time you render a graph can get a little laggy. Recording rules allow PromQL expressions to be evaluated on a regular basis and their results ingested into the storage engine.

Alerting rules are another form of recording rules. They also evaluate PromQL expressions regularly, and any results from those expressions become alerts. Alerts are sent to the *Alertmanager*.

Alert Management

The Alertmanager receives alerts from Prometheus servers and turns them into notifications. Notifications can include email, chat applications such as Slack, and services such as PagerDuty.

The Alertmanager does more than blindly turn alerts into notifications on a one-to-one basis. Related alerts can be aggregated into one notification, throttled to reduce pager storms,[11] and different routing and notification outputs can be configured for each of your different teams. Alerts can also be silenced, perhaps to snooze an issue you are already aware of in advance when you know maintenance is scheduled.

The Alertmanager's role stops at sending notifications; to manage human responses to incidents you should use services such as PagerDuty and ticketing systems.

 Alerts and their thresholds are configured in Prometheus, not in the Alertmanager.

Long-Term Storage

Since Prometheus stores data only on the local machine, you are limited by how much disk space you can fit on that machine.[12] While you usually care only about the most recent day or so worth of data, for long-term capacity planning, a longer retention period is desirable.

Prometheus does not offer a clustered storage solution to store data across multiple machines, but there are remote read and write APIs that allow other systems to hook in and take on this role. These allow PromQL queries to be run transparently against both local and remote data.

What Prometheus Is Not

Now that you have an idea of where Prometheus fits in the broader monitoring landscape and what its major components are, let's look at some use cases for which Prometheus is not a particularly good choice.

As a metrics-based system, Prometheus is not suitable for storing event logs or individual events. Nor is it the best choice for high-cardinality data, such as email addresses or usernames.

---

11 A *page* is a notification to an on call engineer that they are expected to promptly investigate or deal with. While you may receive a page via a traditional radio pager, these days it more likely comes to your mobile phone in the form of an SMS, notification, or phone call. A pager storm is when you receive a string of pages in rapid succession.

12 However, modern machines can hold a lot of data locally, so a separate clustered storage system may not be necessary for you.

Prometheus is designed for operational monitoring, where small inaccuracies and race conditions due to factors like kernel scheduling and failed scrapes are a fact of life. Prometheus makes trade-offs and prefers giving you data that is 99.9% correct over your monitoring breaking while waiting for perfect data. Thus in applications involving money or billing, Prometheus should be used with caution.

In the next chapter we will show you how to run Prometheus and do some basic monitoring.

## CHAPTER 2

Getting Started with Prometheus

In this chapter you will set up and run Prometheus, the Node Exporter, and the Alertmanager. This simple example will monitor a single machine and give you a small taste of what a full Prometheus deployment looks like. Later chapters will look at each aspect of this setup in detail.

This chapter requires a machine running any reasonable, modern version of Linux. Either bare metal or a virtual machine will do. You will use the command line and access services on the machine using a web browser. For simplicity we will assume that everything is running on localhost; if this is not the case, adjust the URLs as appropriate.

 A basic setup similar to the one used in this chapter is publicly available on the Prometheus demo site (*https://oreil.ly/KHxZC*).

Running Prometheus

Prebuilt versions of Prometheus and other components are available from the Prometheus download page (*https://oreil.ly/e_S6d*). Go to that page and download the latest version of Prometheus for the Linux OS with Arch amd64; the download page will look something like Figure 2-1.

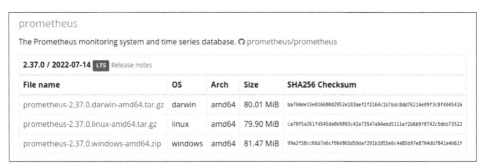

Figure 2-1. Part of the Prometheus download page; the Linux/amd64 version is in the middle

Here we are using Prometheus 2.37.0, so *prometheus-2.37.0.linux-amd64.tar.gz* is the filename.

Long-Term Support

Minor releases of Prometheus are scheduled every six weeks. Upgrading at such a cadence can be challenging, therefore some versions are defined as *Long Term Support (LTS) releases*. LTS releases are supported for a longer period of time than regular releases: instead of six weeks, LTS releases are updated with bug fixes and security fixes for one year. You can find the complete schedule at the Prometheus website (*https://oreil.ly/ZxU-S*).

Prometheus upgrades are intended to be safe between minor versions, such as from 2.0.0 to 2.0.1, 2.1.0, or 2.3.1. Even so, as with all software it is wise to read through the changelog.

Any 2.x.x version of Prometheus should suffice for this chapter.

Extract the tarball on the command line and change into its directory:[1]

```
hostname $ tar -xzf prometheus-*.linux-amd64.tar.gz
hostname $ cd prometheus-*.linux-amd64/
```

---

1 This uses a glob for the version in case you are using a different version than we are. The star will match any text.

Now change the file called *prometheus.yml* to contain the following text:

```
global:
  scrape_interval: 10s
scrape_configs:
 - job_name: prometheus
   static_configs:
    - targets:
       - localhost:9090
```

 The Prometheus ecosystem uses YAML (YAML Ain't Markup Language) for its configuration files, as it is both approachable to humans and can be processed by tools. The format is sensitive to whitespace though, so make sure to copy examples exactly and use spaces rather than tabs.[2]

By default Prometheus runs on TCP port 9090, so this configuration instructs to scrape itself every 10 seconds. You can now run the Prometheus binary with **./prometheus**:

```
hostname $ ./prometheus
level=info ... msg="No time or size retention was set so using the default
    time retention" duration=15d
level=info ... msg="Starting Prometheus" version="(version=2.37.0, branch=HEAD,
    revision=b41e0750abf5cc18d8233161560731de05199330)"
level=info ... build_context="(go=go1.18.4, user=root@0ebb6827e27f,
    date=20220714-15:13:18)"
level=info ... host_details="(Linux 5.18.12 #1-NixOS SMP PREEMPT..."
level=info ... fd_limits="(soft=1024, hard=1048576)"
level=info ... msg="Start listening for connections" address=0.0.0.0:9090
level=info ... msg="Starting TSDB ..."
level=info ... msg="TSDB started"
level=info ... component=web msg="TLS is disabled." http2=false
level=info ... msg="Loading configuration file" filename=prometheus.yml
level=info ... msg="Server is ready to receive web requests."
```

As you can see, Prometheus logs various useful information at startup, including its exact version and details of the machine it is running on. Now you can access the Prometheus UI in your browser at *http://localhost:9090/*, which will look like Figure 2-2.

---

2 You may wonder why Prometheus doesn't use JSON. JSON has its own issues, such as being picky about commas, and unlike YAML, does not support comments. As JSON is a subset of YAML, you can use JSON instead if you really want to.

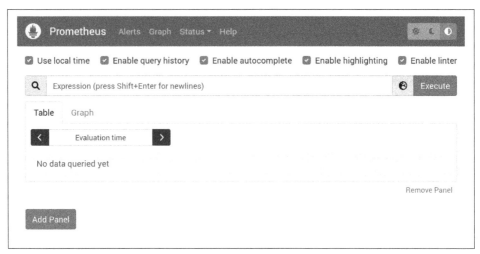

Figure 2-2. The Prometheus expression browser

This is the *expression browser* from which you can run PromQL queries. There are also several other pages in the UI to help you understand what Prometheus is doing, such as the Targets page under the Status tab, which looks like Figure 2-3.

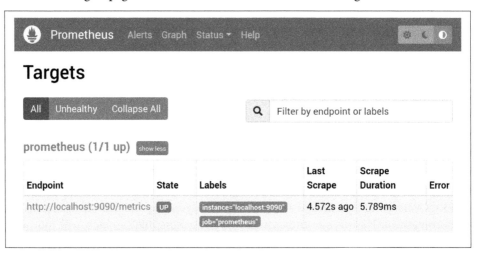

Figure 2-3. The target status page

On this page there is only a single Prometheus server in the UP state, meaning that the last scrape was successful. If there had been a problem with the last scrape, there would be a message in the Error field.

Another page you should look at is the *metrics* page of Prometheus itself, as somewhat unsurprisingly Prometheus is itself instrumented with Prometheus metrics. These are metrics available on *http://localhost:9090/metrics* and are human readable, as you can see in Figure 2-4.

```
# HELP go_gc_duration_seconds A summary of the pause duration of garbage collection cycles.
# TYPE go_gc_duration_seconds summary
go_gc_duration_seconds{quantile="0"} 2.8243e-05
go_gc_duration_seconds{quantile="0.25"} 4.2601e-05
go_gc_duration_seconds{quantile="0.5"} 4.3442e-05
go_gc_duration_seconds{quantile="0.75"} 0.000197572
go_gc_duration_seconds{quantile="1"} 0.000208714
go_gc_duration_seconds_sum 0.000520572
go_gc_duration_seconds_count 5
# HELP go_goroutines Number of goroutines that currently exist.
# TYPE go_goroutines gauge
go_goroutines 27
# HELP go_info Information about the Go environment.
# TYPE go_info gauge
go_info{version="go1.18.4"} 1
# HELP go_memstats_alloc_bytes Number of bytes allocated and still in use.
# TYPE go_memstats_alloc_bytes gauge
go_memstats_alloc_bytes 1.3531248e+07
# HELP go_memstats_alloc_bytes_total Total number of bytes allocated, even if freed.
# TYPE go_memstats_alloc_bytes_total counter
go_memstats_alloc_bytes_total 2.0167168e+07
# HELP go_memstats_buck_hash_sys_bytes Number of bytes used by the profiling bucket hash table.
# TYPE go_memstats_buck_hash_sys_bytes gauge
go_memstats_buck_hash_sys_bytes 1.459769e+06
```

Figure 2-4. The first part of Prometheus's /metrics page

Note that there are not just metrics from the Prometheus code itself, but also about the Go runtime and the process.

Using the Expression Browser

The expression browser is useful for running ad hoc queries, developing PromQL expressions, and debugging both PromQL and the data inside Prometheus.

To start, make sure you are in the Console view, enter the expression **up**, and click Execute.

As Figure 2-5 shows, there is a single result with the value 1 and the name up{instance="localhost:9090",job="prometheus"}. up is a special metric added by Prometheus when it performs a scrape; 1 indicates that the scrape was successful. The instance is a label, indicating the target that was scraped. In this case it indicates it is the Prometheus server itself.

Figure 2-5. The result of up *in the expression browser*

The job label here comes from the job_name in the *prometheus.yml*. Prometheus does not magically know that it is scraping a Prometheus server and thus that it should use a job label with the value prometheus. Rather, this is a convention that requires configuration by the user. The job label indicates the type of application.

Next, you should evaluate **process_resident_memory_bytes**, as shown in Figure 2-6.

Figure 2-6. The result of process_resident_memory_bytes *in the expression browser*

Our Prometheus is using about 73 MB of memory. You may wonder why this metric is exposed using bytes rather than megabytes or gigabytes, which may be more readable. The answer is that what is more readable depends a lot on context, and even the same binary in different environments may have values that differ by many orders of magnitude.[3] An internal RPC may take microseconds, while polling a long-running process might take hours or even days. Thus the convention in Prometheus is to use base units such as bytes and seconds, and leave pretty printing it to frontend tools like Grafana.[4]

Knowing the current memory usage is great and all, but what would be really nice would be to see how it has changed over time. To do so, click Graph to switch to the graph view, as shown in Figure 2-7.

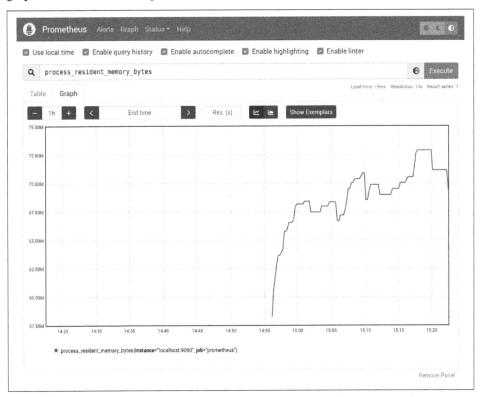

Figure 2-7. A graph of `process_resident_memory_bytes` *in the expression browser*

---

3 You can get the number in MB by running a query like `process_resident_memory_bytes / (1024*1024)`.

4 This is the same logic behind why dates and times are generally best stored in UTC, and time zone transformations only applied just before they are shown to a human.

Metrics like `process_resident_memory_bytes` are called *gauges*. A gauge's current absolute value is what is important to you. There is a second core type of metric called the *counter*. Counters track how many events have happened, or the total size of all the events. Let's look at a counter by graphing **prometheus_tsdb_head_samples_appended_total**, the number of samples Prometheus has ingested, which will look like Figure 2-8.

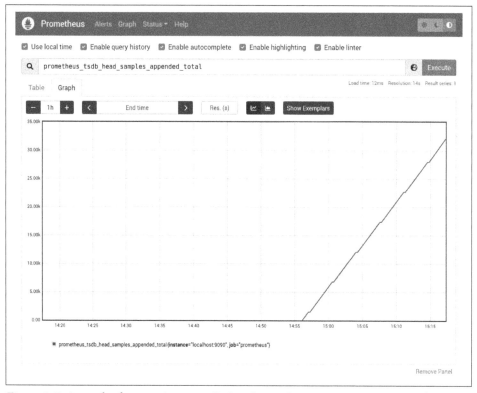

Figure 2-8. A graph of `prometheus_tsdb_head_samples_appended_total` in the expression browser

Counters are always increasing. This creates nice up-and-to-the-right graphs, but the values of counters are not much use on their own. What you really want to know is how fast the counter is increasing, which is where the `rate` function comes in. The `rate` function calculates how fast a counter is increasing per second. Adjust your expression to **rate(prometheus_tsdb_head_samples_appended_total[1m])**, which will calculate how many samples Prometheus is ingesting per second averaged over one minute and produce a result such as that shown in Figure 2-9.

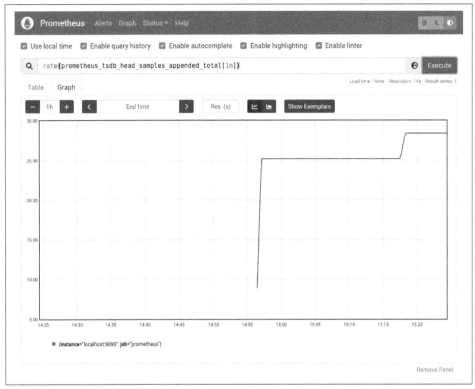

Figure 2-9. A graph of `rate(prometheus_tsdb_head_samples_appended_total[1m])` *in the expression browser*

You can see now that Prometheus is ingesting 28 or so samples per second on average. The `rate` function automatically handles counters resetting due to processes restarting and samples not being exactly aligned.[5]

Running the Node Exporter

The Node Exporter exposes kernel- and machine-level metrics on Unix systems, such as Linux.[6] It provides all the standard metrics such as CPU, memory, disk space, disk I/O, and network bandwidth. In addition it provides myriad additional metrics exposed by the kernel, from load average to motherboard temperature.

---

5 This can lead to rates on integers returning noninteger results, but the results are correct on average. For more information, see "rate" on page 289.

6 Windows users should use the Windows Exporter (*https://oreil.ly/dB6ZZ*) rather than the Node Exporter.

What the Node Exporter does not expose is metrics about individual processes, nor proxy metrics from other exporters or applications. In the Prometheus architecture you monitor applications and services directly, rather than entwining them into the machine metrics.

You can download a prebuilt version of the Node Exporter from the Prometheus download page (*https://oreil.ly/Bc4js*). Go to that page and download the latest version of Node Exporter for the Linux OS with Arch amd64.

Again, the tarball will need to be extracted, but no configuration file is required, so it can be run directly:

```
hostname $ tar -xzf node_exporter-*.linux-amd64.tar.gz
hostname $ cd node_exporter-*.linux-amd64/
hostname $ ./node_exporter
level=info ... msg="Starting node_exporter" version="(version=1.3.1,
    branch=HEAD, revision=a2321e7b940ddcff26873612bccdf7cd4c42b6b6)"
level=info ... msg="Build context" build_context="(go=go1.17.3,
    user=root@243aafa5525c, date=20211205-11:09:49)"
level=info ... msg="Enabled collectors"
level=info ... collector=arp
level=info ... collector=bcache
level=info ... collector=bonding
...
various other collectors
...
level=info ... msg="Listening on" address=:9100
level=info ... msg="TLS is disabled." http2=false
```

You can now access the Node Exporter in your browser at *http://localhost:9100/* and visit its */metrics* endpoint.

To get Prometheus to monitor the Node Exporter, you need to update the *prometheus.yml* by adding an additional scrape config:

```
global:
  scrape_interval: 10s
scrape_configs:
 - job_name: prometheus
   static_configs:
    - targets:
        - localhost:9090
 - job_name: node ❶
   static_configs:
    - targets:
        - localhost:9100
```

❶ The Node Exporter scrape job.

Restart Prometheus to pick up the new configuration by using Ctrl-C to shut it down and then start it again.[7] If you look at the Targets page, you should now see two targets, both in the UP state, as shown in Figure 2-10.

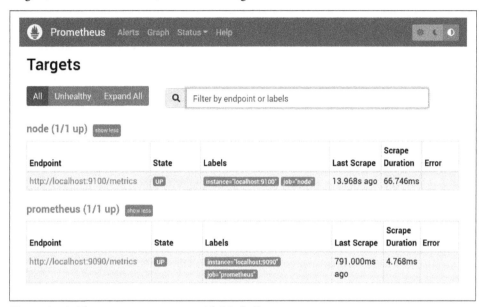

Figure 2-10. *The target status page with Node Exporter*

If you now evaluate **up** in the Console view of the expression browser, you will see two entries, as shown in Figure 2-11.

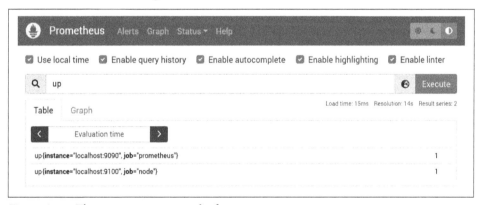

Figure 2-11. *There are now two results for up*

---

7 It is possible to get Prometheus to reload the configuration file without restarting by using a SIGHUP.

As you add more jobs and scrape configs, it is rare that you will want to look at the same metric from different jobs at the same time. The memory usage of a Prometheus and a Node Exporter are very different, for example, and extraneous data makes debugging and investigation harder. You can graph the memory usage of just the Node Exporters with **process_resident_memory_bytes{job="node"}**. The job="node" is called a *label matcher*, and it restricts the metrics that are returned, as you can see in Figure 2-12.

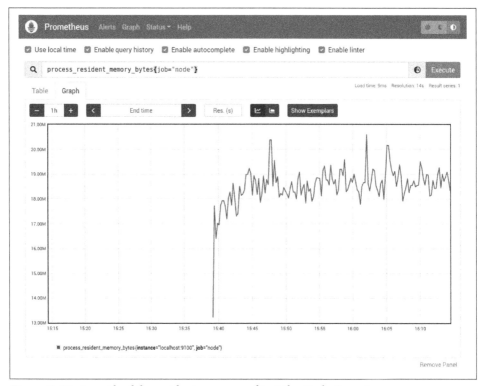

Figure 2-12. A graph of the resident memory of just the Node Exporter

The process_resident_memory_bytes here is the memory used by the Node Exporter process itself (as is hinted by the process prefix) and not the machine as a whole. Knowing the resource usage of the Node Exporter is handy and all, but it is not why you run it.

As a final example, evaluate **rate(node_network_receive_bytes_total[1m])** in Graph view to produce a graph like the one shown in Figure 2-13.

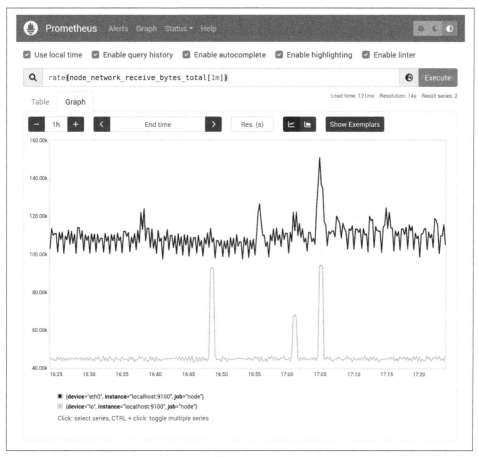

Figure 2-13. A graph of the network traffic received on several interfaces

`node_network_receive_bytes_total` is a counter for how many bytes have been received by network interfaces. The Node Exporter automatically picked up all the network interfaces, and they can be worked with as a group in PromQL. This is useful for alerting, as labels avoid the need to exhaustively list every single thing you wish to alert on.

Alerting

There are two parts to alerting. First, adding alerting rules to Prometheus, defining the logic of what constitutes an alert. Second, the Alertmanager converts firing alerts into notifications, such as emails, pages, and chat messages.

Let's start off by creating a condition that you might want to alert on. Stop the Node Exporter with Ctrl-C. After the next scrape, the Targets page will show the Node Exporter in the DOWN state, as shown in Figure 2-14, with the error *connection refused*, as nothing is listening on the TCP port and the HTTP request is being rejected.[8]

 Prometheus does not include failed scrapes in its application logs, as a failed scrape is an expected occurrence that does not indicate any problems in Prometheus itself. Aside from the Targets page, scrape errors are also available in the debug logs of Prometheus, which you can enable by passing the --log.level debug command-line flag.

Figure 2-14. The target status page showing the Node Exporter as down

Manually looking at the Targets page for down instances is not a good use of your time. Luckily, the up metric has your back, and when evaluating **up** in the Console view of the expression browser, you will see that it now has a value of 0 for the Node Exporter, as shown in Figure 2-15.

---

8 Another common error is *context deadline exceeded*. This indicates a timeout, usually due either to the other end being too slow or the network dropping packets.

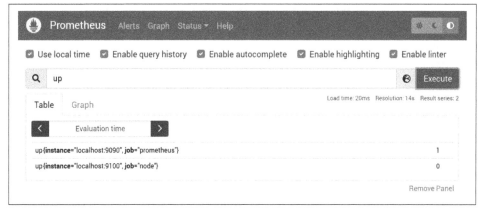

Figure 2-15. up is now 0 for the Node Exporter

For alerting rules, you need a PromQL expression that returns only the results that you wish to alert on. In this case, that is easy to do using the == operator. == will filter[9] away any time series whose values don't match. If you evaluate **up == 0** in the expression browser, only the down instance is returned, as Figure 2-16 shows.

Figure 2-16. Only up metrics with the value 0 are returned

---

9 There is also a `bool` mode that does not filter, covered in the section "bool modifier" on page 264.

Next, you need to add this expression in an alerting rule in Prometheus. We are also going to jump ahead a little and have you tell Prometheus which Alertmanager it will be talking to. You will need to expand your *prometheus.yml* to have the content from Example 2-1.

Example 2-1. prometheus.yml scraping two targets, loading a rule file, and talking to an Alertmanager

```
global:
  scrape_interval: 10s
  evaluation_interval: 10s
rule_files: ❶
 - rules.yml
alerting: ❷
  alertmanagers:
  - static_configs:
    - targets:
       - localhost:9093
scrape_configs: ❸
 - job_name: prometheus
   static_configs:
    - targets:
       - localhost:9090
 - job_name: node
   static_configs:
    - targets:
       - localhost:9100
```

❶ The rule files configuration.

❷ The alerting configuration.

❸ The scrape jobs.

Next, create a new *rules.yml* file with the contents from Example 2-2, and then restart Prometheus.

Example 2-2. rules.yml with a single alerting rule

```
groups:
 - name: example
   rules:
   - alert: InstanceDown
     expr: up == 0
     for: 1m
```

The `InstanceDown` alert will be evaluated every 10 seconds in accordance with the `evaluation_interval`. If a series is continuously returned for at least a minute[10] (the `for`), then the alert will be considered to be firing. Until the required minute is up, the alert will be in a *pending* state. On the Alerts page you can click this alert and see more detail, including its labels, as shown in Figure 2-17.

Figure 2-17. A firing alert on the Alerts page

Now that you have a firing alert, you need an Alertmanager to do something with it. Download the latest version (*https://oreil.ly/Bc4js*) of the Alertmanager for the Linux OS with Arch amd64. Untar the Alertmanager and **cd** into its directory:

```
hostname $ tar -xzf alertmanager-*.linux-amd64.tar.gz
hostname $ cd alertmanager-*.linux-amd64/
```

You now need a configuration for the Alertmanager. There are a variety of ways that the Alertmanager can notify you, but most of the ones that work out of the box use commercial providers and have setup instructions that tend to change over time. Thus we are going to presume that you have an open SMTP smarthost available.[11] You should base your *alertmanager.yml* on Example 2-3, adjusting `smtp_smarthost`, `smtp_from`, and to to match your setup and email address.

---

10 Usually a for of at least 5 minutes is recommended to reduce noise and mitigate various races inherent in monitoring. We are only using a minute here, so you don't have to wait too long when trying this out.

11 Given how email security has evolved over the past decade, this is not a good assumption, but your ISP will probably have one.

Example 2-3. alertmanager.yml sending all alerts to email

```
global:
  smtp_smarthost: 'localhost:25'
  smtp_from: 'yourprometheus@example.org' ❶
route:
  receiver: example-email
  group_by: [alertname]
receivers:
 - name: example-email
   email_configs:
     - to: 'youraddress@example.org' ❷
```

❶   The email address that will be used as the *From* field.

❷   The email address the emails will be sent to.

You can now start the Alertmanager with **./alertmanager**:

```
hostname $ ./alertmanager
level=info ... msg="Starting Alertmanager" version="(version=0.24.0,
    branch=HEAD, revision=f484b17fa3c583ed1b2c8bbcec20ba1db2aa5f11)"
level=info ... build_context="(go=go1.17.8, user=root@265f14f5c6fc,
    date=20220325-09:31:33)"
level=info ... component=cluster msg="setting advertise address
    explicitly" addr=192.168.10.52 port=9094
level=info ... component=cluster msg="Waiting for gossip to settle..."
    interval=2s
level=info ... component=configuration msg="Loading configuration file"
    file=alertmanager.yml
level=info ... component=configuration msg="Completed loading of
    configuration file" file=alertmanager.yml
level=info ... msg=Listening address=:9093
level=info ... msg="TLS is disabled." http2=false
level=info component=cluster ... msg="gossip not settled" polls=0 before=0
    now=1 elapsed=2.00004715s
level=info component=cluster ... msg="gossip settled; proceeding"
    elapsed=10.001771352s
    polls=0 before=0 now=1 elapsed=2.00011639s
```

You can now access the Alertmanager in your browser at *http://localhost:9093/* where
you will see your firing alert, which should look similar to Figure 2-18.

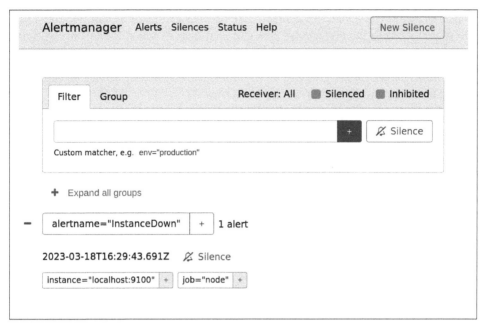

Figure 2-18. An InstanceDown alert in the Alertmanager

If everything is set up and working correctly, after a minute or two you should receive a notification from the Alertmanager in your email inbox that looks like Figure 2-19.

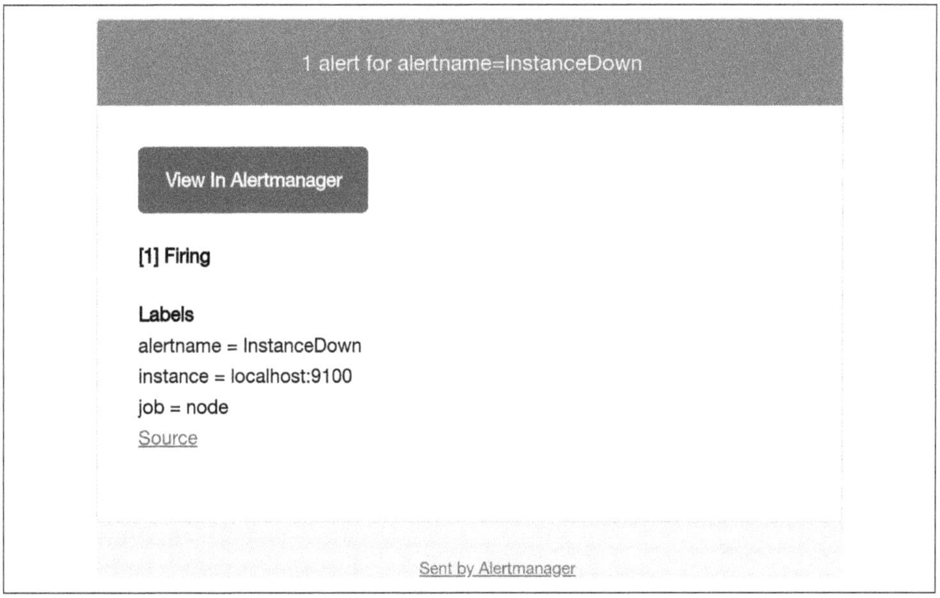

Figure 2-19. An email notification for an InstanceDown alert

This basic setup has given you a small taste of what Prometheus can do. You could add more targets to the *prometheus.yml*, and your alert would automatically work for them too.

In the next chapter we are going to focus on a specific aspect of using Prometheus—adding instrumentation to your own applications.

PART II
Application Monitoring

You will realize the full benefits of Prometheus when you have easy access to the metrics you added to your own applications. This section covers adding and using this instrumentation.

In Chapter 3 you will learn how to add basic instrumentation, and what is beneficial instrumentation to have.

In Chapter 4 we cover making the metrics from your application available to Prometheus.

In Chapter 5 you will learn about one of the most powerful features of Prometheus and how to use it in instrumentation.

After you have your application metrics in Prometheus, Chapter 6 will show you how you can create dashboards that group related graphs together.

## CHAPTER 3

Instrumentation

The largest payoffs you will get from Prometheus are through instrumenting your own applications using *direct instrumentation* and a *client library*. Client libraries are available in a variety of languages, with official client libraries in Go, Python, Java, Rust, and Ruby.

We use Python 3 here as an example, but the same general principles apply to other languages and runtimes, although the syntax and utility methods will vary.

Most modern OSes come with Python 3. In the unlikely event that you don't already have it, download and install Python 3 (*https://oreil.ly/6sAX9*).

You will also need to install the latest Python client library. You can do this with **pip install prometheus_client**. You can find the instrumentation examples on GitHub (*https://oreil.ly/-IbFJ*).

A Simple Program

To start things off, we have written a simple HTTP server shown in Example 3-1. If you run it with Python 3 and then visit *http://localhost:8001/* in your browser, you will get a Hello World response.

Example 3-1. A simple Hello World program that also exposes Prometheus metrics

```
import http.server
from prometheus_client import start_http_server

class MyHandler(http.server.BaseHTTPRequestHandler):
    def do_GET(self):
        self.send_response(200)
        self.end_headers()
        self.wfile.write(b"Hello World")
```

```
if __name__ == "__main__":
    start_http_server(8000)
    server = http.server.HTTPServer(('localhost', 8001), MyHandler)
    server.serve_forever()
```

The start_http_server(8000) starts up an HTTP server on port 8000 to serve metrics to Prometheus. You can view these metrics at *http://localhost:8000/*, which will look like Figure 3-1. Which metrics are returned out of the box varies based on the platform, with Linux platforms tending to have the most metrics.

```
# HELP python_gc_objects_collected_total Objects collected during gc
# TYPE python_gc_objects_collected_total counter
python_gc_objects_collected_total{generation="0"} 131.0
python_gc_objects_collected_total{generation="1"} 244.0
python_gc_objects_collected_total{generation="2"} 0.0
# HELP python_gc_objects_uncollectable_total Uncollectable object found during GC
# TYPE python_gc_objects_uncollectable_total counter
python_gc_objects_uncollectable_total{generation="0"} 0.0
python_gc_objects_uncollectable_total{generation="1"} 0.0
python_gc_objects_uncollectable_total{generation="2"} 0.0
# HELP python_gc_collections_total Number of times this generation was collected
# TYPE python_gc_collections_total counter
python_gc_collections_total{generation="0"} 38.0
python_gc_collections_total{generation="1"} 3.0
python_gc_collections_total{generation="2"} 0.0
# HELP python_info Python platform information
# TYPE python_info gauge
python_info{implementation="CPython",major="3",minor="9",patchlevel="13",version="3.9.13"} 1.0
```

Figure 3-1. The /metrics page when the simple program runs on Linux with CPython

Although you can manually review a */metrics* page, getting the metrics into Prometheus is what you really want. To do this, set up Prometheus with the configuration in Example 3-2 and get it running.

Example 3-2. prometheus.yml to scrape http://localhost:8000/metrics

```
global:
  scrape_interval: 10s
scrape_configs:
 - job_name: example
   static_configs:
    - targets:
      - localhost:8000
```

If you enter the PromQL expression **python_info** in the expression browser at *http://localhost:9090/*, you should see something like Figure 3-2.

Figure 3-2. Evaluating the expression `python_info` *produces one result*

In the rest of this chapter we will presume that you have Prometheus running and scraping your example application. You will use the expression browser as you go along to work with the metrics you create.

The Counter

Counters are the type of metric you will probably use most often in instrumentation. Counters track either the number or size of events. They are mainly used to track how often a particular code path is executed.

Enhance Example 3-1 by including a new metric that tracks the number of times "Hello World" has been requested, as demonstrated in Example 3-3.

Example 3-3. REQUESTS tracks the number of Hello Worlds returned

```
from prometheus_client import Counter

REQUESTS = Counter('hello_worlds_total',
        'Hello Worlds requested.')

class MyHandler(http.server.BaseHTTPRequestHandler):
    def do_GET(self):
        REQUESTS.inc()
        self.send_response(200)
        self.end_headers()
        self.wfile.write(b"Hello World")
```

There are three parts here—the import, the metric definition, and the instrumentation:

Import

Python requires that you import functions and classes from other modules in order to use them. Accordingly, you must import the `Counter` class from the `prometheus_client` library at the top of the file.

Definition

Prometheus metrics must be defined before they are used. Here we define a counter called `hello_worlds_total`. It has a help string of `Hello Worlds requested.`, which will appear on the */metrics* page to help you understand what the metric means.

Metrics are automatically registered with the client library in the *default registry*.[1] A registry is a place where metrics are registered, to be exposed. The default registry is the registry used by default when querying */metrics*. There are some cases when passing a custom registry can be useful; one of the main cases is when writing libraries used by other software.

In the Java library, for example, an extra function call is required, and depending on how you use the Go library, you may also need to explicitly register metrics. You do not need to pull the metric back to the `start_http_server` call; in fact, how the code is instrumented is completely decoupled from the exposition. If you have a transient dependency that includes Prometheus instrumentation, it will appear on your */metrics* page automatically.

Metrics must have unique names, and client libraries should report an error if you try to register the same metric twice. To avoid this, define your metrics at file level, not at class, function, or method level. An alternative pattern is to use custom explicit registries and local definitions.

Instrumentation

Now that you have the metric object defined, you can use it. The `inc` method increments the counter's value by one.

Prometheus client libraries take care of all the nitty-gritty details like bookkeeping and thread safety for you, so that is all there is to it.

When you run the program, the new metric will appear on the */metrics* page. It will start at zero and increase by one[2] every time you view the main URL of the application. You can view this in the expression browser and use the PromQL expression `rate(hello_worlds_total[1m])` to see how many Hello World requests are happening per second, as Figure 3-3 shows.

---

1 Unfortunately, not all client libraries can have this happen automatically for various technical reasons.

2 It may increase by two due to your browser also hitting the */favicon.ico* endpoint.

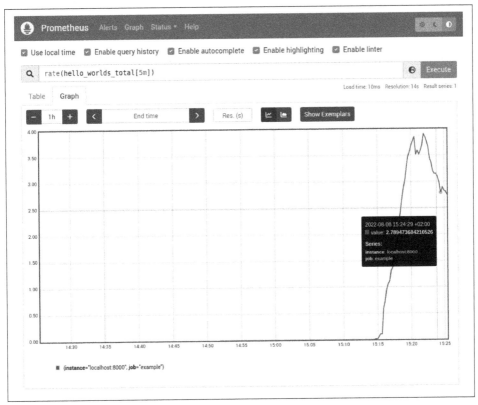

Figure 3-3. A graph of Hello Worlds per second

With just two lines of code, you can add a counter to any library or application. These counters are useful to track how many times errors and unexpected situations occur. While you probably don't want to alert every single time there is an error, knowing how errors are trending over time is useful for debugging. But this is not restricted to errors. Knowing which are the most popular features and code paths of your application allows you to optimize how you allocate your development efforts.

Counting Exceptions

Client libraries provide not just core functionality, but also utilities and methods for common use cases. One of these in Python is the ability to count exceptions. You don't have to write your own instrumentation using a try...except; instead, you can take advantage of the count_exceptions context manager and decorator, as shown in Example 3-4.

Example 3-4. EXCEPTIONS counts the number of exceptions using a context manager

```python
import random
from prometheus_client import Counter

REQUESTS = Counter('hello_worlds_total',
        'Hello Worlds requested.')
EXCEPTIONS = Counter('hello_world_exceptions_total',
        'Exceptions serving Hello World.')

class MyHandler(http.server.BaseHTTPRequestHandler):
    def do_GET(self):
        REQUESTS.inc()
        with EXCEPTIONS.count_exceptions():
          if random.random() < 0.2:
            raise Exception
        self.send_response(200)
        self.end_headers()
        self.wfile.write(b"Hello World")
```

count_exceptions will take care of passing the exception up by raising it, so it does not interfere with application logic. You can see the rate of exceptions with **rate(hello_world_exceptions_total[1m])**. The number of exceptions isn't that useful without knowing how many requests are going through. You can calculate the more useful ratio of exceptions with:

```
rate(hello_world_exceptions_total[1m])
/
rate(hello_worlds_total[1m])
```

in the expression browser. This is how to generally expose ratios: expose two counters, then rate and divide them in PromQL.

 You may notice gaps in the exception ratio graph for periods when there are no requests. This is because you are dividing by zero, which in floating-point math results in a *NaN*, or Not a Number. Returning a zero would be incorrect as the exception ratio is not zero, it is undefined.

You can also use count_exceptions as a function decorator:

```python
EXCEPTIONS = Counter('hello_world_exceptions_total',
        'Exceptions serving Hello World.')

class MyHandler(http.server.BaseHTTPRequestHandler):
    @EXCEPTIONS.count_exceptions()
    def do_GET(self):
        ...
```

Counting Size

Prometheus uses 64-bit floating-point numbers for values so you are not limited to incrementing counters by one. You can in fact increment counters by any non-negative number. This allows you to track the number of records processed, bytes served, or sales in euros, as shown in Example 3-5.

Example 3-5. SALES tracks sale value in euros

```
import random
from prometheus_client import Counter

REQUESTS = Counter('hello_worlds_total',
        'Hello Worlds requested.')
SALES = Counter('hello_world_sales_euro_total',
        'Euros made serving Hello World.')

class MyHandler(http.server.BaseHTTPRequestHandler):
    def do_GET(self):
        REQUESTS.inc()
        euros = random.random()
        SALES.inc(euros)
        self.send_response(200)
        self.end_headers()
        self.wfile.write("Hello World for {} euros.".format(euros).encode())
```

You can see the rate of sales in euros per second in the expression browser using the expression **rate(hello_world_sales_euro_total[1m])**, the same as for integer counters.

 Attempting to increase a counter by a negative number is considered to be a programming error on your part, and will cause an exception to be raised.

It is important for PromQL that counters only ever increase, so that rate and friends don't misinterpret the decrease as counters resetting to zero when an application restarts. This also means there's no need to persist counter state across runs of an application, or reset counters on every scrape. This allows multiple Prometheus servers to scrape the same application without affecting each other.

The Gauge

Gauges are a snapshot of some current state. While for counters how fast it is increasing is what you care about, for gauges it is the actual value of the gauge. Accordingly, the values can go both up and down.

Examples of gauges include:

- The number of items in a queue
- Memory usage of a cache
- Number of active threads
- The last time a record was processed
- Average requests per second in the last minute[3]

Using Gauges

Gauges have three main methods you can use: inc,[4] dec, and set. Similar to the methods on counters, inc and dec default to changing a gauge's value by one. You can pass an argument with a different value to change by if you want. Example 3-6 shows how gauges can be used to track the number of calls in progress and determine when the last one was completed.

Example 3-6. INPROGRESS and LAST track the number of calls in progress and when the last one was completed

```
import time
from prometheus_client import Gauge

INPROGRESS = Gauge('hello_worlds_inprogress',
        'Number of Hello Worlds in progress.')
LAST = Gauge('hello_world_last_time_seconds',
        'The last time a Hello World was served.')

class MyHandler(http.server.BaseHTTPRequestHandler):
    def do_GET(self):
        INPROGRESS.inc()
        self.send_response(200)
        self.end_headers()
        self.wfile.write(b"Hello World")
        LAST.set(time.time())
        INPROGRESS.dec()
```

These metrics can be used directly in the expression browser without any additional functions. For example, **hello_world_last_time_seconds** can be used to determine when the last Hello World was served. The main use case for such a metric is

---

3 While this is a gauge, it is best exposed using a counter. You can convert a requests over time counter to a gauge in PromQL with the rate function.

4 Unlike counters, gauges can decrease, so it is fine to pass negative numbers to a gauge's inc method.

detecting if it has been too long since a request was handled. The PromQL expression `time() - hello_world_last_time_seconds` will tell you how many seconds it is since the last request.

These are both very common use cases, so utility functions are also provided for them, as you can see in Example 3-7. `track_inprogress` has the advantage of being both shorter and taking care of correctly handling exceptions for you. `set_to_current_time` is a little less useful in Python, as `time.time()` returns Unix time, in seconds;[5] but in other languages' client libraries, the `set_to_current_time` equivalents make usage simpler and clearer.

Example 3-7. The same example as Example 3-6 but using the gauge utilities

```
from prometheus_client import Gauge

INPROGRESS = Gauge('hello_worlds_inprogress',
        'Number of Hello Worlds in progress.')
LAST = Gauge('hello_world_last_time_seconds',
        'The last time a Hello World was served.')

class MyHandler(http.server.BaseHTTPRequestHandler):
    @INPROGRESS.track_inprogress()
    def do_GET(self):
        self.send_response(200)
        self.end_headers()
        self.wfile.write(b"Hello World")
        LAST.set_to_current_time()
```

Metric Suffixes

You may have noticed that the example counter metrics all ended with _total, while there is no such suffix on gauges. This is a convention within Prometheus that makes it easier to identify what type of metric you are working with.

With OpenMetrics, this suffix is mandated. As the prometheus_client Python library is the reference implementation for OpenMetrics, if you do not add the suffix, the library will add it for you.

In addition to _total, the _count, _sum, and _bucket suffixes also have other meanings and should not be used as suffixes in your metric names to avoid confusion.

---

5 Seconds are the base unit for time, and thus preferred in Prometheus to other time units such as minutes, hours, days, milliseconds, microseconds, and nanoseconds.

It is also strongly recommended that you include the unit of your metric at the end of its name. For example, a counter for bytes processed might be `myapp_requests_processed_bytes_total`.

Callbacks

To track the size or number of items in a cache, you should generally add `inc` and `dec` calls in each function where items are added or removed from the cache. With more complex logic this can get a bit tricky to get right and maintain as the code changes. The good news is that client libraries offer a shortcut to implement this, without having to use the interfaces that writing an exporter require.

In Python, gauges have a `set_function` method, which allows you to specify a function to be called at exposition time. Your function must return a floating-point value for the metric when called, as demonstrated in Example 3-8. However, this strays a bit outside of direct instrumentation, so you will need to consider thread safety and may need to use mutexes when designing those callback functions.

Example 3-8. A trivial example of `set_function` *to have a metric return the current time*[6]

```
import time
from prometheus_client import Gauge

TIME = Gauge('time_seconds',
        'The current time.')
TIME.set_function(lambda: time.time())
```

The Summary

Knowing how long your application took to respond to a request or the latency of a backend are vital metrics when you are trying to understand the performance of your systems. Other instrumentation systems offer some form of Timer metric, but Prometheus views things more generically. Just as counters can be incremented by values other than one, you may wish to track things about events other than their latency. For example, in addition to backend latency you may also wish to track the size of the responses you get back.

---

6 In practice, there is not much need for such a metric. The `timestamp` PromQL function will return the timestamp of a sample, and the `time` PromQL function will return the query evaluation time.

The primary method of a summary is observe, to which you pass the size of the event. This must be a nonnegative value. Using time.time() you can track latency, as shown in Example 3-9.

Example 3-9. LATENCY tracks how long the Hello World handler takes to run

```
import time
from prometheus_client import Summary

LATENCY = Summary('hello_world_latency_seconds',
        'Time for a request Hello World.')

class MyHandler(http.server.BaseHTTPRequestHandler):
    def do_GET(self):
        start = time.time()
        self.send_response(200)
        self.end_headers()
        self.wfile.write(b"Hello World")
        LATENCY.observe(time.time() - start)
```

If you look at the */metrics* page, you will see that the hello_world_latency_seconds metric has two time series: hello_world_latency_seconds_count and hello_world_latency_seconds_sum.

hello_world_latency_seconds_count is the number of observe calls that have been made, so **rate(hello_world_latency_seconds_count[1m])** in the expression browser would return the per-second rate of Hello World requests.

hello_world_latency_seconds_sum is the sum of the values passed to observe, so rate(hello_world_latency_seconds_sum[1m]) is the amount of time spent responding to requests per second.

If you divide these two expressions, you get the average latency over the last minute. The full expression for average latency would be:

$$\frac{\text{rate(hello\_world\_latency\_seconds\_sum[1m])}}{\text{rate(hello\_world\_latency\_seconds\_count[1m])}}$$

Let's take an example. Say in the last minute you had three requests that took 2, 4, and 9 seconds. The count would be 3 and the sum would be 15 seconds, so the average latency is 5 seconds. rate is per second rather than per minute, so in principle you need to divide both sides by 60, but that cancels out.

Even though the `hello_world_latency_seconds` metric is using seconds as its unit in line with Prometheus conventions, this does not mean it only has second precision. Prometheus uses 64-bit floating-point values that can handle metrics ranging from days to nanoseconds. The preceding example takes about a quarter of a millisecond on our machine, for example.

As summaries are usually used to track latency, there is a `time` context manager and function decorator that makes this simpler, as you can see in Example 3-10. It also handles exceptions and time going backward for you.[7]

Example 3-10. LATENCY tracking latency using the `time` function decorator

```
from prometheus_client import Summary

LATENCY = Summary('hello_world_latency_seconds',
        'Time for a request Hello World.')

class MyHandler(http.server.BaseHTTPRequestHandler):
    @LATENCY.time()
    def do_GET(self):
        self.send_response(200)
        self.end_headers()
        self.wfile.write(b"Hello World")
```

Summary metrics may also include quantiles, although the Python client does not currently support these client-side quantiles. These should generally be avoided as you cannot do math such as averages on top of quantiles, preventing you from aggregating client-side quantiles from across the instances of your service. In addition, client-side quantiles are expensive compared to other instrumentation in terms of CPU usage (a factor of a hundred slower is not unusual). While the benefits of instrumentation generally greatly outweigh their resource costs, this may not be the case for quantiles.

The Histogram

A summary will provide the average latency, but what if you want a quantile? Quantiles tell you that a certain proportion of events had a size below a given value. For example, the 0.95 quantile being 300 ms means that 95% of requests took less than 300 ms.

---

7 System time can go backward if the date is manually set in the kernel, or if a daemon is trying to keep things in sync with the Network Time Protocol (NTP).

Quantiles are useful when reasoning about actual end-user experience. If a user's browser makes 20 concurrent requests to your application, then it is the slowest of them that determines the user-visible latency. In this case, the 95th percentile captures that latency.

 The 95th percentile is the 0.95 quantile. As Prometheus prefers base units, it always uses quantiles, in the same way that ratios are preferred to percentages.

The instrumentation for histograms is the same as for summaries. The observe method allows you to do manual observations, and the time context manager and function decorator allow for easier timings, as shown in Example 3-11.

Example 3-11. LATENCY histogram tracking latency using the time function decorator

```
from prometheus_client import Histogram

LATENCY = Histogram('hello_world_latency_seconds',
        'Time for a request Hello World.')

class MyHandler(http.server.BaseHTTPRequestHandler):
    @LATENCY.time()
    def do_GET(self):
        self.send_response(200)
        self.end_headers()
        self.wfile.write(b"Hello World")
```

This will produce a set of time series with the name hello_world_latency_sec onds_bucket, which are a set of counters. A histogram has a set of buckets, such as 1 ms, 10 ms, and 25 ms, that track the number of events that fall into each bucket. The histogram_quantile PromQL function can calculate a quantile from the buckets. For example, the 0.95 quantile (95th percentile) would be:

```
histogram_quantile(0.95, rate(hello_world_latency_seconds_bucket[1m]))
```

The rate is needed as the buckets' time series are counters.

Buckets

The default buckets cover a range of latencies from 1 ms to 10 s. This is intended to capture the typical range of latencies for a web application. But you can also override them and provide your own buckets when defining metrics. This might be done if the defaults are not suitable for your use case, or to add an explicit bucket for latency quantiles mentioned in your Service-Level Agreements (SLAs). In order to help you detect typos, the provided buckets must be sorted:

```
LATENCY = Histogram('hello_world_latency_seconds',
        'Time for a request Hello World.',
        buckets=[0.0001, 0.0002, 0.0005, 0.001, 0.01, 0.1])
```

If you want linear or exponential buckets, you can use Python list comprehensions. Client libraries for languages that do not have an equivalent to list comprehensions may include utility functions for these:

```
buckets=[0.1 * x for x in range(1, 10)]    # Linear
buckets=[0.1 * 2**x for x in range(1, 10)] # Exponential
```

Cumulative Histograms

If you have looked at a */metrics* page for a histogram, you probably noticed that the buckets aren't just a count of events that fall into them. The buckets also include a count of events in all the smaller buckets, all the way up to the +Inf bucket, which is the total number of events. This is known as a cumulative histogram, and why the bucket label is called le, standing for less than or equal to.

This is in addition to buckets being counters, so Prometheus histograms are cumulative in two different ways.

The reason they're cumulative is that if the number of buckets becomes a performance problem, some extraneous buckets[8] can be dropped using metric_relabel_configs (see "metric_relabel_configs" on page 164) in Prometheus while still allowing quantiles to be calculated. There is an example of this in Example 8-27.

You may be wondering how many buckets you should have for sufficient accuracy. We recommend sticking to somewhere around 10. This may seem like a small number, but buckets are not free, as each is an extra time series to be stored.[9] Fundamentally, a metrics-based system like Prometheus is not going to provide 100% accurate quantiles. For that you would need to calculate the quantiles from a log-based system. But what Prometheus provides is good enough for most practical alerting and debugging purposes.

The best way to think of buckets (and metrics generally) is that while they may not always be perfect, they generally give you sufficient information to determine the next step when you are debugging. So, for example, if Prometheus indicates that the 0.95 quantile jumped from 300 ms to 350 ms, but it was actually from 305 ms to 355 ms, that doesn't matter that much. You still know that there was a big jump, and the next step in your investigation would be the same either way.

---

8 The +Inf bucket is required, and should never be dropped.

9 Particularly if the histogram has labels.

At the time of writing this book, there is a new experimental feature in Prometheus and some client libraries, called Native Histograms. They use dynamic buckets and fix most of the issues of "old" histograms.

Ganesh Vernekar and Björn Rabenstein talked about that experimental feature at PromCon 2022:

- Native Histograms in Prometheus talk (*https://oreil.ly/uLAxm*)
- PromQL for Native Histograms talk (*https://oreil.ly/8CNJx*)

SLAs and Quantiles

Latency SLAs will often be expressed as *95th percentile latency is at most 500 ms.* There is a nonobvious trap here, in that you may focus on the wrong number.

Calculating the 95th percentile accurately is tricky, requiring what may be significant computing resources if you want to get it perfect. Calculating how the proportion of requests that took more than 500 ms is easy though—you only need two counters: one for all requests and another for requests that took up to 500 ms.

By having a 500 ms bucket in your histogram, you can accurately calculate the ratio of requests that take over 500 ms using:

```
    my_latency_seconds_bucket{le="0.5"}
  / ignoring(le)
    my_latency_seconds_bucket{le="+Inf"}
```

to determine if you are meeting your SLA. The rest of the buckets will still give you a good estimate of the 95th percentile latency.

Tools like Pyrra (*https://pyrra.dev*) can assist in managing your SLOs, calculating error budget, and producing recording and alerting rules.

Quantiles are limited in that once you calculate them, you cannot do any further math on them. It is not statistically correct to add, subtract, or average them, for example. This affects not just what you might attempt in PromQL, but also how you reason about a system while debugging it. A frontend may report a latency increase in the 0.95 quantile, yet the backend that caused it may show no such increase (or even a decrease!).

This can be very counterintuitive, especially when you have been woken up in the middle of the night to debug a problem. Averages, on the other hand, do not have this problem; they can be added and subtracted.[10] For example, if you see a 20 ms increase in latency in a frontend due to one of its backends, you will see a matching latency increase of around 20 ms in the backend. But there is no such guarantee with quantiles. So while quantiles are good for capturing end-user experience, they are tricky to debug with.

We recommend debugging latency issues primarily with averages rather than quantiles. Averages work the way you think they do, and once you have narrowed down the subsystem to blame for a latency increase using averages, you can switch back to quantiles if appropriate. To this end, the histogram also includes _sum and _count time series. Just like with a summary, you can calculate average latency with:

```
    rate(hello_world_latency_seconds_sum[1m])
/
    rate(hello_world_latency_seconds_count[1m])
```

Unit Testing Instrumentation

Unit tests are a good way to avoid accidentally breaking your code as it changes over time. You should approach unit testing instrumentation the same way you approach unit tests for logs. Just as you would probably not test a debug-level log statement, neither should you test the majority of metrics that you sprinkle across your code base.

You would usually only unit test log statements for transaction logs and sometimes request logs.[11] Similarly, it usually makes sense to unit test metrics where the metric is a key part of your application or library. For example, if you are writing an RPC library, it would make sense to have at least some basic tests to make sure the key requests, latency, and error metrics are working.

Without tests, some of the noncritical metrics you might use for debugging may not work, and in our experience this will be the case for around 5% of debug metrics. Requiring all metrics to be unit tested would add friction to instrumentation, so rather than ending up with 20 metrics of which 19 are usable, you might instead end up with only 5 tested metrics. It would no longer be a case of adding two lines of code to add a metric. When it comes to using metrics for debugging and deep performance analysis, a wider breadth of metrics is always useful.

The Python client offers a `get_sample_value` function that will effectively scrape the registry and look for a time series. You can use `get_sample_value` as shown in

---

10 However, it is not correct to average a set of averages. For example, if you had 3 events with an average of 5, and 4 events with an average of 6, the overall average would not be 5 + 6 / 2 = 5.5, but rather (3 * 5 + 4 * 6) / (3 + 4) = 5.57.

11 Categories of logs were mentioned in "Logging" on page 9.

Example 3-12 to test counter instrumentation. It is the increase of a counter that you care about, so you should compare the value of the counter before and after, rather than the absolute value. This will work even if other tests have also caused the counter to be incremented.

Example 3-12. Unit testing a counter in Python

```
import unittest
from prometheus_client import Counter, REGISTRY

FOOS = Counter('foos_total', 'The number of foo calls.')

def foo():
    FOOS.inc()

class TestFoo(unittest.TestCase):
    def test_counter_inc(self):
        before = REGISTRY.get_sample_value('foos_total')
        foo()
        after = REGISTRY.get_sample_value('foos_total')
        self.assertEqual(1, after - before)
```

Approaching Instrumentation

Now that you know how to use instrumentation, it is important to know where and how much you should apply it.

What Should I Instrument?

When instrumenting, you will usually be looking to either instrument services or libraries.

Service instrumentation

Broadly speaking, there are three types of services, each with their own key metrics: online-serving systems, offline-serving systems, and batch jobs.

Online-serving systems are those where either a human or another service is waiting on a response. These include web servers and databases. The key metrics to include in service instrumentation are the request rate, latency, and error rate. Having request rate, latency, and error rate metrics is sometimes called the RED method, for Rate, Errors, and Duration. These metrics are not just useful to you from the server side, but also the client side. If you notice that the client is seeing more latency than the server, you might have network issues or an overloaded client.

When instrumenting duration, don't be tempted to exclude failures. If you were to include only successes, then you might not notice high latency caused by many slow but failing requests.

Offline-serving systems do not have someone waiting on them. They usually batch up work and have multiple stages in a pipeline with queues between them. A log processing system is an example of an offline-serving system. For each stage you should have metrics for the amount of queued work, how much work is in progress, how fast you are processing items, and errors that occur. These metrics are also known as the USE method, for Utilization, Saturation, and Errors. Utilization is how full your service is, saturation is the amount of queued work, and errors is self-explanatory. If you are using batches, then it is useful to have metrics both for the batches and the individual items.

Batch jobs are the third type of service, and they are similar to offline-serving systems. However, batch jobs run on a regular schedule, whereas offline-serving systems run continuously. As batch jobs are not always running, scraping them doesn't work too well, so techniques such as the Pushgateway (discussed in "Pushgateway" on page 76) and the Node Exporter textfile collector (discussed in "Textfile Collector" on page 134) are used. At the end of a batch job you should record how long it took to run, how long each stage of the job took, and the time at which the job last succeeded. You can add alerts if the job hasn't succeeded recently enough, allowing you to tolerate individual batch job run failures.

Idempotency for Batch Jobs

Idempotency is the property of getting the same result from an operation or function regardless of how many times you run it. This is a useful property for batch jobs as it means handling a failed job is simply a matter of retrying, so you don't have to worry as much about individual failures.

To achieve this you should avoid passing which items of work (such as the previous day's data) a batch job should work on. Instead, you should have the batch job infer that and continue from where it left off.

This has the additional benefit that you can have your batch jobs retry themselves. For example, you might have a daily batch job run instead a few times per day, so that even if there is a transient failure, the next run will take care of it. Alert thresholds can be increased accordingly, as you will need to manually intervene less often.

Library instrumentation

Services are what you care about at a high level. Within each of your services there are libraries that you can think of as mini services. The majority will be online-serving subsystems, which is to say, synchronous function calls, and benefit from the same metrics of requests, latency, and errors. For a cache, you would want these metrics both for the cache overall and the cache misses that then need to calculate the result or request it from a backend.

With metrics for failures and total, it is easy to calculate the failure ratio by division. With success and failures this is trickier,[12] as you first need to calculate the total.

Similarly, for caches it is best to have either hits and total requests, or failures and total requests. All of total, hits, and misses works fine too.

It is beneficial to add metrics for any errors that occur and anywhere that you have logging. You might only keep your debug logs for a few days due to their volume, but with a metric you can still have a good of idea of the frequency of that log line over time.

Thread and worker pools should be instrumented similarly to offline-serving systems. You will want to have metrics for the queue size, active threads, any limit on the number of threads, and errors encountered.

Background maintenance tasks that run no more than a few times an hour are effectively batch jobs, and you should have similar metrics for these tasks.

How Much Should I Instrument?

While Prometheus is extremely efficient, there are limits to how many metrics it can handle. At some point the operational and resource costs outweigh the benefits for certain instrumentation strategies.

The good news is that most of the time you don't need to worry about this. Let's say that you had a Prometheus server that could handle 10 million metrics[13] and 1,000 application instances. A single new metric on each of these instances would use 0.01% of your resources, making it effectively free.[14] This means you are able to add individual metrics by hand where it is useful.

---

12 You should not try dividing the failures by the successes.

13 This was roughly the performance limit of Prometheus 1.x.

14 This calculation is valid for a Counter or a Gauge without labels.

Where you need to be careful is when things get industrial. If you automatically add a metric for the duration of every function, that can add up fast (it is classic profiling, after all). If you have metrics broken out by request type and HTTP URL,[15] all the potential combinations can easily take up a significant chunk of your resources. Histogram buckets expand that again. A metric with a cardinality of a hundred on each instance would take up 1% of your Prometheus server's resources, which is a less clear win and certainly not free. We discuss this further in "Cardinality" on page 99.

It is common for the 10 biggest metrics in a Prometheus instance to constitute over half of its resource usage. If you are trying to manage the resource usage of your Prometheus, you will get a better return for your efforts by focusing on the 10 biggest metrics.

As a rule of thumb, a simple service like a cache might have a hundred metrics in total, while a complex and well-instrumented service might have a thousand.

What Should I Name My Metrics?

The naming of metrics is more of an art than a science. There are some simple rules you can follow to avoid the more obvious pitfalls, and also general guidelines to construct your metric names.

 Renaming metrics can make it difficult to track and analyze data accurately over time, as it can break existing queries and dashboards. Complex workarounds such as editing PromQL queries may be required to maintain the integrity of your data when a metric gets renamed.

The overall structure of a metric name is generally *library_name_unit_suffix*.

Characters

Prometheus metric names should start with a letter, and can be followed with any number of letters, numbers, and underscores.

While [a-zA-Z_:][a-zA-Z0-9_:]* is a regular expression for valid metric names for Prometheus, you should avoid some of the valid values. You should not use colons in instrumentation as they are reserved for user use in recording rules, as discussed in "Naming of Recording Rules" on page 304. Underscores at the start of metric names are reserved for internal Prometheus use.

---

15 Chapter 5 looks at labels, which are a powerful feature of Prometheus that make this possible.

snake_case

The convention with Prometheus is to use snake case for metric names; that is, each component of the name should be lowercase and separated by an underscore.

Metric suffixes

The _total, _count, _sum, and _bucket suffixes are used by the counter, summary, and histogram metrics. Aside from always having a _total suffix on counters, you should avoid putting these suffixes on the end of your metric names to avoid confusion.

Units

You should prefer using unprefixed base units such as seconds, bytes, and ratios.[16] This is because Prometheus uses seconds in functions such as time, and it avoids ugliness such as kilomicroseconds.

Using only one unit avoids confusion as to whether this particular metric is seconds or milliseconds,[17] so you should always include the unit of your metric in the name. For example, mymetric_seconds_total for a counter with a unit of seconds.

There is not always an obvious unit for a metric, so don't worry if your metric name is missing a unit. You should avoid count as a unit, as aside from clashing with summaries and histograms, most metrics are counts of something so it doesn't tell you anything. Similarly with total.

Name

The meat of a metric name is, um, the name. The name of a metric should give someone who has no knowledge of the subsystem the metric is from a good idea of what it means. requests is not very insightful, http_requests is better, and http_requests_authenticated is better again. The metric description can expand further, but often the user will only have the metric name to go on.

As you can see from the preceding examples, a name may have several underscore-separated components. Try to have the same prefix on related metrics, so that it's easier to understand their relationship. queue_size and queue_limit are more useful than size_queue and limit_queue. You might even have items and items_limit. Names generally go from less to more specific as you go from left to right.

---

16 As a general rule, ratios typically go from 0...1 and percentages go from 0...100.

17 At one point Prometheus itself was using seconds, milliseconds, microseconds, and nanoseconds for metrics.

Do not put what should be labels (covered in Chapter 5) in metric names. When implementing direct instrumentation, you should never procedurally generate metrics or metric names.

 You should avoid putting the names of labels that a metric has into a metric's name because it will be incorrect when that label is aggregated away with PromQL.

Library

As metrics names are effectively a global namespace, it is important to both try to avoid collisions between libraries and indicate where a metric is coming from. A metric name is ultimately pointing you to a specific line of code in a specific file in a specific library. A library could be a stereotypical library that you have pulled in as a dependency, a subsystem in your application, or even the main function of the application itself.

You should provide sufficient distinction in the library part of the metric name to avoid confusion, but there's no need to include complete organization names and paths in source control. There is a balance between succinctness and full qualification.

For example, Cassandra is a well-established application so it would be appropriate for it to use just `cassandra` as the library part of its metric names. On the other hand, using `db` for a company's internal database connection pool library would be unwise, as database libraries and database connection pool libraries are both quite common. You might even have several inside the same application. `robustperception_db_pool` or `rp_db_pool` would be better choices there.

Some library names are already established. The `process` library exposes process-level metrics such as CPU and memory usage, and is standardized across client libraries. Thus you should not expose additional metrics with this prefix. Client libraries also expose metrics relating to their runtime. Python metrics use `python`, Java Virtual Machine (JVM) metrics use `jvm`, and Go uses `go`.

Combining these steps produces metric names like go_memstats_heap_inuse_bytes. This is from the go_memstats library, memory statistics from the Go runtime. heap_inuse indicates the metric is related to the amount of heap being used, and bytes tells us that it is measured in bytes. From just the name you can tell that it is the amount of the heap memory[18] that Go is currently using. While the meaning of a metric will not always be this obvious from the name, it is something to strive for.

 You should not prefix all metric names coming from an application with the name of the application. process_cpu_seconds_total is process_cpu_seconds_total no matter which application exposes it. The way to distinguish metrics from different applications is with target labels, not metric names. See "Target Labels" on page 153.

Now that you have instrumented your application, let's look at how you can expose those metrics to Prometheus.

---

18 The heap is the memory of your process that is dynamically allocated. It is used for memory allocation by functions such as malloc.

## CHAPTER 4

Exposition

In Chapter 3 we mainly focused on adding instrumentation to your code. But all the instrumentation in the world isn't much use if the metrics produced don't end up in your monitoring system. The process of making metrics available to Prometheus is known as *exposition*.

Exposition to Prometheus is done over HTTP. Usually you expose metrics under the */metrics* path, and the request is handled for you by a client library. Prometheus supports two human-readable text formats: the Prometheus text format and Open-Metrics. You have the option of producing the exposition format by hand, in which case it will be easier with the Prometheus text format, which is less strict. You may choose to do this if there is no suitable library for your language, but it is recommended you use a library as it'll get all the little details like escaping correct. Most of the libraries will also provide the ability to produce metrics using both the OpenMetrics and Prometheus text format.

Exposition is typically done either in your main function or another top-level function and only needs to be configured once per application.

Metrics are usually registered with the *default registry* when you define them. If one of the libraries you are depending on has Prometheus instrumentation, the metrics will be in the default registry and you will gain the benefit of that additional instrumentation without having to do anything. Some users prefer to explicitly pass a registry all the way down from the main function, so you'd have to rely on every library between your application's main function and the Prometheus instrumentation being aware of the instrumentation. This presumes that every library in the dependency chain cares about instrumentation and agrees on the choice of instrumentation libraries.

This design allows for instrumentation for Prometheus metrics with no exposition at all.[1] In that case, aside from still paying the (tiny) resource cost of instrumentation, there is no impact on your application. If you are the one writing a library, you can add instrumentation for your users using Prometheus without requiring extra effort for your users who don't monitor. To better support this use case, the instrumentation parts of client libraries try to minimize their dependencies.

Let's take a look at exposition in some of the popular client libraries. We are going to presume here that you know how to install the client libraries and any other required dependencies.

Python

You have already seen `start_http_server` in Chapter 3. It starts up a background thread with an HTTP server that only serves Prometheus metrics, as follows:

```
from prometheus_client import start_http_server

if __name__ == '__main__':
    start_http_server(8000)
    // Your code goes here.
```

`start_http_server` is very convenient to get up and running quickly. But it is likely that you already have an HTTP server in your application that you would like your metrics to be served from.

In Python there are various ways this can be done depending on which frameworks you are using.

WSGI

Web Server Gateway Interface (WSGI) (*https://oreil.ly/5B1tz*) is a Python standard for web applications. The Python client provides a WSGI app that you can use with your existing WSGI code. In Example 4-1, the `metrics_app` is delegated to by `my_app` if the */metrics* path is requested; otherwise, it performs its usual logic. By chaining WSGI applications, you can add middleware such as authentication, which client libraries do not offer out of the box.

Example 4-1. Exposition using WSGI in Python

```
from prometheus_client import make_wsgi_app
from wsgiref.simple_server import make_server

metrics_app = make_wsgi_app()
```

---

[1] No exposition means that the metrics are not scraped by a Prometheus server.

```
def my_app(environ, start_fn):
    if environ['PATH_INFO'] == '/metrics':
        return metrics_app(environ, start_fn)
    start_fn('200 OK', [])
    return [b'Hello World']

if __name__ == '__main__':
    httpd = make_server('', 8000, my_app)
    httpd.serve_forever()
```

Does It Have to Be /metrics?

/metrics is the HTTP path where Prometheus metrics are served by convention, but it's just a convention, so you can put the metrics on other paths. For example, if /metrics is already in use in your application or you want to put administrative endpoints under an /admin/ prefix.

Even if it is on another path, it is still common to refer to such an endpoint as your /metrics.

Twisted

Twisted (*https://twisted.org*) is a Python event-driven network engine. It supports WSGI so you can plug in `make_wsgi_app`, as shown in Example 4-2.

Example 4-2. Exposition using Twisted in Python

```
from prometheus_client import make_wsgi_app
from twisted.web.server import Site
from twisted.web.wsgi import WSGIResource
from twisted.web.resource import Resource
from twisted.internet import reactor

metrics_resource = WSGIResource(
        reactor, reactor.getThreadPool(), make_wsgi_app())

class HelloWorld(Resource):
    isLeaf = False
    def render_GET(self, request):
        return b"Hello World"

root = HelloWorld()
root.putChild(b'metrics', metrics_resource)

reactor.listenTCP(8000, Site(root))
reactor.run()
```

Multiprocess with Gunicorn

Prometheus assumes that the applications it is monitoring are long-lived and multi-threaded. But this can fall apart a little with runtimes such as CPython.[2] CPython is effectively limited to one processor core due to the Global Interpreter Lock (GIL). To work around this, some users spread the workload across multiple processes using a tool such as Gunicorn (*https://gunicorn.org*).

If you were to use the Python client library in the usual fashion, each worker would track its own metrics. Each time Prometheus went to scrape the application, it would randomly get the metrics from only one of the workers, which would be only a fraction of the information and would also have issues such as counters appearing to be going backward. Workers can also be relatively short-lived.

The solution to this problem offered by the Python client is to have each worker track its own metrics. At exposition time all the metrics of all the workers are combined in a way that provides the semantics you would get from a multithreaded application. There are some limitations to the approach used: the process_ metrics and custom collectors will not be exposed, and the Pushgateway cannot be used.[3]

Using Gunicorn, you need to let the client library know when a worker process exits.[4] This is done in a config file like the one in Example 4-3.

Example 4-3. Gunicorn config.py to handle worker processes exiting

```
from prometheus_client import multiprocess

def child_exit(server, worker):
    multiprocess.mark_process_dead(worker.pid)
```

You will also need an application to serve the metrics. Gunicorn uses WSGI, so you can use make_wsgi_app. You must create a *custom registry* containing only a Multi ProcessCollector for exposition, so that it does not include both the multiprocess metrics and metrics from the local default registry (Example 4-4).

Example 4-4. Gunicorn application in app.py

```
from prometheus_client import multiprocess, make_wsgi_app, CollectorRegistry
from prometheus_client import Counter, Gauge
```

---

2 CPython is the official name of the standard Python implementation. Do not confuse it with Cython, which can be used to write C extensions in Python.

3 The Pushgateway is not suitable for this use case, so this is not a problem in practice.

4 child_exit was added in Gunicorn version 19.7 released in March 2017.

```
REQUESTS = Counter("http_requests_total", "HTTP requests")
IN_PROGRESS = Gauge("http_requests_inprogress", "Inprogress HTTP requests",
        multiprocess_mode='livesum')

@IN_PROGRESS.track_inprogress()
def app(environ, start_fn):
    REQUESTS.inc()
    if environ['PATH_INFO'] == '/metrics':
        registry = CollectorRegistry()
        multiprocess.MultiProcessCollector(registry)
        metrics_app = make_wsgi_app(registry)
        return metrics_app(environ, start_fn)
    start_fn('200 OK', [])
    return [b'Hello World']
```

As you can see in Example 4-4, counters work normally, as do summaries and histograms. For gauges there is additional optional configuration using multiproc ess_mode. You can configure the gauge based on how you intended to use it, as follows:

all

The default, which returns a time series from each process, whether it is alive or dead. This allows you to aggregate the series as you wish in PromQL. They will be distinguished by a pid label.

liveall

Returns a time series from each alive process.

livesum

Returns a single time series that is the sum of the value from each alive process. You would use this for things like in-progress requests or resource usage across all processes. A process might have aborted with a nonzero value, so dead processes are excluded.

max

Returns a single time series that is the maximum of the value from each alive or dead process. This is useful if you want to track the last time something happened, such as a request being processed, which could have been in a process that is now dead.

min

Returns a single time series that is the minimum of the value from each alive or dead process.

There is a small bit of setup before you can run Gunicorn, as shown in Example 4-5. You must set an environment variable called prometheus_multiproc_dir. This points to an empty directory the client library uses for tracking metrics. Before starting the application, you should always wipe this directory to handle any potential changes to your instrumentation.

Example 4-5. Preparing the environment before starting Gunicorn with two workers

```
hostname $ export prometheus_multiproc_dir=$PWD/multiproc
hostname $ rm -rf $prometheus_multiproc_dir
hostname $ mkdir -p $prometheus_multiproc_dir
hostname $ gunicorn -w 2 -c config.py app:app
[2018-01-07 19:05:30 +0000] [9634] [INFO] Starting gunicorn 19.7.1
[2018-01-07 19:05:30 +0000] [9634] [INFO] Listening at: http://127.0.0.1:8000 (9634)
[2018-01-07 19:05:30 +0000] [9634] [INFO] Using worker: sync
[2018-01-07 19:05:30 +0000] [9639] [INFO] Booting worker with pid: 9639
[2018-01-07 19:05:30 +0000] [9640] [INFO] Booting worker with pid: 9640
```

When you look at the */metrics* path, you will see the two defined metrics, but python_info and the process_ metrics will not be there.

Multiprocess Mode Under the Covers

Performance is vital for client libraries. This excludes designs where work processes send UDP packets or any other use of networks, due to the system call overhead it would involve. What is needed is something that is about as fast as normal instrumentation, which means something that is as fast as local process memory but can be accessed by other processes.

The approach taken is to use mmap. Each process has its own set of mmaped files where it tracks its own metrics. At exposition time all the files are read and the metrics combined. There is no locking between the instrumentation writing to the files and the exposition reading it to ensure isolation metric values are aligned in memory and a two-phase write is used when adding a new time series.

Counters (including summaries and histograms) must not go backward, so files relating to counters are kept after a worker exits. Whether this makes sense for a gauge depends on how it is used. For a metric like in-progress requests, you only want it from live processes, whereas for the last time a request was processed, you want the maximum across both live and dead processes. This can be configured on a per-gauge basis.

Each process creates several files that must be read at exposition time in `prometheus_multiproc_dir`. If your workers stop and start a lot, this can make exposition slow when you have thousands of files.

It is not safe to delete individual files as that could cause counters to incorrectly go backward, but you can either try to reduce the churn (for example, by increasing or removing a limit on the number of requests workers handle before exiting[5]), or regularly restarting the application and wiping the files.

These steps are for Gunicorn. The same approach also works with other Python multiprocess setups, such as using the `multiprocessing` module.

OpenMetrics Support

The Python client library natively produces an OpenMetrics format. Prometheus always prefers OpenMetrics when it is available. Prometheus uses an `Accept` HTTP Header to indicate that it supports scraping the OpenMetrics format. You can simulate this behavior with the `-H` option when using `curl`:

```
curl -v -H 'Accept: application/openmetrics-text; version=1.0.0;
         charset=utf-8' http://127.0.0.1:8000/metrics
```

Go

In Go, `http.Handler` is the standard interface for providing HTTP handlers, and `promhttp.Handler` provides that interface for the Go client library. To demonstrate how this works, place the code in Example 4-6 in a file called *example.go*.

Example 4-6. A simple Go program demonstrating instrumentation and exposition

```
package main

import (
  "log"
  "net/http"

  "github.com/prometheus/client_golang/prometheus"
  "github.com/prometheus/client_golang/prometheus/promauto"
  "github.com/prometheus/client_golang/prometheus/promhttp"
)
```

---

5 Gunicorn's `--max-requests` flag is one example of such a limit.

```
var (
  requests = promauto.NewCounter(
    prometheus.CounterOpts{
      Name: "hello_worlds_total",
      Help: "Hello Worlds requested.",
    })
)

func handler(w http.ResponseWriter, r *http.Request) {
  requests.Inc()
  w.Write([]byte("Hello World"))
}

func main() {
  http.HandleFunc("/", handler)
  http.Handle("/metrics", promhttp.Handler())
  log.Fatal(http.ListenAndServe(":8000", nil))
}
```

You can fetch dependencies and run this code in the usual way:

```
hostname $ go get -d -u github.com/prometheus/client_golang/prometheus
hostname $ go run example.go
```

This example uses promauto, which will automatically register your metric with the default registry. If you do not wish to do so, you can use prometheus.NewCounter instead and then use MustRegister in an init function:

```
func init() {
  prometheus.MustRegister(requests)
}
```

This is a bit more fragile, as it is easy for you to create and use the metric but forget the MustRegister call.

Java

The Java client library is also known as the *simpleclient*. It replaced the *original client*, which was developed before many of the current practices and guidelines around how to write a client library were established. The Java client should be used for any instrumentation for languages running on a Java Virtual Machine (JVM).

HTTPServer

Similar to `start_http_server` in Python, the `HTTPServer` class in the Java client gives you an easy way to get up and running (Example 4-7).

Example 4-7. A simple Java program demonstrating instrumentation and exposition

```
import io.prometheus.client.Counter;
import io.prometheus.client.hotspot.DefaultExports;
import io.prometheus.client.exporter.HTTPServer;

public class Example {
  private static final Counter myCounter = Counter.build()
      .name("my_counter_total")
      .help("An example counter.").register();

  public static void main(String[] args) throws Exception {
    DefaultExports.initialize();
    HTTPServer server = new HTTPServer(8000);
    while (true) {
      myCounter.inc();
      Thread.sleep(1000);
    }
  }
}
```

You should generally have Java metrics as class static fields, so that they are only registered once.

The call to `DefaultExports.initialize` is needed for the various `process` and `jvm` metrics to work. You should generally call it once in all of your Java applications, such as in the main function. However, `DefaultExports.initialize` is idempotent and thread safe, so additional calls are harmless.

In order to run the code in Example 4-7, you will need the simpleclient dependencies. If you are using Maven, Example 4-8 is what the `dependencies` in your *pom.xml* should look like.

Example 4-8. pom.xml dependencies for Example 4-7

```xml
<dependencies>
  <dependency>
    <groupId>io.prometheus</groupId>
    <artifactId>simpleclient</artifactId>
    <version>0.16.0</version>
  </dependency>
  <dependency>
    <groupId>io.prometheus</groupId>
    <artifactId>simpleclient_hotspot</artifactId>
    <version>0.16.0</version>
  </dependency>
  <dependency>
    <groupId>io.prometheus</groupId>
    <artifactId>simpleclient_httpserver</artifactId>
    <version>0.16.0</version>
  </dependency>
</dependencies>
```

Servlet

Many Java and JVM frameworks support using subclasses of *HttpServlet* in their HTTP servers and middleware. Jetty is one such server, and you can see how to use the Java client's `MetricsServlet` in Example 4-9.

Example 4-9. A Java program demonstrating exposition using `MetricsServlet` *and Jetty*

```java
import io.prometheus.client.Counter;
import io.prometheus.client.exporter.MetricsServlet;
import io.prometheus.client.hotspot.DefaultExports;
import javax.servlet.http.HttpServlet;
import javax.servlet.http.HttpServletRequest;
import javax.servlet.http.HttpServletResponse;
import javax.servlet.ServletException;
import org.eclipse.jetty.server.Server;
import org.eclipse.jetty.servlet.ServletContextHandler;
import org.eclipse.jetty.servlet.ServletHolder;
import java.io.IOException;


public class Example {
  static class ExampleServlet extends HttpServlet {
    private static final Counter requests = Counter.build()
        .name("hello_worlds_total")
        .help("Hello Worlds requested.").register();

    @Override
    protected void doGet(final HttpServletRequest req,
```

```
          final HttpServletResponse resp)
          throws ServletException, IOException {
        requests.inc();
        resp.getWriter().println("Hello World");
    }
  }

  public static void main(String[] args) throws Exception {
      DefaultExports.initialize();

      Server server = new Server(8000);
      ServletContextHandler context = new ServletContextHandler();
      context.setContextPath("/");
      server.setHandler(context);
      context.addServlet(new ServletHolder(new ExampleServlet()), "/");
      context.addServlet(new ServletHolder(new MetricsServlet()), "/metrics");

      server.start();
      server.join();
  }
}
```

You will also need to specify the Java client as a dependency. If you are using Maven, this will look like Example 4-10.

Example 4-10. pom.xml dependencies for Example 4-9

```
<dependencies>
  <dependency>
    <groupId>io.prometheus</groupId>
    <artifactId>simpleclient</artifactId>
    <version>0.16.0</version>
  </dependency>
  <dependency>
    <groupId>io.prometheus</groupId>
    <artifactId>simpleclient_hotspot</artifactId>
    <version>0.16.0</version>
  </dependency>
  <dependency>
    <groupId>io.prometheus</groupId>
    <artifactId>simpleclient_servlet</artifactId>
    <version>0.16.0</version>
  </dependency>
  <dependency>
    <groupId>org.eclipse.jetty</groupId>
    <artifactId>jetty-servlet</artifactId>
    <version>11.0.11</version>
  </dependency>
</dependencies>
```

Pushgateway

Batch jobs are typically run on a regular schedule, such as hourly or daily. They start up, do some work, and then exit. As they are not continuously running, Prometheus can't exactly scrape them.[6] This is where the *Pushgateway* comes in.

The Pushgateway[7] is a metrics cache for service-level batch jobs. Its architecture is shown in Figure 4-1. It remembers only the last push that you make to it for each batch job. You use it by having your batch jobs push their metrics just before they exit. Prometheus scrapes these metrics from your Pushgateway and you can then alert and graph them. Usually you run a Pushgateway beside a Prometheus.

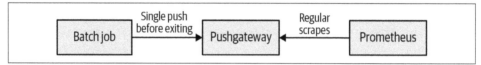

Figure 4-1. The Pushgateway architecture

A service-level batch job is one where there isn't really an `instance` label to apply to it. That is to say it applies to all of one of your services, rather than being innately tied to one machine or process instance.[8] If you don't particularly care where a batch job runs but do care that it happens (even if it happens to currently be set up to run via cron on one machine), it is a service-level batch job. Examples include a per-datacenter batch job to check for bad machines, or one that performs garbage collection across a whole service.

> The Pushgateway is not a way to convert Prometheus from pull to push. If, for example, there are several pushes between one Prometheus scrape and the next, the Pushgateway will only return the last push for that batch job. This is discussed further in "Networks and Authentication" on page 368.

You can download the Pushgateway from the Prometheus download page (*https://oreil.ly/hoXpK*). It is an exporter that runs by default on port 9091, and Prometheus should be set up to scrape it. However, you should also provide the `honor_labels: true` setting in the *scrape config*, as shown in Example 4-11. This is because the metrics you push to the Pushgateway should not have an `instance` label, and you

---

6 Though for batch jobs that take more than a few minutes to run, it may also make sense to scrape them normally over HTTP to help debug performance issues.

7 You may see it referenced as *pgw* in informal contexts.

8 For batch jobs such as database backups that are tied to a machine's lifecycle, the Node Exporter textfile collector is a better choice. This is discussed in "Textfile Collector" on page 134.

do not want the Pushgateway's own `instance` target label to end up on the metrics when Prometheus scrapes them.[9] `honor_labels` is discussed in "Label Clashes and honor_labels" on page 166.

Example 4-11. prometheus.yml scrape config for a local Pushgateway

```
scrape_configs:
 - job_name: pushgateway
   honor_labels: true
   static_configs:
    - targets:
       - localhost:9091
```

You can use client libraries to push to the Pushgateway. Example 4-12 shows the structure you would use for a Python batch job. A *custom registry* is created so that only the specific metrics you choose are pushed. The duration of the batch job is always pushed,[10] and the time it ended is pushed only if the job is successful.

There are three different ways you can write to the Pushgateway. In Python these are the `push_to_gateway`, `pushadd_to_gateway`, and `delete_from_gateway` functions:

push

> Any existing metrics for this job are removed and the pushed metrics added. This uses the PUT HTTP method under the covers.

pushadd

> The pushed metrics override existing metrics with the same metric names for this job. Any metrics that previously existed with different metric names remain unchanged. This uses the POST HTTP method under the covers.

delete

> The metrics for this job are removed. This uses the DELETE HTTP method under the covers.

As Example 4-12 is using `pushadd_to_gateway`, the value of `my_job_duration_sec` `onds` will always get replaced. However, `my_job_last_success_seconds#` will only get replaced if there are no exceptions; it is added to the registry and then pushed.

---

9 The Pushgateway explicitly exports empty `instance` labels for metrics without an `instance` label. Combined with `honor_labels: true`, this results in Prometheus not applying an `instance` label to these metrics. Usually, empty labels and missing labels are the same thing in Prometheus, but this is the exception.

10 Just like summaries and histograms, gauges have a *time* function decorator and context manager. It is intended only for use in batch jobs.

Example 4-12. Instrumenting a batch job and pushing its metrics to a Pushgateway

```python
from prometheus_client import CollectorRegistry, Gauge, pushadd_to_gateway

registry = CollectorRegistry()
duration = Gauge('my_job_duration_seconds',
        'Duration of my batch job in seconds', registry=registry)
try:
    with duration.time():
        # Your code here.
        pass

    # This only runs if there wasn't an exception.
    g = Gauge('my_job_last_success_seconds',
            'Last time my batch job successfully finished', registry=registry)
    g.set_to_current_time()
finally:
    pushadd_to_gateway('localhost:9091', job='batch', registry=registry)
```

You can see pushed data on the status page, as Figure 4-2 shows. An additional metric push_time_seconds has been added by the Pushgateway because Prometheus will always use the time at which it scrapes as the timestamp of the Pushgateway metrics. push_time_seconds gives you a way to know the actual time the data was last pushed. Another metric, push_failure_time_seconds, has been introduced, which represents the last time when an update to this group in the Pushgateway failed.

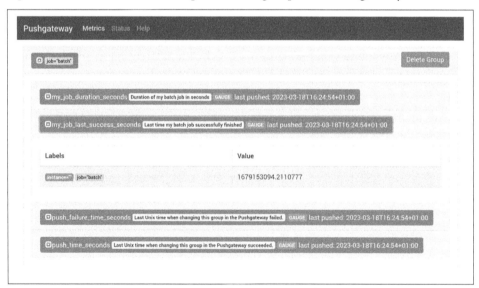

Figure 4-2. The Pushgateway status page showing metrics from a push

You might have noticed in Figure 4-2 that the push is referred to as a *group*. You can provide labels in addition to the job label when pushing, and all of these labels are known as the *grouping key*. In Python this can be provided with the grouping_key keyword argument. You would use this if a batch job was sharded or split up somehow. For example, if you have 30 database shards and each had its own batch job, you might distinguish them with a shard label.

 Once pushed, groups stay forever in the Pushgateway. You should avoid using grouping keys that vary from one batch job run to the next, as this will make the metrics difficult to work with and cause performance issues. When decommissioning a batch job, don't forget to delete its metrics from the Pushgateway.

Bridges

Prometheus client libraries are not limited to outputting metrics in the Prometheus format. There is a separation of concerns between instrumentation and exposition so that you can process the metrics in any way you like.

For example, the Go, Python, and Java clients each include a *Graphite bridge*. A bridge takes metrics output from the client library registry and outputs it to something other than Prometheus. So the Graphite bridge will convert the metrics into a form that Graphite can understand[11] and write them out to Graphite, as shown in Example 4-13.

Example 4-13. Using the Python GraphiteBridge to push to Graphite every 10 seconds

```
import time
from prometheus_client.bridge.graphite import GraphiteBridge

gb = GraphiteBridge(['graphite.your.org', 2003])
gb.start(10)
while True:
    time.sleep(1)
```

This works because the registry has a method that allows you to get a snapshot of all the current metrics. This is CollectorRegistry.collect in Python, CollectorRegistry.metricFamilySamples in Java, and Registry.Gather in Go. This is the method that HTTP exposition uses, and you can use it too. For example, you could use this method to feed data into another non-Prometheus instrumentation library.[12]

---

11 The labels are flattened into the metric name. Tag (i.e., label) support for Graphite was only recently added in 1.1.0.

12 This works both ways. Other instrumentation libraries with an equivalent feature can have their metrics fed into a Prometheus client library. This is discussed in "Custom Collectors" on page 219.

If you ever want to hook into direct instrumentation, you should instead use the metrics output by a registry. Wanting to know every time a counter is incremented does not make sense in terms of a metrics-based monitoring system. However, the count of increments is already provided for you by `CollectorRegistry.collect` and works for custom collectors.

Parsers

In addition to a client library's registry allowing you to access metric output, the Go[13] and Python clients also feature a parser for the Prometheus and OpenMetrics exposition formats. Example 4-14 only prints the samples, but you could feed Prometheus metrics into other monitoring systems or into your local tooling.

Example 4-14. Parsing the Prometheus text format with the Python client

```
from prometheus_client.parser import text_string_to_metric_families

for family in text_string_to_metric_families(u"counter_total 1.0\n"):
  for sample in family.samples:
    print("Name: {0} Labels: {1} Value: {2}".format(*sample))
```

DataDog, InfluxDB, Sensu, and Metricbeat[14] are some of the monitoring systems that have components that can parse the text format. Using one of these monitoring systems, you could take advantage of the Prometheus ecosystem without ever running the Prometheus server. We believe that this is a good thing, as there is currently a lot of duplication of effort between the various monitoring systems. Each of them has to write similar code to support the myriad custom metric outputs provided by the most commonly used software.

Text Exposition Format

The Prometheus text exposition format is relatively easy to produce and parse. Although you should almost always rely on a client library to handle it for you, there are cases such as with the Node Exporter textfile collector (discussed in "Textfile Collector" on page 134) where you may have to produce it yourself.

We will be showing you version 0.0.4 of the text format, which has the content type header:

```
Content-Type: text/plain; version=0.0.4; charset=utf-8
```

---

13 The Go client's parser is the reference implementation.

14 Part of the Elasticsearch stack.

In the simplest cases, the text format is just the name of the metric followed by a 64-bit floating-point number. Each line is terminated with a line-feed character (\n):

```
my_counter_total 14
a_small_gauge 8.3e-96
```

Metric Types

More complete Prometheus text format output would include the HELP and TYPE of the metrics, as shown in Example 4-15. HELP is a description of what the metric is, and should not generally change from scrape to scrape. TYPE is one of counter, gauge, summary, histogram, or untyped. untyped is used when you do not know the type of the metric, and is the default if no type is specified. It is invalid for you to have a duplicate metric, so make sure all the time series that belong to a metric are grouped together.

Example 4-15. Exposition format for a gauge, counter, summary, and histogram

```
# HELP example_gauge An example gauge
# TYPE example_gauge gauge
example_gauge -0.7
# HELP my_counter_total An example counter
# TYPE my_counter_total counter
my_counter_total 14
# HELP my_summary An example summary
# TYPE my_summary summary
my_summary_sum 0.6
my_summary_count 19
# HELP latency_seconds An example histogram
# TYPE latency_seconds histogram
latency_seconds_bucket{le="0.1"} 7     ❶
latency_seconds_bucket{le="0.2"} 18
latency_seconds_bucket{le="0.4"} 24
latency_seconds_bucket{le="0.8"} 28
latency_seconds_bucket{le="+Inf"} 29
latency_seconds_sum 0.6
latency_seconds_count 29     ❷
```

❶ For histograms, the le labels have floating-point values and must be sorted. You should note how the histogram buckets are cumulative, as le stands for less than or equal to.

❷ The _count must match the +Inf bucket, and the +Inf bucket must always be present. Buckets should not change from scrape to scrape, as this will cause problems for PromQL's histogram_quantile function.

Labels

The histogram in the preceding example also shows how labels are represented. Multiple labels are separated by commas, and it is OK to have a trailing comma before the closing brace.

The ordering of labels does not matter, but it is a good idea to have the ordering consistent from scrape to scrape. This will make writing your unit tests easier, and consistent ordering ensures the best ingestion performance in Prometheus.

Here is an example of a summary in text format:

```
# HELP my_summary An example summary
# TYPE my_summary summary
my_summary_sum{foo="bar",baz="quu"} 1.8
my_summary_count{foo="bar",baz="quu"} 453
my_summary_sum{foo="blaa",baz=""} 0
my_summary_count{foo="blaa",baz="quu"} 0
```

It is possible to have a metric with no time series, if no children have been initialized, as discussed in "Child" on page 91:

```
# HELP a_counter_total An example counter
# TYPE a_counter_total counter
```

Escaping

The text exposition format is encoded in UTF-8, and full UTF-8[15] is permitted in both HELP and label values. Thus you need to use backslashes to escape characters that would cause issues using backslashes. For HELP this is line feeds and backslashes. For label values this is line feeds, backslashes, and double quotes.[16] The format ignores extra whitespace.

Here is an example demonstrating escaping in the text exposition format:

```
# HELP escaping A newline \\n and backslash \\ escaped
# TYPE escaping gauge
escaping{foo="newline \\n backslash \\ double quote \" "} 1
```

Timestamps

It is possible to specify a timestamp on a time series. It is an integer value in milliseconds since the Unix epoch,[17] and it goes after the value. Timestamps in the

---

15 The null byte is a valid UTF-8 character.

16 Yes, there are two different sets of escaping rules within the text format. In OpenMetrics, this has been unified to just one rule, as double quotes must be escaped in HELP as well.

17 Midnight January 1st 1970 UTC.

exposition format should generally be avoided as they are only applicable in certain limited use cases (such as federation) and come with limitations. Timestamps for scrapes are usually applied automatically by Prometheus. It is not defined as to what happens if you specify multiple lines with the same name and labels but different timestamps.

This gauge has a timestamp:

```
# HELP foo I'm trapped in a client library
# TYPE foo gauge
foo 1 15100992000000
```

 Timestamps are expressed in *milliseconds* since epoch in the Prometheus text format, while in OpenMetrics they are expressed in *seconds* since epoch.

check metrics

Prometheus 2.0 uses a custom parser for efficiency. So, just because a */metrics* endpoint can be scraped doesn't mean that the metrics are compliant with the format.

Promtool is a utility included with Prometheus that among other things can verify that your metric output is valid and perform lint checks:

```
curl http://localhost:8000/metrics | promtool check metrics
```

Common mistakes include forgetting the line feed on the last line, using carriage return and line feed rather than just line feed,[18] and invalid metric or label names. As a brief reminder, metric and label names cannot contain hyphens, and cannot start with a number.

You now have a working knowledge of the text format. You can find the full specification in the official Prometheus documentation (*https://oreil.ly/20X3R*).

OpenMetrics

The OpenMetrics format is similar to the Prometheus text exposition format but contains several incompatible changes with the Prometheus text format. Even if they look similar, for a given set of metrics, the output they generate would generally be different.

---

18 \r\n is the line ending on Windows, while on Unix, \n is used. Prometheus has a Unix heritage, so it uses \n.

We will be showing you version 1.0.0 of the OpenMetrics format, which has the content type header:

```
Content-Type: application/openmetrics-text; version=1.0.0; charset=utf-8
```

In the simplest cases, the text format is just the name of the metric followed by a 64-bit floating-point number. Each line is terminated with a line-feed character (\n). The file is terminated by # EOF:

```
my_counter_total 14
a_small_gauge 8.3e-96
# EOF
```

Metric Types

The metric types supported by the Prometheus text exposition format are also supported in OpenMetrics. In addition to counters, gauges, summaries, and histograms, specific types have been added: StateSet, GaugeHistograms, and Info.

StateSets represent a series of related boolean values, also called a bitset. A value of 1 means true and 0 means false.

GaugeHistograms measure current distributions. The difference with histograms is that buckets values and sum can go up and down.

Info metrics are used to expose textual information that does not change during process lifetime. An application's version, revision control commit, and the version of a compiler are good candidates. The value of these metrics is always 1.

In addition to HELP and TYPE, metric families in OpenMetrics have an optional UNIT metadata that specifies a metric's unit.

All the types are demonstrated in Example 4-16.

Example 4-16. Exposition format for different types of metrics

```
# HELP example_gauge An example gauge
# TYPE example_gauge gauge
example_gauge -0.7
# HELP my_counter An example counter
# TYPE my_counter counter
my_counter_total 14
my_counter_created 1.640991600123e+09
# HELP my_summary An example summary
# TYPE my_summary summary
my_summary_sum 0.6
my_summary_count 19
# HELP latency_seconds An example histogram
# TYPE latency_seconds histogram
# UNIT latency_seconds seconds
```

```
latency_seconds_bucket{le="0.1"} 7
latency_seconds_bucket{le="0.2"} 18
latency_seconds_bucket{le="0.4"} 24
latency_seconds_bucket{le="0.8"} 28
latency_seconds_bucket{le="+Inf"} 29
latency_seconds_sum 0.6
latency_seconds_count 29
# TYPE my_build_info info
my_build_info{branch="HEAD",version="0.16.0rc1"} 1.0
# TYPE my_stateset stateset
# HELP my_stateset An example stateset
my_stateset{feature="a"} 1
my_stateset{feature="b"} 0
# TYPE my_gaugehistogram gaugehistogram
# HELP my_gaugehistogram An example gaugehistogram
my_gaugehistogram_bucket{le="1.0"} 0
my_gaugehistogram_bucket{le="+Inf"} 3
my_gaugehistogram_gcount 3
my_gaugehistogram_gsum 2
# EOF
```

In OpenMetrics, as shown in Example 4-16, GaugeHistograms use distinct _gcount and _gsum suffixes for counts and sums, differentiating them from Histograms' _count and _sum.

Labels

The Histogram and GaugeHistogram in the preceding example also showed how labels are represented. Multiple labels are separated by commas, but unlike in the Prometheus wire format, commas before the closing brace are not allowed in OpenMetrics.

Timestamps

It is possible to specify a timestamp on a time series. It is a float value in seconds since the Unix epoch,[19] and it goes after the value, as shown in this example:

```
# HELP foo I'm trapped in a client library
# TYPE foo gauge
foo 1 1.5100992e9
```

Timestamps are expressed in *seconds* since epoch in OpenMetrics, while in the Prometheus text format they are expressed in *milliseconds* since epoch.

---

19 Midnight January 1st 1970 UTC.

You now have a working knowledge of the OpenMetrics format. You can find the full specification in the OpenMetrics GitHub repository (*https://oreil.ly/EUEZa*).

We have mentioned labels a few times now. In the following chapter you'll learn what they are in detail.

## CHAPTER 5

Labels

Labels are a key part of Prometheus, and one of the things that make it powerful. In this chapter you will learn what labels are, where they come from, and how you can add them to your own metrics.

What Are Labels?

Labels are key-value pairs associated with time series that, in addition to the metric name, uniquely identify them. That's a bit of a mouthful, so let's look at an example.

If you had a metric for HTTP requests that was broken out by path, you might try putting the path in the metric name, such as is common in Graphite:[1]

```
http_requests_login_total
http_requests_logout_total
http_requests_adduser_total
http_requests_comment_total
http_requests_view_total
```

These metrics would be difficult for you to work with in PromQL. In order to calculate the total requests, you would either need to know every possible HTTP path or do some form of potentially expensive matching across all metric names. Accordingly, this is an antipattern you should avoid. Instead, to handle this common use case, Prometheus has labels. In the preceding case you might use a path label:

```
http_requests_total{path="/login"}
http_requests_total{path="/logout"}
http_requests_total{path="/adduser"}
http_requests_total{path="/comment"}
http_requests_total{path="/view"}
```

---

1 Graphite would use periods rather than underscores.

You can then work with the `http_requests_total` metric with all its `path` labels as one. With PromQL you could get an overall aggregated request rate, the rate of just one of the paths, or what proportion each request is of the whole.

You can also have metrics with more than one label. There is no ordering on labels, so you can aggregate by any given label while ignoring the others, or even aggregate by several of the labels at once.

Instrumentation and Target Labels

Labels come from two sources, *instrumentation labels* and *target labels*. When you are working in PromQL there is no difference between the two, but it's important to distinguish between them in order to get the most benefits from labels.

Instrumentation labels, as the name indicates, come from your instrumentation. They are about things that are known inside your application or library, such as the type of HTTP requests it receives, which databases it talks to, and other internal specifics.

Target labels identify a specific monitoring target; that is, a target that Prometheus scrapes. A target label relates more to your architecture and may include which application it is, what datacenter it lives in, if it is in a development or production environment, which team owns it, and of course, which exact instance of the application it is. Target labels are attached by Prometheus as part of the process of scraping metrics.

Different Prometheus servers run by different teams may have different views of what a "team," "region," or "service" is, so an instrumented application should not try to expose such labels itself. Accordingly, you will not find any features in client libraries to add labels[2] across all metrics of a target. Target labels come from service discovery and relabeling[3] and are discussed further in Chapter 8.

Instrumentation

Let's extend Example 3-3 to use a label. In Example 5-1 you can see `labelnames=['pa th']` in the definition,[4] indicating that your metric has a single label called `path`. When using the metric in instrumentation you must add a call to the `labels` method with an argument for the label value.[5]

---

2 Or prefixes to metric names.

3 When using the Pushgateway, target labels may come from the application, as each Pushgateway group is in a way a monitoring target. Depending on who you ask, this is either a feature or a limitation of push-based monitoring.

4 In Python be careful not to do `labelnames='path'`, which is the same as `labelnames=['p', 'a', 't', 'h']`. This is one of the more common gotchas in Python.

Example 5-1. A Python application using a label for a counter metric

```python
import http.server
from prometheus_client import start_http_server, Counter

REQUESTS = Counter('hello_worlds_total',
        'Hello Worlds requested.',
        labelnames=['path'])

class MyHandler(http.server.BaseHTTPRequestHandler):
    def do_GET(self):
        REQUESTS.labels(self.path).inc()
        self.send_response(200)
        self.end_headers()
        self.wfile.write(b"Hello World")

if __name__ == "__main__":
    start_http_server(8000)
    server = http.server.HTTPServer(('localhost', 8001), MyHandler)
    server.serve_forever()
```

If you visit *http://localhost:8001/* and *http://localhost:8001/foo*, then on the */metrics* page at *http://localhost:8000/metrics* you will see the time series for each of the paths:

```
# HELP hello_worlds_total Hello Worlds requested.
# TYPE hello_worlds_total counter
hello_worlds_total{path="/favicon.ico"} 6.0
hello_worlds_total{path="/"} 4.0
hello_worlds_total{path="/foo"} 1.0
```

Label names are limited in terms of what characters you can use. They should begin with a letter (a–z or A–Z) and be followed with letters, numbers, and underscores. This is the same as for metric names, except without colons.

Unlike metric names, label names are not generally namespaced. However, you should take care when defining instrumentation labels to avoid labels likely to be used as target labels, such as env, cluster, service, team, zone, and region. We also recommend avoiding type as a label name, as it is very generic. Snake case is the convention for label names.

The instance and job label names are used natively by Prometheus, so we don't recommend them either, as they will collide with the target labels.

Label values can be any UTF-8 characters. You can also have an empty label value, but this can be a little confusing in the Prometheus server as at first glance it looks the same as not having that label.

---

5 In Java the method is also labels, and the Go equivalent is WithLabelValues.

Metric

As you may have noticed, the word *metric* is a bit ambiguous and means different things depending on context. It could refer to a metric family, a child, or a time series:

```
# HELP latency_seconds Latency in seconds.
# TYPE latency_seconds summary
latency_seconds_sum{path="/foo"} 1.0
latency_seconds_count{path="/foo"} 2.0
latency_seconds_sum{path="/bar"} 3.0
latency_seconds_count{path="/bar"} 4.0
```

latency_seconds_sum{path="/bar"} is a time series, distinguished by a name and labels. This is what PromQL works with.

latency_seconds{path="/bar"} is a child, and is what the return value of labels() in the Python client represents. For a summary it contains both the _sum and _count time series with those labels.

latency_seconds is a metric family. It is only the metric name and its associated type. This is the metric definition when using a client library.

For a gauge metric with no labels, the metric family, child, and time series are the same.

Multiple Labels

You can specify any number of labels when defining a metric, and then the values in the same order in the labels call (Example 5-2).

Example 5-2. hello_worlds_total has path and method labels

```
REQUESTS = Counter('hello_worlds_total',
        'Hello Worlds requested.',
        labelnames=['path', 'method'])
```

---

6 This is different from the __name__ in the Python code examples.

```
class MyHandler(http.server.BaseHTTPRequestHandler):
    def do_GET(self):
        REQUESTS.labels(self.path, self.command).inc()
        self.send_response(200)
        self.end_headers()
        self.wfile.write(b"Hello World")
```

Python and Go also allow you to supply a map with both label names and values, though the label names must still match those in the metric definitions. This can make it harder to mix up the order of your arguments, but if that is a real risk, then you may have too many labels.

It is not possible to have varying label names for a metric, and client libraries will prevent it. When working with metrics it is important that you know what labels you have in play, so you must know your label names in advance when doing direct instrumentation. If you don't know your labels, you probably want a logs-based monitoring tool for that specific use case instead.

Child

The value returned to you by the labels method in Python is called a *child*. You can store this child for later use, which saves you from having to look it up at each instrumentation event, saving time in performance-critical code that is called hundreds of thousands of times a second. In benchmarks with the Java client, we have found that with no contention the child lookup took 30 ns, while the actual increment took 12 ns.[7]

A common pattern, when an object refers to only one child of a metric, is to call labels once and then store that in the object, as shown in Example 5-3.

Example 5-3. A simple Python cache that stores the child in each named cache

```
from prometheus_client import Counter

FETCHES = Counter('cache_fetches_total',
        'Fetches from the cache.',
        labelnames=['cache'])

class MyCache(object):
    def __init__(self, name):
        self._fetches = FETCHES.labels(name)
        self._cache = {}
```

---

7 For this reason you should also resist the temptation to write a facade or wrapper around a Prometheus client library that takes the metric name as an argument, as that would also incur this lookup cost. It is cheaper, simpler, and better semantically to have a file-level variable track the address of the metric object rather than having to look it up all the time.

```
    def fetch(self, item):
        self._fetches.inc()
        return self._cache.get(item)

    def store(self, item, value):
        self._cache[item] = value
```

Another place where you will run into children is in initializing them. Children only appear on the /metrics page after you call labels.[8] This can cause issues in PromQL, as time series that appear and disappear can be very challenging to work with. Accordingly, where possible you should initialize children at startup, such as in Example 5-4, although if you follow the pattern in Example 5-3, you get this for free.

Example 5-4. Initializing children of a metric at application startup

```
from prometheus_client import Counter

REQUESTS = Counter('http_requests_total',
        'HTTP requests.',
        labelnames=['path'])
REQUESTS.labels('/foo')
REQUESTS.labels('/bar')
```

When using Python decorators, you may also use labels without immediately calling a method on the return value, as shown in Example 5-5.

Example 5-5. Using a decorator with labels in Python

```
from prometheus_client import Summary

LATENCY = Summary('http_requests_latency_seconds',
        'HTTP request latency.',
        labelnames=['path'])

foo = LATENCY.labels('/foo')
@foo.time()
def foo_handler(params):
    pass
```

---

8 This happens automatically for metrics with no labels.

Client libraries usually offer methods to remove children from a metric. You should only consider using these for unit tests. From a PromQL semantic standpoint, once a child exists it should continue to exist until the process dies, otherwise functions such as rate may return undesirable results. These methods also invalidate previous values returned from labels.

Aggregating

Now that your instrumentation is bursting with labels, let's actually use them in PromQL. We will be going into more detail about aggregation operators in Chapter 14, but want to give you a taste of the power of labels now.

In Example 5-2, hello_worlds_total has path and method labels. As hello_worlds_total is a counter, you must first use the rate function. Table 5-1 is one possible output, showing results for two application instances with different HTTP paths and methods.

Table 5-1. Output of rate(hello_worlds_total[5m])

{job="myjob",instance="localhost:1234",path="/foo",method="GET"}	1
{job="myjob",instance="localhost:1234",path="/foo",method="POST"}	2
{job="myjob",instance="localhost:1234",path="/bar",method="GET"}	4
{job="myjob",instance="localhost:5678",path="/foo",method="GET"}	8
{job="myjob",instance="localhost:5678",path="/foo",method="POST"}	16
{job="myjob",instance="localhost:5678",path="/bar",method="GET"}	32

This can be a little hard for you to consume, especially if you have far more time series than in this simple example. Let's start by aggregating away the path label. You do this using the sum aggregation, as you want to add samples together. The without clause indicates what label you want to remove. This gives you the expression sum without(path)(rate(hello_worlds_total[5m])) that produces the output in Table 5-2.

Table 5-2. Output of sum without(path)(rate(hello_worlds_total[5m]))

{job="myjob",instance="localhost:1234",method="GET"}	5
{job="myjob",instance="localhost:1234",method="POST"}	2
{job="myjob",instance="localhost:5678",method="GET"}	40
{job="myjob",instance="localhost:5678",method="POST"}	16

It is not uncommon for you to have tens or hundreds of instances, and in our experience, looking at individual instances on dashboards breaks down somewhere around three to five. You can expand the `without` clause to include the `instance` label, which gives the output shown in Table 5-3. As you would expect from the values in Table 5-1, 1 + 4 + 8 + 32 = 45 requests per second for `GET` and 2 + 16 = 18 requests per second for `POST`.

Table 5-3. Output of `sum without(path, instance)(rate(hello_worlds_total[5m]))`

{job="myjob",method="GET"}	45
{job="myjob",method="POST"}	18

Labels are not ordered in any way, so just as you can remove `path` you can also remove `method`, as seen in Table 5-4.

Table 5-4. Output of `sum without(method, instance)(rate(hello_worlds_total[5m]))`

{job="myjob",path="/foo"}	27
{job="myjob",path="/bar"}	36

> There is also a `by` clause that keeps only the labels you specify. `without` is preferred because if there are additional labels such as `env` or `region` across all of a job, they will not be lost. This helps when you are sharing your rules with others.

Label Patterns

Prometheus only supports 64-bit floating-point numbers as time series values, not any other data types such as strings. But label values are strings, and there are certain limited use cases where it is OK to (ab)use them without getting too far into logs-based monitoring.

Enum

The first common case for strings is *enums*. For example, you may have a resource that could be in exactly one of the states of `STARTING`, `RUNNING`, `STOPPING`, or `TERMINATED`.

You could expose this as a gauge with `STARTING` being 0, `RUNNING` being 1, `STOPPING` being 2, and `TERMINATED` being 3.[9] But this is a bit tricky to work with in PromQL. The numbers 0–3 are a bit opaque, and there is not a single expression you can write to tell you what proportion of the time your resource spent `STARTING`.

---

9 Which is how an enum in a language like C works.

The solution to this is to add a label for the state to the gauge, with each potential state becoming a child. When exposing a boolean value in Prometheus, you should use 1 for true and 0 for false. Accordingly, one of the children will have the value 1 and all the others 0, which would produce metrics like those in Example 5-6.

Example 5-6. An enum example; the blaa resource is in the RUNNING state

```
# HELP gauge The current state of resources.
# TYPE gauge resource_state
resource_state{resource_state="STARTING",resource="blaa"} 0
resource_state{resource_state="RUNNING",resource="blaa"} 1
resource_state{resource_state="STOPPING",resource="blaa"} 0
resource_state{resource_state="TERMINATED",resource="blaa"} 0
```

Because the 0s are always present, the PromQL expression avg_over_time (resource_state[1h]) would give you the proportion of time spent in each state. You could also aggregate by resource_state using sum without(resource) (resource_state) to see how many resources are in each state.

To produce such metrics you could use set on a gauge, but that would bring with it race conditions. A scrape might see a 1 on either zero or two of the states, depending on when exactly it happened. You need some isolation so that the gauge isn't exposed in the middle of an update.

The solution to this is to use a *custom collector*, which will be discussed further in "Custom Collectors" on page 219. To give you an idea of how to go about this, you can find a basic implementation in Example 5-7. In reality you would usually add code like this into an existing class rather than having a standalone class.[10]

Example 5-7. A custom collector for a gauge used as an enum

```
from threading import Lock
from prometheus_client.core import GaugeMetricFamily, REGISTRY

class StateMetric(object):
    def __init__(self):
        self._resource_states = {}
        self._STATES = ["STARTING", "RUNNING", "STOPPING", "TERMINATED",]
        self._mutex = Lock()

    def set_state(self, resource, state):
        with self._mutex:
            self._resource_states[resource] = state
```

---

10 It is likely that future versions of the client libraries will offer you utilities to make working with enums easier. OpenMetrics, for example, currently plans on having a *state set* type, of which enums are a special case.

```
    def collect(self):
        family = GaugeMetricFamily("resource_state",
                "The current state of resources.",
                labels=["resource_state", "resource"])
        with self._mutex:
            for resource, state in self._resource_states.items():
                for s in self._STATES:
                    family.add_metric([s, resource], 1 if s == state else 0)
        yield family

sm = StateMetric()
REGISTRY.register(sm)

# Use the StateMetric.
sm.set_state("blaa", "RUNNING")
```

Enum gauges are normal gauges that follow all the usual gauge semantics, so no special metric suffix is needed.

Note that there are limits to this technique that you should be aware of. If your number of states combined with the number of other labels gets too high, performance issues due to the volume of samples and time series can result. You could try combining similar states together, but in the worst case you may have to fall back to using a gauge with values such as 0–3 to represent the enum, and deal with the complexity that brings to PromQL. This is discussed further in "Cardinality" on page 99.

Info

The second common case for strings are *info metrics*, which you may also find called the *machine roles approach* for historical reasons.[11] Info metrics are useful for annotations such as version numbers and other build information that would be useful to query on, but it doesn't make sense to use them as target labels, which apply to all metrics from a target (discussed in "Target Labels" on page 153) that applies to every metric from a target.

The convention that has emerged is to use a gauge with the value 1 and all the strings you'd like to have annotating the target as labels. The gauge should have the suffix _info. This was shown in Figure 3-2 with the python_info metric, which would look something like Example 5-8 when exposed.

---

[11] Brian's article (*https://oreil.ly/eu_jZ*) was the first place this technique was documented.

Example 5-8. The `python_info` metric the Python client exposes by default

```
# HELP python_info Python platform information
# TYPE python_info gauge
python_info{implementation="CPython",major="3",minor="5",patchlevel="2",
        version="3.5.2"} 1.0
```

To produce this in Python you could use either direct instrumentation or a custom collector. Example 5-9 takes the direct instrumentation route, and also takes advantage of the ability to pass in labels as keyword arguments with the Python client.

Example 5-9. An info metric using direct instrumentation

```
from prometheus_client import Info

version_info = {
    "implementation": "CPython",
    "major": "3",
    "minor": "5",
    "patchlevel": "2",
    "version": "3.5.2",
}

INFO = Info("my_python", "Python platform information")
INFO.labels(version_info)
```

An info metric can be joined to any other metric using the multiplication operator and the `group_left` modifier. Any operator can be used to join the metrics, but as the value of the info metric is 1, multiplication won't change the value of the other metric.[12]

The value of 1 is inferred by the type of metric, in this case Info.

To add the `version` label from `python_info` to all `up` metrics, you would use the PromQL expression:

```
up
* on (instance, job) group_left(version)
  python_info
```

The `group_left(version)` indicates that this is a many-to-one match[13] and that the `version` label should be copied over from `python_info` into all `up` metrics that have the same `job` and `instance` labels. We will look at `group_left` in more detail in "Many-to-One and group_left" on page 268.

---

12 More formally, 1 is the identity element for multiplication.

13 In this case it is only one-to-one as there is only one up time series per `python_info`; however, you could use same expression for metrics with multiple time series per target.

You can tell from looking at this expression that the output will have the labels of the up metric, with a `version` label added. Adding all the labels from `python_info` is not possible, as you could potentially have unknown labels from both sides of the expression,[14] which is not workable semantically. It is important to always know what labels are in play.

Breaking Changes and Labels

If you add or remove a label from instrumentation, it is always a breaking change. Removing a label removes a distinction a user may have been depending on. Adding a label breaks aggregation that uses the `without` clause.

The one exception to this is for info metrics. For those, the PromQL expressions are constructed such that extra labels aren't a problem, so it's safe for you to add labels to info metrics.

Info metrics also have a value of 1 so it is easy to calculate how many time series have each label value using `sum`. The number of application instances running each version of Python would be `sum by (version)(python_info)`. If it were a different value such as 0, a mix of `sum` and `count` would be required in your aggregation hierarchy, which would be both more complicated and error prone.

When to Use Labels

For a metric to be useful, you need to be able to aggregate it somehow. The rule of thumb is that either summing or averaging across a metric should produce a meaningful result. For a counter of HTTP requests split by path and method, the sum is the total number of requests. For a queue, combining the items in it and its size limit into one metric would not make sense, as neither summing nor averaging it produces anything useful.

One hint that an instrumentation label is not useful is if any time you use the metric you find yourself needing to specify that label in PromQL.[15] In such a case you should probably move the label to be in the metric name instead.

Another thing to avoid is having a time series that is a total of the rest of the metric, such as:

---

14 Target labels for up and any additional instrumentation labels added to `python_info` in the future.

15 Unless the label is a target label.

```
some_metric{label="foo"} 7
some_metric{label="bar"} 13
some_metric{label="total"} 20
```

or:

```
some_metric{label="foo"} 7
some_metric{label="bar"} 13
some_metric{} 20
```

Both of these break aggregation with sum in PromQL as you'd be double counting. PromQL already provides you with the ability to calculate this aggregate.

Table Exception

Astute readers probably noticed that summary metric quantiles break the rule about the sum or average being meaningful because you can't do math on quantiles.

This is what we call the *table exception*, where even though you can't do math across a metric, it's better to (ab)use a label than to have to do regexes against a metric name. Regexes on metric names are a very bad smell, and should never be used in graphs or alerts.

For you, this exception should only ever come up when writing exporters, never for direct instrumentation. For example, you might have an unknown mix of voltages, fan speeds, and temperatures coming from hardware sensors. As you lack the information needed to split them into different metrics, the only thing you can really do is shove them all into one metric and leave it to the person consuming the metric to interpret it.

 The label names used for a metric should not change during the lifetime of an application process. If you feel the need for this, you probably want a logs-based monitoring solution for that use case.

Cardinality

Don't go too far when using labels. Monitoring is a means to an end, so more time series and more monitoring aren't always better. For a monitoring system, whether you run it yourself on-premises or pay a company to run it for you in the cloud, every time series and sample has both a resource cost and a human cost in terms of ongoing operations to keep the monitoring system up and running.

In this context we would like to talk about cardinality, which in Prometheus is the number of time series you have. If your Prometheus is provisioned to handle, say, 10 million time series, how would you best spend those? At what point do you move certain use cases to logs-based monitoring instead?

The way we look at it is to assume that someone running your code has a large setup with a thousand instances of a particular application.[16] Adding a simple counter metric to an obscure subsystem will add a thousand time series to your Prometheus, which is 0.01% of its capacity. That is basically free, and it might help you debug a weird problem one day. Across all of the application and its libraries, you might have a hundred of these obscure metrics, which total to 1% of your monitoring capacity and is still quite cheap even given the rarity that you'll likely use any one of them.

Now consider a metric with a label with 10 values and in addition was a histogram that by default has 12 time series.[17] That is a 120 series, or 1.2% of your monitoring capacity. That this is a good trade-off is less clear. It might be OK to have a handful of these, but you might also consider switching to a quantile-less summary metric instead.[18]

The next stage is where things get a little troublesome. If a label already has a cardinality of 10, there is a good chance that it will only increase over time as new features are introduced to your application. A cardinality of 10 today might be 15 next year, and 200 might change to 300. Increased traffic from users usually means more application instances. If you have more than one of these expanding labels on a metric, the impact is compounded, resulting in a combinatorial explosion of time series. And this is just one of the ever-growing applications that Prometheus is monitoring.

In this way cardinality can sneak up on you. It is usually obvious that email addresses, customers, and IP addresses are poor choices for label values on cardinality grounds. It is less clear that the HTTP path is going to be a problem. Given that the HTTP request metric is regularly used, removing labels from it, switching away from a histogram, or even reducing the number of buckets in the histogram can be challenging politically.

The rule of thumb we use is that the cardinality of an arbitrary metric on one application instance should be kept below 10. It is also OK to have a handful of metrics that have a cardinality around 100, but you should be prepared to reduce metric cardinality and rely on logs as that cardinality grows.

---

16 It is possible to have more, but it's a reasonably conservative upper bound.

17 So 10 buckets, plus the _sum and _count.

18 With only the _sum and _count time series, quantileless summary metrics are a very cheap way to get an idea of latency.

The handful of a hundred cardinality metrics per Prometheus presumes a thousand instances exposing such cardinality. If you are 100% certain that you will not reach these numbers, such as with applications you will run exactly one of, you can adjust the rule of thumb accordingly.

There is a common pattern that we have seen when Prometheus is introduced to an organization. It is common for organizations to experience a learning curve when introducing Prometheus. At some point it clicks, and they start to grasp the power of labels. It usually follows quickly that your Prometheus has performance issues due to label cardinality. We advise talking about the limitations of cardinality with your users early on, and also consider using `sample_limit` as an emergency safety valve (see "Reducing Load" on page 376).

The 10 biggest metrics in a Prometheus commonly constitute over half of its resource usage, and this is almost always due to label cardinality. There is sometimes confusion that if the issue is the number of label values, wouldn't moving the label value into the metric name fix the problem? As the underlying resource constraint is actually time series cardinality (which manifests due to label values), moving label values to the metric name doesn't change the cardinality, it just makes the metrics harder to use.[19]

Now that you can add metrics to your applications and know some basic PromQL expressions, in the following chapter we will show you how you can create dashboards in Grafana.

---

19 It would also make it harder to pinpoint the metrics responsible for your resource usage.

## CHAPTER 6

Dashboarding with Grafana

When you get an alert or want to check on the current performance of your systems, dashboards will be your first port of call. The expression browser that you have seen up to now is fine for ad hoc graphing and when you need to debug your PromQL, but it's not designed to be used as a dashboard.

What do we mean by dashboard? A set of graphs, tables, and other visualizations of your systems. You might have a dashboard for global traffic, which services are getting how much traffic, and with what latency. For each of those services you would likely have a dashboard of its latency, errors, request rate, instance count, CPU usage, memory usage, and service-specific metrics. Drilling down, you could have a dashboard for particular subsystems or each service, or a garbage collection dashboard that can be used with any Java application.

Grafana is a popular tool with which you can build such dashboards for many different monitoring and nonmonitoring systems, including Graphite, InfluxDB, Jaeger, Elasticsearch, and PostgreSQL. It is the recommended tool for you to create dashboards when using Prometheus, and is continuously improving its Prometheus support.

In this chapter we introduce using Grafana with Prometheus, extending the Prometheus and Node Exporter you set up in Chapter 2.

Promdash and Console Templates

Originally the Prometheus project had its own dashboarding tool called *Promdash*. Even though Promdash was better at the time for Prometheus use cases, the Prometheus developers decided in 2016 to rally around Grafana rather than have to continue to work on their own dashboarding solution. These days, Prometheus is a first-class plug-in in Grafana, and also one of the most popular.[1]

There is a feature included with Prometheus called *console templates* that can be used for dashboards. Unlike Promdash and Grafana, which store dashboards in relational databases, it is built right into Prometheus and is configured from the filesystem. It allows you to render web pages using Go's templating language[2] and easily keep your dashboards in source control. Console templates are a very raw feature upon which you could build a dashboard system, and as such it is recommended only for niche use cases and advanced users.

Installation

You can download Grafana from the Grafana website (*https://oreil.ly/ANoWC*). The site includes installation instructions, but if you're using Docker, for example, you would use:

```
docker run -d --name=grafana --net=host grafana/grafana:9.1.6
```

Note that this doesn't use a volume mount,[3] so it will store all state inside the container.

We use Grafana 9.1.6 here. You can use a newer version but be aware that what you see will likely differ slightly.

Once Grafana is running you should be able to access it in your browser at *http://localhost:3000/*, and you will see a login screen like the one in Figure 6-1.

---

1 Grafana by default reports anonymous usage statistics. This can be disabled with the `reporting_enabled` setting in its configuration file.

2 This is the same templating language that is used for alert templating, with some minor differences in available functionality.

3 A way to have filesystems shared across containers over time, as by default a Docker container's storage is specific to that container. Volume mounts can be specified with the `-v` flag to `docker run`.

Figure 6-1. Grafana login screen

Log in with the default username of **admin** and the default password, which is also **admin**. You will be prompted to change your password, which we recommend you to do.

You should then see the Home Dashboard, as shown in Figure 6-2. We have switched to the Light theme in the Org Settings in order to make things easier to see in our screenshots.

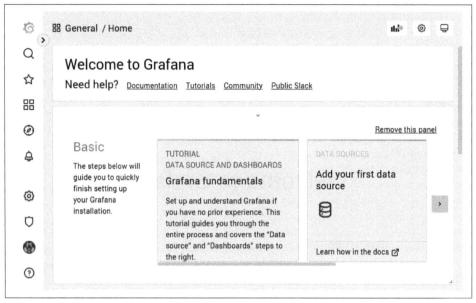

Figure 6-2. Grafana Home Dashboard on a fresh install

Data Source

Grafana connects to Prometheus through *data sources* to fetch information used for graphs. A variety of data source types are supported out of the box, including InfluxDB, PostgreSQL, and of course, Prometheus. You can have many data sources of the same type, and usually you would have one per running Prometheus. A Grafana dashboard can have graphs from a variety of sources, and you can even mix sources in a time series panel.

More recent versions of Grafana make it easy to add your first data source. Click "Add your first data source" and add a data source with a Name of **Prometheus**, a Type of Prometheus, and a URL of *http://localhost:9090* (or whatever other URL your Prometheus from Chapter 2 is listening on). The form should look like Figure 6-3. Leave all other settings at their defaults, and finally click Save & Test at the bottom of the form. Depending on your screen size, you might need to scroll to see the buttons. If it works, you will get a message that the data source is working. If you don't, check that the Prometheus is indeed running and that it is accessible from Grafana.[4]

---

4 The Access server setting has Grafana make the requests to your Prometheus. By contrast, the direct setting has your browser make the request. Direct setting is deprecated and will be removed in future Grafana releases.

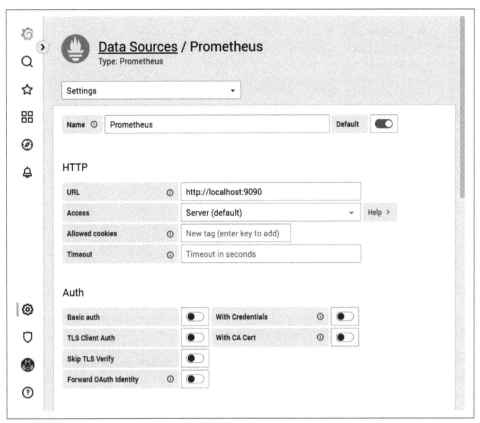

Figure 6-3. Adding a Prometheus data source to Grafana

Dashboards and Panels

Go again to *http://localhost:3000/* in your browser, and this time click "Create your first dashboard," which will bring you to a page that looks like Figure 6-4.

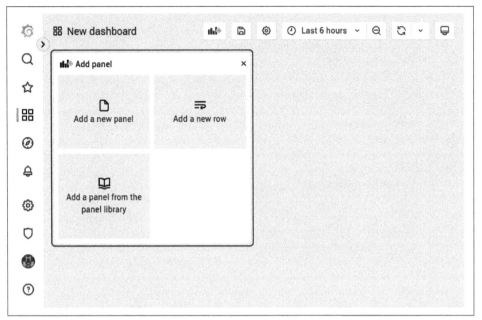

Figure 6-4. A new Grafana dashboard

From here you can click "Add a new panel" and select the first panel you'd like to add. Panels are rectangular areas containing a graph, table, or other visual information. You can add new panels beyond the first with the "Add panel" button, which is the button on the top row with the orange plus sign. Panels are organized within a grid system, and can be rearranged using drag-and-drop.

 After making any changes to a dashboard or panels, if you want them to be remembered you must explicitly save them. You can do this with the save button at the top of the page or using the Ctrl-S keyboard shortcut.

You can access the dashboard settings, such as its name, using the gear icon at the top. From the settings menu you can also duplicate dashboards using Save As, which is handy when you want to experiment with a dashboard.

Avoiding the Wall of Graphs

It is not unusual to end up with multiple dashboards per service you run. It is easy for dashboards to gradually get bloated with too many graphs, making it challenging for you to interpret what is actually going on. To mitigate this you should try to avoid dashboards that serve more than one team or purpose, and instead give them a dashboard each.

The more high-level a dashboard is, the fewer rows and panels it should have. A global overview should fit on one screen and be understandable at a distance. Dashboards commonly used for on call might have a row or two more than that, whereas a dashboard for in-depth performance tuning by experts might run to several screens.

Why do we recommend that you limit the amount of graphs on each of your dashboards? The answer is that every graph, line, and number on a dashboard makes it harder to understand, due to cognitive load to understand everything you are looking at. This is particularly relevant when you are on call and handling alerts. When you are stressed, need to act quickly, and are possibly only half awake, having to remember the subtler points of what each graph on your dashboard means is not going to aid you in terms of either response time or taking an appropriate action.

To give an extreme example, one service Brian worked on had a dashboard (singular) with over 600 graphs.[5] This was hailed as superb monitoring, due to the vast wealth of data on display. The sheer volume of data meant he was never able to get his head around that dashboard, plus it took rather a long time to load. He likes to call this style of dashboarding the Wall of Graphs antipattern.

You should not confuse having lots of graphs with having good monitoring. Monitoring is ultimately about outcomes, such as faster incident resolution and better engineering decisions, not pretty graphs.

Time Series Panel

The Time series panel is the main panel you will be using. As the name indicates, it displays time series. As shown in Figure 6-4, click the "Add a new panel" button to add a Time series panel. You are directly entering editing mode for this new panel. To configure it again later, click Panel Title and then Edit, as shown in Figure 6-5.[6]

---

5 The worst case of this we have heard of weighed in at over 1,000 graphs.

6 You can also use the e keyboard shortcut to open the editor while hovering over the panel. You can press ? to view a full list of keyboard shortcuts.

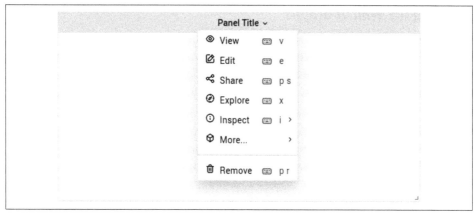

Figure 6-5. Opening the editor for a Time series panel

The panel editor will open on the Query tab. In the text box beside A,[7] enter **process_resident_memory_bytes** for the query expression, as shown in Figure 6-6, and then click "Run queries." You will see a graph of memory usage similar to what Figure 2-7 showed when the same expression was used in the expression browser.

Figure 6-6. The expression `process_resident_memory_bytes` *in the graph editor*

---

7 The A indicates that it is the first query.

Grafana offers more than the expression browser. You can configure the legend to display something other than the full-time series name. Select Custom in the Legend dropdown and type **{{job}}** in the text box. On the right side, under "Standard options," change the unit to "data/bytes (IEC)." Under "Panel options," change the Title to **Memory Usage**. The graph will now look something like Figure 6-7, with a more useful legend, appropriate units on the axis, and a title.

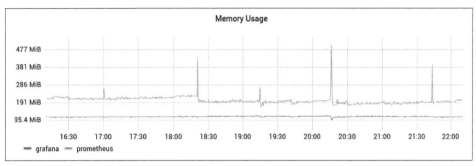

Figure 6-7. Memory Usage graph with custom legend, title, and axis units configured

These are the settings you will want to configure on virtually all of your graphs, but this is only a small taste of what you can do with graphs in Grafana. You can configure colors, draw style, tool tips, stacking, filling, and even include metrics from multiple data sources.

Don't forget to save the panel and dashboard before continuing! Click Apply, then save the dashboard. New dashboard is a special dashboard name for Grafana, so you should choose something more memorable.

Time Controls

You may have noticed Grafana's time controls on the top right of the page. By default, it should say "Last 6 hours." Clicking the time controls will show the page in Figure 6-8 where you can choose a time range. The dropdown next to the circular arrow in Figure 6-9 is where you can choose how often to refresh. The time controls apply to an entire dashboard at once, though you can also configure some overrides on a per-panel basis.

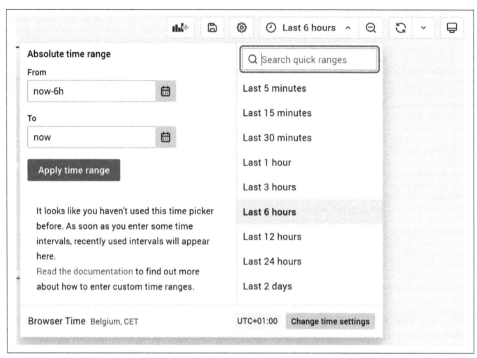

Figure 6-8. Grafana's time control menu

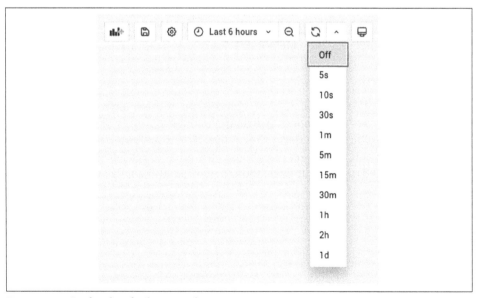

Figure 6-9. Grafana's refresh interval menu

Stat Panel

The Stat panel displays single values of a time series. It can also show a Prometheus label value.

We will start this example by adding a time series value. Click Apply (the back arrow on the top right) to return from the Time series panel to the dashboard view. Click the "Add panel" button and select "Stat panel" from the dropdown on the right.[8] For the query expression on the Metrics tab, use **prometheus_tsdb_head_series**, which is (roughly speaking) the number of different time series Prometheus is ingesting. By default the Stat panel will calculate the last value of the time series over the dashboard's time range. The default text can be a bit small, so change the Font Size to 200%. Under Panel options, change the Title to **Prometheus Time Series**. Under Thresholds, click the trash bin image next to the predefined threshold at 80 to remove the threshold. Finally, click Apply and you should see something like Figure 6-10.

---

8 The dropdown should display Time series by default.

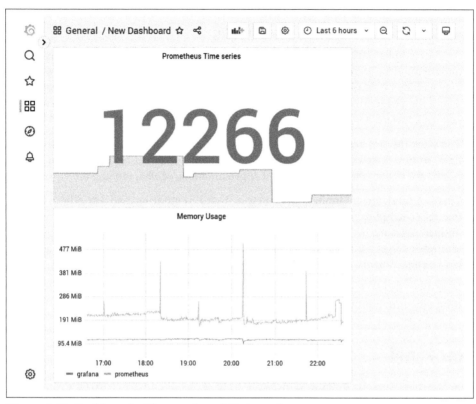

Figure 6-10. Dashboard with a graph and Stat panel

Displaying label values is handy for software versions on your graphs. Add another Stat panel; this time you will use the query expression **node_uname_info**, which contains the same information as the uname -a command. Set "Format as" to Table, and under "Value options," set the Fields to "release." Under "Panel options," the Title should be **Kernel version**. After clicking "Back to dashboard" and rearranging the panels using drag-and-drop, you should see something like Figure 6-11.

The Stat panel has further features, including different colors depending on the time series value, and displaying sparklines behind the value.

Figure 6-11. Dashboard with a graph and two Stat panels, one numeric and one text

Table Panel

While the Stat panel can display multiple time series, each unique time series takes quite a lot of space. The Table panel allows you to display multiple time series in a more concise way, and offers advanced features like pagination. Table panels tend to require more configuration than other panels, and all the text can look cluttered on your dashboards.

Add a new panel, this time a Table panel. As before, click "Add panel" and then "Add a new panel." Select Table in the dropdown on the right. Use the query expression `rate(node_network_receive_bytes_total[1m])` on the Metrics tab, and change the Type from Range to Instant. Change the Format to Table.

There are more columns that you need here. Go to the Transform tab, and click "Organize fields." Select the fields you want to hide by clicking the eye icon, as in Figure 6-12.

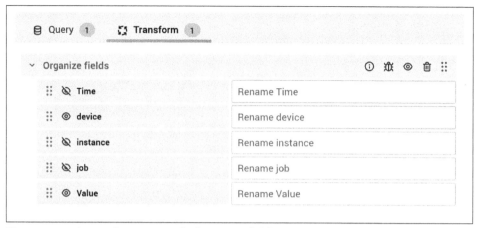

Figure 6-12. A transformation to hide certain fields

In the sidebar, under "Standard options," set the unit to "bytes/sec (IEC)" under "data rate." Finally, under "Panel options," set the title to **Network Traffic Received**. After all that, if you go back to the dashboard and rearrange the panels, you should see a dashboard like the one in Figure 6-13.

Figure 6-13. Dashboard with several panels, including a table for per-device network traffic

State Timeline Panel

When visualizing metrics that represent a state, such as the up metrics, the State timeline panel comes in handy. It shows how discrete state changes over time.

Let's use it to display our up metrics.

Let's add a State timeline panel. As before, Click "Add panel" and then "Add a new panel." Select "State Timeline" in the dropdown on the right. Use the query expression **up** on the Metrics tab. Set the legend to custom: {{job}} / {{instance}}.

In the sidebar, under "Standard options," set "Color scheme" to "Single Color." Under "Value mappings," click "Add value mappings" and add two value mappings: Value 1 to display the text UP, with a green color, and Value 2 to display DOWN, with a red color as seen in Figure 6-14.

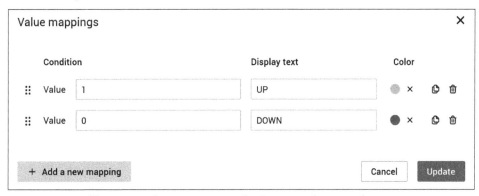

Figure 6-14. Adding two value mappings to the State timeline panel

You see the finished State timeline panel in Figure 6-15.

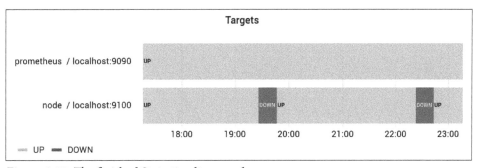

Figure 6-15. The finished State timeline panel

Template Variables

All the dashboard examples we have shown you so far have applied to a single Prometheus and a single Node Exporter. This is fine for demonstration of the basics, but not great when you have hundreds or even tens of machines to monitor. The good news is that you don't have to create a dashboard for every individual machine. You can use Grafana's templating feature.

You only have monitoring for one machine set up, so for this example we will template based on network devices, as you should have at least two of those.[9]

To start with, create a new dashboard by hovering on the four squares icon in the sidebar and then clicking "+New dashboard," as you can see in Figure 6-16.

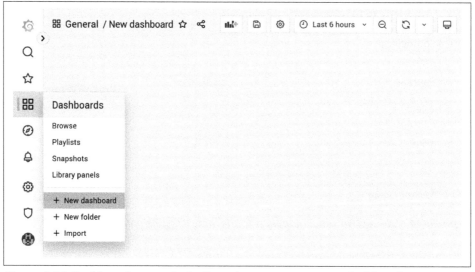

Figure 6-16. Dashboards menu, including a button to create new dashboards

---

9 Loopback and your wired and/or WiFi device.

Click the gear icon up top and then Variables.[10] Click "+Add variable" to add a template variable. The Name should be **Device**, and the "Data source" is Prometheus with a Refresh of "On time range change." The Query you will use is `label_val ues(node_network_receive_bytes_total, device)`.[11] The page should look like Figure 6-17. Click Update to add the variable.

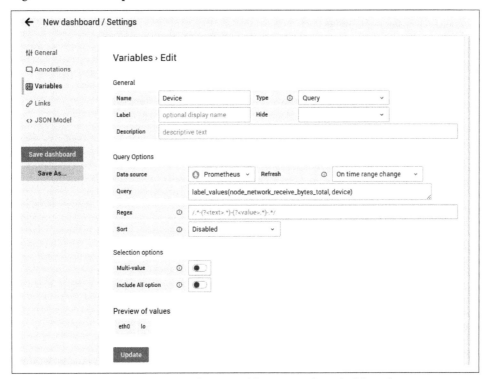

Figure 6-17. Adding a Device template variable to a Grafana dashboard

When you click the arrow to go back to the dashboard, a dropdown for the variable will now be available, as shown in Figure 6-18.

---

10 This was called templating in previous Grafana versions.

11 Note that this is not a PromQL query. `label_values` is specific to Grafana and used only for templating.

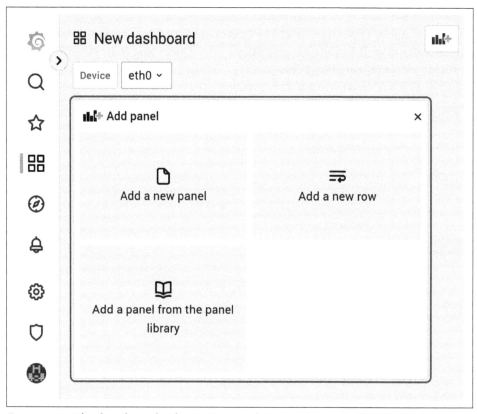

Figure 6-18. The dropdown for the Device template variable is visible

You now need to use the variable. Click the X to close the Templating section, then click the three dots, and add a new Time series panel. Configure the query expression to be `rate(node_network_receive_bytes_total{device="$Device"}[$__rate_interval])`, and $Device will be substituted with the value of the template variable. If you're using the Multi-value option, you would use device=~"$Device" as the variable would be a regular expression in that case. Regexes should also be used in case the value is complex, as Grafana would try to escape them anyway. Set the Legend Format to Custom then `{{device}}`, the Title to `Bytes Received`, and the Unit to "bytes/sec" under "data rate."

> As you have seen, we are using `$__rate_interval` in our PromQL expression. This is a Grafana feature that selects the best interval depending on the scrape interval set in the datasource configuration, and other parameters such as the step used in the panel. If you look at 24 hours of data, the value of `$__rate_interval` would be greater than if you only look at the last hour.

Click Apply and click the panel title, and this time click More and then Duplicate. This will create a copy of the existing panel. Alter the settings on this new panel to use the expression `rate(node_network_transmit_bytes_total {device=~"$Device"})[$__rate_interval]`, and set the Title to **Bytes Transmitted**. The dashboard will now have panels for bytes sent in both directions, as shown in Figure 6-19, and you can look at each network device by selecting it in the dropdown.

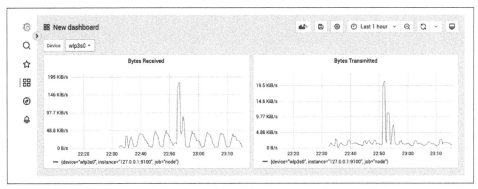

Figure 6-19. A basic network traffic dashboard using a template variable

In the real world you would probably template based on the `instance` label and display all the network-related metrics for one machine at once. You might even have multiple variables for one dashboard. This is how a generic dashboard for Java garbage collection might work: one variable for the `job`, one for the `instance`, and one to select which Prometheus data source to use.

You may have noticed that as you change the value of the variable, the URL parameters change, and similarly if you use the time controls. This allows you to share dashboard links, or have your alerts link to a dashboard with just the right variable values, as shown in "Notification templates" on page 337. There is a "Share dashboard" icon at the top of the page you can use to create the URLs and take snapshots of the data in the dashboard. Snapshots are perfect for postmortems and outage reports, where you want to preserve how the dashboard looked.

In the next chapter we will go into more detail on the Node Exporter and some of the metrics it offers.

PART III
Infrastructure Monitoring

The entire world does not (yet) revolve around Prometheus, nor provide Prometheus metrics out of the box. Exporters are tools that let you translate metrics from other systems into a format that Prometheus understands.

In Chapter 7 one of the first exporters you will probably use, the Node Exporter, is covered in detail.

In Chapter 8 you will learn how Prometheus knows what to pull metrics from and how to do so.

Chapter 9 dives into monitoring of container technologies such as Docker and Kubernetes.

There are literally hundreds of exporters in the Prometheus ecosystem. Chapter 10 shows you how to use various typical exporters.

As you may already have another metric-based monitoring system, Chapter 11 looks at how you can integrate those into Prometheus.

Exporters don't appear from thin air. If the exporter you want doesn't exist, you can use Chapter 12 to create one.

## CHAPTER 7

Node Exporter

The Node Exporter[1] is likely one of the first exporters you will use, as already seen in Chapter 2. It exposes machine-level metrics, largely from your operating system's kernel, such as CPU, memory, disk space, disk I/O, network bandwidth, and motherboard temperature. The Node Exporter is used with Unix systems; Windows users should use the Windows Exporter (*https://oreil.ly/mVsAX*) instead.[2]

The Node Exporter is intended only to monitor the machine itself, not individual processes or services on it. Other monitoring systems often have what we like to call an *uberagent*; that is, a single process that monitors everything on the machine. In the Prometheus architecture each of your services will expose its own metrics, using an exporter if needed, which is then directly scraped by Prometheus. This avoids you ending up with uberagent as either an operational or performance bottleneck, and enables you to think in terms more of dynamic services rather than machines.

The guidelines to use when you are creating metrics with direct instrumentation, such as those discussed in "What Should I Name My Metrics?" on page 60, are relatively clear. This is not the case with exporters, where by definition the data is coming from a source not designed with the Prometheus guidelines in mind. Depending on the volume and quality of metrics, trade-offs have to be made by the exporter developers between engineering effort and getting perfect metrics.

In the case of Linux, there are thousands of metrics on offer. Some are well documented and understood, such as CPU usage; others, like memory usage, have varied from kernel version to kernel version as the implementation has changed. You will

---

1 The Node Exporter has nothing to do with Node.js; it's node in the sense of compute node.

2 The Windows Exporter was previously known as the WMI Exporter.

even find metrics that are completely undocumented, where you would have to read the kernel source code to try to figure out what they do.

The Node Exporter is designed to be run as a nonroot user, and should be run directly on the machine in the same way you run a system daemon like sshd or cron.

 While running Node Exporter within Docker[3] is possible, you will need to use some volumes and command-line parameters (`--path.procfs`, `--path.rootfs`, `--path.sysfs`) to mount the host filesystem inside of the container. If possible, run the Node Exporter as a service on the node, without Docker. Docker attempts to isolate a container from the inner workings of the machine, which doesn't work well with the Node Exporter trying to get to those inner workings.

Unlike most other exporters, due to the broad variety of metrics available from operating systems, the Node Exporter allows you to configure which categories of metrics it fetches. You can do this with command-line flags such as `--collector.wifi`, which would enable the WiFi collector, and `--no-collector.wifi`, which would disable it. `--collector.disable-defaults` will disable all collectors except those explicitly enabled as command-line flags. There are reasonable defaults set, so this is not something you should worry about when starting out.

Different kernels expose different metrics, as, for example, Linux and FreeBSD do things in different ways. Metrics may move between collectors over time as the Node Exporter is refactored. If you are using a different Unix system, you will find that the metrics and collectors on offer vary.

In this chapter we explain some of the key metrics Node Exporter version 1.4.0 exposes with a 5.18.0 Linux kernel. This is not intended to be an exhaustive list of available metrics. As with most exporters and applications, you will want to look through the */metrics* path to see what is available. You can try out the example PromQL expressions using your setup from Chapter 2.

CPU Collector

The main metric from the CPU collector is `node_cpu_seconds_total`, which is a counter indicating how much time each CPU spent in each mode. The labels are `cpu` and `mode`:

---

3 Docker is a platform for developers and system administrators to build, package, and deploy applications in containers. A container is a lightweight, portable, and self-sufficient packaging technology that allows developers to deploy an application and its dependencies as a single unit.

```
# HELP node_cpu_seconds_total Seconds the CPUs spent in each mode.
# TYPE node_cpu_seconds_total counter
node_cpu_seconds_total{cpu="0",mode="idle"} 13024.48
node_cpu_seconds_total{cpu="0",mode="iowait"} 9.53
node_cpu_seconds_total{cpu="0",mode="irq"} 0
node_cpu_seconds_total{cpu="0",mode="nice"} 0.11
node_cpu_seconds_total{cpu="0",mode="softirq"} 109.74
node_cpu_seconds_total{cpu="0",mode="steal"} 0
node_cpu_seconds_total{cpu="0",mode="system"} 566.67
node_cpu_seconds_total{cpu="0",mode="user"} 1220.36
node_cpu_seconds_total{cpu="1",mode="idle"} 13501.28
node_cpu_seconds_total{cpu="1",mode="iowait"} 5.96
node_cpu_seconds_total{cpu="1",mode="irq"} 0
node_cpu_seconds_total{cpu="1",mode="nice"} 0.09
node_cpu_seconds_total{cpu="1",mode="softirq"} 23.74
node_cpu_seconds_total{cpu="1",mode="steal"} 0
node_cpu_seconds_total{cpu="1",mode="system"} 423.84
node_cpu_seconds_total{cpu="1",mode="user"} 936.05
```

For each CPU, the modes will in aggregate increase by one second per second. This allows you to calculate the proportion of idle time across all CPUs using the PromQL expression:

```
avg without(cpu, mode)(rate(node_cpu_seconds_total{mode="idle"}[1m]))
```

This works as it calculates the idle time per second per CPU and then averages that across all the CPUs in the machine.

You could generalize this to calculate the proportion of time spent in each mode for a machine using:

```
avg without(cpu)(rate(node_cpu_seconds_total[1m]))
```

CPU usage by guests (i.e., virtual machines running under the kernel) is already included in the user and nice modes. You can see guest time separately in the node_cpu_guest_seconds_total metric.

Filesystem Collector

The filesystem collector unsurprisingly collects metrics about your *mounted* filesystems, just as you would obtain from the df command. The --collector.file system.mount-points-exclude and --collector.filesystem.fs-types-exclude flags allow restricting which filesystems are included (the defaults exclude various pseudofilesystems). As you will not have Node Exporter running as root, you will need to ensure that file permissions allow it to use the statfs system call on mount-points of interest to you.

All metrics from this collector are prefixed with node_filesystem_ and have device, fstype, and mountpoint labels:

```
# HELP node_filesystem_size_bytes Filesystem size in bytes.
# TYPE node_filesystem_size_bytes gauge
node_filesystem_size_bytes{device="/dev/sda5",fstype="ext4",mountpoint="/"} 9e+10
```

The filesystem metrics are largely self-evident. The one subtlety you should be aware of is the difference between node_filesystem_avail_bytes and node_file system_free_bytes. On Unix filesystems some space is reserved for the root user, so that they can still do things when users fill up all available space. node_filesys tem_avail_bytes is the space available to users, and when trying to calculate used disk space you should accordingly use:

```
  node_filesystem_avail_bytes
/
  node_filesystem_size_bytes
```

node_filesystem_files and node_filesystem_files_free indicate the number of inodes and how many of them are free, which are roughly speaking the number of files your filesystem has. You can also see this with df -i.

Diskstats Collector

The diskstats collector exposes disk I/O metrics from */proc/diskstats*. By default, the --collector.diskstats.device-exclude flag attempts to exclude things that are not real disks, such as partitions and loopback devices:

```
# HELP node_disk_io_now The number of I/Os currently in progress.
# TYPE node_disk_io_now gauge
node_disk_io_now{device="sda"} 0
```

All metrics have a device label, and almost all are counters, as follows:

node_disk_io_now
    The number of I/Os in progress

node_disk_io_time_seconds_total
    Incremented when I/O is in progress

node_disk_read_bytes_total
    Bytes read by I/Os

```
node_disk_read_time_seconds_total
```
The time taken by read I/Os

```
node_disk_reads_completed_total
```
The number of complete I/Os

```
node_disk_written_bytes_total
```
Bytes written by I/Os

```
node_disk_write_time_seconds_total
```
The time taken by write I/Os

```
node_disk_writes_completed_total
```
The number of complete write I/Os

These mostly mean what you think, but take a look at the kernel documentation (*https://oreil.ly/xcAUs*)[4] for more details.

You can use `node_disk_io_time_seconds_total` to calculate disk I/O utilization, as would be shown by `iostat -x`:

```
rate(node_disk_io_time_seconds_total[1m])
```

You can calculate the average time for a read I/O with:

```
    rate(node_disk_read_time_seconds_total[1m])
/
    rate(node_disk_reads_completed_total[1m])
```

Netdev Collector

The netdev collector exposes metrics about your network devices with the prefix `node_network_` and a `device` label:

```
# HELP node_network_receive_bytes_total Network device statistic receive_bytes.
# TYPE node_network_receive_bytes_total counter
node_network_receive_bytes_total{device="lo"} 8.3213967e+07
node_network_receive_bytes_total{device="wlan0"} 7.0854462e+07
```

`node_network_receive_bytes_total` and `node_network_transmit_bytes_total` are the main metrics you will care about as you can calculate network bandwidth in and out with them:

```
rate(node_network_receive_bytes_total[1m])
```

---

4 A sector is always 512 bytes in */proc/diskstats*; you do not need to worry if your disks are using larger sector sizes. This is an example of something that is only apparent from reading the Linux source code.

You may also be interested in `node_network_receive_packets_total` and `node_net work_transmit_packets_total`, which track packets in and out, respectively.

Meminfo Collector

The meminfo collector has all your standard memory-related metrics with a `node_memory_` prefix. These all come from your */proc/meminfo*, and this is the first collector where semantics get a bit muddy. The collector does convert kilobytes to preferred bytes, but beyond that it's up to you to know enough from the documentation (*https://oreil.ly/F-0JW*) and experience with Linux internals to understand what these metrics mean:

```
# HELP node_memory_MemTotal_bytes Memory information field MemTotal.
# TYPE node_memory_MemTotal_bytes gauge
node_memory_MemTotal_bytes 3.285016576e+10
```

For example, `node_memory_MemTotal_bytes` is the total[5] amount of physical memory in the machine—nice and obvious. But note that there is no used memory metric, so you have to somehow calculate it and thus how much memory is not used from other metrics.

`node_memory_MemFree_bytes` is the amount of memory that isn't used by anything, but that doesn't mean it is all the memory you have to spare. In theory your page cache (`node_memory_Cached_bytes`) can be reclaimed, as can your write buffers (`node_memory_Buffers_bytes`), but that could adversely affect performance for some applications.[6] In addition, there are various other kernel structures using memory such as slab and page tables.

`node_memory_MemAvailable` is a heuristic from the kernel for how much memory is really available, but was only added in version 3.14 of Linux. If you are running a new enough kernel, this is a metric you could use to detect memory exhaustion.

Hwmon Collector

When on bare metal, the hwmon collector provides metrics such as temperature and fan speeds with a `node_hwmon_` prefix. This is the same information you can obtain with the `sensors` command:

```
# HELP node_hwmon_sensor_label Label for given chip and sensor
# TYPE node_hwmon_sensor_label gauge
node_hwmon_sensor_label{chip="platform_coretemp_0",
    label="core_0",sensor="temp2"} 1
```

---

5 Almost.

6 Prometheus 2.0, for example, relies on page cache.

```
node_hwmon_sensor_label{chip="platform_coretemp_0",
    label="core_1",sensor="temp3"} 1
# HELP node_hwmon_temp_celsius Hardware monitor for temperature (input)
# TYPE node_hwmon_temp_celsius gauge
node_hwmon_temp_celsius{chip="platform_coretemp_0",sensor="temp1"} 42
node_hwmon_temp_celsius{chip="platform_coretemp_0",sensor="temp2"} 42
node_hwmon_temp_celsius{chip="platform_coretemp_0",sensor="temp3"} 41
```

node_hwmon_temp_celsius is the temperature of various of your components, which may also have sensor labels[7] exposed in node_hwmon_sensor_label.

While it is not the case for all hardware, for some[8] you will need the sensor label to understand what the sensor is. In the preceding metrics, temp3 represents CPU core number 1.

You can join the label label from node_hwmon_sensor_label to node_hwmon_temp_celsius using group_left, which is further discussed in "Many-to-One and group_left" on page 268:

```
    node_hwmon_temp_celsius
  * ignoring(label) group_left(label)
    node_hwmon_sensor_label
```

Stat Collector

The stat collector is a bit of a mix, as it provides metrics from */proc/stat*.[9]

node_boot_time_seconds is when the kernel started, from which you can calculate how long the kernel has been up:

```
    time() - node_boot_time_seconds
```

node_intr_total indicates the number of hardware interrupts you have had. It isn't called node_interrupts_total, as that is used by the interrupts collector, which is disabled by default due to high cardinality.

The other metrics relate to processes. node_forks_total is a counter for the number of fork syscalls, node_context_switches_total is the number of context switches, while node_procs_blocked and node_procs_running indicate the number of processes that are blocked or running.

---

7 *Labels* here does not mean Prometheus labels; they are sensor labels and come from files such as */sys/devices/platform/coretemp.0/hwmon/hwmon1/temp3_label*.

8 Such as our laptop, which the preceding metric output is from.

9 It used to also provide CPU metrics, which have now been refactored into the CPU collector.

Uname Collector

The uname collector exposes a single metric, `node_uname_info`, which you already saw in "Stat Panel" on page 113:

```
# HELP node_uname_info Labeled system information as provided by the uname
    system call.
# TYPE node_uname_info gauge
node_uname_info{domainname="(none)",machine="x86_64",nodename="kozo",
    release="4.4.0-101-generic",sysname="Linux",
    version="#124-Ubuntu SMP Fri Nov 10 18:29:59 UTC 2017"} 1
```

The `nodename` label is the hostname of the machine, which may differ from the `instance` target label (see "Target Labels" on page 153) or any other names, such as in DNS, that you may have for it.

To count how many machines run which kernel version, you could use:

```
count by(release)(node_uname_info)
```

OS Collector

The OS collector exposes two metrics, `node_os_info` and `node_os_version`, which provide you with operating system information:

```
# HELP node_os_info A metric with a constant '1' value labeled by
    build_id, id, id_like, image_id, image_version, name,
    pretty_name, variant, variant_id, version, version_codename,
    version_id.
# TYPE node_os_info gauge
node_os_info{build_id="22.05.20220912.bf014ca",id="nixos",
    id_like="",image_id="",image_version="",name="NixOS",
    pretty_name="NixOS 22.05 (Quokka)",variant="",
    variant_id="",version="22.05 (Quokka)",
    version_codename="quokka",version_id="22.05"} 1
# HELP node_os_version Metric containing the major.minor
    part of the OS version.
# TYPE node_os_version gauge
node_os_version{id="nixos",id_like="",name="NixOS"} 22.05
```

To count how many machines run which distro version, you could use:

```
count by(name, version)(node_os_info)
```

Loadavg Collector

The loadavg collector provides the 1-, 5-, and 15-minute load averages as `node_load1`, `node_load5`, and `node_load15`, respectively.

The meaning of this metric varies across platforms, and may not mean what you think it does. For example, on Linux it is not just the number of processes waiting in the run queue, but also uninterruptible processes such as those waiting for I/O.

> If your kernel is recent enough, we recommend that you use the pressure collector, as described in "Pressure Collector" on page 133.

Load averages can be useful for a quick idea if a machine has gotten busier (for some definition of busier) recently, but they are not a good choice to alert on. For a more detailed look we recommend Brendan Gregg's blog, "Linux Load Averages: Solving the Mystery" (*https://oreil.ly/JVKfd*).

> Its a silly number but people think its important.
>
> —A comment in the Linux loadavg.c

Pressure Collector

Pressure Stall Information (PSI) was introduced in Linux kernel 4.20. These metrics measure resource pressure for three resources: CPU, memory, and I/O. It needs to be enabled in the kernel during compilation time.

Your kernel might be built with PSI support but it could be disabled by default, in which case you can pass `psi=1` on the kernel command line during boot to enable it.

Five different metrics are exposed by the PSI collector:

```
# HELP node_pressure_cpu_waiting_seconds_total
    Total time in seconds that processes have waited for CPU time
# TYPE node_pressure_cpu_waiting_seconds_total counter
node_pressure_cpu_waiting_seconds_total 113.6605130
# HELP node_pressure_io_stalled_seconds_total
    Total time in seconds no process could make progress due to IO congestion
# TYPE node_pressure_io_stalled_seconds_total counter
node_pressure_io_stalled_seconds_total 8.630361
# HELP node_pressure_io_waiting_seconds_total
    Total time in seconds that processes have waited due to IO congestion
# TYPE node_pressure_io_waiting_seconds_total counter
node_pressure_io_waiting_seconds_total 9.609997
# HELP node_pressure_memory_stalled_seconds_total
    Total time in seconds no process could make progress
# TYPE node_pressure_memory_stalled_seconds_total counter
node_pressure_memory_stalled_seconds_total 0
# HELP node_pressure_memory_waiting_seconds_total
    Total time in seconds that processes have waited for memory
# TYPE node_pressure_memory_waiting_seconds_total counter
node_pressure_memory_waiting_seconds_total 0
```

waiting metrics indicate the total amount of seconds that some tasks have been waiting, and stalled means that all tasks were delayed by lack of resources. Memory and I/O have both waiting and stalled metrics, where CPU only has waiting. This is because a CPU is always executing a process.

As those are counters, you can use them with the rate() function to determine whether some resources are overloaded:

```
rate(node_pressure_memory_waiting_seconds_total[1m])
```

Textfile Collector

The textfile collector is a bit different from the collectors we have already shown you. It doesn't obtain metrics from the kernel, but rather from files that you produce.

The Node Exporter is not meant to run as root, so metrics such as those from SMART[10] require root privileges to run the smartctl command.

In addition to metrics that require root, you can only obtain some information by running a command such as iptables. For reliability, the Node Exporter does not start processes.

To use the textfile collector you would create a cronjob that regularly runs commands such as smartctl or iptables, converts its output into the Prometheus text exposition format, and atomically writes it to a file in a specific directory. On every scrape, the Node Exporter will read the files in that directory and include their metrics in its output.

 The Prometheus server cannot read text files directly, therefore you need a software to expose the file as HTTP. While you could use any HTTP server, the Node Exporter also checks that the metrics are correct and is able to expose metrics coming from multiple files.

You can use this collector to add in your own metrics via cronjobs, or you could have more static information that comes from files written out by your machine configuration management system to provide some info metrics (discussed in "Info" on page 96), such as which Chef[11] roles it has, about the machine.

---

10 Self-Monitoring, Analysis, and Reporting Technology, metrics from hard drives that can be useful to predict and detect failure.

11 Chef is a configuration management tool that allows for automated infrastructure provisioning and management through the use of reusable scripts called "cookbooks."

As with the Node Exporter generally, the textfile collector is intended for metrics about a machine. For example, there might be some kernel metric that the Node Exporter does not yet expose, or that requires root to access. You might want to track more operating system-level metrics, such as if there are pending package updates or a reboot due. While it is technically a service rather than an operating system metric, recording when batch jobs such as backups last completed for the Cassandra[12] node running on the machine would also be a good use of the textfile collector, as your interest in whether the backups worked on that machine goes away when the machine does. That is to say the Cassandra node has the same lifecycle as the machine.[13]

The textfile collector should not be used to try to convert Prometheus to push. Nor should you use the textfile collector as a way to take metrics from other exporters and applications running on the machine and expose them all on the Node Exporter's /metrics, but rather have Prometheus scrape each exporter and application individually.

Using the Textfile Collector

The textfile collector is enabled by default, but you must provide the --collector.textfile.directory command-line flag to the Node Exporter for it to work. This should point to a directory that you use solely for this purpose to avoid mixups.

To try this out you should create a directory, write out a simple file in the exposition format (as discussed in "Text Exposition Format" on page 80), and start the Node Exporter with it configured to use this directory, as shown in Example 7-1. The textfile collector only looks at files with the .prom extension.

Example 7-1. Using the textfile collector with a simple example

```
hostname $ mkdir textfile
hostname $ echo example_metric 1 > textfile/example.prom
hostname $ ./node_exporter --collector.textfile.directory=$PWD/textfile
```

Example 7-2 shows the content of the file created by Example 7-1.

Example 7-2. The content of textfile/example.prom

```
example_metric 1
```

---

12 A distributed database.

13 If a metric about a batch job has a different lifecycle than the machine, it is likely a service-level batch job and you may wish to use the Pushgateway, as discussed in "Pushgateway" on page 76.

If you look at the Node Exporter's */metrics*, you will now see your metric:

```
# HELP example_metric Metric read from /some/path/textfile/example.prom
# TYPE example_metric untyped
example_metric 1
```

 If no HELP is provided, the textfile collector will provide one for you. If you are putting the same metric in multiple files (with different labels of course), you need to provide the same HELP for each, as otherwise the mismatched HELP will cause an error.

Usually you will create and update the *.prom* files with a cronjob. As a scrape can happen at any time, it is important that the Node Exporter does not see partially written files. To this end you should write first to a temporary file in the same directory and then move the complete file to the final filename.[14]

Example 7-3 shows a cronjob that outputs to the textfile collector. It creates the metrics in a temporary file,[15] and renames them to the final filename. This is a trivial example that uses short commands, but in most real-world use cases you will want to create a script to keep things readable.

Example 7-3. /etc/crontab that exposes the number of lines in /etc/shadow as the shadow_entries metric using the textfile collector

```
TEXTFILE=/path/to/textfile/directory

# This must all be on one line
*/5 * * * * root (echo -n 'shadow_entries '; grep -c . /etc/shadow)
    > $TEXTFILE/shadow.prom.$$
    && mv $TEXTFILE/shadow.prom.$$ $TEXTFILE/shadow.prom
```

A number of example scripts for use with the textfile collector are available in the textfile collector example scripts GitHub repository (*https://oreil.ly/HMkDo*).

---

14 The `rename` system call is atomic, but can only be used on the same filesystem.

15 $$ in shell expands to the current process ID (pid).

Timestamps

While the exposition format supports timestamps, you cannot use them with the textfile collector. This is because it doesn't make sense semantically, as your metrics would not appear with the same timestamp as other metrics from the scrape.

Instead, the mtime[16] of the file is available to you in the node_textfile_mtime_seconds metric. You can use this to alert on your cronjobs not working, because if this value is from too long ago it can indicate a problem:

```
# HELP node_textfile_mtime_seconds Unixtime mtime of textfiles successfully read.
# TYPE node_textfile_mtime_seconds gauge
node_textfile_mtime_seconds{file="example.prom"} 1.516205651e+09
```

Now that you have the Node Exporter running, let's look at how you can tell Prometheus about all the machines you have it running on.

---

16 The mtime is the last time the file was modified.

## CHAPTER 8

Service Discovery

Thus far you've had Prometheus find what to scrape using static configuration via `static_configs`. This is fine for simple use cases,[1] but having to manually keep your *prometheus.yml* up to date as machines are added and removed would get annoying, particularly if you were in a dynamic environment where new instances might be brought up every minute. This chapter will show you how you can let Prometheus know what to scrape.

You already know where all of your machines and services are, and how they are laid out. Service discovery (SD) enables you to provide that information to Prometheus from whichever database you store it in. Prometheus supports many common sources of service information, such as Consul, Amazon EC2, and Kubernetes out of the box. If your particular source isn't already supported, you can use the file-based and HTTP-based service discovery mechanisms to hook it in. For file-based service discovery, this could be by having your configuration management system, such as Ansible or Chef, write the list of machines and services they know about in the right format, or a script running regularly to pull it from whatever data source you use. For HTTP-based service discovery, third-party tools such as NetBox (*https://oreil.ly/-cbF3*) offer plug-ins that can be installed to offer Prometheus-compatible HTTP service discovery endpoints. Note that some SD projects[2] support both HTTP-based service discovery and file-based service discovery.

Knowing what your monitoring targets are, and thus what should be scraped, is only the first step. Labels are a key part of Prometheus (see Chapter 5), and assigning *target labels* to targets allows them to be grouped and organized in ways that make

---

1 Brian's home Prometheus uses a hardcoded static configuration, for example, as I only have a handful of machines.

2 Like Prometheus vCloud Director SD (*https://oreil.ly/sxi0j*)

sense to you. Target labels allow you to aggregate targets performing the same role, that are in the same environment, or are run by the same team.

As target labels are configured in Prometheus rather than in the applications and exporters themselves, this allows your different teams to have label hierarchies that make sense to them. Your infrastructure team might care only about which rack and PDU[3] a machine is on, while your database team would care that it is the PostgreSQL master for their production environment. If you had a kernel developer who was investigating a rarely occurring problem, they might just care which kernel version was in use.

Service discovery and the pull model allow all these views of the world to coexist, as each of your teams can run their own Prometheus with the target labels that make sense to them.

Service Discovery Mechanisms

Service discovery is designed to integrate with the machine and service databases that you already have. Out of the box, Prometheus 2.37.0 has support for Azure, Consul, DigitalOcean, Docker, Docker Swarm, DNS, Eureka, EC2,[4] file-based service discovery, GCE,[5] Hetzner, HTTP-based service discovery, IONOS Cloud, Kubernetes, Kuma, LightSail, Linode (Akamai), Marathon, Nerve, Nomad, OpenStack, PuppetDB, Scaleway, Serverset, Uyuni, Triton, and Vultr service discovery in addition to the static discovery you have already seen.

Service discovery isn't just about you providing a list of machines to Prometheus, or monitoring. It is a more general concern that you will see across your systems; applications need to find their dependencies to talk to, and hardware technicians need to know which machines are safe to turn off and repair. Accordingly, you should not only have a raw list of machines and services, but also conventions around how they are organized and their lifecycles.

A good service discovery mechanism will provide you with *metadata*. This may be the name of a service, its description, which team owns it, structured tags about it, or anything else that you may find useful. Metadata is what you will convert into target labels, and generally the more metadata you have, the better.

---

3 The Power Distribution Unit (PDU), part of the electrical system in a datacenter. PDUs usually feed a group of racks with electricity, and knowing the CPU load on each machine could be useful to ensure each PDU can provide the power required.

4 Amazon Elastic Compute Cloud

5 Google Compute Engine

A full discussion of service discovery is beyond the scope of this book. If you haven't gotten around to formalizing your configuration management and service databases yet, Consul tends to be a good place to start.

Top-Down Versus Bottom-Up

There are two broad categories of service discovery mechanisms you will come across. Those where the service instances register with service discovery, such as Consul, are bottom-up. Those where instead the service discovery knows what should be there, such as EC2, are top-down.

Both approaches are common. Top-down makes it easy for you to detect if something is meant to be running but isn't. However, for bottom-up you would need a separate reconciliation process to ensure things are in sync, so that cases such as an application instance that stalls before it can register are caught.

Static

You have already seen static configuration in Chapter 2, where targets are provided directly in *prometheus.yml*. It is useful if you have a small and simple setup that rarely changes. This might be your home network, a scrape config that is only for a local Pushgateway, or even Prometheus scraping itself, as in Example 8-1.

Example 8-1. Using static service discovery to have Prometheus scrape itself

```
scrape_configs:
 - job_name: prometheus
   static_configs:
    - targets:
      - localhost:9090
```

If you are using a configuration management tool such as Ansible, you could have its Jinja2 templating system write out a list of all the machines it knows about to have their Node Exporters scraped, such as in Example 8-2.

Example 8-2. Using Ansible's templating to create targets for the Node Exporter on all machines

```
scrape_configs:
 - job_name: node
   static_configs:
    - targets:
{% for host in groups["all"] %}
     - {{ host }}:9100
{% endfor %}
```

In addition to providing a list of targets, a static config can also provide labels for those targets in the `labels` field. If you find yourself needing this, then file SD, covered in "File" on page 142, tends to be a better approach.

The plural in `static_configs` indicates that it is a list, and you can specify multiple static configs in one scrape config, as shown in Example 8-3. While there is not much point to doing this for static configs, it can be useful with other service discovery mechanisms if you want to talk to multiple data sources. You can even mix and match service discovery mechanisms within a scrape config, though that is unlikely to result in a particularly understandable configuration.

Example 8-3. Two monitoring targets are provided, each in its own static config

```
scrape_configs:
 - job_name: node
   static_configs:
    - targets: ❶
      - host1:9100
      labels:
        datacenter: paris
    - targets: ❷
      - host2:9100
      - host3:9100
      labels:
        datacenter: montreal
```

❶ The first static config, containing a single target, with a label `datacenter` set to `paris`.

❷ The second static config, containing two targets, with a label `datacenter` set to `montreal`.

The same applies to `scrape_configs`, a list of scrape configs in which you can specify as many as you like. The only restriction is that the `job_name` must be unique.

File

File service discovery, usually referred to as *file SD*, does not use the network. Instead, it reads monitoring targets from files you provide on the local filesystem. This allows you to integrate with service discovery systems Prometheus doesn't support out of the box, or when Prometheus can't quite do the things you need with the metadata available.

You can provide files in either JSON or YAML formats. The file extension must be *.json* for JSON, and either *.yml* or *.yaml* for YAML. You can see a JSON example in Example 8-4, which you would put in a file called *filesd.json*. You can have as many or as few targets as you like in a single file.

Example 8-4. filesd.json with three targets

```
[
  {
    "targets": [ "host1:9100", "host2:9100" ],
    "labels": {
      "team": "infra",
      "job": "node"
    }
  },
  {
    "targets": [ "host1:9090" ],
    "labels": {
      "team": "monitoring",
      "job": "prometheus"
    }
  }
]
```

 The JSON format is not perfect. One issue you will likely encounter here is that the last item in a list or hash cannot have a trailing comma. We would recommend using a JSON library to generate JSON files rather than trying to do it by hand.

Configuration in Prometheus uses `file_sd_configs` in your scrape config, as shown in Example 8-5. Each file SD config takes a list of filepaths, and you can use globs in the filename.[6] Paths are relative to Prometheus's working directory, which is to say the directory you start Prometheus in.

Example 8-5. prometheus.yml using file service discovery

```
scrape_configs:
 - job_name: file
   file_sd_configs:
     - files:
         - '*.json'
```

---

6 You cannot, however, put globs in the directory, so a/b/*.json is fine, a/*/file.json is not.

Usually you would not provide metadata for use with relabeling when using file SD, but rather the ultimate target labels you would like to have.

If you visit *http://localhost:9090/service-discovery* in your browser[7] and click "show more," you will see Figure 8-1, with both job and team labels from *filesd.json*.[8] As these are made-up targets, the scrapes will fail, unless you actually happen to have a host1 and host2 on your network.

Figure 8-1. Service discovery status page showing three discovered targets from file SD

---

7 This endpoint was added in Prometheus 2.1.0. On older versions you can hover over the Labels on the Targets page to see the metadata.

8 job_name is only a default, which we will look at further in "Duplicate Jobs" on page 163. The other __ labels are special and will be covered in "How to Scrape" on page 162.

Providing the targets with a file means it could come from templating in a configuration management system, a daemon that writes it out regularly, or even from a web service via a cronjob using `wget`. Changes are picked up automatically using inotify, so it would be wise to ensure file changes are made atomically using `rename`, similarly to how you did in "Textfile Collector" on page 134.

HTTP

HTTP service discovery, usually referred to as *HTTP SD*, fetches a target list using HTTP. This mechanism makes it possible to integrate any application directly with Prometheus, without the need to produce files locally on the Prometheus server.

With HTTP service discovery, Prometheus will refresh the target list every minute.[9] As shown in Example 8-6, the minimum configuration to provide to Prometheus is the URL of the service discovery endpoint.

Example 8-6. prometheus.yml with `http_sd_configs`

```
scrape_configs:
 - job_name: cmdb
   http_sd_configs:
    - url: http://cmdb.local/prometheus-service-discovery
```

Service discovery endpoints must use the same JSON format as in Example 8-4. The HTTP Header `Content-Type` must be `application/json` and the HTTP response code must be 200. Unlike file SD, YAML is not supported by HTTP SD.

> In case of a failure, the last discovered targets are kept by Prometheus. As this targets list is not persisted on disk, failures happening directly after a Prometheus restart will produce an empty target list.
>
> You can monitor the health of the HTTP service discovery with the counter `prometheus_sd_http_failures_total`. If it is continuously increasing, Prometheus can't refresh its targets.

The HTTP SD provides all the necessary HTTP options to authenticate. An example with TLS certificates and credentials is shown in Example 8-7.

---

9 By default, one request is made every 60 seconds. This can be changed with the `refresh_interval` parameter.

Example 8-7. prometheus.yml with `http_sd_configs` and security options

```
scrape_configs:
 - job_name: cmdb
   http_sd_configs:
    - url: http://cmdb.local/prometheus-service-discovery
      authorization:
        credentials_file: token
      tls_config:
        ca_file: ca.crt
```

Consul

Consul service discovery is a service discovery mechanism from HashiCorp. If you do not already have a service discovery system within your organization, Consul is one of the easier ones to get up and running. Consul has an agent that runs on each of your machines, and these gossip among themselves. Applications talk only to the local agent on a machine. Some number of agents are also servers, providing persistence and consistency.

To try it out, you can set up a development Consul agent by following Example 8-8. If you wish to use Consul in production, you should follow the official Getting Started (*https://oreil.ly/SmhRW*) guide.

Example 8-8. Setting up a Consul agent in development mode

```
hostname $ wget https://releases.hashicorp.com/consul/1.0.2/
    consul_1.0.2_linux_amd64.zip
hostname $ unzip consul_1.0.2_linux_amd64.zip
hostname $ ./consul agent -dev
```

The Consul UI should now be available in your browser on *http://localhost:8500/*. Consul has a notion of services, and in the development setup has a single service, which is Consul itself. Next, run a Prometheus with the configuration in Example 8-9.

Example 8-9. prometheus.yml using Consul service discovery

```
scrape_configs:
 - job_name: consul
   consul_sd_configs:
    - server: 'localhost:8500'
```

Go to *http://localhost:9090/service-discovery* in your browser and you will see the screen in Figure 8-2, showing that the Consul service discovery has discovered a single target with some metadata, which became a target with instance and job labels. If you had more agents and services, they would also show up here.

Figure 8-2. Service discovery status page showing one discovered target, its metadata, and target labels from Consul

Consul does not expose metrics behind a */metrics* path, so the scrapes from your Prometheus will fail. But it does still provide enough to find all your machines running a Consul agent, and thus should be running a Node Exporter that you can scrape. We will look at how in "Relabeling" on page 149.

> If you want to monitor Consul itself, you will need to config-
> ure both Prometheus and Consul accordingly. See the Consul
> documentation (*https://oreil.ly/Sz3bP*) for more details. A Con-
> sul Exporter (*https://oreil.ly/4ZDhM*) provides cluster-level and kv-
> based metrics.

EC2

Amazon Elastic Compute Cloud, more commonly known as EC2, is a popular provider of virtual machines. It is one of several cloud providers that Prometheus allows you to use out of the box for service discovery.

To use it you must provide Prometheus with credentials to use the EC2 API. One way you can do this is by setting up an IAM user with the `AmazonEC2ReadOnlyAccess` policy[10] and providing the access key and secret key in the configuration file, as shown in Example 8-10.

Example 8-10. prometheus.yml using EC2 service discovery

```
scrape_configs:
 - job_name: ec2
   ec2_sd_configs:
    - region: <region>
      access_key: <access key>
      secret_key: <secret key>
```

If you aren't already running some, start at least one EC2 instance in the EC2 region you have configured Prometheus to look at. If you go to *http://localhost:9090/ service-discovery* in your browser, you can see the discovered targets and the metadata extracted from EC2. `__meta_ec2_tag_Name="My Display Name"`, for example, is the `Name` tag on this instance, which is the name you will see in the EC2 Console (Figure 8-3).

You may notice that the `instance` label is using the private IP. This is a sensible default as it is presumed that Prometheus will be running beside what it is monitoring. Not all EC2 instances have public IPs, and there are network charges for talking to an EC2 instance's public IP.

You will find that service discovery for other cloud providers is broadly similar, but the configuration required and metadata returned vary.

---

10 Only the `EC2:DescribeInstances` permission is needed, but policies are generally easier for you to set up initially.

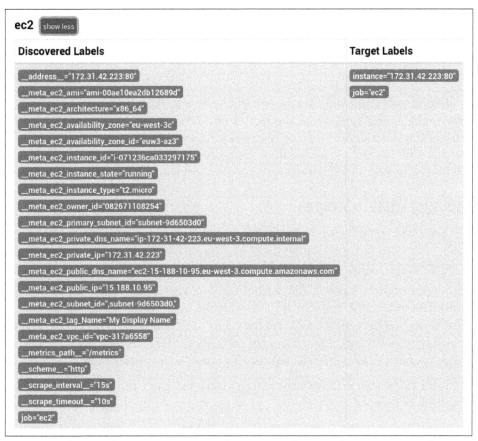

Figure 8-3. Service discovery status page showing one discovered target, its metadata, and target labels from EC2

Relabeling

As seen in the preceding examples of service discovery mechanisms, the targets and their metadata can be a little raw. You could integrate with file SD and provide Prometheus with exactly the targets and labels you want, but in most cases you won't need to. Instead, you can tell Prometheus how to map from metadata to targets using *relabeling*.

Many characters, such as periods and asterisks, are not valid in Prometheus label names, so will be sanitized to underscores in service discovery metadata.

In an ideal world you will have service discovery and relabeling configured so that new machines and applications are picked up and monitored automatically. In the real world it is not unlikely that as your setup matures it will get sufficiently intricate that you have to regularly update the Prometheus configuration file, but by then you will likely also have an infrastructure so complex that it is only a minor hurdle.

Choosing What to Scrape

The first thing you will want to configure is which targets you actually want to scrape. If you are part of one team running one service, you don't want your Prometheus to be scraping every target in the same EC2 region.

Continuing on from Example 8-5, what if you just wanted to monitor the infrastructure team's machines? You can do this with the keep *relabel action*, as shown in Example 8-11. The regex is applied to the values of the labels listed in source_labels (joined by a semicolon), and if the regex matches, the target is kept. As there is only one action here, this results in all targets with team="infra" being kept.

But for a target with a team="monitoring" label, the regex will not match, and the target will be dropped.

Regular expressions in relabeling are *fully anchored*, meaning that the pattern infra will not match fooinfra or infrabar.

Example 8-11. Using a keep relabel action to only monitor targets with a team="infra" label

```
scrape_configs:
 - job_name: file
   file_sd_configs:
    - files:
       - '*.json'
   relabel_configs:
    - source_labels: [team]
      regex: infra
      action: keep
```

You can have multiple relabel actions in a `relabel_configs`; all of them will be processed in order unless either a `keep` or `drop` action drops the target. For example, Example 8-12 will drop all targets, as a label cannot have both `infra` and `monitoring` as a value.

Example 8-12. Two relabel actions requiring contradictory values for the `team` label

```
scrape_configs:
 - job_name: file
   file_sd_configs:
    - files:
       - '*.json'
   relabel_configs:
    - source_labels: [team]
      regex: infra
      action: keep
    - source_labels: [team]
      regex: monitoring
      action: keep
```

To allow multiple values for a label you would use | (the pipe symbol) for the alternation operator, which is a fancy way of saying one or the other. Example 8-13 shows the right way to keep only targets for either the infrastructure or monitoring teams.

Example 8-13. Using | to allow one label value or another

```
scrape_configs:
 - job_name: file
   file_sd_configs:
    - files:
       - '*.json'
   relabel_configs:
    - source_labels: [team]
      regex: infra|monitoring
      action: keep
```

In addition to the `keep` action that drops targets that do not match, you can also use the `drop` action to drop targets that do match. You can also provide multiple labels in `source_labels`; their values will be joined with a semicolon.[11] If you don't want to scrape the Prometheus jobs of the monitoring team, you can combine these, as in Example 8-14.

---

11 You can override the character used to join with the `separator` field.

Example 8-14. Using multiple source labels

```
scrape_configs:
 - job_name: file
   file_sd_configs:
    - files:
       - '*.json'
   relabel_configs:
    - source_labels: [job, team]
      regex: prometheus;monitoring
      action: drop
```

How you use relabeling is up to you. You should define some conventions. For example, EC2 instances should have a `team` tag with the name of the team that owns it, or all production services should have a `production` tag in Consul. Without conventions every new service will require special handling for monitoring, which is probably not the best use of your time.

If your service discovery mechanism includes health checking of some form, do not use this to drop unhealthy instances. Even when an instance is reporting as unhealthy, it could be producing useful metrics, particularly around startup and shutdown.

 Prometheus needs to have a target for each of your individual application instances. Scraping through load balancers will not work, as you can hit a different instance on each scrape, which could, for example, make counters appear to go backward.

Regular Expressions

Prometheus uses the *RE2* engine for regular expressions that comes with Go. RE2 is designed to be linear-time but does not support back references, lookahead assertions, and some other advanced features.

If you are not familiar with regular expressions, they let you provide a rule (called a *pattern*) that is then tested against text. The following table is a quick primer on regular expressions.

	Matches
a	The character a
.	Any single character
\.	A single period
.*	Any number of characters
.+	At least one character
a+	One or more a characters

	Matches
[0-9]	Any single digit, 0–9
\d	Any single digit, 0–9
\d*	Any number of digits
[^0-9]	A single character that is not a digit
ab	The character a followed by the character b
a(b|c*)	An a, followed by a single b, or any number of c characters

In addition, parentheses create a capture group. So if you had the pattern (.)(\d+) and the text a123, then the first capture group would contain a and the second 123. Capture groups are useful to extract parts of a string for later use.

Target Labels

Target labels are labels that are added to the labels of every time series returned from a scrape. They are the identity of your targets,[12] and accordingly they should not generally vary over time as might be the case with version numbers or machine owners.

Every time your target labels change the labels of the scraped time series, their identities also change. This will cause discontinuities in your graphs, and can cause issues with rules and alerts.

So what does make a good target label? You have already seen job and instance, target labels all targets have. It is also common to add target labels for the broader scope of the application, such as whether it is in development or production, their region, datacenter, and which team manages them. Labels for structure within your application can also make sense, for example, if there is sharding.

Target labels ultimately allow you to select, group, and aggregate targets in PromQL. For example, you might want alerts for development to be handled differently than production, to know which shard of your application is the most loaded, or which team is using the most CPU time.

But target labels come with a cost. While it is quite cheap to add one more label in terms of resources, the real cost comes when you are writing PromQL. Every additional label is one more you need to keep in mind for every single PromQL expression you write. For example, if you were to add a host label that was unique per target, that would violate the expectation that only instance is unique per target,

---

12 It is possible for two of your targets to have the same target labels, with other settings different, but this should be avoided because metrics such as up will clash.

which could break all of your aggregation that used without(instance). This is discussed further in Chapter 14.

As a rule of thumb your target labels should be a hierarchy, with each one adding additional distinctiveness. For example, you might have a hierarchy where regions contain datacenters that contain environments that contain services that contain jobs that contain instances. This isn't a hard-and-fast rule; you might plan ahead a little and have a datacenter label even if you only have one datacenter today.[13]

For labels the application knows about but don't make sense to have as target labels, such as version numbers, you can expose them using info metrics, as discussed in "Info" on page 96.

If you find that you want every target in a Prometheus to share some labels such as region, you should instead use external_labels for them, as discussed in "External Labels" on page 323.

replace

So how do you use relabeling to specify your target labels? The answer is the replace action. The replace action allows you to copy labels around, while also applying regular expressions.

Continuing on from Example 8-5, let's say that the monitoring team was renamed to the monitor team and you can't change the file SD input yet so you want to use relabeling instead. Example 8-15 looks for a team label that matches the regular expression monitoring (which is to say, the exact string monitoring), and if it finds it, puts the replacement value monitor in the team label.

Example 8-15. Using a replace relabel action to replace team="monitoring" with team="monitor"

```
scrape_configs:
 - job_name: file
   file_sd_configs:
    - files:
       - '*.json'
   relabel_configs:
    - source_labels: [team]
      regex: monitoring
      replacement: monitor
```

---

13 On the other hand, don't try to plan too far in advance. It's not unusual that, as your architecture changes over the years, your target label hierarchy will need to change with it. Predicting exactly how it will change is usually impossible. Consider, for example, if you were moving from a traditional datacenter setup to a provider like EC2, which has availability zones.

```
    target_label: team
    action: replace
```

That's fairly simple, but in practice having to specify replacement label values one by one would be a lot of work for you. Let's say it turns out that the problem was the ing in monitoring, and you wanted relabeling to strip any trailing "ings" in team names. Example 8-16 does this by applying the regular expression (.*)ing, which matches all strings that end with ing and puts the start of the label value in the first capture group. The replacement value consists of that first capture group, which will be placed in the team label.

Example 8-16. Using a replace relabel action to remove a trailing "ing" from the team label

```
scrape_configs:
 - job_name: file
   file_sd_configs:
    - files:
       - '*.json'
   relabel_configs:
    - source_labels: [team]
      regex: '(.*)ing'
      replacement: '${1}'
      target_label: team
      action: replace
```

If one of your targets does not have a label value that matches, such as team="infra", then the replace action has no effect on that target, as you can see in Figure 8-4.

Figure 8-4. The "ing" is removed from monitoring, while the "infra" targets are unaffected

A label with an empty value is the same as not having that label, so if you wanted to you could remove the team label using Example 8-17.

Example 8-17. Using a `replace` relabel action to remove the `team` label

```
scrape_configs:
 - job_name: file
   file_sd_configs:
    - files:
      - '*.json'
   relabel_configs:
    - source_labels: []
      regex: '(.*)'
      replacement: '${1}'
      target_label: team
      action: replace
```

 All labels beginning with __ are discarded at the end of relabeling for target labels, so you don't need to do this yourself.

Since performing a regular expression against the whole string, capturing it, and using it as the replacement is common, these are all defaults. Thus you can omit them,[14] and Example 8-18 will have the same effect as Example 8-17.

Example 8-18. Using the defaults to remove the `team` label succinctly

```
scrape_configs:
 - job_name: file
   file_sd_configs:
    - files:
      - '*.json'
   relabel_configs:
    - source_labels: []
      target_label: team
```

Now that you have more of a sense of how the `replace` action works, let's look at a more realistic example. Example 8-9 produced a target with port 80, but it'd be useful if you could change that to port 9100 where the Node Exporter is running. In Example 8-19 we take the address from Consul and append `:9100` to it, placing it in the `__address__` label.

---

14 You could also omit `source_labels: []`. We left it in here to make it clearer that the label was being removed.

Example 8-19. Using the IP from Consul with port 9100 for the Node Exporter

```
scrape_configs:
 - job_name: node
   consul_sd_configs:
     - server: 'localhost:8500'
   relabel_configs:
     - source_labels: [__meta_consul_address]
       regex: '(.*)'
       replacement: '${1}:9100'
       target_label: __address__
```

 If relabeling produces two identical targets from one of your scrape configs, they will be deduplicated automatically. So if you have many Consul services running on each machine, only one target per machine would result from Example 8-19.

job, instance, and __address__

In the preceding examples you may have noticed that there was an instance target label, but no matching instance label in the metadata. So where did it come from? The answer is that if your target has no instance label, it is defaulted to the value of the __address__ label.

instance along with job are two labels your targets will always have, job being defaulted from the job_name configuration option. The job label indicates a set of instances that serve the same purpose, and will generally all be running with the same binary and configuration.[15] The instance label identifies one instance within a job.

The __address__ is the host and port your Prometheus will connect to when scraping. While it provides a default for the instance label, it is separate so you can have a different value for it. For example, you may wish to use the Consul node name in the instance label, while leaving the address pointing to the IP address, as in Example 8-20. This is a better approach than adding an additional host, node, or alias label with a nicer name, as it avoids adding a second label unique to each target, which would cause complications in your PromQL.

---

15 A job could potentially be further divided into shards with another label.

Example 8-20. Using the IP from Consul with port 9100 as the address, with the node name in the instance *label*

```
scrape_configs:
 - job_name: consul
   consul_sd_configs:
    - server: 'localhost:8500'
   relabel_configs:
    - source_labels: [__meta_consul_address]
      regex: '(.*)'
      replacement: '${1}:9100'
      target_label: __address__
    - source_labels: [__meta_consul_node]
      regex: '(.*)'
      replacement: '${1}:9100'
      target_label: instance
```

> Prometheus will perform DNS resolution on the __address__, so one way you can have more readable instance labels is by providing host:port rather than ip:port.

labelmap

The labelmap action is different from the drop, keep, and replace actions you have already seen in that it applies to label names rather than label values.

Where you might find this useful is if the service discovery you are using already has a form of key-value labels, and you would like to use some of those as target labels. This might be to allow configuration of arbitrary target labels, without having to change your Prometheus configuration every time there is a new label.

EC2's tags, for example, are key-value pairs. You might have an existing convention to have the name of the service go in the service tag, and its semantics align with what the job label means in Prometheus. You might also declare a convention that any tags prefixed with monitor_ will become target labels. For example, an EC2 tag of mon itor_foo=bar would become a Prometheus target label of foo="bar". Example 8-21 shows this setup, using a replace action for the job label and a labelmap action for the monitor_ prefix.

Example 8-21. Use the EC2 service tag as the job label, with all tags prefixed with monitor_ as additional target labels

```
scrape_configs:
 - job_name: ec2
   ec2_sd_configs:
     - region: <region>
       access_key: <access key>
       secret_key: <secret key>
   relabel_configs:
     - source_labels: [__meta_ec2_tag_service]
       target_label: job
     - regex: __meta_ec2_public_tag_monitor_(.*)
       replacement: '${1}'
       action: labelmap
```

But you should be wary of blindly copying all labels in a scenario like this, as it is unlikely that Prometheus is the only consumer of metadata such as this within your overall architecture. For example, a new cost center tag might be added to all of your EC2 instances for internal billing reasons. If that tag automatically became a target label due to a labelmap action, that would change all of your target labels and likely break graphing and alerting. Thus, using either well-known names (such as the service tag here) or clearly namespaced names (such as monitor_) is wise.

Case

Sometimes, it is useful to change the case of label values. This enables you to make labels consistent across multiple service discoveries. You can change the case with the lowercase and uppercase relabel actions, as shown in Example 8-22.

Example 8-22. prometheus.yml with lowercase relabel config

```
- job_name: ionos
  ionos_sd_configs:
    - basic_auth:
        username: john.doe@example.com
        password: <secret>
      datacenter_id: 57375146-e890-4b84-8d59-c045d3eb6f4c
  relabel_configs:
    - source_labels: [__meta_ionos_server_type]
      target_label: server_type
      action: lowercase
```

Lists

Not all service discovery mechanisms have key-value labels or tags; some just have a list of tags, with the canonical example being Consul's tags. While Consul is the most likely place that you will run into this, there are various other places where a service discovery mechanism must somehow convert a list into key-value metadata such as the EC2 subnet ID.[16]

This is done by joining the items in the list with a comma and using the now-joined items as a label value. A comma is also put at the start and the end of the value to make writing correct regular expressions easier.

As an example, say a Consul service had dublin and prod tags. The __meta_consul_tags label could have the value ,dublin,prod, or ,prod,dublin, as tags are unordered. If you wanted to only scrape production targets, you would use a keep action, as shown in Example 8-23.

Example 8-23. Keeping only Consul services with the prod tag

```
scrape_configs:
 - job_name: node
   consul_sd_configs:
    - server: 'localhost:8500'
   relabel_configs:
    - source_labels: [__meta_consul_tags]
      regex:  '.*,prod,.*'
      action: keep
```

Sometimes you will have tags that are only the value of a key-value pair. You can convert such values to labels, but you need to know the potential values. Example 8-24 shows how a tag indicating the environment of a target can be converted into an env label.

Example 8-24. Using prod, staging, and dev tags to fill an env label

```
scrape_configs:
 - job_name: node
   consul_sd_configs:
    - server: 'localhost:8500'
   relabel_configs:
    - source_labels: [__meta_consul_tags]
      regex:  '.*,(prod|staging|dev),.*'
      target_label: env
```

---

16 An EC2 instance can have multiple network interfaces, each of which could be in different subnets.

With sophisticated relabeling rules you may find yourself needing a temporary label to put a value in. The __tmp prefix is reserved for this purpose.

How to Scrape

You now have targets with their target labels and the __address__ to connect to. There are some additional things you may wish to configure, such as a path other than */metrics* or client authentication.

Example 8-25 shows some of the more common options you can use. As these change over time, check the documentation (*https://oreil.ly/xHd-o*) for the most up-to-date settings.

Example 8-25. A scrape config showing several of the available options

```
scrape_configs:
 - job_name: example
   consul_sd_configs:
    - server: 'localhost:8500'
   scrape_timeout: 5s
   metrics_path: /admin/metrics
   params:
     foo: [bar]
   scheme: https
   tls_config:
     insecure_skip_verify: true
   basic_auth:
     username: brian
     password: hunter2
```

metrics_path is only the path of the URL, and if you tried to put */metrics?foo=bar*, for example, it would get escaped to */metrics%3Ffoo=bar*. Instead, any URL parameters should be placed in params, though you usually only need this for federation and the classes of exporters that include the SNMP and Blackbox Exporters. It is not possible to add arbitrary headers, as that would make debugging more difficult. If you need flexibility beyond what is offered, you can always use a proxy server with proxy_url to tweak your scrape requests.

scheme can be http or https; and with https you can provide additional options, including the key_file and cert_file if you wish to use TLS client authentication. insecure_skip_verify allows you to disable validation of a scrape target's TLS cert, which is not advisable security-wise.

Aside from TLS client authentication, HTTP Basic Authentication and HTTP Bearer Token Authentication are offered via basic_auth, OAuth2, and authorization. The

token can also be read from a file, rather than from the configuration, using `authori`
`zation`'s `credentials_file`. As the tokens and basic authentication passwords are
expected to contain secrets, they will be masked on the status pages of Prometheus so
that you don't accidentally leak them.

In addition to overriding the `scrape_timeout` in a scrape config, you can also override the `scrape_interval`, but in general you should aim for a single scrape interval
in a Prometheus for sanity.

Of these scrape config settings, the scheme, path, and URL parameters are available
to you and can be overridden by you via relabeling, with the label names `__scheme__`,
`__metrics_path__`, and `__param_<name>`. If there are multiple URL parameters with
the same name, only the first is available. It is not possible to relabel other settings for
reasons varying from sanity to security.

Service discovery metadata is not considered security sensitive[17] and will be accessible
to anyone with access to the Prometheus UI. As secrets can only be specified per
scrape config, it is recommended that any credentials you use are made standard
across your services.

Duplicate Jobs

While `job_name` must be unique, as it is only a default, you are not prevented from
having different scrape configs producing targets with the same `job` label.

For example, if you had some jobs that required a different secret which were indica-
ted by a Consul tag, you could segregate them using `keep` and `drop` actions, and then
use a `replace` to set the `job` label:

```
- job_name: my_job
  consul_sd_configs:
   - server: 'localhost:8500'
  relabel
   - source_labels: [__meta_consul_tag]
     regex:  '.*,specialsecret,.*'
     action: drop
  basic_auth:
    username: brian
    password: normalSecret

- job_name: my_job_special_secret
  consul_sd_configs:
   - server: 'localhost:8500'
  relabel
   - source_labels: [__meta_consul_tag]
```

---

17 Nor are the service discovery systems typically designed to hold secrets.

```
      regex:  '.*,specialsecret,.*'
      action: keep
    - replacement: my_job
      target_label: job
  basic_auth:
    username: brian
    password: specialSecret
```

metric_relabel_configs

In addition to relabeling being used for its original purpose of mapping service discovery metadata to target labels, relabeling has also been applied to other areas of Prometheus. One of those is *metric relabeling*: relabeling applied to the time series scraped from a target.

The keep, drop, replace, lowercase, uppercase, and labelmap actions you have already seen can all be used in metric_relabel_configs as there are no restrictions on which relabel actions can be used where.[18]

 To help you remember which is which, relabel_configs occurs when figuring out what to scrape, and metrics_relabel_configs happens after the scrape has occurred.

There are two cases where you might use metric relabeling: when dropping expensive metrics and when fixing bad metrics. While it is better to fix such problems at the source, it is always good to know that you have tactical options while the fix is in progress.

Metric relabeling gives you access to the time series after it is scraped but before it is written to storage. The keep and drop actions can be applied to the __name__ label (discussed in "Reserved Labels and __name__" on page 90) to select which time series you actually want to ingest. If, for example, you discovered that the http_request_size_bytes[19] metric of Prometheus had excessive cardinality and was causing performance issues, you could drop it, as shown in Example 8-26. It is still being transferred over the network and parsed, but this approach can still offer you some breathing room.

---

18 Which is not to say that all relabel actions make sense in all relabel contexts.

19 In Prometheus 2.3.0 this metric was changed to a histogram and renamed to prometheus_http_response_size_bytes.

Example 8-26. Dropping an expensive metric using `metric_relabel_configs`

```
scrape_configs:
 - job_name: prometheus
   static_configs:
    - targets:
       - localhost:9090
   metric_relabel_configs:
    - source_labels: [__name__]
      regex: http_request_size_bytes
      action: drop
```

The `le` labels are also available. As mentioned in "Cumulative Histograms" on page 54, you can also drop certain buckets (but not `+Inf`) of histograms and you will still be able to calculate quantiles. Example 8-27 shows this with the `prometheus_tsdb_compaction_duration_seconds` histogram in Prometheus.

Example 8-27. Dropping histogram buckets to reduce cardinality

```
scrape_configs:
 - job_name: prometheus
   static_configs:
    - targets:
       - localhost:9090
   metric_relabel_configs:
    - source_labels: [__name__, le]
      regex: 'prometheus_tsdb_compaction_duration_seconds_bucket;(4|32|256)'
      action: drop
```

> `metric_relabel_configs` only applies to metrics that you scrape from the target. It does not apply to metrics like up, which are about the scrape itself, and which will have only the target labels.

You could also use `metric_relabel_configs` to rename metrics, rename labels, or even extract labels from metric names.

labeldrop and labelkeep

There are two further relabel actions that are unlikely to be ever required for target relabeling, but that can come up in metric relabeling. Sometimes exporters can be overly enthusiastic in the labels they apply, or confuse instrumentation labels with target labels and return what they think should be the target labels in a scrape. The `replace` action can only deal with label names you know the name of in advance, which sometimes isn't the case.

This is where `labeldrop` and `labelkeep` come in. Similar to `labelmap`, they apply to label names rather than to label values. Instead of copying labels, `labeldrop` and `labelkeep` remove labels. Example 8-28 uses `labeldrop` to drop all labels with a given prefix.

*Example 8-28. Dropping all scraped labels that begin with node_*

```
scrape_configs:
 - job_name: misbehaving
   static_configs:
    - targets:
       - localhost:1234
   metric_relabel_configs:
    - regex: 'node_.*'
      action: labeldrop
```

When you have to use these actions, prefer using `labeldrop` where practical. With `labelkeep` you need to list every single label you want to keep, including __name__, le, and `quantile`.

Label Clashes and honor_labels

While `labeldrop` can be used when an exporter incorrectly presumes it knows what labels you want, there is a small set of exporters where the exporter does know the labels you want. For example, metrics in the Pushgateway should not have an `instance` label, as was mentioned in "Pushgateway" on page 76, so you need some way of not having the Pushgateway's instance target label apply.

But first let's look at what happens when there is a target label with the same name as an instrumentation label from a scrape. To avoid misbehaving applications interfering with your target label setup, it is the target label that wins. If you had a clash on the `job` label, for example, the instrumentation label would be renamed to `exported_job`.

If instead you want the instrumentation label to win and override the target label, you can set `honor_labels: true` in your scrape config. This is the one place in Prometheus where an empty label is not the same thing as a missing label. If a scraped metric explicitly has an `instance=""` label, and `honor_labels: true` is configured, the resultant time series will have no instance label. This technique is used by the Pushgateway.

Aside from the Pushgateway, honor_labels can also come up when ingesting metrics from other monitoring systems if you do not follow the recommendation in Chapter 11 to run one exporter per application instance.

 If you want more fine-grained control for handling clashing target and instrumentation labels, you can use metric_relabel_configs to adjust the labels before the metrics are added to the storage. Handling of label clashes and honor_labels is performed before metric_relabel_configs.

Now that you understand service discovery, you're ready to look at monitoring containers and how service discovery can be used with Kubernetes.

## CHAPTER 9

Containers and Kubernetes

Container deployments are becoming more common with technologies such as Docker and Kubernetes—you may even already be using them. In this chapter we will cover exporters that you can use with containers, and explain how to use Prometheus with Kubernetes.

All Prometheus components run happily in containers, with the sole exception of the Node Exporter, as noted in Chapter 7.

cAdvisor

In the same way the Node Exporter provides metrics about the machine, cAdvisor (*https://oreil.ly/tvOmH*) is an exporter that provides metrics about *cgroups*. Cgroups are a Linux kernel isolation feature that are usually used to implement containers on Linux, and are also used by runtime environments such as systemd.

You can run cAdvisor with Docker:

```
docker run \
  --volume=/:/rootfs:ro \
  --volume=/var/run:/var/run:rw \
  --volume=/sys:/sys:ro \
  --volume=/var/lib/docker/:/var/lib/docker:ro \
  --volume=/dev/disk/:/dev/disk:ro \
  --publish=8080:8080 \
  --detach=true \
  --name=cadvisor \
  gcr.io/cadvisor/cadvisor:v0.45.0
```

If you visit *http://localhost:8080/metrics*, you will see a long list of metrics, as Figure 9-1 shows.

```
# HELP cadvisor_version_info A metric with a constant '1' value labeled by kernel version, OS
version, docker version, cadvisor version & cadvisor revision.
# TYPE cadvisor_version_info gauge
cadvisor_version_info{cadvisorRevision="86b11c65",cadvisorVersion="v0.45.0",dockerVersion="",kernel
Version="5.18.19",osVersion="Alpine Linux v3.16"} 1
# HELP container_blkio_device_usage_total Blkio Device bytes usage
# TYPE container_blkio_device_usage_total counter
container_blkio_device_usage_total{device="/dev/disk/by-uuid/6451bb4f-81d7-4739-9638-
ca9b79ef6f38",id="/",image="",major="254",minor="3",name="",operation="Read"} 1.37632256e+09
1664884883416
container_blkio_device_usage_total{device="/dev/disk/by-uuid/6451bb4f-81d7-4739-9638-
ca9b79ef6f38",id="/",image="",major="254",minor="3",name="",operation="Write"} 1.62582528e+09
1664884883416
container_blkio_device_usage_total{device="/dev/dm-
0",id="/",image="",major="254",minor="0",name="",operation="Read"} 2.548012032e+09 1664884883416
container_blkio_device_usage_total{device="/dev/dm-
0",id="/",image="",major="254",minor="0",name="",operation="Write"} 6.952341504e+09 1664884883416
container_blkio_device_usage_total{device="/dev/dm-
0",id="/init.scope",image="",major="254",minor="0",name="",operation="Read"} 1.196032e+06
1664884884114
```

Figure 9-1. The start of a /metrics page from cAdvisor

The container metrics are prefixed with container_, and you will notice that they all
have an id label. The id labels starting with /docker/ or /system.slice/docker- are
from Docker and its containers, and if you have /user.slice/ and /system.slice/,
they come from systemd running on your machine. If you have other software using
cgroups, its cgroups will also be listed.

These metrics can be scraped with a *prometheus.yml* such as:

```
scrape_configs:
  - job_name: cadvisor
    static_configs:
      - targets:
          - localhost:8080
```

CPU

You will find three metrics for container CPU: container_cpu_usage_seconds_
total, container_cpu_system_seconds_total, and container_cpu_user_seconds_
total.

container_cpu_usage_seconds_total is split out by CPU, but not by mode.
container_cpu_system_seconds_total and container_cpu_user_seconds_total
are the user and system modes, respectively, similar to the Node Exporter's CPU
collector, as described in "CPU Collector" on page 126. These are all counters with
which you can use the rate function.

With many containers and CPUs in one machine, you may find
that the aggregate cardinality of metrics from cAdvisor becomes a
performance issue. You can use a drop relabel action, as discussed
in "metric_relabel_configs" on page 164, to drop less-valuable met‐
rics at scrape time.

Memory

Similar to the Node Exporter, the memory usage metrics are less than perfectly clear and require digging through code and documentation (*https://oreil.ly/VzlVe*) to understand them.

`container_memory_cache` is the page cache used by the container, in bytes. `container_memory_rss` is the resident set size (RSS), in bytes. This is not the same RSS or physical memory used as a process would have, as it excludes the sizes of mapped files.[1] `container_memory_usage_bytes` is the RSS and the page cache, and is limited by `container_spec_memory_limit_bytes` if the limit is nonzero. `container_memory_working_set_bytes` is calculated by subtracting the inactive file-backed memory (`total_inactive_file` from the kernel) from `container_memory_usage_bytes`.

In practice, `container_memory_working_set_bytes` is the closest to RSS that is exposed, and you may also wish to keep an eye on `container_memory_usage_bytes` as it includes page cache.

In general, we would recommend relying on metrics such as `process_resident_memory_bytes` from the process itself rather than metrics from the cgroups. If your applications do not expose Prometheus metrics, then cAdvisor is a good stopgap, and cAdvisor metrics are still important for debugging and profiling.

Labels

Cgroups are organized in a hierarchy, with the / cgroup at the root of the hierarchy. The metrics for each of your cgroups include the usage of the cgroups below it. This goes against the usual rule that within a metric the sum or average is meaningful, and is thus an example of the table exception, as discussed in "Table Exception" on page 99.

In addition to the `id` label, cAdvisor adds in more labels about containers if it has them. For Docker containers there will always be the `image` and `name` labels, for the specific Docker image being run and Docker's name for the container.

Any metadata labels Docker has for a container will also be included with a `container_label_` prefix. Arbitrary labels like these from a scrape can break your monitoring, so you may wish to remove them with a `labeldrop`, as shown in Example 9-1, and as we talked about in "labeldrop and labelkeep" on page 165.[2]

---

1 Mapped files include both `mmap` and any libraries used by a process. This is exposed by the kernel as `file_mapped` but is not used by cAdvisor, thus the standard RSS is not available from cAdvisor.

2 The behavior of cAdvisor is the main reason the `labeldrop` and `labelkeep` relabel actions were originally added.

Example 9-1. Using labeldrop to drop container_label_ labels from cAdvisor

```
scrape_configs:
 - job_name: cadvisor
   static_configs:
     - targets:
         - localhost:9090
   metric_relabel_configs:
     - regex: 'container_label_.*'
       action: labeldrop
```

Kubernetes

Kubernetes is a popular platform for orchestrating containers. Like Prometheus, the Kubernetes project is part of the Cloud Native Computing Foundation (CNCF). Here we are going to cover running Prometheus on Kubernetes and working with its service discovery.

As Kubernetes is a large and fast-moving target, we are not going to cover it in exhaustive detail. If you would like more depth, we suggest the book *Kubernetes: Up and Running, 3rd Edition* by Brendan Burns, Joe Beda, Kelsey Hightower, and Lachlan Evenson (O'Reilly).

Running in Kubernetes

To demonstrate using Prometheus with Kubernetes, we will use Minikube (*https://oreil.ly/Sl3or*), a tool used to run a single-node Kubernetes cluster inside a virtual machine.

Follow the steps in Example 9-2. We are using a Linux amd64 machine with VirtualBox already installed. If you are running in a different environment, follow the Minikube installation documentation (*https://oreil.ly/9oMjE*). Here we are using Minikube 1.27.0 and Kubernetes 1.25.0.

Example 9-2. Downloading and running Minikube

```
hostname $ curl -LO \
    https://storage.googleapis.com/minikube/releases/latesn/minikube-linux-amd64
hostname $ mv minikube-linux-amd64 minikube
hostname $ chmod +x minikube
hostname $ ./minikube start --kubernetes-version=v1.25.0
minikube v1.27.0 on Nixos 22.05 (Quokka)
Starting control plane node minikube in cluster minikube
Pulling base image ...
Downloading Kubernetes v1.25.0 preload ...
Creating docker container (CPUs=2, Memory=7800MB) ...
Preparing Kubernetes v1.25.0 on Docker 20.10.17 ...
> Generating certificates and keys ...
```

```
> Booting up control plane ...
> Configuring RBAC rules ...
Verifying Kubernetes components...
> Using image gcr.io/k8s-minikube/storage-provisioner:v5
Enabled addons: storage-provisioner, default-storageclass
```

 minikube dashboard --url will provide you with a URL for the Kubernetes Dashboard, from which you can inspect your Kubernetes cluster.

You will also need to install kubectl, which is a command-line tool used to interact with Kubernetes clusters. Example 9-3 shows how to install it and confirm that it can talk to your Kubernetes cluster.

Example 9-3. Downloading and testing kubectl

```
hostname $ wget \
    https://storage.googleapis.com/kubernetes-release/release/v1.25.0/bin/linux
    /amd64/kubectl
hostname $ chmod +x kubectl
hostname $ ./kubectl get services
NAME         TYPE        CLUSTER-IP    EXTERNAL-IP   PORT(S)   AGE
kubernetes   ClusterIP   10.96.0.1     <none>        443/TCP   44s
```

Example 9-4 shows how to get an example Prometheus running on Minikube. *prometheus-deployment.yml* contains permissions so that your Prometheus can access resources such as pods and nodes in the cluster, a *configMap* is created to hold the Prometheus configuration file, a *deployment* to run Prometheus, and a *service* to make it easier for you to access the Prometheus UI. The final command, the ./mini kube service, will provide you with a URL where you can access the Prometheus UI.

Example 9-4. Setting up permissions and running Prometheus on Kubernetes

```
hostname $./kubectl apply -f prometheus-deployment.yml
hostname $./minikube service prometheus --url
http://192.168.99.100:30114
```

The target status page should look like Figure 9-2. You can find *prometheus-deployment.yml* on GitHub (*https://oreil.ly/Qdwvp*).

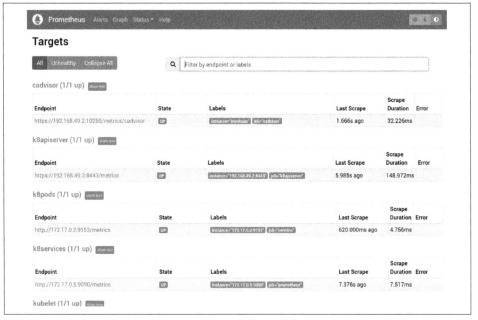

Figure 9-2. Targets of the example Prometheus running on Kubernetes

This is a basic Kubernetes setup to demonstrate the core ideas behind monitoring on Kubernetes, and it is not intended for you to use directly in production; for example, all data is lost every time Prometheus restarts.

Service Discovery

There are currently six different types of Kubernetes service discoveries you can use with Prometheus, namely *node*, *endpoints*, *endpointslice*, *service*, *pod*, and *ingress*.[3] Prometheus uses the Kubernetes API to discover targets.

Node

Node service discovery is used to discover the nodes comprising the Kubernetes cluster, and you will use it to monitor the infrastructure around Kubernetes. The *Kubelet* is the name of the agent that runs on each node, and you should scrape it as part of monitoring the health of the Kubernetes cluster (Example 9-5).

---

3 Endpoints are deprecated in Kubernetes, and we recommend using endpointslice.

Example 9-5. prometheus.yml fragment to scrape the Kubelet

```
scrape_configs:
- job_name: 'kubelet'
  kubernetes_sd_configs:
  - role: node
  scheme: https
  tls_config:
    ca_file: /var/run/secrets/kubernetes.io/serviceaccount/ca.crt
    insecure_skip_verify: true
  authorization:
    credentials_file: /var/run/secrets/kubernetes.io/serviceaccount/token
```

Example 9-5 shows the configuration being used by Prometheus to scrape the Kubelet. We are going to break down the scrape config:

```
job_name: 'kubelet'
```

A default `job` label is provided, and as there are no `relabel_configs`, `kubelet` will be the `job` label:[4]

```
kubernetes_sd_configs:
- role: node
```

A single Kubernetes service discovery is provided with the `node` role. The `node` role discovers one target for each of your Kubelets. As Prometheus is running inside the cluster, the defaults for the Kubernetes service discovery are already set up to authenticate with the Kubernetes API:

```
scheme: https
tls_config:
  ca_file: /var/run/secrets/kubernetes.io/serviceaccount/ca.crt
  insecure_skip_verify: true
authorization:
  credentials_file: /var/run/secrets/kubernetes.io/serviceaccount/token
```

The Kubelet serves its */metrics* over HTTPS, so we must specify the `scheme`. Kubernetes clusters usually have their own *certificate authority* that are used to sign their TLS certs, and the `ca_file` provides that for the scrape. Unfortunately Minikube doesn't get this quite right, so `insecure_skip_verify` is required to bypass security checks.

The `authorization` block and `credentials_file` parameters make Prometheus use the service account token as the Bearer token when scraping targets.

The returned target points at the Kubelet, and authentication/authorization is turned off in this Minikube setup, so no further configuration is needed.

---

4 We don't use `node` as the `job` label, as that's typically used for the Node Exporter.

The `tls_config` in the scrape config contains TLS settings for the scrape. `kubernetes_sd_configs` also has a `tls_config` that contains TLS settings for when service discovery talks to the Kubernetes API.

The metadata available includes node annotations and labels, as you can see in Figure 9-3. You could use this metadata with `relabel_configs` to add labels to distinguish interesting subsets of nodes, such as those with different hardware.

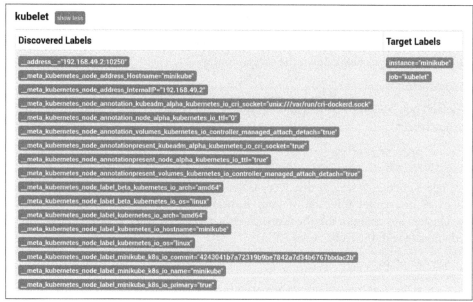

Figure 9-3. The Kubelet on the service discovery status page of Prometheus

The Kubelet's own */metrics* only contains metrics about the Kubelet itself, not container-level information. The Kubelet has an embedded cAdvisor on its */metrics/cadvisor* endpoint. Scraping the embedded cAdvisor only requires adding a `metrics_path` to the scrape config used with the Kubelet, as shown in Example 9-6. The embedded cAdvisor includes labels for the Kubernetes `namespace` and `pod_name`.

Example 9-6. prometheus.yml fragment to scrape the Kubelet's embedded cAdvisor

```
- job_name: 'cadvisor'
  kubernetes_sd_configs:
  - role: node
  scheme: https
  tls_config:
    ca_file: /var/run/secrets/kubernetes.io/serviceaccount/ca.crt
    insecure_skip_verify: true
```

```
  authorization:
    credentials_file: /var/run/secrets/kubernetes.io/serviceaccount/token
  metrics_path: /metrics/cadvisor
```

Node service discovery can be used for anything you want to monitor that runs on each machine in a Kubernetes cluster. If the Node Exporter was running on your Minikube node, you could scrape it by relabeling the port, for example.

Service

Node service discovery is useful for monitoring the infrastructure of and under Kubernetes, but not much use for monitoring your applications running on Kubernetes.

There are several ways that you can organize your applications on Kubernetes, and no single clear standard has emerged yet. But you are likely using *services*, which is how applications on Kubernetes find each other.

While there is a `service` role, it is not what you usually want. The `service` role returns a single target for each port[5] of your services. Services are basically load balancers, and scraping targets through load balancers is not wise, as Prometheus can scrape a different application instance each time. However, the `service` role can be useful for blackbox monitoring to check if the service is responding at all.

Endpointslice

Prometheus should be configured to have a target for each application instance, and the `endpointslice` role provides just that. Services are backed by *pods*. Pods are a group of tightly coupled containers that share network and storage. For each Kubernetes service port, the endpoints service discovery role returns a target for each pod backing that service. Additionally, any other ports of the pods will be returned as targets.

That's a bit of a mouthful, so let's look at an example. One of the services that is running in your Minikube is the `kubernetes` service, which is the Kubernetes API servers. Example 9-7 is a scrape config that will discover and scrape the API servers.

Example 9-7. prometheus.yml fragment used to scrape the Kubernetes API servers

```
scrape_configs:
- job_name: 'k8apiserver'
  kubernetes_sd_configs:
   - role: endpointslice
  scheme: https
```

---

5 A service can have multiple ports.

```
  tls_config:
    ca_file: /var/run/secrets/kubernetes.io/serviceaccount/ca.crt
    insecure_skip_verify: true
  authorization:
    credentials_file: /var/run/secrets/kubernetes.io/serviceaccount/token
  relabel_configs:
   - source_labels:
      - __meta_kubernetes_namespace
      - __meta_kubernetes_service_name
      - __meta_kubernetes_endpoint_port_name
     action: keep
     regex: default;kubernetes;https
```

Breaking down this scrape config:

```
  job_name: 'k8apiserver'
```

The job label is going to be k8apiserver, as there's no target relabeling to change it:

```
  kubernetes_sd_configs:
  - role: endpointslice
```

 Note that we are using the role endpointslice here, which is a replacement for endpoints. In recent Kubernetes versions, the endpoint role can only list up to 1,000 entries. In order to be able to list all the targets, we recommend you use endpointslices, which do not have that limitation, to address future growth of your infrastructure.

There is a single Kubernetes service discovery using the endpointslice role, which will return a target for every port of every pod backing each of your services:

```
  scheme: https
  tls_config:
    ca_file: /var/run/secrets/kubernetes.io/serviceaccount/ca.crt
    insecure_skip_verify: true
  authorization:
    credentials_file: /var/run/secrets/kubernetes.io/serviceaccount/token
```

As with the Kubelet, the API servers are served over HTTPS. In addition, authentication is required, which is provided by the credentials_file:

```
  relabel_configs:
  - source_labels:
      - __meta_kubernetes_namespace
      - __meta_kubernetes_service_name
      - __meta_kubernetes_endpointslice_port_name
     action: keep
     regex: default;kubernetes;https
```

This relabel configuration will only return targets that are in the `default` namespace, and are part of a service called `kubernetes` with a port called `https`.

You can see the resulting target in Figure 9-4. The API server is special, so there isn't much metadata. All the other potential targets were dropped.

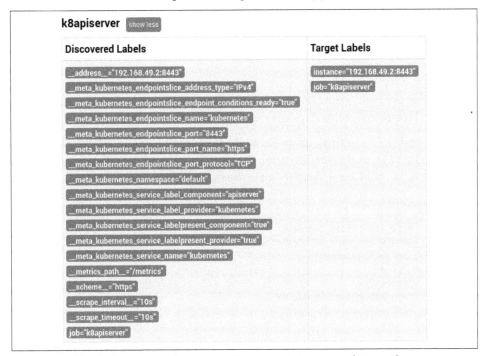

Figure 9-4. The API server on the service discovery status page of Prometheus

While you will want to scrape the API servers, most of the time you'll be focused on your applications. Example 9-8 shows how you can automatically scrape the pods for all of your services.

Example 9-8. prometheus.yml fragment to scrape pods backing all Kubernetes services, except the API servers

```
scrape_configs:
 - job_name: 'k8services'
   kubernetes_sd_configs:
    - role: endpointslice
   relabel_configs:
    - source_labels:
       - __meta_kubernetes_namespace
       - __meta_kubernetes_service_name
      regex: default;kubernetes
      action: drop
```

```
- source_labels:
  - __meta_kubernetes_namespace
  regex: default
  action: keep
- source_labels: [__meta_kubernetes_service_name]
  target_label: job
```

Once again we will break it down:

```
job_name: 'k8services'
kubernetes_sd_configs:
 - role: endpointslice
```

As with the previous example, this is providing a job name and the Kubernetes endpointslice role, but this does not end up as the job label due to later relabeling.

There are no HTTPS settings, as we know the targets are all plain HTTP. There is no credentials_file, as no authentication is required, and sending a bearer token to all of your services could allow them to impersonate you:[6]

```
relabel_configs:
- source_labels:
    - __meta_kubernetes_namespace
    - __meta_kubernetes_service_name
  regex: default;kubernetes
  action: drop
- source_labels:
    - __meta_kubernetes_namespace
  regex: default
  action: keep
```

We excluded the API server, as there is already another scrape config handling it. We also only looked at the default namespace, which is where we are launching applications:[7]

```
- source_labels: [__meta_kubernetes_service_name]
  target_label: job
```

This relabel action takes the Kubernetes service name and uses it as the job label. The job_name we provided for the scrape config is only a default, and does not apply.

In this way you can have your Prometheus automatically pick up new services and start scraping them with a useful job label. In this case that's just Prometheus itself, as shown in Figure 9-5.

---

6 This is also the case with basic auth, but not for a challenge-response mechanism like TLS client certificate authentication.

7 And to not cause confusion with Example 9-10, as kube-dns is in the kube-system namespace.

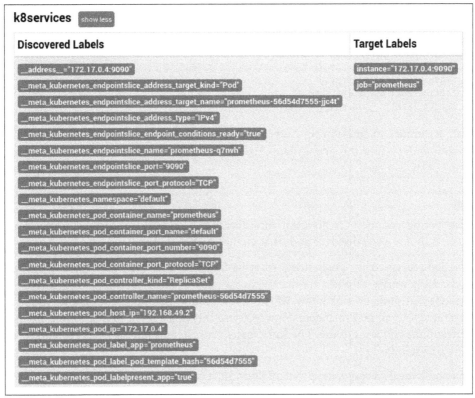

Figure 9-5. Prometheus has automatically discovered itself using endpoint service discovery

You could go a step further and use relabeling to add additional labels from service or pod metadata, or even set __scheme__ or __metrics_path__ based on a Kubernetes annotation, as shown in Example 9-9. These would look for prometheus.io/scheme, prometheus.io/path, and prometheus.io/port service annotations,[8] and use them if present.

Example 9-9. Relabeling using Kubernetes service annotations to optionally configure the scheme, path, and port of targets

```
relabel_configs:
 - source_labels: [__meta_kubernetes_service_annotation_prometheus_io_scheme]
   regex: (.+)
   target_label: __scheme__
 - source_labels: [__meta_kubernetes_service_annotation_prometheus_io_path]
```

---

8 Forward slashes are not valid in label names, so they are sanitized to underscores.

```
    regex: (.+)
    target_label: __metrics_path__
  - source_labels:
    - __address__
    - __meta_kubernetes_service_annotation_prometheus_io_port
    regex: ([^:]+)(:\d+)?;(\d+)
    replacement: ${1}:${3}
    target_label: __address__
```

This is limited to monitoring only one port per service. You could have another scrape config using the `prometheus.io/port2` annotation, and so on for however many ports you need.

Pod

Discovering endpoints is great for monitoring the primary processes backing your services, but it won't discover pods that are not part of services.

The pod role discovers pods. It will return a target for each port of every one of your pods. As it works off pods, service metadata such as labels and annotations are not available, as pods do not know which services they are members of. But you will have access to all pod metadata. How you use this boils down to a question of what conventions you want to use. The Kubernetes ecosystem is rapidly evolving, and there is no one standard yet.

You could create a convention that all pods must be part of a service, and then use the `endpointslice` role in service discovery. You could have a convention that all pods have a label indicating the (single) Kubernetes service they are a part of, and use the pod role for service discovery. As all ports have names, you could base a convention off that and have ports named with a prefix of `prom-http` be scraped with HTTP, and `prom-https` be scraped with HTTPS.

One of the components that comes with Minikube is *kube-dns*, which provides DNS services. Its pod has multiple ports, including a port named `metrics` that serves Prometheus metrics. Example 9-10 shows how you could discover this port and use the name of the container as the `job` label, as Figure 9-6 shows.

Example 9-10. prometheus.yml to discover all pod ports with the name `metrics` and to use the container name as the `job` label

```
scrape_configs:
- job_name: 'k8pods'
  kubernetes_sd_configs:
   - role: pod
  relabel_configs:
   - source_labels: [__meta_kubernetes_pod_container_port_name]
     regex: metrics
```

```
    action: keep
- source_labels: [__meta_kubernetes_pod_container_name]
  target_label: job
```

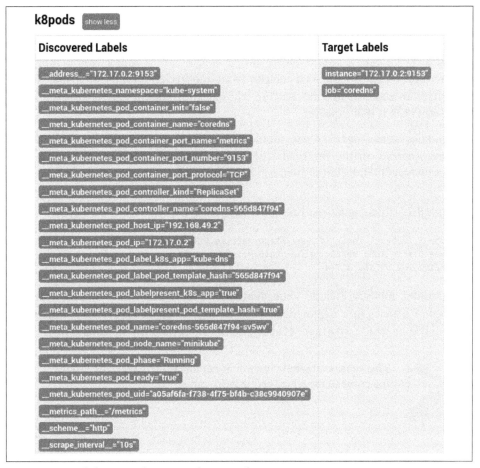

Figure 9-6. Pod discovered using pod service discovery

Ingress

An *ingress* is a way for a Kubernetes service to be exposed outside the cluster. As it is a layer on top of services, similar to the `service` role, the `ingress` role is also basically a load balancer. If multiple pods backed the service and thus ingress, this would cause problems when scraping with Prometheus. Accordingly, you should only use this role for blackbox monitoring.

kube-state-metrics

Using Kubernetes service discovery you can have Prometheus scrape your applications and Kubernetes infrastructure, but this will not include metrics about what Kubernetes knows about your services, pods, deployments, and other resources. This is because applications such as the Kubelet and Kubernetes API servers should expose information about their own performance, not dump their internal data structures.[9]

Instead, you would obtain such metrics from another endpoint,[10] or if that doesn't exist, have an exporter that extracts the relevant information. For Kubernetes, kube-state-metrics is that exporter.

To run kube-state-metrics you should follow the steps in Example 9-11 and then visit the */metrics* on the returned URL in your browser. You can find *kube-state-metrics.yml* on GitHub (*https://oreil.ly/xY3SK*).

Example 9-11. Running kube-state-metrics

```
hostname $./kubectl apply -f kube-state-metrics.yml
hostname $./minikube service kube-state-metrics --url
http://192.168.99.100:31774
```

Some useful metrics include kube_deployment_spec_replicas for the intended number of metrics in a deployment, kube_node_status_condition for node problems, and kube_pod_container_status_restarts_total for pod restarts.

 This kube-state-metrics will be automatically scraped by Prometheus due to the scrape config in Example 9-8.

kube-state-metrics features several examples of enum and info metrics, as discussed in "Enum" on page 94 and "Info" on page 96 metrics, such as kube_node_status_condition and kube_pod_info, respectively.

---

9 Put another way, a database exporter does not dump the contents of the database as metrics.

10 Such as the Kubelet exposing cAdvisor's metrics on another endpoint.

Alternative Deployments

So far, you've learned how to deploy Prometheus in Kubernetes from scratch. While the task is not complex, there are a few projects that provide additional resources, CRD,[11] and helpers, to make your life easier. While they are out of scope for this book, we encourage you to look at two of them in particular:

- The Prometheus Operator (*https://oreil.ly/8S74Q*) is a project supported by a large community, which includes CRD, configuration of Prometheus, and its targets.
- The Prometheus Community Kubernetes Helm Charts (*https://oreil.ly/Mg824*) provide more than 30 charts to spin up components from the Prometheus ecosystem using Helm.

Now that you have an idea about how to use Prometheus in container environments, let's look at some of the common exporters you will run into.

---

11 Kubernetes Custom Resources Definition

## CHAPTER 10

Common Exporters

You already saw the Node Exporter in Chapter 7, but there are literally hundreds of other exporters you can use.

We are not going to go through all of the ever-growing number of exporters out there; instead, we will show you some examples of the types of things you will come across when using exporters. This will prepare you to use exporters in your own environment.

At the simplest, exporters work out of the box, with no configuration required on your part, as you already saw for the Node Exporter. Usually you will need to do minimal configuration to tell the exporter which application instance to scrape. At the far end, some exporters require extensive configuration as the data they are working with is very general.

You will generally have one exporter for every application instance that needs one. This is because the intended way to use Prometheus is for every application to have direct instrumentation and have Prometheus discover it and scrape it directly. When that isn't possible, exporters are used, and you want to keep to that architecture as much as possible. Having the exporter live right beside the application instance it is exporting from is easier to manage as you grow, and keeps your failure domains aligned. You will find that some exporters violate this guideline and offer the ability to scrape multiple instances, but you can still deploy them in the intended fashion and use the techniques shown in "metric_relabel_configs" on page 164 to remove any extraneous labels.

Consul

You already installed and ran Consul in "Consul" on page 146. Assuming it is still running, you can download and run the Consul Exporter with the commands in

Example 10-1. Because Consul usually runs on port 8500, you don't need to do any extra configuration as the Consul Exporter uses that port by default.

Example 10-1. Downloading and running the Consul Exporter

```
hostname $ wget https://github.com/prometheus/consul_exporter/releases/
    download/v0.3.0/consul_exporter-0.8.0.linux-amd64.tar.gz
hostname $ tar -xzf consul_exporter-0.8.0.linux-amd64.tar.gz
hostname $ cd consul_exporter-0.8.0.linux-amd64/
hostname $ ./consul_exporter
msg="Starting consul_exporter" version="(version=0.8.0, branch=HEAD,
    revision=176aef0f2d437e9fd1cb3a9e29dc4730de717e05)"
build_context="(go=go1.17.6, user=root@566e953b1722, date=20220210-16:54:21)"
msg="Listening on address" address=:9107
```

If you open *http://localhost:9107/metrics* in your browser, you will see the metrics available.

The first metric you should make note of is `consul_up`. Some exporters will return an HTTP error to Prometheus when fetching data fails, which results in up being set to 0 in Prometheus. But many exporters will still be successfully scraped in this scenario and use a metric such as `consul_up` to indicate if there was a problem. Accordingly, when alerting on Consul being down, you should check both up and `consul_up`. If you stop Consul and then check the */metrics*, you will see the value changes to 0, and back to 1 again when Consul is started again.

`consul_catalog_service_node_healthy` tells you about the health of the various services in the Consul node, similar to how `kube-state-metrics` (discussed in "kube-state-metrics" on page 184) tells you about the health of nodes and containers but across an entire Kubernetes cluster.

`consul_serf_lan_members` is the number of Consul agents in the cluster. You may wonder if this could come just from the *leader* of the Consul cluster, but remember that each agent might have a different view of how many members the cluster has if there is an issue such as a network partition. In general, you should expose metrics like this from every member of a cluster, and synthesize the value you want using aggregation in PromQL.

There are also metrics about your Consul Exporter. `consul_exporter_build_info` is its build information, and there are a variety of `process_` and `go_` metrics about the process and the Go runtime. These are useful for debugging issues with the Consul Exporter itself.

You can configure Prometheus to scrape the Consul Exporter, as shown in Example 10-2. Even though the scrape is going via an exporter, we used the `job` label of `consul`, as it is really Consul we are scraping.

Exporters can be considered as a form of proxy. They take in a scrape request from Prometheus, fetch metrics from a process, munge them into a format that Prometheus can understand, and respond with them to Prometheus.

Example 10-2. prometheus.yml to scrape a local Consul Exporter

```
global:
  scrape_interval: 10s
scrape_configs:
 - job_name: consul
   static_configs:
    - targets:
       - localhost:9107
```

MySQLd

The MySQLd Exporter is a typical exporter. To demonstrate it you will need to launch an instance of MySQL and set up a Prometheus user.

You can then run MySQL and create the user, as shown in Example 10-3.

Example 10-3. Downloading and running the MySQL Exporter

```
hostname $ docker run -it --net=host --rm mysql mysql -h 127.0.0.1 -P 3306
    -uroot -pmy-secret-pw
mysql: [Warning] Using a password on the command line interface can be insecure.
mysql> CREATE USER 'prometheus'@'127.0.0.1' IDENTIFIED BY 'my-secret-prom-pw'
    WITH MAX_USER_CONNECTIONS 3;
Query OK, 0 rows affected (0.03 sec)

mysql> GRANT PROCESS, REPLICATION CLIENT, SELECT ON *.* TO 'prometheus'@'127.0.0.1';
Query OK, 0 rows affected (0.01 sec)
```

Create a *my.cnf* file with the credentials shown in Example 10-4.

Example 10-4. ~/.my.cnf with Prometheus credentials

```
[client]
user = prometheus
password = my-secret-prom-pw
host = 127.0.0.1
```

Next, you should download and run the MySQLd exporter, as shown in Example 10-5.

Example 10-5. Downloading and running the MySQLd Exporter

```
hostname $ wget https://github.com/prometheus/mysqld_exporter/releases/download/
    v0.9.0/mysqld_exporter-0.9.0.linux-amd64.tar.gz
hostname $ tar -xzf mysqld_exporter-0.9.0.linux-amd64.tar.gz
hostname $ cd mysqld_exporter-0.9.0.linux-amd64/
hostname $ ./mysqld_exporter
```

If you go to *http://localhost:9104/metrics*, you will see the metrics being produced. Similar to the Consul Exporter's `consul_up`, there is a `mysql_up` metric, indicating if talking to MySQLd succeeded.

 The name of the exporter is MySQLd Exporter. However, it also works with forks of MySQL, such as MariaDB.

You will notice that many MySQL-related metrics are presents: `mysql_global_vari ables_` shows the value of global configuration variables, and `mysql_global_status_` metrics show the current values returned by `SHOW STATUS`.

Exporter Default Ports

You may have noticed that Prometheus, the Node Exporter, Alertmanager, and other exporters in this chapter have similar port numbers.

Back when there were only a handful of exporters, many had the same default port number. Both the Node and HAProxy exporters used port 8080 by default, for example. This was annoying when trying out or deploying Prometheus, so a wiki page (*https://oreil.ly/Cx_7b*) was started to keep the official exporters on different ports.

This organically grew to being a comprehensive list of exporters, and aside from some users skipping over numbers, it now serves a purpose beyond its initial one.

You can configure the MySQLd Exporter to be scraped by Prometheus in the same way as any other exporter, as you can see in Example 10-6.

Example 10-6. prometheus.yml to scrape a local MySQLd Exporter

```
global:
  scrape_interval: 10s
scrape_configs:
 - job_name: mysqld
   static_configs:
```

```
    - targets:
      - localhost:9104
```

Grok Exporter

Not all applications produce metrics in a form that can be converted into something that Prometheus understands using an exporter. But such applications may produce logs, and the Grok Exporter (*https://oreil.ly/6NaQL*) can be used to convert those into metrics.[1] Grok is a way to parse unstructured logs that is commonly used with Logstash.[2] The Grok Exporter reuses the same pattern language, allowing you to reuse patterns that you already have.

Say that you had a simple log that looks like:

```
GET /foo 1.23
GET /bar 3.2
POST /foo 4.6
```

which was in a file called *example.log*. You could convert these logs into metrics by using the Grok Exporter. First, download the 0.2.8 Grok Exporter Linux amd64 release (*https://oreil.ly/StPAZ*) and unzip it. Next, create a file called *grok.yml* with the content in Example 10-7.

Example 10-7. grok.yml to parse a simple logfile and produce metrics

```
global:
  config_version: 2
input:
  type: file
  path: example.log
  readall: true  # Use false in production
grok:
  additional_patterns:
    - 'METHOD [A-Z]+'
    - 'PATH [^ ]+'
    - 'NUMBER [0-9.]+'
metrics:
 - type: counter
   name: log_http_requests_total
   help: HTTP requests
   match: '%{METHOD} %{PATH:path} %{NUMBER:latency}'
   labels:
     path: '{{.path}}'
 - type: histogram
   name: log_http_request_latency_seconds_total
```

---

1 There is also *https://oreil.ly/1phnz* in this space.

2 The L in the ELK stack.

```
    help: HTTP request latency
    match: '%{METHOD} %{PATH:path} %{NUMBER:latency}'
    value: '{{.latency}}'
server:
  port: 9144
```

Finally, run the Grok Exporter:

```
./grok_exporter -config grok.yml
```

We'll break this down. First, there is some boilerplate:

```
global:
  config_version: 2
```

Next, you need to define the file to be read. Here we are using `readall: true`, so you will see the same results as in this example. In production you would leave it to the default of `false` so that the file is tailed:

```
input:
  type: file
  path: example.log
  readall: true  # Use false in production
```

Grok works with patterns based on regular expressions. We have defined all of our patterns here manually so you can better understand what's going on, but you can also reuse ones you already have:

```
grok:
  additional_patterns:
    - 'METHOD [A-Z]+'
    - 'PATH [^ ]+'
    - 'NUMBER [0-9.]+'
```

We have two metrics. The first is a counter called `log_http_requests_total`, which has a label `path`:

```
metrics:
  - type: counter
    name: log_http_requests_total
    help: HTTP requests
    match: '%{METHOD} %{PATH:path} %{NUMBER:latency}'
    labels:
      path: '{{.path}}'
```

Our second is a histogram called `log_http_request_latency_seconds_total`, which is observing the latency value, and has no labels:

```
  - type: histogram
    name: log_http_request_latency_seconds_total
    help: HTTP request latency
    match: '%{METHOD} %{PATH:path} %{NUMBER:latency}'
    value: '{{.latency}}'
```

Finally, we define where we want the exporter to expose its metrics:

```
server:
    port: 9144
```

When you visit *http://localhost:9144*, among its output you will find the following metrics:

```
# HELP log_http_request_latency_seconds_total HTTP request latency
# TYPE log_http_request_latency_seconds_total histogram
log_http_request_latency_seconds_total_bucket{le="0.005"} 0
log_http_request_latency_seconds_total_bucket{le="0.01"} 0
log_http_request_latency_seconds_total_bucket{le="0.025"} 0
log_http_request_latency_seconds_total_bucket{le="0.05"} 0
log_http_request_latency_seconds_total_bucket{le="0.1"} 1
log_http_request_latency_seconds_total_bucket{le="0.25"} 2
log_http_request_latency_seconds_total_bucket{le="0.5"} 3
log_http_request_latency_seconds_total_bucket{le="1"} 3
log_http_request_latency_seconds_total_bucket{le="2.5"} 3
log_http_request_latency_seconds_total_bucket{le="5"} 3
log_http_request_latency_seconds_total_bucket{le="10"} 3
log_http_request_latency_seconds_total_bucket{le="+Inf"} 3
log_http_request_latency_seconds_total_sum 0.57
log_http_request_latency_seconds_total_count 3
# HELP log_http_requests_total HTTP requests
# TYPE log_http_requests_total counter
log_http_requests_total{path="/bar"} 1
log_http_requests_total{path="/foo"} 2
```

As you can see, the Grok Exporter is more involved to configure than your typical exporter; it's closer to direct instrumentation in terms of effort, as you must individually define each metric you want to expose. You would generally run one per application instance that needs to be monitored, and scrape it with Prometheus in the usual way, as shown in Example 10-8.

Example 10-8. prometheus.yml to scrape a local Grok Exporter

```
global:
  scrape_interval: 10s
scrape_configs:
 - job_name: grok
   static_configs:
    - targets:
       - localhost:9144
```

Blackbox

While the recommended way to deploy exporters is to run one right beside each application instance, there are cases where this is not possible for technical reasons.[3] This is usually the case with blackbox monitoring—monitoring the system from the outside with no special knowledge of the internals. We like to think of blackbox monitoring as similar to smoke tests when unit testing; their purpose is primarily to quickly tell you when things have gone hilariously wrong.

If you are monitoring whether a web service works from the standpoint of a user, you usually want to monitor that through the same load balancers and virtual IP (VIP) addresses the user is hitting. You can't exactly run an exporter on a VIP as it is, well, virtual. A different architecture is needed.

In Prometheus there is a class of exporters usually referred to as Blackbox-style or SNMP-style, after the two primary examples of exporters that cannot run beside an application instance. The Blackbox Exporter by necessity usually needs to run somewhere else on the network, and there is no application instance to run on. For the SNMP[4] Exporter, it's rare for you to be able to run your own code on a network device—and if you could, you would use the Node Exporter instead.

So how are Blackbox-style or SNMP-style exporters different? Instead of you configuring them to talk to only one target, they take in the target as a URL parameter. Any other configuration is provided by you on the exporter side as usual. This keeps the responsibilities of service discovery and scrape scheduling with Prometheus, and the responsibility of translating metrics into a form understandable by Prometheus with your exporter.

The Blackbox Exporter allows you to perform ICMP, TCP, HTTP, and DNS probing. We will show you each in turn, but first you should get the Blackbox Exporter running, as shown in Example 10-9.

Example 10-9. Downloading and running the Blackbox Exporter

```
hostname $ wget https://github.com/prometheus/blackbox_exporter/releases/download/
    v0.22.0/blackbox_exporter-0.22.0.linux-amd64.tar.gz
hostname $ tar -xzf blackbox_exporter-0.22.0.linux-amd64.tar.gz
hostname $ cd blackbox_exporter-0.22.0.linux-amd64/
hostname $ sudo ./blackbox_exporter
msg="Starting blackbox_exporter" version="(version=0.22.0,
  branch=HEAD, revision=0bbd65d1264722f7afb87a72ec4128b9214e5840)"
```

---

3 As distinct from cases where it's not possible for political reasons.

4 Simple Network Management Protocol, a standard for (among other things) exposing metrics on network devices. It can also sometimes be found on other hardware.

```
msg="Loaded config file"
msg="Listening on address" address=:9115
```

If you visit *http://localhost:9115/* in your browser, you should see a status page like the one in Figure 10-1.

Blackbox Exporter

Probe prometheus.io for http_2xx

Debug probe prometheus.io for http_2xx

Metrics

Configuration

Recent Probes

Module	Target	Result	Debug

Figure 10-1. The Blackbox Exporter's status page

ICMP

The Internet Control Message Protocol (ICMP) is a part of the Internet Protocol (IP). In the context of the Blackbox exporter, it is the *echo reply* and *echo request* messages that are of interest to you, more commonly known as *ping*.[5]

 ICMP uses raw sockets so it requires more privileges than a typical exporter, which is why Example 10-9 uses sudo. On Linux you could instead give the Blackbox Exporter the CAP_NET_RAW capability.

To start, you should ask the Blackbox Exporter to ping localhost by visiting *http://localhost:9115/probe?module=icmp&target=localhost* in your browser, which should produce something like:

---

5 Some pings can also work via UDP or TCP instead, but those are relatively rare.

```
# HELP probe_dns_lookup_time_seconds Returns the time taken for probe dns
    lookup in seconds
# TYPE probe_dns_lookup_time_seconds gauge
probe_dns_lookup_time_seconds 0.000580415
# HELP probe_duration_seconds Returns how long the probe took to complete
    in seconds
# TYPE probe_duration_seconds gauge
probe_duration_seconds 0.001044791
# HELP probe_icmp_duration_seconds Duration of icmp request by phase
# TYPE probe_icmp_duration_seconds gauge
probe_icmp_duration_seconds{phase="resolve"} 0.000580415
probe_icmp_duration_seconds{phase="rtt"} 0.000123794
probe_icmp_duration_seconds{phase="setup"} 0.000130416
# HELP probe_icmp_reply_hop_limit Replied packet hop limit (TTL for ipv4)
# TYPE probe_icmp_reply_hop_limit gauge
probe_icmp_reply_hop_limit 64
# HELP probe_ip_addr_hash Specifies the hash of IP address. It's useful
    to detect if the IP address changes.
# TYPE probe_ip_addr_hash gauge
probe_ip_addr_hash 1.751717746e+09
# HELP probe_ip_protocol Specifies whether probe ip protocol is IP4 or IP6
# TYPE probe_ip_protocol gauge
probe_ip_protocol 6
# HELP probe_success Displays whether or not the probe was a success
# TYPE probe_success gauge
probe_success 1
```

The key metric here is `probe_success`, which is 1 if your probe succeeded and 0 otherwise. This is similar to `consul_up`, and you should check that neither up nor `probe_success` are 0 when alerting. There is an example of this in "for" on page 314.

The */metrics* of the Blackbox Exporter provides metrics about the Blackbox Exporter itself, such as how much CPU it has used. To perform blackbox probes, you use */probe*.

There are also other useful metrics that all types of probes produce. `probe_ip_proto col` indicates the IP protocol used, IPv4 in this case; `probe_ip_addr_hash` is a hash of the IP address, useful to detect when it changes; and `probe_duration_seconds` is how long the entire probe took, including DNS resolution.

The name resolution used by Prometheus and the Blackbox Exporter is DNS resolution, not the `gethostbyname` syscall. Other potential sources of name resolution, such as */etc/hosts* and *nsswitch.conf*, are not considered by the Blackbox Exporter. This can lead to the `ping` command working, but the Blackbox Exporter failing due to not being able to resolve its target via DNS.

If you look inside *blackbox.yml*, you will find the `icmp` module:

```
icmp:
  prober: icmp
```

This says that there is a module called `icmp`, which you had requested with the `?module=icmp` in the URL. This module uses the `icmp` prober, with no additional options specified. ICMP is quite simple, so only in niche use cases might you need to specify `dont_fragment` or `payload_size`.

You can also try other targets. For example, to probe *google.com* you can visit *http://localhost:9115/probe?module=icmp& target=www.google.com* in your browser. For the `icmp` probe, the `target` URL parameter is an IP address or hostname.

You may find that this probe fails, with output like:

```
# HELP probe_dns_lookup_time_seconds Returns the time taken for probe dns
    lookup in seconds
# TYPE probe_dns_lookup_time_seconds gauge
probe_dns_lookup_time_seconds 0.018805905
# HELP probe_duration_seconds Returns how long the probe took to complete
    in seconds
# TYPE probe_duration_seconds gauge
probe_duration_seconds 0.019061888
# HELP probe_icmp_duration_seconds Duration of icmp request by phase
# TYPE probe_icmp_duration_seconds gauge
probe_icmp_duration_seconds{phase="resolve"} 0.018805905
probe_icmp_duration_seconds{phase="rtt"} 0
probe_icmp_duration_seconds{phase="setup"} 9.8677e-05
# HELP probe_ip_addr_hash Specifies the hash of IP address. It's useful to
detect if the IP address changes.
# TYPE probe_ip_addr_hash gauge
probe_ip_addr_hash 4.125764906e+09
# HELP probe_ip_protocol Specifies whether probe ip protocol is IP4 or IP6
# TYPE probe_ip_protocol gauge
probe_ip_protocol 6
# HELP probe_success Displays whether or not the probe was a success
# TYPE probe_success gauge
probe_success 0
```

`probe_success` is 0 here, indicating the failure. Notice that `probe_ip_protocol` is 6, indicating IPv6. In this case the machine we are using doesn't have a working IPv6 setup. Why is the Blackbox Exporter using IPv6?

When resolving the Blackbox Exporter, targets will prefer a returned IPv6 address if there is one; otherwise, it will use an IPv4 address. *google.com* has both, so IPv6 is chosen and fails on our machine.

You can see this in more detail if you add `&debug=true` on to the end of the URL, giving *http://localhost:9115/probe?module=icmp&target=www.google.com&debug=true*, which will produce output like:

```
Logs for the probe:
... module=icmp target=www.google.com level=info
        msg="Beginning probe" probe=icmp timeout_seconds=119.5
... module=icmp target=www.google.com level=info
        msg="Resolving target address" preferred_ip_protocol=ip6
... module=icmp target=www.google.com level=info
        msg="Resolved target address" ip=2a00:1450:400c:c07::69
... module=icmp target=www.google.com level=info
        msg="Creating socket"
... module=icmp target=www.google.com level=info
        msg="Creating ICMP packet" seq=10 id=3483
... module=icmp target=www.google.com level=info
        msg="Writing out packet"
... module=icmp target=www.google.com level=warn
        msg="Error writing to socket" err="write udp
        [::]:3->[2a00:1450:400c:c07::69]:0: sendto: network is unreachable"
... module=icmp target=www.google.com level=error
        msg="Probe failed" duration_seconds=0.001902969

Metrics that would have been returned:
# HELP probe_dns_lookup_time_seconds Returns the time taken for probe dns
    lookup in seconds
# TYPE probe_dns_lookup_time_seconds gauge
probe_dns_lookup_time_seconds 0.001635165
# HELP probe_duration_seconds Returns how long the probe took to complete
    in seconds
# TYPE probe_duration_seconds gauge
probe_duration_seconds 0.001902969
# HELP probe_icmp_duration_seconds Duration of icmp request by phase
# TYPE probe_icmp_duration_seconds gauge
probe_icmp_duration_seconds{phase="resolve"} 0.001635165
probe_icmp_duration_seconds{phase="rtt"} 0
probe_icmp_duration_seconds{phase="setup"} 9.6612e-05
# HELP probe_ip_addr_hash Specifies the hash of IP address. It's useful to
    detect if the IP address changes.
# TYPE probe_ip_addr_hash gauge
probe_ip_addr_hash 4.142542525e+09
# HELP probe_ip_protocol Specifies whether probe ip protocol is IP4 or IP6
# TYPE probe_ip_protocol gauge
probe_ip_protocol 6
# HELP probe_success Displays whether or not the probe was a success
# TYPE probe_success gauge
probe_success 0

Module configuration:
prober: icmp
http:
    ip_protocol_fallback: true
    follow_redirects: true
    enable_http2: true
tcp:
    ip_protocol_fallback: true
```

```
icmp:
    ip_protocol_fallback: true
    ttl: 64
dns:
    ip_protocol_fallback: true
    recursion_desired: true
```

The debug output is extensive, and by carefully reading through it you can understand exactly what the probe is doing. The error you see here is from the `sendto` syscall, which cannot assign an IPv6 address. To prefer IPv4 instead, you can add a new module with the `preferred_ip_protocol: ipv4` option to *blackbox.yml*:

```
icmp_ipv4:
  prober: icmp
  icmp:
    preferred_ip_protocol: ip4
```

After restarting the Blackbox Exporter,[6] if you use this module via *http://localhost:9115/probe?module=icmp_ipv4&target=www.google.com*, it will now work via IPv4.

TCP

The Transmission Control Protocol is the TCP in TCP/IP. Many standard protocols use it, including websites (HTTP), email (SMTP), remote login (Telnet and SSH), and chat (IRC). The `tcp` probe of the Blackbox Exporter allows you to check TCP services, and perform simple conversations for those that use line-based text protocols.

To start, you can check if your local SSH server is listening on port 22 with *http://localhost:9115/probe?module=tcp_connect&target=localhost:22*:

```
# HELP probe_dns_lookup_time_seconds Returns the time taken for probe dns lookup
    in seconds
# TYPE probe_dns_lookup_time_seconds gauge
probe_dns_lookup_time_seconds 0.000202381
# HELP probe_duration_seconds Returns how long the probe took to complete in
    seconds
# TYPE probe_duration_seconds gauge
probe_duration_seconds 0.000881654
# HELP probe_failed_due_to_regex Indicates if probe failed due to regex
# TYPE probe_failed_due_to_regex gauge
probe_failed_due_to_regex 0
# HELP probe_ip_protocol Specifies whether probe ip protocol is IP4 or IP6
# TYPE probe_ip_protocol gauge
probe_ip_protocol 4
# HELP probe_success Displays whether or not the probe was a success
```

---

6 Similar to Prometheus, you can also send a `SIGHUP` to the Blackbox Exporter to have it reload its
   configuration.

```
# TYPE probe_success gauge
probe_success 1
```

This is quite similar to the metrics produced by the ICMP probe, and you can see that this probe succeeded as `probe_success` is 1. The definition of the `tcp_connect` module in *blackbox.yml* is:

```
tcp_connect:
  prober: tcp
```

This will try to connect to your target, and once it is connected immediately, it will close the connection. The `ssh_banner` module goes further, checking for a particular response from the remote server:

```
ssh_banner:
  prober: tcp
  tcp:
    query_response:
    - expect: "^SSH-2.0-"
```

As the very start of an SSH session is in plain text, you can check for this part of the protocol with the `tcp` probe. This is better than `tcp_connect`, as you are not only checking that the TCP port is open, but that the server on the other end is responding with an SSH banner.

If your server returned something different, the `expect` regex will not match, and `probe_success` will be 0. In addition, `probe_failed_due_to_regex` would be 1. Since Prometheus is a metrics-based system, the full debug output cannot be saved, as that would be event logging.[7] However, the Blackbox Exporter can provide a small number of metrics to help you to piece together what went wrong after the fact.

> If you find that every service needs a different module, consider standardizing what your health checks look like across services. If a service exposes a */metrics* page, then there is not much need for basic connectivity checks with the Blackbox Exporter, as Prometheus's scrapes will already provide that.

The `tcp` probe can also connect via TLS. Add a `tcp_connect_tls` to your *blackbox.yml* file with the following configuration:

```
tcp_connect_tls:
  prober: tcp
  tcp:
    tls: true
```

---

7 However, the debug information for the most recent probes is available from the Blackbox Exporter's status page.

After restarting the Blackbox Exporter, if you now visit *http://localhost:9115/probe? module=tcp_connect_tls&target=www.oreilly.com:443*, you can check if O'Reilly's website can be contacted with HTTPS.[8] For the `tcp` prober, the `target` URL parameter is an IP address or hostname, followed by a colon, and then the port number.

You may notice among the metrics output:

```
# HELP probe_ssl_last_chain_expiry_timestamp_seconds Returns last SSL chain
    expiry in timestamp
# TYPE probe_ssl_last_chain_expiry_timestamp_seconds gauge
probe_ssl_last_chain_expiry_timestamp_seconds 1.686095999e+09
```

`probe_ssl_last_chain_expiry_timestamp_seconds` is produced as a side effect of probing, indicating when your TLS/SSL certificate[9] will expire. You can use this to catch expiring certificates before they become outages.

While HTTP is a line-oriented text protocol[10] that you could use the `tcp` probe with, there is an `http` probe that is more suitable for this purpose.

HTTP

The HyperText Transfer Protocol (HTTP) is the basis for the modern web, and likely what most of the services you provide use. While most monitoring of web applications is best done by Prometheus scraping metrics over HTTP, sometimes you will want to perform blackbox monitoring of your HTTP services.

The `http` prober takes a URL[11] for the `target` URL parameter. If you visit *http://localhost:9115/probe?module=http_2xx&target=https://www.oreilly.com/*, you can check O'Reilly's website over HTTPS using the `http_2xx` module,[12] producing output similar to:

```
# HELP probe_dns_lookup_time_seconds Returns the time taken for probe
    dns lookup in seconds
# TYPE probe_dns_lookup_time_seconds gauge
probe_dns_lookup_time_seconds 0.001481084
# HELP probe_duration_seconds Returns how long the probe took to complete
    in seconds
# TYPE probe_duration_seconds gauge
probe_duration_seconds 0.165316519
# HELP probe_failed_due_to_regex Indicates if probe failed due to regex
# TYPE probe_failed_due_to_regex gauge
```

---

8 443 is the standard port for HTTPS.

9 More exactly, the first certificate that will expire in your certificate chain.

10 At least for HTTP versions prior to 2.0.

11 You can even include URL parameters, if they are appropriately encoded.

12 The `http_2xx` module is incidentally the default module name if you don't provide one as a URL parameter.

```
probe_failed_due_to_regex 0
# HELP probe_http_content_length Length of http content response
# TYPE probe_http_content_length gauge
probe_http_content_length -1
# HELP probe_http_duration_seconds Duration of http request by phase, summed
    over all redirects
# TYPE probe_http_duration_seconds gauge
probe_http_duration_seconds{phase="connect"} 0.02226464
probe_http_duration_seconds{phase="processing"} 0.05238605
probe_http_duration_seconds{phase="resolve"} 0.001481084
probe_http_duration_seconds{phase="tls"} 0.043717698
probe_http_duration_seconds{phase="transfer"} 0.044905889
# HELP probe_http_last_modified_timestamp_seconds Returns the Last-Modified
    HTTP response header in unixtime
# TYPE probe_http_last_modified_timestamp_seconds gauge
probe_http_last_modified_timestamp_seconds 1.665390603e+09
# HELP probe_http_redirects The number of redirects
# TYPE probe_http_redirects gauge
probe_http_redirects 0
# HELP probe_http_ssl Indicates if SSL was used for the final redirect
# TYPE probe_http_ssl gauge
probe_http_ssl 1
# HELP probe_http_status_code Response HTTP status code
# TYPE probe_http_status_code gauge
probe_http_status_code 200
# HELP probe_http_uncompressed_body_length Length of uncompressed response body
# TYPE probe_http_uncompressed_body_length gauge
probe_http_uncompressed_body_length 75719
# HELP probe_http_version Returns the version of HTTP of the probe response
# TYPE probe_http_version gauge
probe_http_version 2
# HELP probe_ip_addr_hash Specifies the hash of IP address. It's useful to
    detect if the IP address changes.
# TYPE probe_ip_addr_hash gauge
probe_ip_addr_hash 1.793027101e+09
# HELP probe_ip_protocol Specifies whether probe ip protocol is IP4 or IP6
# TYPE probe_ip_protocol gauge
probe_ip_protocol 4
# HELP probe_ssl_earliest_cert_expiry Returns earliest SSL cert expiry
    in unixtime
# TYPE probe_ssl_earliest_cert_expiry gauge
probe_ssl_earliest_cert_expiry 1.697068799e+09
# HELP probe_ssl_last_chain_expiry_timestamp_seconds Returns last SSL chain
    expiry in timestamp seconds
# TYPE probe_ssl_last_chain_expiry_timestamp_seconds gauge
probe_ssl_last_chain_expiry_timestamp_seconds 1.697068799e+09
# HELP probe_ssl_last_chain_info Contains SSL leaf certificate information
# TYPE probe_ssl_last_chain_info gauge
probe_ssl_last_chain_info{fingerprint_sha256="849c8863b"} 1
# HELP probe_success Displays whether or not the probe was a success
# TYPE probe_success gauge
probe_success 1
```

```
# HELP probe_tls_version_info Contains the TLS version used
# TYPE probe_tls_version_info gauge
probe_tls_version_info{version="TLS 1.3"} 1
```

You can see `probe_success`, but also a number of other useful metrics for debugging, such as the status code, HTTP version, and timings for different phases of the request.

The `http` probe has many options to both affect how the request is made, and whether the response is considered successful. You can specify HTTP authentication, headers, POST body, and then in the response, check that the status code, HTTP version, and body are acceptable.

For example, we may want to test that users of *http://www.oreilly.com* end up redirected to an HTTPS website, with a 200 status code, and that the word "Prometheus" is in the body. To do so you could create a module like:

```
http_200_ssl_prometheus:
  prober: http
  http:
    valid_status_codes: [200]
    fail_if_not_ssl: true
    fail_if_not_matches_regexp:
      - oreillymedia
```

Visiting *http://localhost:9115/probe?module=http_200_ssl_prometheus&target=https:// oreilly.com* in your browser, you should see that this works as `probe_success` is 1. You could also use the same request against *http://prometheus.io* if you visit *http:// localhost:9115/probe?module=http_200_ssl_prometheus&target=http://prometheus.io* in your browser.[13]

 While the Blackbox Exporter will follow HTTP redirects,[14] not all features work perfectly across redirects.

This example is a little contrived, but each module of the Blackbox Exporter is a specific test that you can run against different targets by providing different `target` URL parameters as you did here with *http://www.oreilly.com* and *http://prometheus.io*. For example, you might check that each frontend application instance serving your website is returning the right result. If different services need different tests, then you can create modules for each of them. It is not possible to override modules via URL

---

13 Presuming you have a working IPv6 setup; if not, add **preferred_ip_protocol: ip4**.

14 Unless `follow_redirects` is set to `false`.

parameters, as that would lead to the Blackbox Exporter being an open proxy[15] and would confuse the division of responsibilities between Prometheus and exporters.

The http probe is the most configurable of the Blackbox Exporter's probes (the documentation (*https://oreil.ly/Jj0mf*) lists all of the options). While flexible, the Blackbox Exporter cannot handle all possible use cases, as it is a relatively simple HTTP probe at the end of the day. If you need something more sophisticated, you may need to write your own exporter, or take advantage of existing exporters such as the WebDriver Exporter (*https://oreil.ly/qTbHY*), which simulates a browser visiting a URL.

DNS

The dns probe is primarily for testing DNS servers; for example, checking that all of your DNS replicas are returning results.

If you wanted to test that your DNS servers were responding over TCP,[16] you could create a module in your *blackbox.yml* like this:

```
dns_tcp:
  prober: dns
  dns:
    transport_protocol: "tcp"
    query_name: "www.prometheus.io"
```

After restarting the Blackbox Exporter, you can visit *http://localhost:9115/probe?module=dns_tcp&target=8.8.8.8* to check if Google's Public DNS service[17] works via TCP. Note that the target URL parameter is the DNS server that is talked to, and the query_name is the DNS request sent to the DNS server. This is the same as if you ran the command dig -tcp @8.8.8.8 www.prometheus.io.

For the dns prober, the target URL parameter is an IP address or hostname, followed by a colon, and then the port number. You can also provide just the IP address or hostname, in which case the standard DNS port of 53 will be used.

Aside from testing DNS servers, you could also use a dns probe to confirm that specific results are being returned by DNS resolution. But usually you want to go further and communicate to the returned service via HTTP, TCP, or ICMP, in which case one of those probes makes more sense as you get the DNS check for free.

---

15 Which would be unwise from a security standpoint.

16 While DNS usually uses UDP, it can also use TCP in cases such as for large responses. Unfortunately, many site operators are not aware of this and block TCP on port 53, which is the DNS port.

17 Which is offered on the IPs 8.8.8.8, 8.8.4.4, 2001:4860:4860::8888, and 2001:4860:4860::8844.

An example of using the `dns` probe to check for specific results would be to check that your MX records[18] have not disappeared.

You could create a module in your *blackbox.yml* like this:

```
dns_mx_present_rp_io:
  prober: dns
  dns:
    query_name: "prometheus.io"
    query_type: "MX"
    validate_answer_rrs:
      fail_if_not_matches_regexp:
        - ".+"
```

After restarting the Blackbox Exporter, you can visit *http://localhost:9115/probe?module=dns_mx_present_rp_io&target=8.8.8.8* to check that `prometheus.io` has MX records. Note that as the `query_name` is specified per module, you will need a module for every domain that you want to check. We are using 8.8.8.8 here, as Google's Public DNS is a public DNS resolver, but you could also use a local resolver.

The `dns` probe has more features intended to help check for aspects of DNS responses, such as authority and additional records, which you can find out more about in the documentation (*https://oreil.ly/3pY9E*). For a better understanding of DNS, we recommend RFCs 1034 (*https://oreil.ly/y7Rra*) and 1035 (*https://oreil.ly/dtwcY*),[19] or a book such as *DNS and BIND* by Paul Albitz and Cricket Liu (O'Reilly).

Prometheus Configuration

As you have seen, the Blackbox Exporter takes a `module` and `target` URL parameter on the */probe* endpoint. Using the `params` and `metrics_path`, as discussed in "How to Scrape" on page 162, you can provide these in a scrape config, but that would mean having a scrape config per target, which would be unwieldy as you could not take advantage of Prometheus's ability to do service discovery.

The good news is that you can take advantage of service discovery, as the `__param_<name>` label can be used to provide URL parameters in relabeling. In addition, the `instance` and `__address__` labels are distinct, as discussed in "job, instance, and `__address__`" on page 158, so you can have Prometheus talk to the Blackbox Exporter while having an `instance` label of your actual target.

Example 10-10 shows an example of this in practice.

---

18 Used for email, MX stands for Mail eXchanger.

19 We learned DNS from these RFCs; they're a little outdated but still give a good sense of how DNS operates.

Example 10-10. prometheus.yml to check if several websites work

```
scrape_configs:
 - job_name: blackbox
   metrics_path: /probe
   params:
     module: [http_2xx]
   static_configs:
    - targets:
       - http://www.prometheus.io
       - http://www.robustperception.io
       - http://demo.robustperception.io
   relabel_configs:
    - source_labels: [__address__]
      target_label: __param_target
    - source_labels: [__param_target]
      target_label: instance
    - target_label: __address__
      replacement: 127.0.0.1:9115
```

To break it down:

```
 - job_name: 'blackbox'
   metrics_path: /probe
   params:
     module: [http_2xx]
```

A default job label, custom path, and one URL parameter are specified:

```
   static_configs:
    - targets:
       - https://www.prometheus.io
       - https://www.oreilly.com
       - https://demo.do.prometheus.io
```

There are three websites that you will be probing:

```
   relabel_configs:
    - source_labels: [__address__]
      target_label: __param_target
    - source_labels: [__param_target]
      target_label: instance
    - target_label: __address__
      replacement: 127.0.0.1:9115
```

The relabel_configs is where the magic happens. First, the __address__ label becomes the target URL parameter and secondly also the instance label. At this point, the instance label and target URL parameter have the value you want, but the __address__ is still a URL rather than the Blackbox Exporter. The final relabeling action sets the __address__ to the host and port of the local Blackbox Exporter.

If you run Prometheus with this configuration and look at the Targets status page, you will see something like Figure 10-2. The endpoint has the desired URL parameters, and the instance label is the URL.

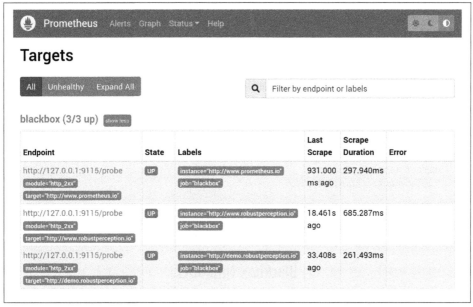

Figure 10-2. The Blackbox Exporter's status page

 That the State is UP for the Blackbox Exporter does not mean that the probe was successful, merely that the Blackbox Exporter was scraped successfully.[20] You need to check that `probe_success` is 1.

This approach is not limited to `static_configs`. You can use any other service discovery mechanism (as discussed in Chapter 8). For example, building on Example 8-19, which scraped the Node Exporter for all nodes registered in Consul, Example 10-11 will check that SSH is responding for all nodes registered in Consul.

---

20 Indeed, in Figure 10-2 the probe of *http://www.prometheus.io* is failing, as our machine has a broken IPv6 setup.

Example 10-11. Checking SSH on all nodes registered in Consul

```
scrape_configs:
 - job_name: node
   metrics_path: /probe
   params:
     module: [ssh_banner]
   consul_sd_configs:
    - server: 'localhost:8500'
   relabel_configs:
    - source_labels: [__meta_consul_address]
      regex: '(.*)'
      replacement: '${1}:22'
      target_label: __param_target
    - source_labels: [__param_target]
      target_label: instance
    - target_label: __address__
      replacement: 127.0.0.1:9115
```

The power of this approach allows you to reuse service discovery for not just scraping of */metrics*, but also to do blackbox monitoring of your applications.

Blackbox Timeouts

You may be wondering how to configure timeouts for your probes. The good news is that the Blackbox prober determines the timeout automatically based on the `scrape_timeout` in Prometheus.

Prometheus sends an HTTP header called `X-Prometheus-Scrape-Timeout-Seconds` with every scrape. The Blackbox Exporter uses this for its timeouts, less a buffer.[21] The end result is that the Blackbox Exporter will usually return with some metrics that will be useful in debugging in the event of the target being slow, rather than the scrape as a whole failing.

You can reduce the timeout further using the `timeout` field in *blackbox.yml*.

Now that you have an idea of the sorts of exporters you will run into, you're ready to learn how to pull metrics from your existing monitoring systems.

---

21 Specified by the `--timeout-offset` command-line flag.

## CHAPTER 11

Working with Other Monitoring Systems

In an ideal world all of your applications would be directly exposing Prometheus metrics, but this is unlikely to be the world you inhabit. You may have other monitoring systems already in use, and doing a big switchover one day to Prometheus is not practical.

The good news is that among the hundreds of exporters for Prometheus there are several that convert data from other monitoring systems into the Prometheus format. While your ideal end goal would be to move completely to Prometheus, exporters like the ones you'll learn about in this chapter are very helpful when you are still transitioning.

Other Monitoring Systems

Monitoring systems vary in how compatible they are with Prometheus; some require notable effort, while others require close to none. For example, InfluxDB has a data model fairly similar to Prometheus, so you can have your application push the InfluxDB line protocol to the InfluxDB Exporter (*https://oreil.ly/NPmXE*), which can then be scraped by Prometheus.

Other systems like collectd do not have labels, but it is possible to automatically convert the metrics it outputs into an OK Prometheus metric with no additional configuration using the Collectd Exporter (*https://oreil.ly/ErtjW*). As of version 5.7, collectd even includes this natively with the Write Prometheus plug-in (*https://oreil.ly/mWhRg*).

But not all monitoring systems have data models that can be automatically converted into reasonable Prometheus metrics. Historically, Graphite did not not support key-value labels, and some configuration labels can be extracted from the dotted strings it uses using the Graphite Exporter (*https://oreil.ly/6ah0Q*).[1] StatsD has basically the same dotted-string model as Graphite; StatsD uses events rather than metrics, so the StatsD Exporter (*https://oreil.ly/ECuBA*) aggregates the events into metrics, and can also extract labels.

In the Java/JVM space, JMX (Java Management eXtensions) is a standard often used for exposing metrics, but how it is used varies quite a bit from application to application. The JMX Exporter (*https://oreil.ly/A549a*) has OK defaults, but given the lack of standardization of the mBean structure, the only sane way to configure it is via regular expressions. The good news is that there are a variety of example configurations provided, and that the JMX Exporter is intended to run as a Java agent so you don't have to manage a separate exporter process.

SNMP actually has a data model that is quite close to that of Prometheus, and by using MIBs,[2] SNMP metrics can be automatically produced by the SNMP Exporter (*https://oreil.ly/HW3wu*). The bad news is twofold. First, MIBs from vendors are often not freely available, so you need to acquire the MIBs yourself and use the *generator* included with the SNMP Exporter to convert the MIBs into a form the SNMP Exporter can understand. Second, many vendors follow the letter of the SNMP specification but not the spirit, so additional configuration and/or munging with PromQL is sometimes required. The SNMP Exporter is a Blackbox/SNMP-style exporter, as was discussed in "Blackbox" on page 194, so unlike almost all other exporters, you typically run one per Prometheus rather than one per application instance.

 SNMP is a very chatty network protocol. It is advisable to have SNMP Exporters as close as you can on the network to the network devices they are monitoring to mitigate this. Furthermore, many SNMP devices can speak the SNMP protocol but not return metrics in anything resembling a reasonable time frame. You may need to be judicious in what metrics you request and generous in your scrape_interval.

There are also exporters you can use to extract metrics from a variety of software as a service (SaaS) monitoring systems, including the CloudWatch Exporter (*https://oreil.ly/lQ9Fe*), New Relic Exporter (*https://oreil.ly/YWPcw*), Pingdom Exporter (*https://oreil.ly/UU4br*), and Stackdriver Exporter (*https://oreil.ly/JH2T9*). One thing to watch with such exporters is that there may be rate limits and financial costs for using the APIs they access.

---

1 Version 1.1.0 of Graphite added tag supports that are ingested by the Graphite Exporter as labels.

2 Management Information Base, basically a schema for SNMP objects.

The NRPE Exporter (*https://oreil.ly/BBkqg*) is an SNMP/Blackbox-style exporter that allows you to run NRPE checks. NRPE stands for Nagios Remote Program Execution, a way to run Nagios checks on remote machines. While many existing checks in a Nagios-style monitoring setup can be replaced by metrics from the Node and other exporters, you may have some custom checks that are a bit harder to migrate. The NRPE Exporter gives you a transition option here, allowing you to later convert these checks to another solution such as the textfile collector, as discussed in "Textfile Collector" on page 134.

Integration with other monitoring systems isn't limited to running separate exporters; there are also integrations with popular instrumentation systems such as Dropwizard metrics.[3] The Java client (*https://oreil.ly/IdIHo*) has an integration that can pull metrics from Dropwizard metrics using its reporting feature that will then appear alongside any direct instrumentation you have on */metrics*.

 Dropwizard can also expose its metrics via JMX. If possible (i.e., you control the codebase), you should prefer using the Java client's Dropwizard integration over JMX, since going via JMX has higher overhead and requires more configuration.

InfluxDB

The InfluxDB Exporter accepts the InfluxDB line protocol that was added in version 0.9.0 of InfluxDB. The protocol works over HTTP, so the same TCP port can be used both to accept writes and serve */metrics*. To run the InfluxDB Exporter, follow the steps in Example 11-1.

Example 11-1. Downloading and running the InfluxDB Exporter

```
hostname $ wget https://github.com/prometheus/influxdb_exporter/releases/download/
    v0.10.0/influxdb_exporter-0.10.0.linux-amd64.tar.gz
hostname $ tar -xzf influxdb_exporter-0.10.0.linux-amd64.tar.gz
hostname $ cd influxdb_exporter-0.10.0.linux-amd64/
hostname $ ./influxdb_exporter
msg="Starting influxdb_exporter" version="(version=0.10.0, branch=
    HEAD, revision=6ce7ff5e3f584eb9c2019be71ecb9e586ba3d83e)"
msg="Build context" context="(go=go1.18.3, user=root@de8ee7c667
    c4, date=20220708-19:34:59)"
```

---

3 Previously known as Yammer metrics.

You can then direct your existing applications that speak the InfluxDB line protocol to use the InfluxDB Exporter. To send a metric by hand with labels, you can do:

```
curl -XPOST 'http://localhost:9122/write' --data-binary \
    'example_metric,foo=bar value=43 1517339868000000000'
```

If you then visit *http://localhost:9122/metrics* in your browser, among the output you will see:

```
# HELP example_metric InfluxDB Metric
# TYPE example_metric untyped
example_metric{foo="bar"} 43
```

You may notice that the timestamp that you sent to the exporter is not exposed. There are very few valid use cases for */metrics* to expose timestamps, as scrapes are meant to synchronously gather metrics representing the application state at scrape time. When working with other monitoring systems this is often not the case, and using timestamps would be valid. At the time of writing only the Java client library supports timestamps for custom collectors. When metrics are exported without timestamps, Prometheus will use the time at which the scrape happens. The InfluxDB Exporter will garbage collect the point after a few minutes and stop exposing it. These are the challenges you face when you convert from push to pull. On the other hand, converting from pull to push is quite simple, as shown in Example 4-13.

You can scrape the InfluxDB Exporter like any other exporter, as shown in Example 11-2.

Example 11-2. prometheus.yml to scrape a local InfluxDB Exporter

```
global:
  scrape_interval: 10s
scrape_configs:
 - job_name: application_name
   static_configs:
     - targets:
       - localhost:9122
```

StatsD

StatsD takes in events and aggregates them over time into metrics. You can think of sending an event to StatsD as like calling inc on a counter or observe on a summary. The StatsD Exporter does just that, converting your StatsD events into Prometheus client library metrics and instrumentation calls.

You can run the StatsD Exporter by following the steps in Example 11-3.

Example 11-3. Downloading and running the StatsD Exporter

```
hostname $ wget https://github.com/prometheus/statsd_exporter/releases/download/
    v0.22.8/statsd_exporter-0.22.8.linux-amd64.tar.gz
hostname $ tar -xzf statsd_exporter-0.22.8.linux-amd64.tar.gz
hostname $ cd statsd_exporter-0.22.8.linux-amd64/
hostname $ ./statsd_exporter
msg="Starting StatsD -> Prometheus Exporter" version="(version=0.22.8, branch=
    HEAD, revision=aecad1a2faf31d4a6c27323a29ca8c7a23d88f6b)"
msg="Build context" context="(go=go1.18.6, user=root@56d5d8c6d
    3d1, date=20220913-14:49:05)"
msg="Accepting StatsD Traffic" udp=:9125 tcp=:9125 unixgram=
msg="Accepting Prometheus Requests" addr=:9102
```

As StatsD uses a custom TCP and UDP protocol, you need different ports for sending events than for scraping */metrics.*

You can send a gauge by hand with:[4]

```
echo 'example_gauge:123|g' | nc localhost 9125
```

which will appear on *http://localhost:9102/metrics* as:

```
# HELP example_gauge Metric autogenerated by statsd_exporter.
# TYPE example_gauge gauge
example_gauge 123
```

You can also send counter increments and summary/histogram observations:

```
echo 'example_counter_total:1|c' | nc localhost 9125
echo 'example_latency_total:20|ms' | nc localhost 9125
```

The StatsD protocol isn't fully specified; many implementations only support integer values. While the StatsD Exporter does not have this limitation, note that many metrics will not be in the base units you are used to with Prometheus.

You can also extract labels, as StatsD is often used with the Graphite *dotted string* notation, where position indicates meaning. `app.http.requests.eu-west-1./foo` might, for example, mean what would be `app_http_requests_total{region="eu-west-1",path="/foo"}` in Prometheus. To be able to map from such a string, you need to provide a mapping file in *mapping.yml*, such as:

```
mappings:
- match: app.http.requests.*.*
  name: app_http_requests_total
  labels:
    region: "${1}"
    path: "${2}"
```

---

4 nc is a handy networking utility whose full name is *netcat*. You may need to install it if you don't have it already.

and then run the StatsD Exporter using it:

```
./statsd_exporter -statsd.mapping-config mapping.yml
```

If you now send requests following that pattern to the StatsD Exporter, they will be appropriately named and labeled:

```
echo 'app.http.requests.eu-west-1./foo:1|c' | nc localhost 9125
echo 'app.http.requests.eu-west-1./bar:1|c' | nc localhost 9125
```

If you visit *http://localhost:9102/metrics*, it will now contain:

```
# HELP app_http_requests_total Metric autogenerated by statsd_exporter.
# TYPE app_http_requests_total counter
app_http_requests_total{path="/bar",region="eu-west-1"} 1
app_http_requests_total{path="/foo",region="eu-west-1"} 1
```

The Graphite Exporter has a similar mechanism to convert dotted strings into labels.

You may end up running the StatsD Exporter even after you have completed your transition to Prometheus if you are using languages such as PHP and Perl for web applications. As mentioned in "Multiprocess with Gunicorn" on page 68, Prometheus presumes a multithreaded model with long-lived processes. You typically use languages like PHP in a way that is not only multiprocess, but also often with processes that only live for a single HTTP request. While an approach such as the Python client uses for multiprocess deployments is theoretically possible for typical PHP deployments, you may find that the StatsD Exporter is more practical. There is also the prom-aggregation-gateway (*https://oreil.ly/qrGYk*) in this space.

We would recommend for exporters like the InfluxDB, Graphite, StatsD, and Collectd Exporters that convert from push to pull that you have one exporter per application instance and the same lifecycle as the application. You should start, stop, and restart the exporter at the same time as you start, stop, and restart the application instance. That way is easier to manage, avoids issues with labels changing, and keeps the exporter from becoming a bottleneck.[5]

While there are hundreds of exporters on offer, you may find yourself needing to write or extend one yourself. The next chapter will show you how to write exporters.

---

5 One of the reasons that Prometheus exists is due to scaling issues that SoundCloud had with many applications sending to one StatsD.

## CHAPTER 12

Writing Exporters

Sometimes you will not be able to either add direct instrumentation to an application, nor find an existing exporter that covers it. This leaves you with having to write an exporter yourself. The good news is that exporters are relatively easy to write. The hard part is figuring out what the metrics exposed by applications mean. Units are often unknown, and documentation, if it exists at all, can be vague. In this chapter you will learn how to write exporters.

Consul Telemetry

We are going to write a small exporter for Consul to demonstrate the process. We already saw Consul and the Consul Exporter in "Consul" on page 187, so let's create a simple exporter with metrics from the telemetry API.[1]

While you can write exporters in any programming language, the majority are written in Go, and that is the language we will use here. However, you will find a small number of exporters written in Python, and an even smaller number in Java.

If your Consul is not running, start it again following the instructions in Example 8-8. If you visit *http://localhost:8500/v1/agent/metrics*, you will see the JSON output that you will be working with, which is similar to Example 12-1. Conveniently, Consul provides a Go library that you can use, so you don't have to worry about parsing the JSON yourself.

---

1 These metrics are also exported natively by Consul. This example predates these metrics being natively exposed by Consul.

Example 12-1. An abbreviated example output from a Consul agent's metrics output

```
{
  "Timestamp": "2018-01-31 14:42:10 +0000 UTC",
  "Gauges": [
    {
      "Name": "consul.autopilot.failure_tolerance",
      "Value": 0,
      "Labels": {}
    }
  ],
  "Points": [],
  "Counters": [
    {
      "Name": "consul.raft.apply",
      "Count": 1,
      "Sum": 2, "Min": 1, "Max": 1, "Mean": 1, "Stddev": 0,
      "Labels": {}
    }
  ],
  "Samples": [
    {
      "Name": "consul.fsm.coordinate.batch-update",
      "Count": 1,
      "Sum": 0.13156799972057343,
      "Min": 0.13156799972057343, "Max": 0.13156799972057343,
      "Mean": 0.13156799972057343, "Stddev": 0,
      "Labels": {}
    }
  ]
}
```

You are in luck that Consul has split out the counters and gauges for you.[2] The Samples also look like you can use the Count and Sum in a summary metric. Looking at all the Samples again, we have a suspicion that they are tracking latency. Digging through the documentation (*https://oreil.ly/6RY1Y*) confirms that they are *timers*, which means a Prometheus summary (see "The Summary" on page 50). The timers are also all in milliseconds, so we can convert them to seconds.[3] While the JSON has a field for labels, none are used, so you can ignore that. Aside from that, the only other thing you need to do is ensure any invalid characters in the metric names are sanitized.

---

2 Just because something is called a counter does not mean it is a counter. For example, Dropwizard has counters that can go down, so depending on how the counter is used in practice, it may be a counter, gauge, or untyped in Prometheus terms.

3 If only some of the Samples were timers, you would have to choose between exposing them as is or maintaining a list of which metrics are latencies and which weren't.

You now know the logic you need to apply to the metrics that Consul exposes, so you can write your exporter as in Example 12-2.

Example 12-2. consul_metrics.go, an exporter for Consul metrics written in Go

```go
package main

import (
        "log"
        "net/http"
        "regexp"

        "github.com/hashicorp/consul/api"
        "github.com/prometheus/client_golang/prometheus"
        "github.com/prometheus/client_golang/prometheus/promhttp"
)

var (
        up = prometheus.NewDesc(
                "consul_up",
                "Was talking to Consul successful.",
                nil, nil,
        )
        invalidChars = regexp.MustCompile("[^a-zA-Z0-9:_]")
)

type ConsulCollector struct {
}

// Implements prometheus.Collector.
func (c ConsulCollector) Describe(ch chan<- *prometheus.Desc) {
        ch <- up
}

// Implements prometheus.Collector.
func (c ConsulCollector) Collect(ch chan<- prometheus.Metric) {
        consul, err := api.NewClient(api.DefaultConfig())
        if err != nil {
                ch <- prometheus.MustNewConstMetric(up, prometheus.GaugeValue, 0)
                return
        }

        metrics, err := consul.Agent().Metrics()
        if err != nil {
                ch <- prometheus.MustNewConstMetric(up, prometheus.GaugeValue, 0)
                return
        }
        ch <- prometheus.MustNewConstMetric(up, prometheus.GaugeValue, 1)

        for _, g := range metrics.Gauges {
                name := invalidChars.ReplaceAllLiteralString(g.Name, "_")
```

```
        desc := prometheus.NewDesc(name, "Consul metric "+g.Name, nil,
            g.Labels)
        ch <- prometheus.MustNewConstMetric(
                desc, prometheus.GaugeValue, float64(g.Value))
    }

    for _, c := range metrics.Counters {
        name := invalidChars.ReplaceAllLiteralString(c.Name, "_")
        desc := prometheus.NewDesc(name+"_total", "Consul metric "+c.Name,
            nil, c.Labels)
        ch <- prometheus.MustNewConstMetric(
                desc, prometheus.CounterValue, float64(c.Count))
    }

    for _, s := range metrics.Samples {
        // All samples are times in milliseconds, we convert them to
        // seconds below.
        name := invalidChars.ReplaceAllLiteralString(s.Name, "_") +
            "_seconds"
        countDesc := prometheus.NewDesc(
                name+"_count", "Consul metric "+s.Name, nil, s.Labels)
        ch <- prometheus.MustNewConstMetric(
                countDesc, prometheus.CounterValue, float64(s.Count))
        sumDesc := prometheus.NewDesc(
                name+"_sum", "Consul metric "+s.Name, nil, s.Labels)
        ch <- prometheus.MustNewConstMetric(
                sumDesc, prometheus.CounterValue, s.Sum/1000)
    }
}

func main() {
    c := ConsulCollector{}
    prometheus.MustRegister(c)
    http.Handle("/metrics", promhttp.Handler())
    log.Fatal(http.ListenAndServe(":8000", nil))
}
```

If you have a working Go development environment, you can run the exporter with:

```
go get -d -u github.com/hashicorp/consul/api
go get -d -u github.com/prometheus/client_golang/prometheus
go run consul_metrics.go
```

If you visit *http://localhost:8000/metrics*, you will see metrics like:

```
# HELP consul_autopilot_failure_tolerance Consul metric
    consul.autopilot.failure_tolerance
# TYPE consul_autopilot_failure_tolerance gauge
consul_autopilot_failure_tolerance 0
# HELP consul_raft_apply_total Consul metric consul.raft.apply
# TYPE consul_raft_apply_total counter
consul_raft_apply_total 1
# HELP consul_fsm_coordinate_batch_update_seconds_count Consul metric
```

```
        consul.fsm.coordinate.batch-update
# TYPE consul_fsm_coordinate_batch_update_seconds_count counter
consul_fsm_coordinate_batch_update_seconds_count 1
# HELP consul_fsm_coordinate_batch_update_seconds_sum Consul metric
        consul.fsm.coordinate.batch-update
# TYPE consul_fsm_coordinate_batch_update_seconds_sum counter
consul_fsm_coordinate_batch_update_seconds_sum 1.3156799972057343e-01
```

That's all well and good, but how does the code work? In the next section we will show you how.

Custom Collectors

With direct instrumentation the client library takes in instrumentation events and tracks the values of the metrics over time. Client libraries provide the counter, gauge, summary, and histogram metrics for this, which are all examples of *collectors*. At scrape time each collector in a registry is *collected*, which is to say, asked for its metrics. These metrics will then be returned by the scrape of */metrics*. Counters and the other three standard metric types only ever return one metric family.

If rather than using direct instrumentation you want to provide from some other source, you use a *custom collector*, which is any collector that is not one of the standard four. Custom collectors can return any number of metric families. Collection happens on every single scrape of a */metrics* page, where each collection is a consistent snapshot of the metrics from a collector.

In Go your collectors must implement the `prometheus.Collector` interface. That is to say the collectors must be objects with `Describe` and `Collect` methods with a specific signature.

The `Describe` method returns a description of the metrics it will produce, in particular the metric name, label names, and help string. The `Describe` method is called at registration time, and is used to avoid duplicate metric registration.

There are two types of metrics an exporter can have: ones where it knows the names and labels in advance, and ones where they are only determined at scrape time. In this example, `consul_up` is known in advance so you can create its `Desc` once with `NewDesc` and provide it via `Describe`. All the other metrics are generated dynamically at scrape time, so cannot be included:

```
var (
  up = prometheus.NewDesc(
    "consul_up",
    "Was talking to Consul successful.",
    nil, nil,
  )
)
// Implements prometheus.Collector.
```

```
func (c ConsulCollector) Describe(ch chan<- *prometheus.Desc) {
  ch <- up
}
```

 The Go client requires that at least one Desc is provided by Describe. If all your metrics are dynamic, you can provide a dummy Desc to work around this.

At the core of a custom collector is the Collect method. In this method you fetch all the data you need from the application instance you are working with, munge it as needed, and then send the metrics back to the client library. Here you need to connect to Consul and then fetch its metrics. If an error occurs, consul_up is returned as 0; otherwise, once we know that the collection is going to be successful, it is returned as 1. Only returning a metric sometimes is difficult[4] to deal with in PromQL; having consul_up allows you to alert on issues talking to Consul so you'll know that something is awry.

To return consul_up, prometheus.MustNewConstMetric is used to provide a sample for just this scrape. It takes its Desc, type, and value:

```
// Implements prometheus.Collector.
func (c ConsulCollector) Collect(ch chan<- prometheus.Metric) {
  consul, err := api.NewClient(api.DefaultConfig())
  if err != nil {
    ch <- prometheus.MustNewConstMetric(up, prometheus.GaugeValue, 0)
    return
  }

  metrics, err := consul.Agent().Metrics()
  if err != nil {
    ch <- prometheus.MustNewConstMetric(up, prometheus.GaugeValue, 0)
    return
  }
  ch <- prometheus.MustNewConstMetric(up, prometheus.GaugeValue, 1)
```

There are three possible values: GaugeValue, CounterValue, and UntypedValue. Gauge and Counter you already know, and Untyped is for cases where you are not sure whether a metric is a counter or a gauge. This is not possible with direct instrumentation, but it is not unusual for the type of metrics from other monitoring and instrumentation systems to be unclear and impractical to determine.

---

4 See "or operator" on page 271.

Now that you have the metrics from Consul, you can process the gauges. Invalid characters in the metric name, such as dots and hyphens, are converted to underscores. A `Desc` is created on the fly, and immediately used in a `MustNewConstMetric`:

```
for _, g := range metrics.Gauges {
  name := invalidChars.ReplaceAllLiteralString(g.Name, "_")
  desc := prometheus.NewDesc(name, "Consul metric "+g.Name, nil, g.Labels)
  ch <- prometheus.MustNewConstMetric(
      desc, prometheus.GaugeValue, float64(g.Value))
}
```

 We pass `g.Labels` as the last parameter to `prometheus.NewDesc`. It is a set of labels set by Consul, such as a `datacenter` label. We have to pass them because some of the gauges have a cardinality greater than one, and without those labels, the /metrics page would error out.

Processing of counters is similar, except that a `_total` suffix is added to the metric name:

```
for _, c := range metrics.Counters {
  name := invalidChars.ReplaceAllLiteralString(c.Name, "_")
  desc := prometheus.NewDesc(name+"_total", "Consul metric "+c.Name, nil,
      c.Labels)
  ch <- prometheus.MustNewConstMetric(
      desc, prometheus.CounterValue, float64(s.Count))
}
```

The contents of `metrics.Samples` are more complicated. While the samples are a Prometheus summary, the Go client does not currently support those for `MustNewConstMetric`. Instead, you can emulate it using two counters. `_seconds` is appended to the metric name, and the sum is divided by one thousand to convert from milliseconds to seconds:

```
for _, s := range metrics.Samples {
  // All samples are times in milliseconds, we convert them to seconds below.
  name := invalidChars.ReplaceAllLiteralString(s.Name, "_") + "_seconds"
  countDesc := prometheus.NewDesc(
      name+"_count", "Consul metric "+s.Name, nil, s.Labels)
  ch <- prometheus.MustNewConstMetric(
      countDesc, prometheus.CounterValue, float64(s.Count))
  sumDesc := prometheus.NewDesc(
      name+"_sum", "Consul metric "+s.Name, nil, s.Labels)
  ch <- prometheus.MustNewConstMetric(
      sumDesc, prometheus.CounterValue, s.Sum/1000)
}
```

s.Sum here is a float64, but you must be careful when doing division with integers to ensure you don't unnecessarily lose precision. If sum were an integer, float64(sum)/1000 would convert to floating point first and then divide, which is what you want. On the other hand, float64(sum/1000) will first divide the integer value by one thousand, losing three digits of precision.

Finally, the custom collector object is instantiated and registered with the default registry, in the same way you would one of the direct instrumentation metrics:

```
c := ConsulCollector{}
prometheus.MustRegister(c)
```

Exposition is performed in the usual way, which you already saw in "Go" on page 71:

```
http.Handle("/metrics", promhttp.Handler())
log.Fatal(http.ListenAndServe(":8000", nil))
```

This is, of course, a simplified example. In reality you would have some way to configure the Consul server to talk to, such as a command-line flag, rather than depending on the client's default. You would also reuse the client between scrapes, and allow the various authentication options of the client to be specified.

The min, max, mean, and stddev were discarded from the original output as they are not very useful. You can calculate a mean using the sum and count. min, max, and stddev, on the other hand, cannot be aggregated and you don't know over what time period they were measured.

As the default registry is being used, go_ and process_ metrics are included in the result. These provide you with information about the performance of the exporter itself, and are useful to detect issues such as file descriptor leaks using the process_open_fds. This saves you from having to scrape the exporter separately for these metrics.

The only time you might not use the default registry for an exporter is when writing a Blackbox/SNMP-style exporter, where some interpretation of URL parameters needs to be performed as collectors have no access to URL parameters for a scrape. In that case, you would also scrape the /metrics of the exporter in order to monitor the exporter itself.

For comparison, the equivalent exporter written using Python 3 is shown in Example 12-3. This is largely the same as the one written in Go; the only notable difference is that a SummaryMetricFamily is available to represent a summary, instead of emulating it with two separate counters. The Python client does not have as many sanity checks as the Go client, so you need to be a little more careful with it.

Example 12-3. consul_metrics.py, an exporter for Consul metrics written in Python 3

```python
import json
import re
import time
from urllib.request import urlopen

from prometheus_client.core import GaugeMetricFamily, CounterMetricFamily
from prometheus_client.core import SummaryMetricFamily, REGISTRY
from prometheus_client import start_http_server


def sanitize_name(s):
    return re.sub(r"[^a-zA-Z0-9:_]", "_", s)

class ConsulCollector(object):
  def collect(self):
    out = urlopen("http://localhost:8500/v1/agent/metrics").read()
    metrics = json.loads(out.decode("utf-8"))

    for g in metrics["Gauges"]:
      yield GaugeMetricFamily(sanitize_name(g["Name"]),
          "Consul metric " + g["Name"], g["Value"])

    for c in metrics["Counters"]:
      yield CounterMetricFamily(sanitize_name(c["Name"]) + "_total",
          "Consul metric " + c["Name"], c["Count"])

    for s in metrics["Samples"]:
      yield SummaryMetricFamily(sanitize_name(s["Name"]) + "_seconds",
          "Consul metric " + s["Name"],
          count_value=c["Count"], sum_value=s["Sum"] / 1000)

if __name__ == '__main__':
  REGISTRY.register(ConsulCollector())
  start_http_server(8000)
  while True:
    time.sleep(1)
```

Labels

In the preceding example you only saw metrics without labels. To provide labels you need to specify the label names in `Desc` and then the values in `MustNewConstMetric`.

To expose a metric with the time series `example_gauge{foo="bar", baz="small"}` and `example_gauge{foo="quu", baz="far"}`, you could do, with the Go Prometheus client library:

```go
func (c MyCollector) Collect(ch chan<- prometheus.Metric) {
  desc := prometheus.NewDesc(
    "example_gauge",
```

```
      "A help string.",
      []string{"foo", "baz"}, nil,
    )
  ch <- prometheus.MustNewConstMetric(
    desc, prometheus.GaugeValue, 1, "bar", "small")
  ch <- prometheus.MustNewConstMetric(
    desc, prometheus.GaugeValue, 2, "quu", "far")
}
```

First, you can provide each time series individually. The registry will take care of combining all the time series belonging to the same metric family in the *metrics* output.

 The help strings of all metrics with the same name must be identical. Providing differing Descs will cause the scrape to fail.

The Python client works a little differently; you assemble the metric family and then return it. While that may sound like more effort, it usually works out to be the same level of effort in practice:

```
class MyCollector(object):
  def collect(self):
    mf = GaugeMetricFamily("example_gauge", "A help string.",
        labels=["foo", "baz"])
    mf.add_metric(["bar", "small"], 1)
    mf.add_metric(["quu", "far"], 2)
    yield mf
```

Guidelines

While direct instrumentation tends to be reasonably simple, writing exporters tends to be murky and involve engineering trade-offs. Do you want to spend a lot of ongoing effort to produce perfect metrics, or do something that's good enough and requires no maintenance? Writing exporters is more of an art than a science.

You should try to follow the metric naming practices, in particular, avoiding the _count, _sum, _total, _bucket, and _info suffixes unless the time series is part of a metric that is meant to contain such a time series.

It is often not possible or practical to determine whether a bunch of metrics are gauges, counters, or a mix of the two. In cases where there is a mix you should mark them as *untyped* rather than using gauge or counter, which would be incorrect. If a metric is a counter, don't forget to add the _total suffix.

Where practical you should try to provide units for your metrics, and at the very least try to ensure that the units are in the metric name. Having to determine what the units are from metrics, as in Example 12-1, is not fun for anyone, so you should try to remove this burden from your exporter users. Seconds and bytes are always preferred.

In terms of using labels in exporters, there are a few gotchas to look out for. As with direct instrumentation, cardinality is also a concern for exporters for the same reasons that were discussed in "Cardinality" on page 99. Metrics with high churn in their labels should be avoided.

Labels should create a partition across a metric, and if you take a sum or average across a metric it should be meaningful, as discussed in "When to Use Labels" on page 98. In particular, you should look out for any time series that are just totals of all the other values in a metric, and remove them. If you are ever unsure as to whether a label makes sense when writing an exporter, then it is safest not to use one, though keep in mind the discussion in "Table Exception" on page 99. As with direct instrumentation, you should not apply a label such as env="prod" to all metrics coming from your exporter, as that is what target labels are for, as discussed in "Target Labels" on page 153.

It is best to expose raw metrics to Prometheus, rather than doing calculations on the application side. For example, there is no need to expose a 5-minute rate when you have a counter, as you can use the rate function to calculate a rate over any period you like. Similarly with ratios, drop them in favor of the numerator and denominator. If you have a percentage without its constituent numerator and denominator, at the least convert it to a ratio.[5]

Beyond multiplication and division to standardize units, you should avoid math in exporters, as processing raw data in PromQL is preferred. Race conditions between metrics instrumentation events can lead to artifacts, particularly when you subtract one metric from another. Addition of metrics for the purposes of reducing cardinality can be OK, but if they're counters, make sure there will not be spurious resets due to some of them disappearing.

Some metrics are not particularly useful given how Prometheus is intended to be used. Many applications expose metrics such as machine RAM, CPU, and disk. You should not expose machine-level metrics in your exporter, as that is the responsibility of the Node Exporter.[6] Minimums, maximums, and standard deviations cannot be sanely aggregated so should also be dropped.

---

5 And check that it is actually a ratio/percentage; it's not unknown for metrics to confuse the two.

6 Or Windows Exporter for Windows users.

You should plan on running one exporter per application instance,[7] and fetch metrics synchronously for each scrape without any caching. This keeps the responsibilities of service discovery and scrape scheduling with Prometheus. Note that you should be aware that concurrent scrapes can happen.[8]

Just as Prometheus adds a `scrape_duration_seconds` metric when performing a scrape, you may also add a `myexporter_scrape_duration_seconds` metric for how long it takes your exporter to pull the data from its application. This helps in performance debugging, as you can see if it's the application or your exporter that is getting slow. Additional metrics such as the number of metrics processed can also be helpful.

It can make sense for you to add direct instrumentation to exporters, in addition to the custom collectors that provide their core functionality. For example, the Cloud-Watch Exporter has a `cloudwatch_requests_total` counter tracking the number of API calls it makes, as each API call costs money. But this is usually only something that you will see with Blackbox/SNMP-style exporters.

Now that you know how to get metrics out of both your applications and third-party code, in the next chapter we will start covering PromQL, which allows you to work with these metrics.

---

7 Unless writing a Blackbox/SNMP-style exporter, which is rare.

8 This can happen when your exporters are scraped by multiple servers.

PART IV

PromQL

The Prometheus Query Language offers you the ability to do all sorts of aggregations, analysis, and arithmetic, allowing you to better understand the performance of your systems from your metrics.

In this part you will be reusing the Prometheus and Node Exporter setup you created in Chapter 2, and using the expression browser to execute queries.

Chapter 13 covers the basics of PromQL, and how you can use the HTTP API to evaluate expressions.

Chapter 14 looks in depth into how aggregation works.

Chapter 15 covers operators such as addition and comparisons, and how you can join different metrics.

Chapter 16 goes into the wide variety of functions that PromQL offers you, from knowing the time of day to predicting when your hard disk will fill up.

Chapter 17 covers the recording rule feature of Prometheus, which allows you to precompute metrics for faster and more sophisticated querying with PromQL.

## CHAPTER 13

Introduction to PromQL

PromQL is the Prometheus Query Language. While it ends in *QL*, you will find that it is not an SQL-like language, as SQL languages tend to lack expressive power when it comes to the sort of calculations you would like to perform on time series.

Labels are a key part of PromQL, and you can use them not only to do arbitrary aggregations but also to join different metrics together for arithmetic operations against them. There are a wide variety of functions available to you from prediction to date and math functions.

This chapter will introduce you to the basic concepts of PromQL, including aggregation, basic types, and the HTTP API.

Aggregation Basics

Let's get started with some simple aggregation queries. These queries will likely cover most of your potential uses for PromQL. While PromQL is as powerful as it is possible to be,[1] most of the time your needs will be reasonably simple.

Gauge

Gauges are a snapshot of state, and usually when aggregating them you want to take a sum, average, minimum, or maximum.

Consider the metric `node_filesystem_size_bytes` from your Node Exporter, which reports the size of each of your mounted filesystems, and has `device`, `fstype`, and `mountpoint` labels. You can calculate total filesystem size on each machine with:

---

1 Brian has demonstrated PromQL to be Turing Complete in two (*https://oreil.ly/TQWlz*) different (*https://oreil.ly/kikcz*) ways. Don't try this in production.

```
sum without(device, fstype, mountpoint)(node_filesystem_size_bytes)
```

This works as `without` tells the `sum` aggregator to sum everything up with the same labels, ignoring those three. So if you had the time series:

```
node_filesystem_free_bytes{device="/dev/sda1",fstype="vfat",
    instance="localhost:9100",job="node",mountpoint="/boot/efi"} 70300672
node_filesystem_free_bytes{device="/dev/sda5",fstype="ext4",
    instance="localhost:9100",job="node",mountpoint="/"} 30791843840
node_filesystem_free_bytes{device="tmpfs",fstype="tmpfs",
    instance="localhost:9100",job="node",mountpoint="/run"} 817094656
node_filesystem_free_bytes{device="tmpfs",fstype="tmpfs",
    instance="localhost:9100",job="node",mountpoint="/run/lock"} 5238784
node_filesystem_free_bytes{device="tmpfs",fstype="tmpfs",
    instance="localhost:9100",job="node",mountpoint="/run/user/1000"} 826912768
```

the result would be:

```
{instance="localhost:9100",job="node"} 32511390720
```

You will notice that the `device`, `fstype`, and `mountpoint` labels are now gone. The metric name is also no longer present, as this is no longer `node_filesys tem_free_bytes` because math has been performed on it. Since there is only one Node Exporter being scraped by Prometheus, there is only one result, but if you were scraping more, then you would have a result for each of the Node Exporters.

You could go a step further and remove the `instance` label with:

```
sum without(device, fstype, mountpoint, instance)(node_filesystem_size_bytes)
```

This as expected removes the `instance` label, but the value remains the same as the previous expression because there is only one Node Exporter to aggregate metrics from:

```
{job="node"} 32511390720
```

You can use the same approach with other aggregations. `max` would tell you the size of the biggest mounted filesystem on each machine:

```
max without(device, fstype, mountpoint)(node_filesystem_size_bytes)
```

The outputted labels are exactly the same as when you aggregated using `sum`:

```
{instance="localhost:9100",job="node"} 30792601600
```

This predictability in what labels are returned is important for vector matching with operators, as will be discussed in Chapter 15.

You are not limited to aggregating metrics about one type of job. For example, to find the average number of file descriptors open across all your jobs, you could use:

```
avg without(instance, job)(process_open_fds)
```

Counter

Counters track the number or size of events, and the value your applications expose on their */metrics* is the total since it started. But that total is of little use to you on its own; what you really want to know is how quickly the counter is increasing over time. This is usually done using the `rate` function, though the `increase` and `irate` functions also operate on counter values.

For example, to calculate the amount of network traffic received per second, you could use:

```
rate(node_network_receive_bytes_total[5m])
```

The [`5m`] says to provide `rate` with 5 minutes of data, so the returned value will be an average over the last 5 minutes:

```
{device="lo",instance="localhost:9100",job="node"}   1859.389655172414
{device="wlan0",instance="localhost:9100",job="node"} 1314.5034482758622
```

The values here are not integers, as the 5-minute window `rate` is looking at does not perfectly align with the samples that Prometheus has scraped. Some estimation is used to fill in the gaps between the data points you have and the boundaries of the range.

The output of `rate` is a gauge, so the same aggregations apply as for gauges. The `node_network_receive_bytes_total` metric has a `device` label, so if you aggregate it away you will get the total bytes received per machine per second:

```
sum without(device)(rate(node_network_receive_bytes_total[5m]))
```

Running this query will give you a result like:

```
{instance="localhost:9100",job="node"} 3173.8931034482762
```

You can filter down which time series to request, so you could only look at `eth0` and then aggregate it across all machines by aggregating away the `instance` label:

```
sum without(instance)(rate(node_network_receive_bytes_total{device="eth0"}[5m]))
```

When you run this query the `instance` label is gone, but the `device` label remains as you did not ask for it to be removed:

```
{device="eth0",job="node"} 3173.8931034482762
```

There is no ordering or hierarchy within labels, allowing you to aggregate by as many or as few labels as you like.

Summary

A summary metric will usually contain both a _sum and _count, and sometimes a time series with no suffix with a quantile label. The _sum and _count are both counters.

Your Prometheus exposes an http_response_size_bytes summary for the amount of data some of its HTTP APIs return.[2] http_response_size_bytes_count tracks the number of requests, and as it is a counter, you must use rate before aggregating away its handler label:

```
sum without(handler)(rate(http_response_size_bytes_count[5m]))
```

This gives you the total per-second HTTP request rate, and as the Node Exporter also returns this metric, you will see both jobs in the result:

```
{instance="localhost:9090",job="prometheus"} 0.26868836781609196
{instance="localhost:9100",job="node"} 0.1
```

Similarly, http_response_size_bytes_sum is a counter with the number of bytes each handle has returned, so the same pattern applies:

```
sum without(handler)(rate(http_response_size_bytes_sum[5m]))
```

This will return results with the same labels as the previous query, but the values are larger as responses tend to return many bytes:

```
{instance="localhost:9090",job="prometheus"} 796.0015958275862
{instance="localhost:9100",job="node"} 1581.6103448275862
```

The power of a summary is that it allows you to calculate the average size of an event, in this case the average amount of bytes that are being returned in each response. If you had three responses of size 1, 4, and 7, then the average would be their sum divided by their count, which is to say 12 divided by 3. The same applies to the summary. You divide the _sum by the _count (after taking a rate) to get an average over a time period:

```
  sum without(handler)(rate(http_response_size_bytes_sum[5m]))
/
  sum without(handler)(rate(http_response_size_bytes_count[5m]))
```

The division operator matches the time series with the same labels, and divides, giving you the same two time series out but with the average response size over the past 5 minutes as a value:

```
{instance="localhost:9090",job="prometheus"} 2962.54580091246150133317
{instance="localhost:9100",job="node"} 15816.10344827586200000000
```

---

2 In Prometheus 2.3.0 this was renamed to prometheus_http_response_size_bytes_count.

When calculating an average, it is important that you first aggregate up the sum and count, and only as the last step perform the division. Otherwise, you could end up averaging averages, which is not statistically valid.

For example, if you wanted to get the average response size across all instances of a job, you could do:[3]

```
sum without(instance)(
  sum without(handler)(rate(http_response_size_bytes_sum[5m]))
)
/
sum without(instance)(
  sum without(handler)(rate(http_response_size_bytes_count[5m]))
)
```

However, it'd be incorrect to do:

```
avg without(instance)(
    sum without(handler)(rate(http_response_size_bytes_sum[5m]))
  /
    sum without(handler)(rate(http_response_size_bytes_count[5m]))
)
```

It is incorrect to average an average, and both the division and `avg` would be calculating averages.

> It is not possible for you to aggregate the quantiles of a summary (the time series with the `quantile` label) from a statistical standpoint.

Histogram

Histogram metrics allow you to track the distribution of the size of events, allowing you to calculate quantiles from them. For example, you can use histograms to calculate the 0.9 quantile (which is also known as the 90th percentile) latency.

Prometheus 2.37.1 exposes a histogram metric called `prometheus_tsdb_compaction_duration_seconds` that tracks how many seconds compaction takes for the time series database. This histogram metric has time series with a `_bucket` suffix called `prometheus_tsdb_compaction_duration_seconds_bucket`. Each bucket has a `le` label, which is a counter of how many events have a size less than or equal to the bucket boundary. This is an implementation detail you largely need not worry about

---

3 This can of course be more simply calculated as sum `without(instance, handler)(…)`, but with the recording rules covered in Chapter 17, such an expression could end up split into several expressions.

as the `histogram_quantile` function takes care of this when calculating quantiles. For example, the 0.90 quantile would be:

```
histogram_quantile(
    0.90,
    rate(prometheus_tsdb_compaction_duration_seconds_bucket[1d]))
```

As `prometheus_tsdb_compaction_duration_seconds_bucket` is a counter, you must first take a `rate`. Compaction usually only happens every two hours, so a one-day time range is used here and you will see a result in the expression browser such as:

```
{instance="localhost:9090",job="prometheus"} 7.720000000000001
```

This indicates that the 90th percentile latency of compactions is around 7.72 seconds. As there will usually only be 12 compactions in a day, the 90th percentile says that 10% of compactions take longer than this, which is to say one or two compactions. This is something to be aware of when using quantiles. For example, if you want to calculate a 0.999 quantile, you should have several thousand data points to work with in order to produce a reasonably accurate answer. If you have fewer than that, single outliers could greatly affect the result, and you should consider using lower quantiles to avoid making statements about your system for which you have insufficient data to back up.

 Usually you would use a 5- or 10-minute `rate` with histograms. All the bucket time series combined with any labels, and a long range on the `rate`, can make for a lot of samples that need to be processed. Be wary of PromQL expressions using ranges that are hours or days, as they can be relatively expensive to calculate.[4]

Similar to when taking averages, using `histogram_quantile` should be the last step in a query expression. Quantiles cannot be aggregated, or have arithmetic performed upon them, from a statistical standpoint. Accordingly, when you want to take a histogram of an aggregate, first aggregate up with `sum` and then use `histogram_quantile`:

```
histogram_quantile(
    0.90,
    sum without(instance)(rate(prometheus_tsdb_compaction_duration_bucket[1d])))
```

This calculates the 0.9 quantile compaction duration across all of your Prometheus servers, and will produce a result without an `instance` label:

```
{job="prometheus"} 7.720000000000001
```

---

4 The day-long range is only being used here due to the limited number of histograms that Prometheus and the Node Exporter offer for us to use as examples.

Histogram metrics also include _sum and _count metrics, which work exactly the same as for the summary metric. You can use these to calculate average event sizes, such as the average compaction duration:

```
    sum without(instance)(rate(prometheus_tsdb_compaction_duration_sum[1d]))
  /
    sum without(instance)(rate(prometheus_tsdb_compaction_duration_count[1d]))
```

This would produce a result like:

```
    {job="prometheus"} 3.1766430400714287
```

Selectors

Working with all the different time series with different label values for a metric can be a bit overwhelming, and potentially confusing if a metric is coming from multiple different types of servers.[5] Usually you will want to narrow down which time series you are working on. You almost always will want to limit by job label, and depending on what you are up to, you might want to only look at one instance or one handler, for example.

This limiting by labels is done using *selectors*. You have seen selectors in every example thus far, and now we are going to explain them to you in detail. For example:

```
    process_resident_memory_bytes{job="node"}
```

is a selector that will return all time series with the name process_resident_
memory_bytes and a job label of node. This particular selector is most properly called an *instant vector selector*, as it returns the values of the given time series at a given instant. *Vector* here basically means a one-dimensional list, as a selector can return zero or more time series, and each time series will have one sample.

The job="node" is called a *matcher*, and you can have many matchers in one selector that are ANDed together.

Matchers

There are four matchers (you have already seen the *equality matcher*, which is also the most commonly used):

---

5 Such as process_cpu_seconds_total, which most exporters and client libraries will expose.

=

This is the *equality matcher*; for example, job="node". With this you can specify that the returned time series has a label name with exactly the given label value. As an empty label, value is the same as not having that label, so you could use foo="" to specify that the foo label not be present.

!=

This is the *negative equality matcher*; for example, job!="node". With this you can specify that the returned time series do not have a label name with exactly the given label value.

=~

This is the *regular expression matcher*; for example, job=~"n.*". With this you specify that for the returned time series, the given label's value will be matched by the regular expression. The regular expression is fully anchored, which is to say that the regular expression a will only match the string a, and not xa or ax. You can prepend or suffix your regular expression with .* if you do not want this behavior.[6] As with relabeling, the RE2 regular expression engine is used, as covered in "Regular Expressions" on page 152.

!~

This is the *negative regular expression matcher*. RE2 does not support negative lookahead expressions, so this provides you with an alternative way to exclude label values based on a regular expression.

You can have multiple matchers with the same label name in a selector, which can be a substitute for negative lookahead expressions. For example, to find the size of all filesystems mounted under /run but not /run/user, you could use:[7]

```
node_filesystem_size_bytes{job="node",mountpoint=~"/run/.*",
    mountpoint!~"/run/user/.*"}
```

Internally, the metric name is stored in a label called __name__ (as discussed in "Reserved Labels and __name__" on page 90), so process_resident_memory_bytes{job="node"} is syntactic sugar for {*name*="process_resident_memory_bytes",job="node"}. You can even do regular expressions on the metric name, but this is unwise outside of when you are debugging the performance of the Prometheus server.

---

6 It works this way to avoid accidentally overmatching. This way you usually get immediate feedback if your regular expression is under matching, while an unanchored expression might cause subtle issues down the line.

7 The Node Exporter has a --collector.filesystem.ignored-mount-points flag you could use if you didn't want these filesystems exported in the first place.

Having to use regular expression matchers is a little bit of a smell. If you find yourself using them a lot on a given label, consider if you should instead combine the matched label values into one. For example, for HTTP status codes instead of doing `code~="4.."` to catch 401s, 404s, 405s, etc., you might combine them into a label value 4xx and use the equality matcher `code="4xx"`.

The selector {} returns an error, which is a safety measure to avoid accidentally returning all the time series inside the Prometheus server as that could be expensive. To be more precise, at least one of the matchers in a selector must not match the empty string. So `{foo=""}` and `{foo=~".*"}` will return an error, while `{foo="",bar="x"}`, `{foo!=""}`, or `{foo=~".+"}` are permitted.[8]

Instant Vector

An instant vector selector returns an `instant vector` of the most recent samples before the query evaluation time, which is to say a list of zero or more time series. Each of these time series will have one sample, and a sample contains both a value and a timestamp. While the instant vector returned by an instant vector selector has the timestamp of the original data,[9] any instant vectors returned by other operations or functions will have the timestamp of the query evaluation time for all of their values.

When you ask for current memory usage, you do not want samples from an instance that was turned down days ago to be included, a concept known as *staleness*. In Prometheus 1.x this was handled by returning time series that had a sample no more than 5 minutes before the query evaluation time. This largely worked but had downsides such as double counting if an instance restarted with a new `instance` label within that 5-minute window.

Prometheus 2.x has a more sophisticated approach. If a time series disappears from one scrape to the next, or if a target is no longer returned from service discovery, a special type of sample called a *stale marker*[10] is appended to the time series. When evaluating an instant vector selector, all time series satisfying all the matchers are first found, and the most recent sample in the 5 minutes before the query evaluation time is still considered. If the sample is a normal sample, then it is returned in the instant

---

8 If you do want to return all time series, you can use `{__name__=~".+"}`, but beware of the expense of this expression.

9 You can extract the samples' timestamps using the `timestamp` function.

10 Internally, stale markers are a special type of NaN value. They are an implementation detail, and you cannot access them directly via any of the query APIs that use PromQL. But you could see them if you looked at the Prometheus server's storage directly, such as via Prometheus's remote read endpoint.

vector, but if it is a stale marker, then that time series will not be included in that instant vector.

The outcome of all of this is that when you use an instant vector selector, time series that have gone stale are not returned.

 If you have an exporter exposing timestamps, as described in "Timestamps" on page 82, then stale markers and the Prometheus 2.x staleness logic will not apply. The affected time series will work instead with the older logic that looks back 5 minutes.

Range Vector

There is a second type of selector you have already seen, called the *range vector selector*. Unlike an instant vector selector, which returns one sample per time series, a range vector selector can return many samples for each time series.[11] Range vectors are always used with the rate function, for example:

```
rate(process_cpu_seconds_total[1m])
```

The [1m] turns the instant vector selector into a range vector selector, and instructs PromQL to return for all time series matching the selector all samples for the minute up to the query evaluation time. If you execute just process_cpu_seconds_total[1m] in the Console tab of the expression browser, you will see something like Figure 13-1.

In this case, each time series happens to have six samples in the past minute. You will notice that while the samples for each time series happen to be perfectly 10 seconds apart[12] in line with the scrape interval you configured, the two time series timestamps are not aligned with each other. One time series has a sample with a timestamp of 1517925155.087 and the other 1517925156.245.

---

11 You may also see it referred to as a *matrix* in places, as it is a two-dimensional data structure.

12 This is a very lightly loaded Prometheus, so there is no jitter.

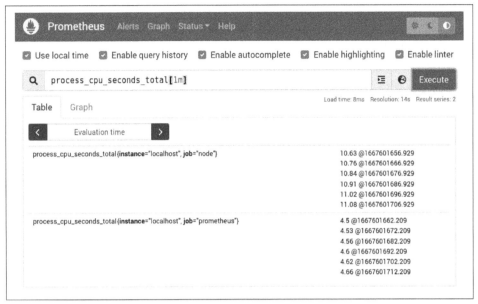

Figure 13-1. A range vector in the Console tab of the expression browser

This is because range vectors preserve the actual timestamps of the samples, and the scrapes for different targets are distributed in order to spread load more evenly. While you can control the frequency of scrapes and rule evaluations, you cannot control their phase or alignment. If you have a 10-second scrape interval and hundreds of targets, then all those targets will be scraped at different points in a given 10-second window. Put another way, your time series all have slightly different ages. This generally won't matter to you in practice, but can lead to artifacts as fundamentally metrics-based monitoring systems like Prometheus produce (quite good) estimates rather than exact answers.

You will very rarely look at range vectors directly. It only comes up when you need to see raw samples when debugging. Almost always you will use a range vector with a function such as `rate` or `avg_over_time` that takes a range vector as an argument.

Staleness and stale markers have no impact on range vectors; you will get all the normal samples in a given range. Any stale markers also in that range are not returned by a range vector selector.

Durations

Durations in Prometheus as used in PromQL and the configuration file support several units. You have already seen m for minute.

Suffix	Meaning
ms	Milliseconds
s	Seconds, which have 1,000 milliseconds
m	Minutes, which have 60 seconds
h	Hours, which have 60 minutes
d	Days, which have 24 hours
w	Weeks, which have 7 days
y	Years, which have 365 days

You can combine multiple units with integers, as long as they are ordered, so 90m is valid, 1h30m and 1.5h are also valid, but 30m1h is not valid.

Leap years and leap seconds are ignored; 1y is always 60*60*24*365 seconds.

Subqueries

While range vectors act on time series, they cannot be used in combination with functions.

If you want to combine max_over_time with rate, you can either use recording rules, which would record the result of the rate function and pass it to the vector function, or you can use a subquery.

A subquery is a part of a query that allows you to do a range query within a query. The syntax for a subquery uses square brackets, like range selectors. But it takes two different durations: the range and the resolution.

The range is the range returned by the subquery, and the resolution acts as a step:

```
max_over_time( rate(http_requests_total[5m])[30m:1m] )
```

The preceding query runs rate(http_requests_total[5m]) every minute (1m) for the last 30 minutes (30m), then feeds the result in a max_over_time() function.

The resolution can be omitted, such as in [30m:]. In this case, the global evaluation interval is used as resolution.

Offset

There is a modifier you can use with either type of vector selector called `offset`. `offset` allows you to take the evaluation time for a query, and on a per-selector basis put it further back in time. For example:

```
process_resident_memory_bytes{job="node"} offset 1h
```

would get memory usage an hour before the query evaluation time.

`offset` is not used much in simple queries like this, as it would be easier to change the evaluation time for the whole query instead. Where this can be useful is when you only want to adjust one selector in a query expression. For example:

```
process_resident_memory_bytes{job="node"}
-
process_resident_memory_bytes{job="node"} offset 1h
```

would give the change in memory usage in the Node Exporter over the past hour.[13]

The same approach works with range vectors:

```
rate(process_cpu_seconds_total{job="node"}[5m])
-
rate(process_cpu_seconds_total{job="node"}[5m] offset 1h)
```

`offset` allows you to look further back into the past, but also in the future, using a negative offset. This can be used when doing prediction or when the sample of the metrics is unaligned with the reality:

```
rate(process_cpu_seconds_total{job="node"}[5m]) offset -1h
-
rate(process_cpu_seconds_total{job="node"}[5m])
```

Note that this query will likely not return anything for the last hour.

> Grafana has a feature to shift in time a panel to a different time range than the rest of the dashboard it is a part of. In Grafana 5.0.0 you can find this in the Time range tab of the panel editor.

---

13 This is susceptible to outliers as it is using only two data points; the `deriv` function discussed in "deriv" on page 293 is more robust.

At Modifier

Similar to the `offset` modifier, PromQL supports an `@` modifier that lets you change the evaluation of vector selectors, range selectors, and subqueries to a fixed revaluation time.

The `@` modifier can be used with a Unix timestamp. The query `http_requests_total @ 1667491200` returns the value of `http_requests_total` at `2022-11-03T16:00:00+00:00`. The query `rate(http_requests_total[5m] @ 1667491200)` returns the 5-minute rate of `http_requests_total` at the same time.

Additionally, `start()` and `end()` can be used as values for the `@` modifier. For a range query, they resolve respectively with the start and the end of the range query. For an instant query, they both resolve to the evaluation time.

In practice, it is possible to use the `@` modifier to graph the evolution of the `http_request_total` that has a high rate at the end of the evaluation interval:

```
rate(http_requests_total[1m])
  and
topk(5, rate(http_requests_total[1h] @ end()))
```

The `topk(5, rate(http_requests_total[1h] @ end()))` acts as a ranking function, filtering only the higher values at the end of the evaluation interval.

HTTP API

Prometheus offers a number of HTTP APIs. The ones you will mostly interact with are `query` and `query_range`, which give you access to PromQL and can be used by dashboarding tools or custom reporting scripts.

All the endpoints of interest are under `/api/v1/`, and beyond executing PromQL you can also look up time series metadata and perform administrative actions, such as taking snapshots and deleting time series. These other APIs are mainly of interest to dashboarding tools such as Grafana, which can use metadata to enhance its UI, and to those administering Prometheus, but are not relevant to PromQL execution.

query

The *query endpoint*, or more formally `/api/v1/query`, executes a PromQL expression at a given time and returns the result. For example, *http://localhost:9090/api/v1/query?query=process_resident_memory_bytes* will return results like:[14]

---

14 We have pretty printed these JSON results for readability.

```json
{
  "status": "success",
  "data": {
    "resultType": "vector",
    "result": [
      {
        "metric": {
          "__name__": "process_resident_memory_bytes",
          "instance": "localhost:9090",
          "job": "prometheus"
        },
        "value": [1517929228.782, "91656192"]
      },
      {
        "metric": {
          "__name__": "process_resident_memory_bytes",
          "instance": "localhost:9100",
          "job": "node"
        },
        "value": [1517929228.782, "15507456"]
      }
    ]
  }
}
```

The status is success, meaning that the query worked. If it had failed, the status would be error, and an error field would provide more details.

This particular result is an instant vector, which you can tell from "resultType": "vector". For each of the samples in the result, the labels are in the metric map, and the sample value is in the value list. The first number in the value list is the timestamp of the sample, in seconds, and the second is the actual value of the sample. The value is inside a string, as JSON cannot represent nonreal values such as NaN and +Inf.

The time of all the samples will be the query evaluation time, even if the expression consisted of only an instant vector selector. Here the query evaluation time defaulted to the current time, but you can specify a time with the time URL parameter, which can be a Unix time, in seconds, or an RFC 3339 time. For example, *http://localhost:9090/api/v1/query?query=process_resident_memory_bytes&time=1514764800* would evaluate the query at midnight of January 1st, 2018.[15]

---

15 Unless your Prometheus has been running since then, this will produce an empty result.

You can also use range vectors with the `query` endpoint. For example, *http://local-host:9090/api/v1/query?query=prometheus_tsdb_head_samples_appended_total[1m]* will return results like:

```
{
  "status": "success",
  "data": {
    "resultType": "matrix",
    "result": [
      {
        "metric": {
          "__name__": "process_resident_memory_bytes",
          "instance": "localhost:9090",
          "job": "prometheus"
        },
        "values": [
          [1518008453.662, "87318528"],
          [1518008463.662, "87318528"],
          [1518008473.662, "87318528"]
        ]
      },
      {
        "metric": {
          "__name__": "process_resident_memory_bytes",
          "instance": "localhost:9100",
          "job": "node"
        },
        "values": [
          [1518008444.819, "17043456"],
          [1518008454.819, "17043456"],
          [1518008464.819, "17043456"]
        ]
      }
    ]
  }
}
```

This is different than the previous instant vector result, as `resultType` is now `matrix`, and each time series has multiple values. When used with a range vector, the `query` endpoint returns the raw samples,[16] but be wary of asking for too much data at once because one end or the other may run out of memory.

There is one other type of result called a *scalar*. Scalars don't have labels, they are just numbers.[17] *http://localhost:9090/api/v1/query?query=42* would produce:

---

[16] Excluding stale markers.

[17] This is different from {}, which is the identity of a time series with no labels.

```
{
  "status": "success",
  "data": {
    "resultType": "scalar",
    "result": [1518008879.023, "42"]
  }
}
```

query_range

The *query range endpoint* at /api/v1/query_range is the main HTTP endpoint of
Prometheus you will use, as it is the endpoint to use for graphing. Under the covers,
query_range is syntactic sugar (plus some performance optimizations) for multiple
calls to the query endpoint.

In addition to a query URL parameter, you provide query_range with a start time,
an end time, and a step. The query is first executed at the start time. Then it is
executed step seconds after the start time. Then it is executed twice step seconds
after the start time and so on, stopping when the query evaluation time would
exceed the end time. All the instant vector[18] results from the different executions are
combined into a range vector and returned.

For example, if you wanted to query the number of samples Prometheus ingested in
the first 15 minutes of 2018, you could run the following: *http://localhost:9090/api/v1/
query_range?query=rate(prometheus_tsdb_head_samples_appended_total[5m])&start
=1514764800&end=1514765700&step=60*, which would produce a result like:

```
{
  "status": "success",
  "data": {
    "resultType": "matrix",
    "result": [
      {
        "metric": {
          "instance": "localhost:9090",
          "job": "prometheus"
        },
        "values": [
          [1514764800, "85.07241379310345"],
          [1514764860, "102.6793103448276"],
          [1514764920, "120.30344827586208"],
          [1514764980, "137.93103448275863"],
          [1514765040, "146.7586206896552"],
          [1514765100, "146.7793103448276"],
          [1514765160, "146.8"],
```

---

18 A scalar result is converted into an instant vector with a single time series with no labels with the same value,
    as if the vector function was used. Range vector results are not supported.

```
                [1514765220, "146.8"],
                [1514765280, "146.8"],
                [1514765340, "146.8"],
                [1514765400, "146.8"],
                [1514765460, "146.8"],
                [1514765520, "146.8"],
                [1514765580, "146.8"],
                [1514765640, "146.8"],
                [1514765700, "146.8"],
            ]
        }
    ]
  }
}
```

There are a few aspects of this that you should take note of. The first is that the sample timestamps align with the start time and step, as each result comes from a different instant query evaluation and instant query results always use their evaluation time as the timestamp of results.

The second is that the last sample here is at the end time, which is to say that the range is inclusive and the last point will be the end time if it happens to line up with the step.

The third is that we selected a range of 5 minutes for the `rate` function, which is larger than the step. Since `query_range` is doing repeated instant query evaluations, there is no state being passed between the evaluations. If the range was smaller than the step, then we would have been skipping over data. For example, a 1-minute range with a 5-minute step would have ignored 80% of the samples. To prevent this you should use ranges that are at least one or two scrape intervals larger than the `step` you are using.

> When using range vectors with `query_range`, you should usually use a range that is longer than your `step` in order to not skip data.

The fourth is that some of the samples are not particularly round, and that any numbers are round at all is due to this being a simple setup of the sample values. When working with metrics your data is rarely perfectly clean; different targets are scraped at different times and scrapes can be delayed. When performing queries that are not perfectly aligned with the underlying data or aggregating across multiple hosts, you will rarely get round results. In addition, the nature of floating-point calculations can lead to numbers that are almost round.

Here, there is a sample for each step. If it happened that there was no result for a given time series for a step, then that sample would simply be missing in the end result.

If there are more than 11,000 steps for a query_range, Prometheus will reject the query with an error. This is to prevent accidentally sending extremely large queries to Prometheus, such as a 1-second step for a week. As monitors with a horizontal resolution of over 11,000 pixels are rare, you are unlikely to run into this when graphing.

If you are writing reporting scripts, you can split up query_range requests that would hit this limit. This limit allows for a minute resolution for a week, or an hour of resolution for a year, so most of the time it should not apply.

Aligned data

When using tools like Grafana it's common for the alignment of query_range to be based on the current time, and so your results will not align perfectly with minutes, hours, or days. While this is fine when you are looking at dashboards, it is rarely what you want with reporting scripts.

query_range does not have an option to specify alignment, instead it is up to you to specify a start parameter with the right alignment. For example, if you wanted to have samples every hour on the hour in Python, the expression (time.time() // 3600) * 3600 will return the start of the current hour,[19] which you can adjust in steps of 3,600 and use as the start and end URL parameters, and then use a step parameter of 3600.

Now that you know the basics of how to use PromQL and execute queries via the HTTP APIs, we will go into more detail on aggregation.

---

19 // performs integer division in Python.

## CHAPTER 14

Aggregation Operators

You already learned about aggregation in "Aggregation Basics" on page 229; however, this is only a small taste of what is possible. Aggregation is important. With applications with thousands or even just tens of instances it's not practical for you to sift through each instance's metrics individually. Aggregation allows you to summarize metrics not just within one application, but across applications too.

There are 12 aggregation operators in PromQL, with 2 optional clauses, without and by. In this chapter you'll learn about the different ways you can use aggregation.

Grouping

Before talking about the aggregation operators themselves, you need to know about how time series are grouped. Aggregation operators work only on instant vectors, and they also output instant vectors.

Let's say you have the following time series in Prometheus:

```
node_filesystem_size_bytes{device="/dev/sda1",fstype="vfat",
    instance="localhost:9100",job="node",mountpoint="/boot/efi"} 100663296
node_filesystem_size_bytes{device="/dev/sda5",fstype="ext4",
    instance="localhost:9100",job="node",mountpoint="/"} 90131324928
node_filesystem_size_bytes{device="tmpfs",fstype="tmpfs",
    instance="localhost:9100",job="node",mountpoint="/run"} 826961920
node_filesystem_size_bytes{device="tmpfs",fstype="tmpfs",
    instance="localhost:9100",job="node",mountpoint="/run/lock"} 5242880
node_filesystem_size_bytes{device="tmpfs",fstype="tmpfs",
    instance="localhost:9100",job="node",mountpoint="/run/user/1000"} 826961920
node_filesystem_size_bytes{device="tmpfs",fstype="tmpfs",
    instance="localhost:9100",job="node",mountpoint="/run/user/119"} 826961920
```

There are three instrumentation labels: device, fstype, and mountpoint. There are also two target labels: job and instance. Target and instrumentation labels are a notion that you and we have, but which PromQL knows nothing about. All labels are the same when it comes to PromQL, no matter where they originated from.

without

Generally you will always know the instrumentation labels, as they rarely change. But you do not always know the target labels in play, as an expression you write might be used by someone else on metrics originating from different scrape configs, or Prometheus servers that might also have added in other target labels across a job, such as an env or cluster label. You might even add in such target labels yourself at some point, and it'd be nice not to have to update all your expressions.

When aggregating metrics you should usually try to preserve such target labels, and thus you should use the without clause when aggregating to specify the labels you want to remove. For example, the query:

```
sum without(fstype, mountpoint)(node_filesystem_size_bytes)
```

will group the time series, ignoring the fstype and mountpoint labels, into three groups:

```
# Group {device="/dev/sda1",instance="localhost:9100",job="node"}
node_filesystem_size_bytes{device="/dev/sda1",fstype="vfat",
    instance="localhost:9100",job="node",mountpoint="/boot/efi"} 100663296

# Group {device="/dev/sda5",instance="localhost:9100",job="node"}
node_filesystem_size_bytes{device="/dev/sda5",fstype="ext4",
    instance="localhost:9100",job="node",mountpoint="/"} 90131324928

# Group {device="tmpfs",instance="localhost:9100",job="node"}
node_filesystem_size_bytes{device="tmpfs",fstype="tmpfs",
    instance="localhost:9100",job="node",mountpoint="/run"} 826961920
node_filesystem_size_bytes{device="tmpfs",fstype="tmpfs",
    instance="localhost:9100",job="node",mountpoint="/run/lock"} 5242880
node_filesystem_size_bytes{device="tmpfs",fstype="tmpfs",
    instance="localhost:9100",job="node",mountpoint="/run/user/1000"} 826961920
node_filesystem_size_bytes{device="tmpfs",fstype="tmpfs",
    instance="localhost:9100",job="node",mountpoint="/run/user/119"} 826961920
```

and the sum aggregator will apply within each of these groups, adding up the values of the time series and returning one sample per group:

```
{device="/dev/sda1",instance="localhost:9100",job="node"} 100663296
{device="/dev/sda5",instance="localhost:9100",job="node"} 90131324928
{device="tmpfs",instance="localhost:9100",job="node"} 2486128640
```

Notice that the instance and job labels are preserved, as would be any other labels that had been present. This is useful because any alerts you created that included this expression somehow would have additional target labels like env or cluster preserved. This provides context for your alerts and makes them more useful (also useful when graphing).

The metric name has also been removed, as this is an aggregation of the `node_file system_size_bytes` metric rather than the original metric. When a PromQL operator or function could change the value or meaning of a time series, the metric name is removed.

It is valid to provide no labels to the `without`. For example:

```
sum without()(node_filesystem_size_bytes)
```

will give you the same result as:

```
node_filesystem_size_bytes
```

with the only difference being the metric name is removed.

by

In addition to `without` there is also the by clause. Where `without` specifies the labels to remove, by specifies the labels to keep. Accordingly, some care is required when using by to ensure you don't remove target labels that you would like to propagate in your alerts or use in your dashboards. You cannot use both by and `without` in the same aggregation.

The query:

```
sum by(job, instance, device)(node_filesystem_size_bytes)
```

will produce the same result as the query in the preceding section using `without`:

```
{device="/dev/sda1",instance="localhost:9100",job="node"} 100663296
{device="/dev/sda5",instance="localhost:9100",job="node"} 90131324928
{device="tmpfs",instance="localhost:9100",job="node"} 2486128640
```

However, if `instance` or `job` had not been specified, then they wouldn't have defined the group and would not be in the output. Generally, you should prefer to use `without` rather than by for this reason.

There are two cases where you might find by more useful. The first is that unlike `without`, by does keep the __name__ label if told explicitly. This allows you to use expressions like:

```
sort_desc(count by(__name__)({__name__=~".+"}))
```

to investigate how many time series have the same metric names.[1]

---

1 This is potentially an expensive query as it touches every active time series; use it carefully.

The second is cases where you do want to remove any labels you do not know about. For example, info metrics, as discussed in "Info" on page 96, are expected to add more labels over time. To count how many machines were running each kernel version, you could use:

```
count by(release)(node_uname_info)
```

which on our single machine test setup returns:

```
{release="4.4.0-101-generic"} 1
```

You can use sum with an empty by, and can even omit the by. That is to say that:

```
sum by()(node_filesystem_size_bytes)
```

and:

```
sum(node_filesystem_size_bytes)
```

are exactly equivalent and will give a result like:

```
{} 92718116864
```

This is a single time series, and that time series has no labels.

If you executed the expression:

```
sum(non_existent_metric)
```

the result would be an instant vector with no time series, which will show up in the expression browser's Console tab as *"no data."*

 If the input to an aggregation operator is an empty instant vector, it will output an empty instant vector. Thus, count by(foo)(non_existent_metric) will be empty rather than 0, as count and other aggregators don't have any labels to work with. count(non_existent_metric) is consistent with this, and also returns an empty instant vector.

Operators

All 11 aggregation operators use the same grouping logic. You can control this with one of without or by. What differs between aggregation operators is what they do with the grouped data.

sum

sum is the most common aggregator; it adds up all the values in a group and returns that as the value for the group. For example:

```
sum without(fstype, mountpoint, device)(node_filesystem_size_bytes)
```

would return the total size of the filesystems of each of your machines.

When dealing with counters,[2] it is important that you take a `rate` before aggregating with `sum`:

```
sum without(device)(rate(node_disk_read_bytes_total[5m]))
```

If you were to take a `sum` across counters directly, the result would be meaningless, as different counters could have been initialized at different times depending on when the exporter started, restarted, or any particular children were first used.

count

The `count` aggregator counts the number of time series in a group, and returns it as the value for the group. For example:

```
count without(device)(node_disk_read_bytes_total)
```

would return the number of disk devices a machine has. Our machine only has one disk, so we get:

```
{instance="localhost:9100",job="node"} 1
```

Here it is OK not to use `rate` with a counter, as you care about the existence of the time series rather than its value.

Unique label values

You can also use `count` to count how many unique values a label has. For example, to count the number of CPUs in each of your machines, you could use:

```
count without(cpu)(count without (mode)(node_cpu_seconds_total))
```

The inner `count`[3] removes the other instrumentation label, `mode`, returning one time series per CPU per instance:

```
{cpu="0",instance="localhost:9100",job="node"} 8
{cpu="1",instance="localhost:9100",job="node"} 8
{cpu="2",instance="localhost:9100",job="node"} 8
{cpu="3",instance="localhost:9100",job="node"} 8
```

The outer `count` then returns the number of CPUs that each instance has:

```
{instance="localhost:9100",job="node"} 4
```

---

2 Including the _sum, _count, and _bucket of histograms and summary metrics.

3 The inner aggregation does not have to be `count`; anything that returns the same set of time series, such as `sum`, would also work. This is because the outer `count` ignores the values of these time series.

If you didn't want a per-machine breakdown, such as if you were investigating whether certain labels had high cardinality, you could use the by modifier to look at only one label:

```
count(count by(cpu)(node_cpu_seconds_total))
```

which would produce a single sample with no labels, such as:

```
{} 4
```

avg

The avg aggregator returns the average of the values[4] of the time series in the group as the value for the group. For example:

```
avg without(cpu)(rate(node_cpu_seconds_total[5m]))
```

would give you the average usage of each CPU mode for each Node Exporter instance with a result such as:

```
{instance="localhost:9100",job="node",mode="idle"} 0.9095948275861836
{instance="localhost:9100",job="node",mode="iowait"} 0.005543103448275879
{instance="localhost:9100",job="node",mode="irq"} 0
{instance="localhost:9100",job="node",mode="nice"} 0.0013620689655172522
{instance="localhost:9100",job="node",mode="softirq"} 0.0001465517241379329
{instance="localhost:9100",job="node",mode="steal"} 0
{instance="localhost:9100",job="node",mode="system"} 0.015836206896552414
{instance="localhost:9100",job="node",mode="user"} 0.06054310344827549
```

This gives you the exact same result as:

```
  sum without(cpu)(rate(node_cpu_seconds_total[5m]))
/
  count without(cpu)(rate(node_cpu_seconds_total[5m]))
```

but it is both more succinct and more efficient to use avg.

When using avg, sometimes you may find that a NaN in the input is causing the entire result to become NaN. This is because any floating-point arithmetic that involves NaN will have NaN as a result.

You may wonder how to filter out these NaNs in the input, but that is the wrong question to ask. Usually this is due to attempting to average averages, and one of the denominators of the first averages was 0.[5] Averaging averages is not statistically valid, so what you should do instead is aggregate using sum and then finally divide, as shown in "Summary" on page 232.

---

4 Technically it is called an *arithmetic mean*. In the unlikely event you need a *geometric mean*, the ln and exp functions combined with the avg aggregator can be used to calculate that.

5 This is as 1 / 0 = NaN.

group

The `group` aggregator returns 1 for each of the time series in the group as the value for the group. For example:

```
count by (instance)(
  group by (fstype,instance) (node_filesystem_files)
)
```

That query would return the number of different filesystem types for each instance.

In this case, any aggregation could have worked (`sum`, `count`) in place of `group`. However, using `group` makes it clear for anyone reading the query that we are interested in the grouping and the resulting labels themselves rather than the value produced by the inner aggregation operator.

stddev and stdvar

The *standard deviation* is a statistical measure of how spread out a set of numbers is. For example, if you had the numbers [2,4,6], then the standard deviation would be 1.633.[6] The numbers [3,4,5] have the same average of 4, but a standard deviation of 0.816.

The main use of the standard deviation in monitoring is to detect outliers. In normally distributed data you would expect that about 68% of samples would be within one standard deviation of the mean, and 95% within two standard deviations.[7] If one instance in a job has a metric several standard deviations away from the average, that's a good indication that something is wrong with it.

For example, you could find all instances that were at least two standard deviations above the average using an expression such as:

```
  some_gauge
> ignoring (instance) group_left()
  (
      avg without(instance)(some_gauge)
    +
      2 * stddev without(instance)(some_gauge)
  )
```

This uses one-to-many vector matching, which will be discussed in "Many-to-One and group_left" on page 268. If your values are all tightly bunched, then this may return some time series that are more than two standard deviations away, but still operating normally and close to the average. You could add an additional filter that

---

6 Prometheus uses the *population standard deviation* rather than the *sample standard deviation*, as you will usually be looking at all the values you are interested in rather than a random subset.

7 For nonnormally distributed data, *Chebyshev's inequality* provides a weaker bound.

the value has to be at least, say, 20% higher than the average to protect against this. This is also a rare case where it is OK to take an average of an average, such as if you applied this to average latency.

The *standard variance* is the standard deviation squared[8] and has statistical uses.

min and max

The min and max aggregators return the minimum or maximum value within a group as the value of the group, respectively. The same grouping rules apply as elsewhere, so the output time series will have the labels of the group.[9] For example:

```
max without(device, fstype, mountpoint)(node_filesystem_size_bytes)
```

will return the size of the biggest filesystem on each instance, which for us returns:

```
{instance="localhost:9100",job="node"} 90131324928
```

The max and min aggregators will only return NaN if all values in a group are NaN.[10]

topk and bottomk

topk and bottomk are different from the other aggregators discussed so far in three ways. First, the labels of time series they return for a group are not the labels of the group; second, they can return more than one time series per group; and third, they take an additional parameter.

topk returns the k time series with the biggest values, so for example:

```
topk without(device, fstype, mountpoint)(2, node_filesystem_size_bytes)
```

would return up to two[11] time series per group, such as:

```
node_filesystem_size_bytes{device="/dev/sda5",fstype="ext4",
    instance="localhost:9100",job="node",mountpoint="/"} 90131324928
node_filesystem_size_bytes{device="tmpfs",fstype="tmpfs",
    instance="localhost:9100",job="node",mountpoint="/run"} 826961920
```

As you can see, topk returns input time series with all their labels, including the __name__ label, which holds the metric name. The result is also sorted.

---

8 If the exponentiation operator had existed at the time we were adding stdvar and stddev, then stdvar would probably not have been added.

9 If you want the input time series returned, use topk or bottomk.

10 In floating-point math, any comparison with NaN always returns false. Aside from causing oddities such as NaN != NaN returning false, a naive implementation of min and max would (and once did) get stuck on a NaN if it was the first value examined.

11 The k is 2 in this case.

bottomk is the same as topk, except that it returns the k time series with the smallest values rather than the k biggest values. Both aggregators will, where possible, avoid returning time series with NaN values.

There is a gotcha when using these aggregators with the query_range HTTP API endpoint. As was discussed in "query_range" on page 245, the evaluation of each step is independent. If you use topk, it is possible that the top time series will change from step to step. So a topk(5, some_gauge) for a query_range with 1,000 steps could in the worst case return 5,000 different time series.

The way to handle this is to use the at (@) modifier, as discussed in "At Modifier" on page 242.

quantile

The quantile aggregator returns the specified quantile of the values of the group as the group's return value. As with topk, quantile takes a parameter.

So, for example, if we wanted to know across the different CPUs in each of our machines what the 90th percentile of the system mode CPU usage is, we could use:

```
quantile without(cpu)(0.9, rate(node_cpu_seconds_total{mode="system"}[5m]))
```

which produces a result like:

```
{instance="localhost:9100",job="node",mode="system"} 0.024558620689654007
```

This means that 90% of our CPUs are spending at least 0.02 seconds per second in the system mode. This would be a more useful query if we had tens of CPUs in our machine, rather than the four it actually has.

In addition to the mean, you could use quantile to show the median, 25th, and 75th percentiles[12] on your graphs. For example, for process CPU usage the expressions would be:

```
# average, arithmetic mean
avg without(instance)(rate(process_cpu_seconds_total[5m]))

# 0.25 quantile, 25th percentile, 1st or lower quartile
quantile without(instance)(0.25, rate(process_cpu_seconds_total[5m]))

# 0.5 quantile, 50th percentile, 2nd quartile, median
quantile without(instance)(0.5, rate(process_cpu_seconds_total[5m]))

# 0.75 quantile, 75th percentile, 3rd or upper quartile
quantile without(instance)(0.75, rate(process_cpu_seconds_total[5m]))
```

---

12 Also known as the 1st and 3rd *quartiles*.

This would give you a sense of how your different instances for a job are behaving, without having to graph each instance individually. This allows you to keep your dashboards readable as the number of underlying instances grows. Personally we find that per-instance graphs break down somewhere around three to five instances.

---

quantile, histogram_quantile, and quantile_over_time

As you may have noticed by now, there is more than one PromQL function or operator with quantile in the name.

The `quantile` aggregator works across an instant vector in an aggregation group.

The `quantile_over_time` function works across a single time series at a time in a range vector.

The `histogram_quantile` function works across the buckets of one histogram metric child at a time in an instant vector.

---

count_values

The final aggregation operator is `count_values`. Like `topk` it takes a parameter and can return more than one time series from a group. What it does is build a *frequency histogram* of the values of the time series in the group, with the count of each value as the value of the output time series and the original value as a new label.

That's a bit of a mouthful, so we will show you an example. Say you had a time series called `software_version` with the following values:

```
software_version{instance="a",job="j"} 7
software_version{instance="b",job="j"} 4
software_version{instance="c",job="j"} 8
software_version{instance="d",job="j"} 4
software_version{instance="e",job="j"} 7
software_version{instance="f",job="j"} 4
```

If you evaluated the query:

```
count_values without(instance)("version", software_version)
```

on these time series, you would get the result:

```
{job="j",version="7"} 2
{job="j",version="8"} 1
{job="j",version="4"} 3
```

There were two time series in the group with a value of 7, so a time series with a version="7" plus the group labels was returned with the value 2. The result is similar for the other time series.

There is no bucketing involved when the frequency histogram is created; the exact values of the time series are used. Thus this is only really useful with integer values and where there will not be too many unique values.

This is most useful with version numbers,[13] or with the number of objects of some type that each instance of your application sees. If you have too many versions deployed at once, or different applications are continuing to see different numbers of objects, something might be stuck somewhere.

count_values can be combined with count to calculate the number of unique values for a given aggregation group. For example, the number of versions of software that are deployed can be calculated with:

```
count without(version)(
  count_values without(instance)("version", software_version)
)
```

which in this case would return:

```
{job="j"} 3
```

You could also combine count_values with count in the other direction; for example, to see how many of your machines had how many disk devices:

```
count_values without(instance)(
  "devices",
  count without(device) (node_disk_io_now)
)
```

In our case we have one machine with five disk devices:

```
{devices="5",job="node"} 1
```

Now that you understand aggregators, we will look at binary operators, like addition and subtraction, and how vector matching works.

---

13 For versions that cannot be represented as floating-point values, you can use an info metric, as discussed in "Info" on page 96.

## CHAPTER 15

Binary Operators

You will want to do more with your metrics than simply aggregate them, which is where the *binary operators* come in. Binary operators are operators that take two operands,[1] such as the addition and equality operators.

Binary operators in allow for more than simple arithmetic on instant vectors; you can also apply a binary operator to two instant vectors with grouping based on labels. This is where the real power of PromQL comes out, allowing classes of analysis that few other metrics systems offer.

PromQL has three sets of binary operators: arithmetic operators, comparison operations, and logical operators. This chapter will show you how to use them.

Working with Scalars

In addition to instant vectors and range vectors, there is another type of value known as a *scalar*.[2] Scalars are single numbers with no dimensionality. For example, 0 is a scalar with the value zero, while {} 0 is an instant vector containing a single sample with no labels and the value zero.[3]

Arithmetic Operators

You can use scalars in arithmetic with an instant vector to change the values in the instant vector. For example:

---

1 In contrast to *unary operators*, which only take one operand. PromQL has + and - unary operators.

2 Internally, PromQL also has a *string* type, but this is only used as an argument to count_values, label_replace, and label_join.

3 You may also see the convention {}: 0 to represent a single sample.

```
process_resident_memory_bytes / 1024
```

would return:

```
{instance="localhost:9090",job="prometheus"} 21376
{instance="localhost:9100",job="node"} 13316
```

which is the process memory usage, in kilobytes.[4] You will note that the division operator was applied to all time series in the instant vector returned by the process_resident_memory_bytes selector, and that the metric name was removed as it is no longer the metric process_resident_memory_bytes.

 Even when you are using arithmetic operators in a way that doesn't change the value, the metric name will still be removed for consistency. For example, the result of some_gauge + 0 will not have a metric name.

All six arithmetic operations work similarly, with the semantics you'd expect from other programming languages. They are:

- + addition
- - subtraction
- * multiplication
- / division
- % modulo
- ^ exponentiation

The *modulo* operator is a floating-point modulo and can return noninteger results if you provide it with noninteger input. For example:

```
5 % 1.5
```

will return:

```
0.5
```

As this example demonstrates, you can also use binary arithmetic operators when both operands are scalars. The result will be a scalar. This is mostly useful for readability, as it is much easier to understand the intent of (1024 * 1024 * 1024) than it is 1073741824.

---

4 If you are using a dashboarding tool like Grafana, it's generally best to let it handle creating human-readable units for metrics that are already in base units, such as bytes.

In addition, you can put the scalar operand on the left side of the operator and an instant vector on the right, so for example:

```
1e9 - process_resident_memory_bytes
```

would subtract the process memory from a billion.

You can also use arithmetic operators with instant vectors on both sides, which is covered in "Vector Matching" on page 265.

Trigonometric Operator

The `atan2` operator returns the arc tangent of the division of two vectors, using the signs of the two to determine the quadrant of the return value:

```
x atan2 y
```

This operator allows you to execute `atan2` on two vectors using vector matching, which isn't available with normal functions. It acts in the same manner as arithmetic operators (+, -, *, ...).

Comparison Operators

The *comparison operators* are as follows, with the usual meanings:

- == equals
- != not equals
- > greater than
- < less than
- >= greater than or equal to
- <= less than or equal to

What is a little different is that the comparison operators in PromQL are *filtering*. That is to say that if you had the samples:

```
process_open_fds{instance="localhost:9090",job="prometheus"} 14
process_open_fds{instance="localhost:9100",job="node"} 7
```

and used an instant vector in a comparison with a scalar, such as in the expression:

```
process_open_fds > 10
```

then you would get the result:

```
process_open_fds{instance="localhost:9090",job="prometheus"}  14
```

As the value can't change, the metric name has been preserved. When comparing a scalar and an instant vector, it doesn't matter which side each is on; it is always elements of the instant vector that are returned.

 As PromQL deals with floating-point numbers, some care is required when using == and !=. Floating-point calculations can produce results that are very slightly different depending on exactly what the values are and in what order the operations are performed.

If you want to do equality on noninteger values, it is better to instead check that their difference is less than some small number which is called an *epsilon*. For example, you could do:

```
(some_gauge - 1) < 1e-6 > -1e-6
```

to check if a gauge has a value of 1 allowing for inaccuracy of one in a million.

You cannot do a filtering comparison between two scalars, as to be consistent with arithmetic operations between two scalars it'd have to return a scalar. This doesn't allow for filtering, as there's no way to have an empty scalar like you can have an empty instant vector.

bool modifier

Filtering comparisons are primarily useful in alerting rules, as discussed in Chapter 18, and generally to be avoided elsewhere.[5] We will show you why.

Continuing on from the preceding example, say you wanted to see how many of your processes for each job had more than 10 open file descriptors. The obvious way to do this would be:

```
count without(instance)(process_open_fds > 10)
```

which would return the result:

```
{job="prometheus"}  1
```

This correctly indicates that there is 1 Prometheus process with more than 10 open file descriptions. It does not report that the Node Exporter has zero such processes. This is can be a subtle gotcha because as long as one time series is not filtered away, everything seems to be OK.

---

5 It is possible to use filtering correctly with careful application of the or operator, but it's more complicated and error prone.

What you need is some way to do the comparison but not have it filter. This is what the bool modifier does; for each comparison it returns a 0 for false or a 1 for true.

For example:

```
process_open_fds > bool 10
```

will return:

```
{instance="localhost:9090",job="prometheus"} 1
{instance="localhost:9100",job="node"} 0
```

which as expected has one output sample per sample in the input instant vector.

From there you can sum up to get the number of processes for each job that have more than 10 open file descriptors:

```
sum without(instance)(process_open_fds > bool 10)
```

which produces the result you originally wanted:

```
{job="prometheus"} 1
{job="node"} 0
```

You could use a similar approach to find the proportion of machines with more than four disk devices:

```
avg without(instance)(
  count without(device)(node_disk_io_now) > bool 4
)
```

This works by first using a count aggregation to find the number of disks reported by each Node Exporter, then seeing how many have more than four, and finally averaging across machines to get the proportion. The trick here is that the values returned by the bool modifier are all 0 and 1, so the count is the total number of machines, and the sum is the number of machines meeting the criteria. The avg is the count divided by the sum, giving you a ratio or proportion.

The bool modifier is the only way you can compare scalars, as:

```
42 <= bool 13
```

will return:

```
0
```

where the 0 indicates false.

Vector Matching

Using operators between scalars and instant vectors will cover many of your needs, but using operators between two instant vectors is where PromQL's power really starts to shine.

When you have a scalar and an instant vector, it is obvious that the scalar can be applied to each sample in the vector. With two instant vectors, which samples should apply to which other samples? This matching of the instant vectors is known as *vector matching*.

One-to-One

In the simplest cases there will be a one-to-one mapping between your two vectors. Say that you had the following samples:

```
process_open_fds{instance="localhost:9090",job="prometheus"} 14
process_open_fds{instance="localhost:9100",job="node"} 7
process_max_fds{instance="localhost:9090",job="prometheus"} 1024
process_max_fds{instance="localhost:9100",job="node"} 1024
```

Then when you evaluated the expression:

```
  process_open_fds
/
  process_max_fds
```

you would get the result:

```
{instance="localhost:9090",job="prometheus"} 0.013671875
{instance="localhost:9100",job="node"} 0.0068359375
```

What has happened here is that samples with exactly the same labels, except for the metric name in the label __name__, were matched together. That is to say that the two samples with the labels {instance="localhost:9090",job="prometheus"} got matched together, and the two samples with the labels {instance="local host:9100",job="node"} got matched together.

In this case there was a perfect match, with each sample on both sides of the operator being matched. If a sample on one side had no match on the other side, then it would not be present in the result, as binary operators need two operands.

 If a binary operator returns an empty instant vector when you were expecting a result, it is probably because the labels of the samples in the operands don't match. This is often due to a label that is present on one side of the operator but not the other.

Sometimes you will want to match two instant vectors whose labels do not quite match. Similar to how aggregation allows you to specify which labels matter, as discussed in "Grouping" on page 249, vector matching also has clauses controlling which labels are considered.

You can use the `ignoring` clause to ignore certain labels when matching, similar to how `without` works for aggregation. Say you were working with `node_cpu_seconds_total`, which has `cpu` and `mode` as instrumentation labels, and wanted to know what proportion of time was being spent in the `idle` mode for each instance. You could use the expression:

```
  sum without(cpu)(rate(node_cpu_seconds_total{mode="idle"}[5m]))
/ ignoring(mode)
  sum without(mode, cpu)(rate(node_cpu_seconds_total[5m]))
```

This will give you a result such as:

```
{instance="localhost:9100",job="node"} 0.8423353718871361
```

Here the first `sum` produces an instant vector with a `mode="idle"` label, whereas the second `sum` produces an instant vector with no `mode` label. Usually vector matching will fail to match the samples, but with `ignoring(mode)` the `mode` label is discarded when the vectors are being grouped, and matching succeeds. As the `mode` label was not in the match group, it is not in the output.[6]

You can tell the preceding expression is correct in terms of vector matching by inspection, without having to know anything about the underlying time series. The removal of `cpu` is balanced on both sides, and `ignoring(mode)` handles one side having a `mode` and the other not.

This can be trickier when there are different time series with different labels in play, but looking at expressions in terms of how the labels flow is a handy way for you to spot errors.

The `on` clause allows you to consider only the labels you provide, similar to how `by` works for aggregation. The expression:

```
  sum by(instance, job)(rate(node_cpu_seconds_total{mode="idle"}[5m]))
/ on(instance, job)
  sum by(instance, job)(rate(node_cpu_seconds_total[5m]))
```

will produce the same result as the previous expression,[7] but as with `by`, the `on` clause has the disadvantage that you need to know all labels that are currently on the time series or that may be present in the future in other contexts.

The value that is returned for the arithmetic operators is the result of the calculation, but you may be wondering what happens for the comparison operators when there

---

6 The `cpu` label was aggregated away by both `sum`s, so is not present in the output either.

7 You could exclude the `on(instance, job)` here as the left- and righthand side both have only `instance` and `job` labels.

are two instant vectors. The answer is that the value from the lefthand side is returned. For example, the expression:

```
process_open_fds
>
(process_max_fds * .5)
```

will return for you the value of `process_open_fds` for all instances whose open file descriptors are more than halfway to the maximum.[8]

If you had instead used:

```
(process_max_fds * .5)
<
process_open_fds
```

you would get half the maximum file descriptors as the return value. While the result will have the same labels, this value might be semantically less useful when alerting[9] or when used in a dashboard! In general, a current value is more informative than the limit, so you should try to structure your math so that the most interesting number is on the lefthand side of a comparison.

Many-to-One and group_left

If you were to remove the matcher on `mode` from the preceding section and try to evaluate:

```
  sum without(cpu)(rate(node_cpu_seconds_total[5m]))
/ ignoring(mode)
  sum without(mode, cpu)(rate(node_cpu_seconds_total[5m]))
```

you would get the error:

```
multiple matches for labels:
  many-to-one matching must be explicit (group_left/group_right)
```

This is because the samples no longer match one-to-one, as there are multiple samples with different mode labels on the lefthand side for each sample on the righthand side. This can be a subtle failure mode, as a time series may appear later on that breaks your expression. You can see that this is a potential issue, as looking at the label flow there's nothing restricting the `mode` label to one potential value[10] on the lefthand side.

---

8 Running out of file descriptors can break applications in fun ways, and you should usually try to ensure that your applications always have enough.

9 Alert templates have ready access to the value of an alert's PromQL expression. This is discussed in "Annotations and Templates" on page 318.

10 A missing mode label due to aggregating it away would count as a single label value of the empty string.

Errors like this are usually due to incorrectly written expressions, so PromQL does not attempt to do anything smart by default. Instead, you must specifically request that you want to do many-to-one matching using the `group_left` modifier.

`group_left` lets you specify that there can be multiple matching samples in the group of the lefthand operand.[11] For example:

```
    sum without(cpu)(rate(node_cpu_seconds_total[5m]))
  / ignoring(mode) group_left
    sum without(mode, cpu)(rate(node_cpu_seconds_total[5m]))
```

will produce one output sample for each different `mode` label within each group on the lefthand side:

```
{instance="localhost:9100",job="node",mode="irq"} 0
{instance="localhost:9100",job="node",mode="nice"} 0
{instance="localhost:9100",job="node",mode="softirq"} 0.00005226389784152013
{instance="localhost:9100",job="node",mode="steal"} 0
{instance="localhost:9100",job="node",mode="system"} 0.01720353303949279
{instance="localhost:9100",job="node",mode="user"} 0.10345203045243238
{instance="localhost:9100",job="node",mode="idle"} 0.8608691486211044
{instance="localhost:9100",job="node",mode="iowait"} 0.01842302398912871
```

`group_left` always takes all of its labels from samples of your operand on the lefthand side. This ensures that the extra labels that are on the left side that require this to be many-to-one vector matching are preserved.[12]

This is much easier than having to run a one-to-one expression with a matcher for each potential `mode` label: `group_left` does it all for you in one expression. You can use this approach to determine the proportion each label value within a metric represents of the whole, as shown in the preceding example, or to compare a metric from a leader of a cluster against the replicas.

There is another use for `group_left`—adding labels from info metrics to other metrics from a target. Instrumentation with info metrics was covered in "Info" on page 96. The role of info metrics is to allow you to provide labels that would be useful for a target or metric to have but that would clutter up the metric if you were to use it as a normal label.

The `prometheus_build_info` metric, for example, provides you with build information from Prometheus:

---

11 There can still only be one sample per group on the righthand side of the operand, as `group_left` only enables many-to-one matching, not many-to-many matching.

12 If the labels from the righthand side were used, you would get the same labels for each sample from the groups on the left, which would clash.

```
prometheus_build_info{branch="HEAD",goversion="go1.10",
    instance="localhost:9090",job="prometheus",
    revision="bc6058c81272a8d938c05e75607371284236aadc",version="2.2.1"}
```

You can join this with metrics such as up:

```
up
* on(instance) group_left(version)
  prometheus_build_info
```

which will produce a result like:

```
{instance="localhost:9090",job="prometheus",version="2.2.1"} 1
```

You can see that the version label has been copied over from the righthand operand
to the lefthand operand as was requested by group_left(version), in addition
to returning all the labels from the lefthand operand as group_left usually does.
You can specify as many labels as you like to group_left, but usually it's only one or
two.[13] This approach works no matter how many instrumentation labels the lefthand
side has, as the vector matching is many-to-one.

The preceding expression used on(instance), which relies on each instance label
only being used for one target within your Prometheus. While this is often the case, it
isn't always, so you may also need to add other labels such as job to the on clause.

prometheus_build_info applies to a whole target. There are also info-style[14] metrics
such as node_hwmon_sensor_label mentioned in "Hwmon Collector" on page 130
that apply to children of a different metric:

```
node_hwmon_sensor_label{chip="platform_coretemp_0",instance="localhost:9100",
    job="node",label="core_0",sensor="temp2"} 1
node_hwmon_sensor_label{chip="platform_coretemp_0",instance="localhost:9100",
    job="node",label="core_1",sensor="temp3"} 1

node_hwmon_temp_celsius{chip="platform_coretemp_0",instance="localhost:9100",
    job="node",sensor="temp1"} 42
node_hwmon_temp_celsius{chip="platform_coretemp_0",instance="localhost:9100",
    job="node",sensor="temp2"} 42
node_hwmon_temp_celsius{chip="platform_coretemp_0",instance="localhost:9100",
    job="node",sensor="temp3"} 41
```

The node_hwmon_sensor_label metric has children that match with some (but not
all) of the time series in node_hwmon_temp_celsius. In this case you know that there

---

13 There's no way for you to request all the labels to be copied over, as then you would no longer know what
   labels the output metric had.

14 The convention for whether a metric that has a single info-style label should have an _info suffix is not fully
   resolved yet.

is only one additional label (which is called `label`), so you can use `ignoring` with `group_left` to add this label to the `node_hwmon_temp_celsius` samples:

```
  node_hwmon_temp_celsius
* ignoring(label) group_left(label)
  node_hwmon_sensor_label
```

which will produce results such as:

```
{chip="platform_coretemp_0",instance="localhost:9100",
    job="node",label="core_0",sensor="temp2"} 42
{chip="platform_coretemp_0",instance="localhost:9100",
    job="node",label="core_1",sensor="temp3"} 41
```

Notice that there is no sample with `sensor="temp1"` as there was no such sample in `node_hwmon_sensor_label` (how to match sparse instant vectors will be covered in "or operator" on page 271).

There is also a `group_right` modifier that works in the same way as `group_left` except that the one and the many sides are switched, with the many side now being your operand on the righthand side. Any labels you specify in the `group_right` modifier are copied from the left to the right. For the sake of consistency, you should prefer `group_left`.

Many-to-Many and Logical Operators

There are three logical or set operators you can use:

- or union
- and intersection
- `unless` set subtraction

There is no *not* operator, but the `absent` function discussed in "Missing Series, absent, and absent_over_time" on page 287 serves a similar role.

All the logical operators work in a many-to-many fashion, and they are the only operators that work many-to-many. They are different from the arithmetic and comparison operators you have already seen in that no math is performed; all that matters is whether a group contains samples.

or operator

In the preceding section, `node_hwmon_sensor_label` did not have a sample to go with every `node_hwmon_temp_celsius`, so results were only returned for samples that were present in both instant vectors. Metrics with inconsistent children, or whose children are not always present, are tricky to work with, but you can deal with them using the or operator.

How the or operator works is that for each group where the group on the lefthand side has samples, then they are returned; otherwise, the samples in the group on the righthand side are returned. If you are familiar with SQL, this operator can be used in a similar way as the SQL COALESCE function, but with labels.

Continuing the example from the preceding section, or can be used to substitute the missing time series from node_hwmon_sensor_label. All you need is some other time series that has the labels you need, which in this case is node_hwmon_temp_celsius. node_hwmon_temp_celsius does not have the label label, but all the other labels match up so you can ignore this using ignoring:

```
    node_hwmon_sensor_label
  or ignoring(label)
    (node_hwmon_temp_celsius * 0 + 1)
```

The vector matching produced three groups of labels. The first two groups had a sample from node_hwmon_sensor_label so that was what was returned, including the metric name as there was nothing to change it. For the third group, however, which included sensor="temp1", there was no sample in the group for the lefthand side, so the values in the group from the righthand side were used. Because arithmetic operators were used on the value, the metric name was removed.

 x * 0 + 1 will change all[15] the values of the x instant vector to 1. This is also useful when you want to use group_left to copy labels, as 1 is the identity element for multiplication, which is to say it does not change the value you are multiplying.

This expression can now be used in the place of node_hwmon_sensor_label:

```
    node_hwmon_temp_celsius
  * ignoring(label) group_left(label)
    (
        node_hwmon_sensor_label
      or ignoring(label)
        (node_hwmon_temp_celsius * 0 + 1)
    )
```

which will produce:

```
{chip="platform_coretemp_0",instance="localhost:9100",
    job="node",sensor="temp1"} 42
{chip="platform_coretemp_0",instance="localhost:9100",
    job="node",label="core_0",sensor="temp2"} 42
```

---

15 NaN will stay as NaN, but in practice there will be another time series with the same labels and no NaN values that you could use instead.

```
{chip="platform_coretemp_0",instance="localhost:9100",
    job="node",label="core_1",sensor="temp3"} 41
```

The sample with `sensor="temp1"` is now present in your result. It has no label called `label`, which is the same as saying that that `label` label has the empty string as a value.

In simpler cases you will be working with metrics without any instrumentation labels. For example, you might be using the textfile collector, as covered in "Textfile Collector" on page 134, and expecting it to expose a metric called `node_custom_metric`. In the event that metric doesn't exist, you would like to return 0 instead. In cases like this, you can use the up metric that is associated with every target:

```
node_custom_metric
or
  up * 0
```

This has a small problem in that it will return a value even for a failed scrape, which is not how scraped metrics work.[16] It will also return results for other jobs. You can fix this with a matcher and some filtering:

```
node_custom_metric
or
  (up{job="node"} == 1) * 0
```

Another way you can use the or operator is to return the larger of two series:

```
(a >= b) or b
```

If a is larger it will be returned by the comparison, and then the or operator since the group on the lefthand side was not empty. If, on the other hand, b is larger, then the comparison will return nothing, and or will return b as the group on the lefthand side was empty.

unless operator

The `unless` operator does vector matching in the same way as the or operator, working based on whether groups from the right and left operands are empty or have samples. The `unless` operator returns the lefthand group, unless the righthand group has members, in which case it returns no samples for that group.

You can use `unless` to restrict what time series are returned based on an expression. For example, if you wanted to know the average CPU usage of processes except those using less than 100 MB of resident memory, you could use the expression:

---

16 up is not a scraped metric; Prometheus adds it after every scrape whether the scrape succeeds or fails.

```
rate(process_cpu_seconds_total[5m])
unless
  process_resident_memory_bytes < 100 * 1024 * 1024
```

`unless` can also be used to spot when a metric is missing from a target. For example:

```
up{job="node"} == 1
unless
  node_custom_metric
```

would return a sample for every instance that was missing the `node_custom_metric` metric, which you could use in alerting.

By default, as with all binary operators, `unless` looks at all labels when grouping. If `node_custom_metric` had instrumentation labels, you could use `on` or `ignoring` to check that at least one relevant time series existed without having to know the values of the other labels:

```
up == 1
unless on (job, instance)
  node_custom_metric
```

Even if there are multiple samples from the right operand in a group, this is OK as `unless` uses many-to-many matching.

and operator

The `and` operator is the opposite of the `unless` operator. It returns a group from the lefthand operand only if the matching righthand group has samples; otherwise, it returns no samples for that match group. You can think of it as an *if* operator.[17]

You will use the `and` operator most commonly in alerting to specify more than one condition. For example, you might want to return when both latency is high and there is more than a trickle of user requests. To do this for Prometheus for handlers that were taking over a second on average and had at least one request per second, you could use:

```
(
    rate(http_request_duration_seconds_sum{job="prometheus"}[5m])
  /
    rate(http_request_duration_seconds_count{job="prometheus"}[5m])
) > 1
and
  rate(http_request_duration_seconds_count{job="prometheus"}[5m]) > 1
```

---

17 Prior to Prometheus 2.x, PromQL had an `IF` keyword that was used in alerting, so while Brian had wondered if renaming the `and` operator to `if` would have been a good idea, it was not possible.

This will return a sample for every individual handler on every prometheus job, so it could get a little spammy even with the one request per second restriction. Usually you would want to aggregate across a job when alerting.

You can use on and ignoring with the and operator, as you can with the other binary operators. In particular, on() can be used to have a condition that has no common labels at all between the two operands. You can use this, for example, to limit the time of day an expression will return results for:

```
(
    rate(http_request_duration_microseconds_sum{job="prometheus"}[5m])
  /
    rate(http_request_duration_microseconds_count{job="prometheus"}[5m])
) > 1000000
and
  rate(http_request_duration_microseconds_count{job="prometheus"}[5m]) > 1
and on()
  hour() >= 9 < 17
```

The hour function is covered in "minute, hour, day_of_week, day_of_month, day_of_year, days_in_month, month, and year" on page 284; it returns an instant vector with one sample with no labels and the hour of the UTC day of the query evaluation time as the value.

Operator Precedence

When evaluating an expression with multiple binary operators, PromQL does not simply go from left to right. Instead, there is an order of operators that is largely the same as the order used in other languages:

1. ^
2. * / % atan2
3. + -
4. == != > < >= <=
5. unless and
6. or

For example, a or b * c + d is the same as a or ((b * c) + d).

All operators except ^ are left-associative. That means that a / b * c is the same as (a / b) * c, but a ^ b ^ c is a ^ (b ^ c).

You can use parentheses to change the order of evaluation. We also recommend adding parentheses where the evaluation order may not be immediately clear for an expression, as not everyone will have memorized the operator precedence.

Now that you understand both aggregators and operators, let's look at the final part of PromQL: functions.

## CHAPTER 16

Functions

PromQL has 69 functions as of 2.37.0, and offers you a wide variety of functionality, from common math to functions specifically for dealing with counter and histogram metrics. In this chapter you will learn about how all the functions work and how they can be used.

Almost all PromQL functions return instant vectors, and the three that don't (`time`, `pi`, and `scalar`) return scalars. No functions return range vectors, though multiple functions, including `rate` and `avg_over_time` that you have already seen, take a range vector as input.

Put another way, functions generally work either across the samples of a single time series at a time or across the samples of an instant vector. If you want to process an entire range vector at once, you would need to use subqueries.

PromQL is statically typed, functions do not change their return value based on the input types. In fact, the input types for each function are also fixed. Where a function needs to work with two different types, two different names are used. For example, you use the `avg` aggregator on instant vectors and the `avg_over_time` function on range vectors.

There are no official categories for the functions, but we have grouped related functions together.

Changing Type

At times you will have a vector but need a scalar, or vice versa. There are two functions that allow you to do so: `vector` and `scalar`.

vector

The `vector` function takes a scalar value, and converts it into an instant vector with one sample without a label and the given value. For example, the expression:

```
vector(1)
```

will produce:

```
{} 1
```

This is useful if you need to ensure an expression returns a result, but can't depend on any particular time series to exist. For example:

```
sum(some_gauge) or vector(0)
```

will always return one sample, even if `some_gauge` has no samples. Depending on the use case, the `bool` modifier, as discussed in "bool modifier" on page 264, may be a better choice than the `or` operator (see "or operator" on page 271).

scalar

The `scalar` function takes an instant vector with a single sample and converts it to a scalar with the value the input sample had. If there is not exactly one sample, then `NaN` will be returned to you.

This is mostly useful when working with scalar constants, but you should use math functions that only work on instant vectors. For example, if you wanted the natural logarithm of two as a scalar, rather than typing out `0.6931471805599453` and hoping anyone reading it recognized the significance of number, you could use:

```
scalar(ln(vector(2)))
```

This can also make certain expressions simpler to write. For example, if you wanted to see which servers were started in the current year, you could do:

```
year(process_start_time_seconds)
==
scalar(year())
```

rather than:

```
year(process_start_time_seconds)
== on() group_left
year()
```

as scalar comparisons are a little easier to understand than vector matching with `group_left`, and this is OK because you know that `year` here will only ever return one sample.

But use of the scalar function should be limited because using scalar loses all of your labels and with it your ability to do vector matching. For example:

```
sum(rate(node_cpu_seconds_total{mode!="idle",instance="localhost:9090"}[5m]))
/
scalar(count(node_cpu_seconds_total{mode="idle",instance="localhost:9090"}))
```

will give you the proportion of time a machine's CPU is not idle, but you would then have to alter and reevaluate this expression for every single instance.

Taking advantage of the full power of PromQL, you can do:

```
sum without (cpu, mode)(
    rate(node_cpu_seconds_total{mode!="idle"}[5m])
)
/
count without(cpu, mode)(node_cpu_seconds_total{mode="idle"})
```

and calculate the proportion of nonidle CPU for all your machines at once.

Math

The math functions perform standard mathematical operations on instant vectors, such as calculating absolute values or taking a logarithm. Each sample in the instant vector is handled independently, and the metric name is removed in the return value.

abs

abs takes an instant vector and returns the absolute value for each of its values, which is to say any negative numbers are changed to positive numbers.

The expression:

```
abs(process_open_fds - 15)
```

will return how far away each process's open file descriptors count is from 15. Counts of 5 and 25 would both return 10.

ln, log2, and log10

The functions ln, log2, and log10 take an instant vector, return the logarithm of the values, and use different bases for the logarithm, Euler's number e, 2, and 10, respectively. ln is also known as the *natural logarithm*.

These functions can be used to get an idea of the different orders of magnitude of numbers. For example, to calculate the number of 9s[1] of successes an API endpoint had over the past hour, you could do:

---

1 A 99% success rate is two 9s.

```
log10(
    sum without(instance)(rate(requests_failed_total[1h]))
  /
    sum without(instance)(rate(requests_total[1h]))
) * -1
```

 If you want a logarithm to a different base, you can use the *change of base* formula. For example, for a logarithm base three on the instant vector x, you would use:

```
ln(x) / ln(3)
```

These can also be useful for graphing in certain circumstances where normal linear graphs can't suitably represent a large variance in values. However, it is usually best to rely on the built-in logarithm graphing options in tools such as Grafana rather than using these functions, as they tend to gracefully handle edge cases such as negative logarithms returning NaN.

exp

The exp function provides the natural exponent, and is the inverse to the ln function. For example:

```
exp(vector(1))
```

returns:

```
{} 2.718281828459045
```

which is Euler's number, *e*.

sqrt

The sqrt function returns a square root of the values in an instant vector. For example:

```
sqrt(vector(9))
```

will return:

```
{} 3
```

sqrt predates the exponent operator ^, so this is equivalent to:

```
vector(9) ^ 0.5
```

 If you need other roots, you can use the same approach. For example, the cube or third root can be calculated with:

```
vector(9) ^ (1/3)
```

ceil and floor

ceil and floor allow you to round the values in an instant vector. ceil always rounds up to the nearest integer, and floor always rounds down. For example:

```
ceil(vector(0.1))
```

will return:

```
{} 1
```

round

round rounds the values in an instant vector to the nearest integer. If you provide a value that is exactly halfway between two integers, it is rounded up. That is to say that:

```
round(vector(5.5))
```

will return:

```
{} 6
```

round is also one of the functions that you can optionally provide with an additional argument. The additional argument is a scalar, and the values will be rounded to the nearest multiple of this number:

```
round(vector(2446), 1000)
```

will return:

```
{} 2000
```

for example. This is equivalent to:

```
round(vector(2446) / 1000) * 1000
```

but easier for you to use and understand.

clamp, clamp_max, and clamp_min

Sometimes you will find that a metric returns spurious values well outside the normal range, such as a gauge that you expect to be positive occasionally being massively negative. clamp_max and clamp_min allow you to put upper and lower bounds, respectively, on the values in an instant vector.

For example, if you didn't believe that your processes could have fewer than 10 open file descriptors, you could use:

```
clamp_min(process_open_fds, 10)
```

which would produce a result like:

```
{instance="localhost:9090",job="prometheus"} 46
{instance="localhost:9100",job="node"} 10
```

clamp enables you to put upper and lower bounds into a single query. On the same data, the following query:

```
clamp(process_open_fds, 10, 20)
```

would produce a result like:

```
{instance="localhost:9090",job="prometheus"} 20
{instance="localhost:9100",job="node"} 10
```

sgn

sgn returns a vector with all sample values converted to their sign, defined as this: 1 if the value is positive, –1 if value is negative, and 0 if the value is equal to zero.

```
sgn(vector(100))
```

will return:

```
{} 1
```

Trigonometric Functions

There are 12 trigonometric functions available. They work in radians:

- acos calculates the arccosine of the values.
- acosh calculates the inverse hyperbolic cosine of the values.
- asin calculates the arcsine of the values.
- asinh calculates the inverse hyperbolic sine of the values.
- atan calculates the arctangent of the values.
- atanh calculates the inverse hyperbolic tangent of the values.
- cos calculates the cosine of the values.
- cosh calculates the hyperbolic cosine of the values.
- sin calculates the sine of the values.
- sinh calculates the hyperbolic sine of the values.
- tan calculates the tangent of the values.
- tanh calculates the hyperbolic tangent of the values.

There are three additional functions that are useful for converting between degrees and radians:

- deg converts values passed as radians to degrees.

- pi returns pi.

- rad converts values passed as degrees to radians.

```
sin(vector(pi()/2))
```

returns:

```
{} 1
```

Time and Date

Prometheus offers you several functions dealing with time, most of which are convenience functions around `time` to save you from having to implement date-related logic yourself. Prometheus works entirely in UTC, and has no notion of time zones.

time

The `time` function is the most basic time-related function. It returns the evaluation time of the query as seconds since the Unix epoch[2] as a scalar. For example:

```
time()
```

might return:

```
1652911202.529
```

If you were to use `time` with the `query_range` endpoint, then every result would be different, as each step has a different evaluation time.

The Prometheus best practice is to expose the Unix time in seconds at which something of interest happened, and not how long it has been since it happened. This is more reliable, as it's not susceptible to failure to update the metric. The `time` function then lets you convert these to durations. For example, if you wanted to see how long your processes have been running, you would use:

```
time() - process_start_time_seconds
```

which will return a result such as:

```
{instance="localhost:9090",job="prometheus"} 313.5699999332428
{instance="localhost:9100",job="node"} 322.25999999046326
```

Here both Node Exporter and Prometheus have been running for a bit over 5 minutes. If you had a batch job pushing the last time it succeeded to the Pushgateway,

---

2 Midnight January 1st, 1970 UTC.

as discussed in "Pushgateway" on page 76, you could find jobs that hadn't succeeded in the past hour with:

```
time() - my_job_last_success_seconds > 3600
```

minute, hour, day_of_week, day_of_month, day_of_year, days_in_month, month, and year

time covers most use cases, but sometimes you will want to have logic based on the clock or calendar. Converting to minutes and hours from time isn't too difficult,[3] but beyond that you have to consider issues like leap days.

All of these functions return the given value for the query evaluation time as an instant vector with one sample and no labels. As we write this it is currently 13:37 on Saturday, November 5, 2022, in the UTC time zone. The outputs of these functions when evaluated at this time are:

Expression	Result
minute()	{} 37
hour()	{} 13
day_of_week()	{} 6
day_of_month()	{} 5
day_of_year()	{} 309
days_in_month()	{} 30
month()	{} 11
year()	{} 2022

day_of_week starts with 0 for Sunday, so the 6 here is Saturday. If you wanted to check if today was the last day of the month, you could compare the output of day_of_month to days_in_month.

You may be wondering why these functions don't return scalars, as that'd seem more convenient to work with. The answer is that these functions all take an optional argument[4] so that you can pass in instant vectors. For example, to see what year your processes started in, you could use:

```
year(process_start_time_seconds)
```

---

3 Minutes are floor(vector(time() / 60 % 60)), for example.

4 The default value of this argument is vector(time()).

---

which would produce a result such as:

```
{instance="localhost:9090",job="prometheus"} 2022
{instance="localhost:9100",job="node"} 2022
```

This could also be used to count how many processes were started this month:

```
sum(
    (year(process_start_time_seconds) == bool scalar(year()))
  *
    (month(process_start_time_seconds) == bool scalar(month()))
)
```

Here we are taking advantage of the fact that the multiplication operator acts like an *and operator* when used on booleans with the value 1 for `true` and 0 for `false`.

timestamp

The `timestamp` function is different from the other time functions in that it looks at the timestamp of the samples in an instant vector rather than the values. As was mentioned in "Instant Vector" on page 237 and "query" on page 242, the timestamps for samples returned from all operators, functions, the `query_range` HTTP API, and query HTTP API when it returns an instant vector will be the query evaluation time.

However, the timestamp of samples in an instant vector from an instant vector selector will be the actual timestamps.[5] The `timestamp` function allows you to access these. For example, you can see when the last scrape started for each target with:

```
timestamp(up)
```

This is because the default timestamp for data from a scrape is the time that the scrape started. Similarly the timestamp for samples from recording rules, as covered in Chapter 17, is the rule group execution time.

If you want to see raw data with samples for debugging, using a range vector selector with the query HTTP API is best, but `timestamp` does have some uses. For example:

```
node_time_seconds - timestamp(node_time_seconds)
```

would return the difference between when the scrape of the Node Exporter was started by Prometheus and what time the Node Exporter thought was the current time. While this isn't 100% accurate (it will vary with machine load), it will allow you to know if time is out of sync by a few seconds without needing a 1-second scrape interval.

---

5 As will the timestamps of samples if you provide a range vector selector to the query HTTP API.

Labels

In an ideal world the label names and label values used by different parts of your system would be consistent; for example, you wouldn't have `customer` in one place and `cust` in another. While it is best to resolve such inconsistencies in the source code, or failing that with `metric_relabel_configs` as discussed in "metric_relabel_configs" on page 164, this is not always possible. Thus the two label functions allow you to change labels.

label_replace

`label_replace` allows you to do regular expression substitution on label values. For example, if you needed the `device` label on `node_disk_read_bytes_total` to be dev instead for vector matching to work as you needed, you could do:[6]

```
label_replace(node_disk_read_bytes_total, "dev", "${1}", "device", "(.*)")
```

which would return a result like:

```
node_disk_read_bytes_total{dev="sda",device="sda",instance="localhost:9100",
    job="node"} 4766305792
```

Unlike most functions, `label_replace` does not remove the metric name, as it is presumed that you are doing something unusual if you have to resort to `label_replace`, and removing the metric name could make that harder for you.

The arguments to `label_replace` are the instant vector input, the name of the output label, the replacement, the name of the source label, and the regular expression. `label_replace` is similar to the `replace` relabeling action, but you can only use one label as a source label. If the regular expression does not match for a given sample, then that sample is returned unchanged.

label_join

`label_join` allows you to join label values, similarly to how `source_labels` is handled in relabeling. For example, if you wanted to join the `job` and `instance` labels into a new label, you could do:

```
label_join(node_disk_read_bytes_total, "combined", "-", "instance", "job")
```

which would return a result such as:

```
node_disk_read_bytes_total{combined="localhost:9100-node",device="sda",
    instance="localhost:9100",job="node"} 4766359040
```

---

6 In reality, as `node_disk_read_bytes_total` is a counter, you would use `rate` first and then `label_replace`.

As with `label_replace`, `label_join` does not remove the metric name. The arguments are the instant vector input, the name of the output label, the separator, and then zero or more label names.

You could combine `label_join` with `label_replace` to provide the full functionality of the `replace` relabel action, but at that point you should seriously consider `metric_relabel_configs` or fixing the source metrics instead.

Missing Series, absent, and absent_over_time

As mentioned in "Many-to-Many and Logical Operators" on page 271, the `absent` function plays the role of a *not* operator. If you pass a nonempty instant vector as the `absent` argument, it returns an empty instant vector. If you pass an empty instant vector, it returns an instant vector with one sample and a value of 1.

You might expect that this sample has no labels, since there are no labels to work with. However, `absent` is a little smarter than that, and if the argument is an instant vector selector, it uses the labels from any equality matchers present.

Expression	Result
`absent(up)`	empty instant vector
`absent(up{job="prometheus"})`	empty instant vector
`absent(up{job="missing"})`	`{job="missing"} 1`
`absent(up{job=~"missing"})`	`{} 1`
`absent(non_existent)`	`{} 1`
`absent(non_existent{job="foo",env="dev"})`	`{job="foo",env="dev"} 1`
`absent(non_existent{job="foo",env="dev"} * 0)`	`{} 1`

`absent` is useful for detecting if an entire job has gone missing from service discovery. Alerting on `up == 0` doesn't work too well when you have no targets to produce up metrics! Even when using `static_configs` it can be wise to have such an alert in case generation of your *prometheus.yml* goes awry.

If you want instead to alert on specific metrics that are missing from a target, you can use `unless`, which was covered in "unless operator" on page 273.

`absent` has a range variant, `absent_over_time`. It returns an empty vector if the range vector passed to it has any elements, and a one-element vector with the value 1 if the range vector passed has no elements.

This is useful for alerting on when no time series exist for a given metric name and label combination for a certain amount of time.

The following query:

```
absent_over_time(up{job="myjob"}[1h])
```

would mean that the job myjob hasn't got any target for at least one hour.

Sorting with sort and sort_desc

PromQL generally does not specify the order of elements within an instant vector, so it can change from evaluation to evaluation. But if you use sort or sort_desc as the last thing that is evaluated in a PromQL expression, then the instant vector will be sorted by value. For example:

```
sort(node_filesystem_size_bytes)
```

might return:

```
node_filesystem_free_bytes{device="tmpfs",fstype="tmpfs",
    instance="localhost:9100",job="node",mountpoint="/run/lock"} 5238784
node_filesystem_free_bytes{device="/dev/sda1",fstype="vfat",
    instance="localhost:9100",job="node",mountpoint="/boot/efi"} 70300672
node_filesystem_free_bytes{device="tmpfs",fstype="tmpfs",
    instance="localhost:9100",job="node",mountpoint="/run"} 817094656
node_filesystem_free_bytes{device="tmpfs",fstype="tmpfs",
    instance="localhost:9100",job="node",mountpoint="/run/user/1000"} 826912768
node_filesystem_free_bytes{device="/dev/sda5",fstype="ext4",
    instance="localhost:9100",job="node",mountpoint="/"} 30791843840
```

The effect of these functions is cosmetic, but may save you some effort in reporting scripts. NaNs are always sorted to the end, so sort and sort_desc are not quite the reverse of each other.

 The instant vectors returned from the topk and bottomk aggregators already come with their samples sorted within the aggregation groups.

Histograms with histogram_quantile

The histogram_quantile function was already touched on in "Histogram" on page 233. It is internally a bit like an aggregator, since it groups samples together like a without(le) clause would and then calculates a quantile from their values. For example:

```
histogram_quantile(
    0.90,
    rate(prometheus_tsdb_compaction_duration_seconds_bucket[1d])
)
```

would calculate the 0.9 quantile (also known as the 90th percentile) latency of Prometheus's compaction latency over the past day. Values outside of the range from zero to one do not make sense for quantiles, and will result in infinities.

As discussed in "Cumulative Histograms" on page 54, the values in the buckets must be cumulative and there must be a +Inf bucket.

You must always use rate first for buckets exposed by Prometheus's histogram metric type, as shown in "The Histogram" on page 52, as histogram_quantile needs gauges to work on. But there are a very small number of exporters that expose histogram-like time series where the buckets are gauges rather than counters. If you come across one of these, it is OK to use histogram_quantile on them directly.

Counters

Counters include not just the counter metric, but also the _sum, _count, and _bucket time series from summary and histogram metrics. Counters can only go up. When an application starts or restarts, counters will initialize to 0, and the counter functions take this into account automatically.

The values of counters are not particularly useful on their own; you will almost always want to convert them to gauges using one of the counter-related functions.

Functions working on counters all take a range vector as an argument and return an instant vector. Each of the time series in the range vector is processed individually, and returns at most one sample. If there is only one sample for one of your time series within the range you provide, you will get no output for it when using these functions.

rate

The rate function is the primary function you will use with counters, and indeed likely the main function you will use from PromQL. rate returns how fast a counter is increasing per second for each time series in the range vector passed to it. You have already seen many examples of rate, such as:

```
rate(process_cpu_seconds_total[1m])
```

which returns a result like:

```
{instance="localhost:9090",job="prometheus"} 0.0018000000000000683
{instance="localhost:9100",job="node"} 0.005
```

rate automatically handles counter resets, and any decrease in a counter is considered to be a counter reset. So, for example, if you had a time series that had values [5,10,4,6], it would be treated as though it was [5,10,14,16]. rate presumes that the targets it is monitoring are relatively long-lived compared to a scrape interval, as it cannot detect multiple resets in a short period of time. If you have targets that are expected to regularly live for less than a handful of scrape intervals, you may wish to consider a log-based monitoring solution instead.

rate has to handle scenarios like time series appearing and disappearing, such as if one of your instances started up and then later crashed. For example, if one of your instances had a counter that was incrementing at a rate of around 10 per second, but was only running for half an hour, then a rate(x_total[1h]) would return a result of around 5 per second.

Values are rarely exact. Since scrapes for different targets happen at different times, there can be jitter over time, the steps of a query_range call will rarely align perfectly with scrapes, and scrapes are expected to fail every now and then. In the face of such challenges, rate is designed to be robust, and the result of rate is intended to be correct when looked at on average over time.

rate is not intended to catch every single increment, as it is expected that increments will be lost, such as if an instance dies between scrapes. This may cause artifacts if you have very slow-moving counters, such as if they're only incremented a few times an hour. rate can also only deal with changes in counters, because if a counter time series appears with a value of 100, rate has no idea if those increments were just now or if the target has been running for years and has only just started being returned by service discovery to be scraped.

It is recommended to use a range for your range vector that is at least four times your scrape interval. This will ensure that you always have two samples to work with even if scrapes are slow, ingestion is slow, and there has been a single scrape failure. Such issues are a fact of life in real-world systems, so it is important to be resilient. For example, for a 1-minute scrape interval you might use a 4-minute rate, but usually that is rounded up to a 5-minute rate.[7]

Generally you should aim to have the same range used on all your rate functions within a Prometheus for the sake of sanity, since outputs from rates over different ranges are not comparable and tend to be hard to keep track of.

You may wonder with all these implementation details and caveats if rate could be changed to be simpler. There are several ways you can approach this problem, but at the end of the day they all have both advantages and disadvantages. If you fix one apparent problem, you will cause a different problem to pop up. The rate function is a good balance across all of these concerns, and provides a robust solution suitable for operational monitoring. If you run into a situation where any rate-like function

---

[7] *Five-minute rate* is a colloquial way to say a rate function on a range vector with a 5-minute range, such as rate(x_total[5m]).

isn't giving you quite what you need, we would suggest continuing your debugging based on logs data, which does not have these particular concerns and can produce exact answers with the trade-off of a bigger price.

increase

increase is merely syntactic sugar on top of rate. increase(x_total[5m]) is exactly equivalent to rate(x_total[5m]) * 300, which is to say the result of rate multiplied by the range of the range vector. The logic is otherwise identical.

Seconds are the base unit for Prometheus, so you should use increase only when displaying values to humans. Within your recording rules and alerts it is best to stick to rate for consistency.

One of the outcomes of the robustness of rate and increase is that they can return noninteger results when given integer inputs. Consider that you had the following data points for a time series:

```
21 at 2s
22 at 7s
24 at 12s
```

and you were to calculate increase(x_total[15s]) with a query time of 15 seconds. The increase here is 3 over a period of 10 seconds, so you might expect a result of 3. However, the rate was taken over a 15-second period, so to avoid underestimating the correct answer, the 10 seconds of data you have is extrapolated out to 15 seconds, producing a result of 4.5 for the increase.

rate and increase presume that a time series continues beyond the bound of the range if the first/last samples is within 110% of the average interval of the data. If this is not the case, it is presumed the time series exists for 50% of an interval beyond the samples you have, but not with the value going below zero.

irate

irate is like rate in that it returns the per-second rate at which a counter is increasing. The algorithm it uses is much simpler though; it only looks at the last two samples of the range vector it is passed. This has the advantage that it is much more responsive to changes and you don't have to care so much about the relationship between the vector's range and the scrape interval, but comes with the corresponding disadvantage that as it is only looking at two samples, it can only be safely used in graphs that are fully zoomed in.[8] Figure 16-1 shows a comparison of a 5-minute rate against an irate.

---

8 If the step for a query_range is greater than the scrape interval, you would skip data when using irate.

Due to the lack of averaging that `irate` brings, the graphs can be more volatile[9] and harder to read. It is not advisable to use `irate` in alerts due to it being sensitive to brief spikes and dips; use `rate` instead.

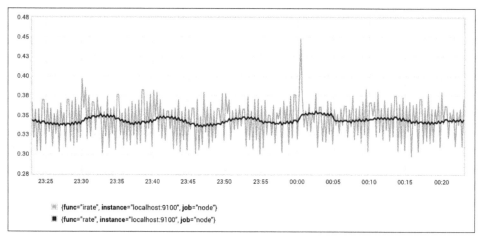

Figure 16-1. CPU usage of a Node Exporter viewed with `rate` and `irate`

resets

You may sometimes suspect that a counter is resetting more often than it should be. The `resets` function returns how many times each time series in a range vector has reset. For example, the expression:

```
resets(process_cpu_seconds_total[1h])
```

will indicate how many times the CPU time of the process has reset in the past hour. This should be the number of times the process has restarted,[10] but if you had a bug that was causing it to go backward, the value would be higher.

`resets` is intended as a debugging tool for counters, since counters might reset too often and nonmonotonic counters will cause artifacts in the form of large spikes in your graphs. However, some users have found occasional uses for it when they want to know how many times a gauge has been seen to decrease.

---

9 `irate` is short for *instant rate*, though that the function is called *irate* still brings Brian minor amusement.

10 `changes(process_start_time_seconds[1h])` is a better way to count restarts, as timestamps are gauges (*https://oreil.ly/EHfl0*).

Changing Gauges

Unlike counters, the values of gauges are useful on their own and you can use binary operators and aggregators directly on them. But sometimes you will want to analyze the history of a gauge, and there are several functions for this purpose.

As with the counter functions, these functions also take a range vector and return an instant vector with at most one sample for each time series in your input.

changes

Some gauges are expected to change very rarely. For example, the start time of a process does not change in the lifetime of a process.[11] The `changes` function allows you to count how many times a gauge has changed value, so:

```
changes(process_start_time_seconds[1h])
```

will tell you how many times your process has restarted in the past hour. If you aggregated this across entire applications, it would allow you to spot if your applications were in a slow crash loop.

Due to the fundamental nature of metrics sampling, Prometheus may not scrape often enough to see every possible change. However, if a process is restarting that frequently, you will still detect it either via this method or by up being 0.

You can use `changes` beyond `process_start_time_seconds` for other situations where the fact that a gauge has changed is interesting to you.

deriv

Often you will want to know how quickly a gauge is changing; for example, how quickly a backlog is increasing if it is increasing at all. This would allow you to alert on not only the backlog being higher than you'd like but also that it has not already started to go down.

You could do `x - x offset 1h`, but this only uses two samples, and thus lacks robustness because it is susceptible to individual outlier values. The `deriv` function uses *least-squares regression*[12] to estimate the slope of each of the time series in a range vector. For example:

```
deriv(process_resident_memory_bytes[1h])
```

---

11 Although there have been cases, such as in Prometheus bug report 289 (*https://oreil.ly/HW1KI*), where a cloud provider's kernel was providing bad metrics.

12 Also known as *simple linear regression*.

would calculate how fast resident memory is changing per second based on samples from the past hour.

predict_linear

predict_linear goes a step further than deriv and predicts what the value of a gauge will be in the future based on data in the provided range. For example:

```
predict_linear(node_filesystem_free_bytes{job="node"}[1h], 4 * 3600)
```

would predict how much free space would be left on each filesystem in four hours based on the past hour of samples. This expression is roughly equivalent to:

```
deriv(node_filesystem_free_bytes{job="node"}[1h]) * 4 * 3600
+
node_filesystem_free_bytes{job="node"}
```

but predict_linear is slightly more accurate because it uses the intercept from the regression.

predict_linear is useful for resource limit alerts, where static thresholds such as 1 GB free or percentage thresholds such as 10% free tend to have false positives and false negatives depending on whether you are working with relatively large or small filesystems. A 1 GB threshold on a 1 TB filesystem would alert you too late, but would also alert you too early on a 2 GB filesystem. predict_linear works better across all sizes.

It can take some tweaking to choose good values for the range and to determine how far to predict forward. If there was a regular sawtooth pattern in the data, you would want to ensure that the range was long enough not to extrapolate the upward part of the cycle out indefinitely.

delta

delta is similar to increase, but without the counter reset handling. This function should be avoided as it can be overly affected by single outlier values. You should use deriv instead, or x - x offset 1h if you really want to compare with the value a given time ago.

idelta

idelta takes the last two samples in a range and returns their difference. idelta is intended for advanced use cases. For example, the way rate and irate work is not to everyone's personal tastes, so using idelta and recording rules allows users to implement what they'd like without polluting PromQL with various subtle variations of the rate function.

holt_winters

The holt_winters function[13] implements *Holt-Winters double exponential smoothing*. Gauges can at times be very spiky and hard to read so some smoothing is often good. At the simplest you could use avg_over_time, but you might want something more sophisticated.

This function works through the samples for a time series, tracks the smoothed value so far, and provides an estimate of the trend in the data. Each new sample is taken into account based on the *smoothing factor*, which indicates how much old data is important relative to new data, and the *trend factor*, which controls how important the trend is. For example:

```
holt_winters(process_resident_memory_bytes[1h], 0.1, 0.5)
```

would smooth memory usage with a smoothing factor of 0.1 and a trend factor of 0.5. Both factors must be between 0 and 1.

Aggregation Over Time

Aggregators such as avg work across the samples in an instant vector. There is also a set of functions such as avg_over_time that apply the same logic, but across the values of a time series in a range vector. These functions are:

- sum_over_time
- count_over_time
- avg_over_time
- stddev_over_time
- stdvar_over_time
- min_over_time
- max_over_time
- quantile_over_time

---

13 It is possible this function is misnamed; see Prometheus issue #2458 (*https://oreil.ly/WTR0v*).

Two extra functions are not directly linked to aggregators:

- `present_over_time` acts like the `group` aggregator, returns the value 1 for any series matched by the range selector.
- `last_over_time` returns the last value for any series matched by the range selector.

For example, to see the peak memory usage that Prometheus saw for a process, you could use:

```
max_over_time(process_resident_memory_bytes[1h])
```

and even go a step further and calculate that across the application:

```
max without(instance)(max_over_time(process_resident_memory_bytes[1h]))
```

These functions only work from the values of the samples; there is no weighting based on the length of time between samples or any other logic relating to timestamps. This means that if you change the scrape interval, for example, there will be a bias toward the time period with the more frequent scrapes for functions such as `avg_over_time` and `quantile_over_time`. Similarly, if there are failed scrapes for a period of time, that period will be less represented in your result.

These functions are used with gauges.[14] If you want to take an `avg_over_time` of a `rate`, this isn't possible as that function returns instant rather than range vectors. However, `rate` already calculates an average over time, so you can increase the range on the `rate`. For example, instead of trying to do:

```
avg_over_time(rate(x_total[5m])[1h])
```

which will produce a parse error, you can instead do:

```
rate(x_total[1h])
```

How to use the instant vector output of functions as the input of functions that require range vectors is covered in the next chapter on recording rules.

---

14 Though as `count_over_time` and `present_over_time` ignore values, they can be useful for debugging any type of metric.

## CHAPTER 17

Recording Rules

The HTTP API is not the only way in which you can access PromQL. You can also use *recording rules* to have Prometheus evaluate PromQL expressions regularly and ingest their results. This is useful to speed up your dashboards, provide aggregated results for use elsewhere, and compose range vector functions. Other monitoring systems might call their equivalent feature standing queries or continuous queries. Alerting rules (covered in Chapter 18) are also a variant of recording rules. This chapter will show you how and when to use recording rules.

Using Recording Rules

Recording rules go in separate files from your *prometheus.yml*, which are known as *rule files*. As with *prometheus.yml*, rule files also use the YAML format. You can specify where your rule files are located using the `rule_files` top-level field in your *prometheus.yml*. For example, Example 17-1 loads a rule file called *rules.yml*, in addition to scraping two targets.

Example 17-1. prometheus.yml scraping two targets and loading a rule file

```
global:
  scrape_interval: 10s
  evaluation_interval: 10s
rule_files:
 - rules.yml
scrape_configs:
 - job_name: prometheus
   static_configs:
     - targets:
       - localhost:9090
 - job_name: node
   static_configs:
```

```
    - targets:
      - localhost:9100
```

Similar to the `files` field of `file_sd_configs`, as covered in "File" on page 142, `rule_files` takes a list of paths, and you can use globs in the filename. Unlike file service discovery, `rule_files` does not use inotify nor does it automatically pick up changes you make to rule files. Instead, you must either restart Prometheus or reload its configuration.

To ask Prometheus to reload its configuration, you can send it the `SIGHUP` signal using a command like:

```
kill -HUP <pid>
```

where `pid` is the process ID of Prometheus. You can also send an HTTP `POST` to the */-/reload* endpoint of Prometheus, but for security reasons this requires that the `--web.enable-lifecycle` flag is specified. If the reload fails, Prometheus will log this, and you will see the `prometheus_config_last_reload_successful` metric change to 0.

To detect bad configuration files or rules in advance, you can use the `promtool check config` command to check your *prometheus.yml*. This will also check all the rule files referenced by the *prometheus.yml*. You might have this as a pre-submit check or unit test that is applied before the configuration file is rolled out. If you want to check the syntax of individual rule files, you can use `promtool check rules`.

Rule files themselves consist of zero[1] or more groups of rules. Example 17-2 shows a rule file.

Example 17-2. rules.yml with one group containing two rules

```
groups:
 - name: example
   rules:
    - record: job:process_cpu_seconds:rate5m
      expr: sum without(instance)(rate(process_cpu_seconds_total[5m]))
    - record: job:process_open_fds:max
      expr: max without(instance)(process_open_fds)
```

You will notice that the group has a `name`. This must be unique within a rule file, and is used in the Prometheus UI and metrics. `expr` is the PromQL expression to be evaluated and output into the metric name specified by `record`.

---

1 Zero groups or zero rules in group is technically possible, but serves no purpose.

It is possible to specify an `evaluation_interval` for a group, but as with `scrape_interval` you should aim for only one interval in a Prometheus for sanity. You can also specify a set of labels in the `labels` field to be added to the output, but this is rarely appropriate for recording rules.[2]

Each rule in a group is evaluated in turn, and the output of your first rule is ingested into the time series database before your second rule is run. While rules within a group are executed sequentially, different groups will be run at different times just as different targets are scraped at different times. This is to spread out the load on your Prometheus.

Once your rules are loaded and running, you can view them on the Rules status page at *http://localhost:9090/rules*, as shown in Figure 17-1.

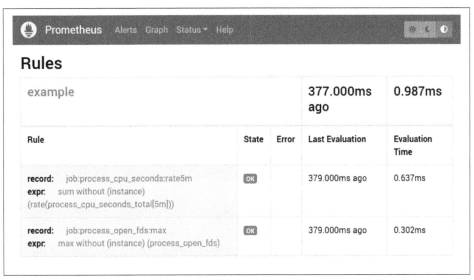

Figure 17-1. Rules status page of Prometheus

In addition to listing your rules, how long each group as a whole took to last evaluate and how long each rule took to execute are also displayed. You can use this to find expensive rules that may need adjustment or reconsideration. The `prometheus_rule_group_last_duration_seconds` metric will also tell you how long the last evaluation of each group took, which you can use to determine if there have been recent changes in the cost of your rules. There is no metric with the duration of individual rules as that could cause cardinality issues. In this case, the rules are taking less than a millisecond, which is well under the evaluation interval, so there is nothing to worry about.

---

2 However, `labels` is used in virtually all alerting rules.

There is no API to upload or change rules. As with Prometheus configuration generally, files are intended to be a base upon which you could build such a system on top of if you so wish.

When to Use Recording Rules

There are several cases when you might want to use recording rules. Recording rules are mainly used to aggregate metrics in order to make your queries more efficient. This is common for dashboards, federation, and before storing the metrics in long-term storage. You might also use recording rules to compose range vector functions, and on occasion offer APIs of metrics to other teams.

Reducing Cardinality

If you have an expression such as:

```
sum without(instance)(rate(process_cpu_seconds_total{job="node"}[5m]))
```

in a dashboard, you will find you get a prompt response from Prometheus if you have a few targets. As the number of targets grows to the hundreds and thousands, you will find that the response time for a `query_range` is not as snappy.

Rather than asking PromQL to access and process thousands of time series for the entire range of each graph on your dashboard, you can precompute this value using a rule group using something like:[3]

```
groups:
  - name: node
    rules:
      - record: job:process_cpu_seconds:rate5m
        expr: >
          sum without(instance)(
            rate(process_cpu_seconds_total{job="node"}[5m])
          )
```

which will output to a metric called `job:process_cpu_seconds:rate5m`.

Now you only need to fetch that one time series when your dashboard is being rendered. The same applies even if you have instrumentation labels in play, as you are reducing the number of time series to process by a factor of how many instances you have. Effectively, you are trading an ongoing resource cost against much lower latency and resource cost for your queries. Due to this trade-off it is not generally

---

3 The > here is one of the ways to have multiline strings in YAML.

wise to have rules that use long vector ranges, as such queries tend to be expensive, and running them regularly can cause performance problems.

You should try to put all rules for one job in one group. That way they will have the same timestamp and avoid artifacts when you do further math on them. All recording rules in a group have the same query evaluation time for an execution, and all output samples will also have that timestamp.

You will find aggregation rules like these are useful beyond making your dashboards faster. When using federation, as discussed in "Going Global with Federation" on page 360, you will always want to pull aggregated metrics, as otherwise you would be pulling in large swathes of instance-level metrics. At that point, the Prometheus using federation would be better off scraping the targets directly itself from a performance standpoint.[4]

Similar logic applies if you want to save some metrics on a long-term basis. When doing capacity planning over months or years of data, details of individual instances are not relevant. By keeping primarily aggregated metrics long term, you can save a lot of resources with little loss in useful information.[5]

You will often have aggregation rules based off the same metric but with different sets of labels. Rather than calculating each aggregation individually, you can be efficient by having one rule use the output of another. For example:

```
groups:
 - name: node
   rules:
    - record: job_device:node_disk_read_bytes:rate5m
      expr: >
        sum without(instance)(
          rate(node_disk_read_bytes_total{job="node"}[5m])
        )
    - record: job:node_disk_read_bytes:rate5m
      expr: >
        sum without(device)(
          job_device:node_disk_read_bytes:rate5m{job="node"}
        )
```

For this to work properly, the rules in a given hierarchy must be in order within a single rule group.[6] It is generally best to explicitly specify the job that your rules apply to in your selectors, so that your groups don't step on each others' toes.

---

4 Performance-wise, many small scrapes staggered over time are better than the samples from all those scrapes being combined into one massive scrape.

5 This can be done via federation, remote write relabeling, or you could delete time series you are no longer interested in via the API. As always, be careful when deleting metrics.

6 Prior to Prometheus 2.0 this approach was not practical. There was no notion of rule groups, so you couldn't guarantee that one rule would only run after another rule had completed.

Composing Range Vector Functions

As mentioned in "Aggregation Over Time" on page 295, you cannot use range vector functions on the output of functions that produce instant vectors. For example, `max_over_time(sum without(instance)(rate(x_total[5m]))[1h])` is not possible, and will produce a parse error. While PromQL features subqueries, you can use recording rules to the same effect:

```
groups:
  - name: j_job_rules
    rules:
      - record: job:x:rate5m
        expr: >
          sum without(instance)(
            rate(x_total{job="j"}[5m])
          )
      - record: job:x:max_over_time1h_rate5m
        expr: max_over_time(job:x:rate5m{job="j"}[1h])
```

This approach can be used with any range vector function, including not only the `_over_time` functions but also `predict_linear`, `deriv`, and `holt_winters`.

However, this technique should not be used with `rate`, `irate`, or `increase`, as an effective expression of `rate(sum(x_total)[5m])` would have massive spikes every time one of its constituent counters reset or disappeared.

 Always `rate` and then `sum`, never `sum` and then `rate`.

You are not required to have the outer function in a recording rule. With the preceding example it might make more sense to have the `max_over_time` performed as you need it. For example, the primary use for this particular example would be capacity planning, as you need to plan for peak rather than average traffic. Since capacity planning is often performed once a month or once a quarter, there is not much point in you evaluating the `max_over_time` at least once a minute rather than running the query just when you need it. Functions over longer time ranges can also get expensive due to the amount of data they have to process. Be careful with ranges over an hour and particularly across many time series.

Rules for APIs

Usually the Prometheus servers you run are going to be used entirely by you and your team. But you may run into situations where other teams wish to pull metrics from your Prometheus. If their usage is just informational or depends on metrics that are unlikely to change, that's generally OK, because if you break things on them it's not the end of the world. But if the metrics are being used as part of automated systems or processes outside of your control, it may be a good idea to create metrics just for other teams to consume as a form of public API. Then if you need to change the labels or rules inside your Prometheus you can do so, while still ensuring that the metrics the other team depends on keep the same semantics.

The naming of such metrics doesn't tend to follow the normal naming conventions, and you will typically put the name of the consuming team either in the metric name or a label.

Such uses of rules are quite rare. If another team's use of your Prometheus is getting to the stage where it is placing a nontrivial maintenance burden on you, you might want to ask them to run their own Prometheus for the metrics they need.

How Not to Use Rules

We have noticed a few common antipatterns with recording rules that we would like to help you avoid.

The first of these is rules that undo the benefits of labels. For example:

```
- record: job_device:node_disk_read_bytes_sda:rate5m
  expr: >
    sum without(instance)(
      rate(node_disk_read_bytes_total{job="node",device="sda"}[5m])
    )
- record: job_device:node_disk_read_bytes_sdb:rate5m
  expr: >
    sum without(instance)(
      rate(node_disk_read_bytes_total{job="node",device="sdb"}[5m])
    )
```

This would require you to have a rule per potential device label, and you cannot easily aggregate across these metrics. This basically defeats the entire purpose of labels, one of the most powerful features of Prometheus. You should avoid moving label values into metric names, and if you want to limit what time series are returned based on a label value, use a matcher at query time. Similarly do not move the job label into the metric name.

Another antipattern is preaggregating every metric an application exposes. While it is true that aggregation is a good idea to reduce cardinality for performance, it is counterproductive to overdo it. In a metrics-based monitoring system it is not uncommon to never use over 90% of your metrics,[7] so aggregating everything by default is a waste of resources and would require unnecessary maintenance as metrics

---

7 Brian has heard numbers around this mark from multiple monitoring systems.

are added and removed over time. Instead, you should add aggregation as you need it. Those other 90% of metrics are still accessible for when you end up debugging some weird issue in the bowels of your system, and the only cost of not aggregating them is that your queries on them will take slightly longer.

The primary purpose of recording rules is to reduce cardinality, so there is often not much point in having recording rules that still have an `instance` label in their output. Querying ten time series at query time isn't notably more expensive than querying one. If you have metrics with high cardinality within a target, recording rules with `instance` labels can make sense, though you should also consider if those instrumentation labels should be removed on cardinality grounds.

With rules such as:

```
- record: job:x:max_over_time1h_rate5m
  expr: max_over_time(job:x:rate5m{job="j"}[1h])
```

from the preceding section, you might be tempted to change their `evaluation_inter val` to an hour in order to save resources. This is not a good idea for three reasons. First, as the input metric came from a recording rule that already reduced cardinality, any resource savings will likely be tiny in the grand scheme of things. Second, Prometheus only guarantees that the rule will be executed once an hour, not when in the hour it will be executed. As you likely want results around the start of the hour, this, combined with staleness handling, will not work out. Third, for the sake of your sanity, you should aim for one interval inside your Prometheus servers.

The final pattern we would advise you to avoid is using recording rules to fix poor metric names and labels. This pattern loses the original timestamps of the data, and makes it harder to figure out where a metric came from and what it means. First, you should try improving the metrics at their source, and if that is not possible for technical or political reasons, consider whether using `metric_relabel_configs`, as described in "metric_relabel_configs" on page 164, to improve them is worth the downsides of them differing from what everyone else expects them to be named.

Unfortunately, there will always be cases where systems expose metrics that are too far outside the Prometheus way of doing things, and you have no choice but to fix them up however you can.

Naming of Recording Rules

By using a good convention for naming recording rules, you can not only tell at a glance what a given recording rule metric name means, but it will also be easier to share your rules with others due to a shared vocabulary.

As mentioned in "What Should I Name My Metrics?" on page 60, colons are valid characters to have in metric names but are to be avoided in instrumentation. The reason for this is so the user can take advantage of them to add your own structure in recording rules. The convention we use here balances precision and succinctness and comes from years of experience.

The way this convention works is to have your metric names contain the labels that are in play, followed by the metric name, followed by the operations that have been performed on the metric. These three sections are separated by colons, so you will always have either zero or two colons in a metric name. For example, given the metric name:

```
job_device:node_disk_read_bytes:rate5m
```

We can tell that it has `job` and `device` labels, the metric it is based off is `node_disk_read_bytes`, and it is a counter that `rate(node_disk_read_bytes_total[5m])` was applied to. These parts are the *level*, *metric*, and *operations*:

level

> The level indicates the aggregation level of the metric by the labels it has. This will always include the instrumentation labels (if they have not been aggregated away yet), the `job` label that should be present, and any other target labels that are relevant. Which target labels to include depends on context. If you have an `env` label across all your targets that doesn't affect your rules, then there's no need to bloat your metric names with it. But if a job was broken up by a `shard` label, you should probably include it.

metric

> The metric is just that—the metric or time series name. It's normal to remove the `_total` on counters to make things more succinct, but otherwise this should be the exact metric name. The benefits of keeping the metric name is that it is then easy to search your code base for that metric name, and vice versa if you are looking at code to find if the metric has been aggregated. For ratios you would use `foo_per_bar`, but there's a special rule for dealing with `_sum` and `_count` ratios.

operations

> The operations are a list of functions and aggregators that have been applied to the metric, the most recent first. If you have two `sum` or `max` operations, you only need to list one, as a sum of a sum is still a sum. Since sum is the default aggregation, you generally don't need to list it. But if you have no other operation to use, or haven't applied any operations yet, `sum` is a good default. Depending on what operations you plan on applying at other levels, `min` and `max` can make sense for a base metric name. The operation you should use for division is `ratio`.

To take some examples, if you had a `foo_total` counter with a `bar` instrumentation label, then aggregating away the `instance` label would look like:

```
- record: job_bar:foo:rate5m
  expr: sum without(instance)(rate(foo_total{job="j"}[5m]))
```

Going from there, to aggregate away the bar label would look like:

```
- record: job:foo:rate5m
  expr: sum without(bar)(job_bar:foo:rate5m{job="j"})
```

You can start to see some of the advantages of this approach. It is clear from inspection that the label handling is as expected here, as the input time series had job_bar as the level, bar was removed using a without clause, and the output had job as the level. In more complex rules and hierarchies this can be helpful to spot mistakes. For example, the rule:

```
- record: job:foo_per_bar:ratio_rate5m
  expr: >
    (
        job:foo:rate5m{job="j"}
      /
        job:bar:rate10m{job="j"}
    )
```

seems to be following the naming scheme for ratios, but there is a mismatch between the rate5m and the rate10m, which you should notice and realize that this expression and the resulting recording rule don't make sense. A correct ratio might look like:

```
- record: job_mountpoint:node_filesystem_avail_bytes_per_
           node_filesystem_size_bytes:ratio
  expr: >
    (
        job_mountpoint:node_filesystem_avail_bytes:sum{job="node"}
      /
        job_mountpoint:node_filesystem_size_bytes:sum{job="node"}
    )
```

Here you can see that the numerator and denominator have the same level and operations, which are propagated to the output metric name.[8] Here the sum is removed, as it doesn't tell you anything. This would not be the case if there was a rate5m operation in the input metrics.

Using the preceding notation for average event sizes would be a bit wordy, so instead the metric name is preserved and mean5m is used as the output operation as it is based on a rate5m and is thus a mean over 5 minutes:

---

8 Arguably, you could remove the _bytes here as it cancels out, but that might make it harder to find the original metrics in the source code.

```
- record: job_instance:go_gc_duration_seconds:mean5m
  expr: >
    (
        job_instance:go_gc_duration_seconds_sum:rate5m{job="prometheus"}
      /
        job_instance:go_gc_duration_seconds_count:rate5m{job="prometheus"}
    )
```

If you later saw the rule:

```
- record: job:go_gc_duration_seconds:mean5m
  expr:
    avg without(instance)(
      job_instance:go_gc_duration_seconds:mean5m{job="prometheus"}
    )
```

it would be immediately obvious that this is attempting to take an average of an average, which doesn't make sense. The correct aggregation would be:

```
- record: job:go_gc_duration_seconds:mean5m
  expr:
    (
        sum without(instance)(
          job_instance:go_gc_duration_seconds_sum:rate5m{job="prometheus"})
        )
      /
        sum without(instance)(
          job_instance:go_gc_duration_seconds_count:rate5m{job="prometheus"})
        )
    )
```

You should sum to aggregate, and only perform division for averaging at the last step of your calculation.

While the preceding cases are straightforward, like metric naming in general, once you get off the beaten track, recording rule naming can be more of an art than a science. You should endeavor to ensure that your recording rule names are clear in what their semantics and labels are, while also attempting to make it easy to tie back recording rule names to the code that produced the original metrics.

Aside from the very rare exception (see "Rules for APIs" on page 302), metric names should indicate the identity of a metric name so that you can know what it is. Metric names should not be used as a way to store annotations for policy.

For example, you should not feel tempted to add `:federate` or `:longterm` or similar to metric names to indicate that you want such and such a metric transferred to another system. This bloats metric names, and will cause problems when your policy changes. Instead, define and implement your policy via matchers when extracting the data, such as, say, pulling all metric names matching `job:.*`, rather than trying to micro-optimize which exact metrics will and won't be fetched. By the time a metric has been through a recording rule, it has likely been aggregated sufficiently that its cardinality is negligible, and thus it is probably not worth your time to worry about the resource costs downstream.

Now that you know how to use recording rules, the next chapter will look at alerting rules. Alerting rules also live in rule groups, and have a similar syntax.

## PART V

Alerting

If you want to be woken up at 3 a.m. by your monitoring system,[1] these are the chapters for you.

Building on the previous chapter, Chapter 18 covers alerting rules in Prometheus, which offer you the ability to alert on far more than simple thresholds.

Once you have alerts firing in Prometheus, the Alertmanager converts those into notifications while attempting to group and throttle notifications to increase the value of each notification, as explained in Chapter 19.

---

1 Hopefully when there's a true emergency.

Alerting

Back in "What Is Monitoring?" on page 4 we stated that alerting was one of the components of monitoring, allowing you to notify a human when there is a problem. Prometheus allows you to define conditions in the form of PromQL expressions that are continuously evaluated, and any resulting time series become alerts. This chapter will show you how to configure *alerts* in Prometheus.

As you saw from the example in "Alerting" on page 31, Prometheus is not responsible for sending out *notifications* such as emails, chat messages, or pages. That role is handled by the *Alertmanager*.

Prometheus is where your logic to determine what is or isn't alerting is defined. Once an alert is *firing* in Prometheus, it is sent to an Alertmanager, which can take in alerts from many Prometheus servers. The Alertmanager then groups alerts together and sends you throttled notifications (Figure 18-1).

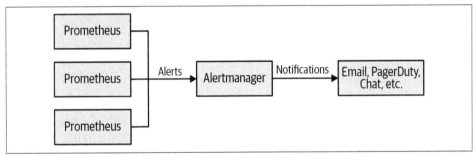

Figure 18-1. Prometheus and Alertmanager architecture

This architecture shown in Figure 18-1 allows you not only flexibility, but also the ability to have a single notification based on alerts from multiple different Prometheus servers. For example, if you had an issue propagating serving data to all of your datacenters, you could configure your alert grouping so that you got only a single notification rather than being spammed by a notification for each datacenter you have.

Alerting Rules

Alerting rules are similar to recording rules, which were covered in Chapter 17. You place alerting rules in the same rule groups as recording rules, and can mix and match as you see fit. For example, it is normal to have all the rules and alerts for a job in one group:[1]

```
groups:
 - name: node_rules
   rules:
    - record: job:up:avg
      expr: avg without(instance)(up{job="node"})
    - alert: ManyInstancesDown
      expr: job:up:avg{job="node"} < 0.5
```

This defines an alert with the name `ManyInstancesDown` that will fire if more than half of your Node Exporters are down. You can tell that it is an alerting rule because it has an `alert` field rather than a `record` field.

In this example we are careful to use `without` rather than by so that any other labels the time series have are preserved and will be passed on to the Alertmanager. Knowing details such as the job, environment, and cluster of your alert is rather useful when you get the eventual notification.

For recording rules, you should avoid filtering in your expressions, as time series appearing and disappearing are challenging to deal with. For alerting rules, filtering is essential. If evaluating your alert expression results in an empty instant vector, then no alerts will fire, but if there are any samples returned, each of them will become an alert.

Due to this, a single alerting rule like:

```
 - alert: InstanceDown
   expr: up{job="node"} == 0
```

automatically applies to every instance in the `node` job that service discovery returns, and if you had a hundred down instances you would get a hundred firing alerts. If on the next evaluation cycle some of those instances are back up, those alerts are considered *resolved*.

---

[1] If a group gets too large to be calculated in one interval, you may have to split it up if trimming it down is not an option.

An alert is identified across evaluation cycles by its labels and does not include the metric name label __name__, but does include an alertname label with the name of the alert.

In addition to sending alerts to the Alertmanager, your alerting rules will also populate two metrics: ALERTS and ALERTS_FOR_STATE. In addition to all the labels of your alert, an alertstate label is also added to ALERTS. The alertstate label will have a value of firing for firing alerts and pending for pending alerts, as discussed in "for" on page 314. Resolved alerts do not have samples added to ALERTS. While you can use ALERTS in your alerting rules as you would any other metric, we would advise caution as it may indicate that you are overcomplicating your setup.

The value of ALERT_FOR_STATE is the Unix timestamp when the alert started. That metric is used internally by Prometheus to restore the state of alerts after a restart.

 Correct staleness handling for resolved alerts in ALERTS depends on alerts always firing from the same alerting rule. If you have multiple alerts with the same name in a rule group, and a given alert can come from more than one of those alerting rules, then you may see odd behavior from ALERTS.[2]

If you want notifications for an alert to be sent only at certain times of the day, the Alertmanager does not support routing based on time. But you can use the date functions described in "minute, hour, day_of_week, day_of_month, day_of_year, days_in_month, month, and year" on page 284. For example:

```
- alert: ManyInstancesDown
  expr: >
    (
        avg without(instance)(up{job="node"}) < 0.5
      and on()
        hour() >= 9 < 17
    )
```

This alert will only fire from 9 a.m. to 5 p.m. UTC. It is common to use and as discussed in "and operator" on page 274 to combine alerting conditions together. Here we used on() as there were no shared labels between the two sides of the and, which is not usually the case.

---

2 This also applies to recording rules, but it is quite rare to have multiple recording rules with the same metric name in a group.

For batch jobs, you will want to alert on the job not having succeeded recently:

```
- alert: BatchJobNoRecentSuccess
  expr: >
    time() - my_batch_job_last_success_time_seconds{job="batch"} > 86400*2
```

As discussed in "Idempotency for Batch Jobs" on page 58, with idempotent batch jobs you can avoid having to care about or be notified by a single failure of a batch job.

for

Metrics-based monitoring involves many race conditions—a scrape may timeout due to a lost network packet, a rule evaluation could be a little delayed due to process scheduling, and the systems you are monitoring could have a brief blip.

You don't want to be woken up in the middle of the night for every artifact or oddity in your systems; you want to save your energy for real problems that affect users. Accordingly, firing alerts based on the result of a single rule evaluation is rarely a good idea. This is where the for field of alerting rules comes in:

```
groups:
- name: node_rules
  rules:
  - record: job:up:avg
    expr: avg without(instance)(up{job="node"})
  - alert: ManyInstancesDown
    expr: avg without(instance)(up{job="node"}) < 0.5
    for: 5m
```

The for field says that a given alert must be returned for at least this long before it starts firing. Until the for condition is met, an alert is considered to be pending. An alert in the pending state but that has not yet fired is not sent to the Alertmanager. You can view the current pending and firing alerts at *http://localhost:9090/alerts*, which will look like Figure 18-2 after you click on an alert name.

Prometheus has no notion of hysteresis or flapping detection for alerting. You should choose your alert thresholds so that the problem is sufficiently bad that it is worth calling in a human, even if the problem subsequently subsides.

We generally recommend using a for of at least 5 minutes for all of your alerts. This will eliminate false positives from the majority of artifacts, including from brief flaps. You may worry that this will prevent you from jumping immediately on an issue, but keep in mind that it will likely take you the guts of 5 minutes to wake up, boot up your laptop, log in, connect to the corporate network, and start debugging. Even if you are sitting in front of your computer all ready to go, it is our experience that once your system is well developed, the alerts you will handle will be nontrivial and it will take you at least 20–30 minutes just to get an idea of what is going on.

Figure 18-2. The Alert status page displays firing and pending alerts

While wanting to immediately jump on every problem is commendable, a high rate of alerts will burn you and your team out and greatly reduce your effectiveness. If you have an alert that requires a human to take an action in less than 5 minutes, then you should work toward automating that action as such a response time comes at a high human cost if you can even reliably react in less than 5 minutes.

You may have some alerts that are less critical or a bit more noisy, with which you would use a longer duration in the for field. As with other durations and intervals, try to keep things simple. For example, across all of your alerts a 5m, 10m, 30m, and 1h for are probably sufficient in practice and there's not much point in micro-optimizing by adding a 12m or 20m on top of that.

Because for requires that your alerting rule return the same time series for a period of time, your for state can be reset if a single rule evaluation does not contain a given time series. For example, if you are using a gauge metric that comes directly from a target, if one of the scrapes fails, then the for state will be reset if you had an alerting rule such as:

```
- alert: FDsNearLimit
  expr: >
    process_open_fds > process_max_fds * .8
  for: 5m
```

To protect against this gotcha you can use the _over_time functions, discussed in "Aggregation Over Time" on page 295. Usually, you will want to use avg_over_time, last_over_time, or max_over_time:

```
- alert: FDsNearLimit
  expr:
    (
```

```
      max_over_time(process_open_fds[5m])
    >
      max_over_time(process_max_fds[5m]) * 0.9
  )
for: 5m
```

The up metric is special in that it is always present even if a scrape fails, so you do not need to use an _over_time function. So if you were running the Blackbox Exporter, as covered in "Blackbox" on page 194, and wanted to catch both failed scrapes or failed probes,[3] you could use:

```
- alert: ProbeFailing
  expr: up{job="blackbox"} == 0 or probe_success{job="blackbox"} == 0
  for: 5m
```

Alert Labels

Just like with recording rules, you can specify labels for an alerting rule. Using labels with recording rules is quite rare, but it is standard practice with alerting rules.

When routing alerts in the Alertmanager, as covered in "Routing Tree" on page 327, you do not want to have to mention the name of every single alert you have individually in the Alertmanager's configuration file. Instead, you should take advantage of labels to indicate intent.

It is usual for you to have a severity label indicating whether an alert is intended to page someone, and potentially wake them up, or that it is a ticket that can be handled less urgently.

For example, a single machine being down should not be an emergency, but half your machines going down requires urgent investigation:

```
- alert: InstanceDown
  expr: up{job="node"} == 0
  for: 1h
  labels:
    severity: ticket
- alert: ManyInstancesDown
  expr: job:up:avg{job="node"} < 0.5
  for: 5m
  labels:
    severity: page
```

The severity label here does not have any special semantic meaning; it's merely a label added to the alert that will be available for your use when you configure the

---

3 While the Blackbox Exporter should return a response before it times out, things can always go wrong, such as the network being slow or the Blackbox Exporter being down.

Alertmanager. As you add alerts in Prometheus, you should set things up so you only need to add a `severity` label to get the alert routed appropriately, and rarely have to adjust your Alertmanager configuration.

In addition to the `severity` label, if a Prometheus can send alerts to different teams, it's not unusual to have a `team` or `service` label. If an entire Prometheus was only sending alerts to one team, you would use external labels (as discussed in "External Labels" on page 323). There should be no need to mention labels like `env` or `region` in alerting rules; they should already either be on the alert due to being target labels that end up in the output of the alerting expression, or will be added subsequently by `external_labels`.

Because all the labels of an alert, from both the expression and the `labels`, define the identity of an alert, it is important that they do not vary from evaluation cycle to evaluation cycle. Aside from such alerts never satisfying the `for` field, they will spam the time series database within Prometheus, the Alertmanager, and you.

Prometheus does not permit an alert to have multiple thresholds, but you can define multiple alerts with different thresholds and labels:

```
- alert: FDsNearLimit
  expr: >
    process_open_fds > process_max_fds * .95
  for: 5m
  labels:
    severity: page
- alert: FDsNearLimit
  expr: >
    process_open_fds > process_max_fds * .8
  for: 5m
  labels:
    severity: ticket
```

Note that if you are over 95% of the file descriptor limit, both of these alerts will fire. Attempting to make only one of them fire would be dangerous, because if the value was oscillating around 95%, then neither alert would ever fire. In addition, an alert firing should be a situation where you have already decided it is worth demanding a human take a look at an issue. If you feel this may be spammy, then you should try to adjust the alerts themselves and consider if they are worth having in the first place, rather than trying to put the genie back in the bottle when the alert is already firing.

Alerts Need Owners

Brian purposefully did not include a severity of `email` or `chat` in the examples. To explain why, let him tell you a story:

I was once on a team that had to create a team mailing list every few months. There was a mailing list for email alerts, but alerts sent there didn't always get the attention that was desired as there were just too many of them and responsibility was diffuse, which is to say it wasn't actually anyone's job to take care of them. There were some alerts considered important, but not important enough to page the on call engineer. So these alerts were sent to the main team mailing list, in the hope that someone would take a look. Fast forward a bit and the exact same thing happened to the team mailing list, which now had regular automated alerts coming in. At some point it got bad enough that a new team mailing list was created, and this story repeated itself, at which point this team had three email alert lists.

Based on this experience and that of others, I strongly discourage email alerts and alerts that are assigned to a team.[4] Instead, I advocate having alert notifications going to a ticketing system of some form, where they will be assigned to a specific person whose job it is to handle them. I have also seen it work out to have a daily email to the on call team members that lists all currently firing alerts.

After an outage it is everyone's fault for not looking at the email alerts,[5] but still not anyone's responsibility. The key point is that there needs to be ownership and not merely using email as logging.

The same applies to chat messages for alerts, with messaging systems such as IRC, Slack, and Telegram. Having your pages duplicated to your messaging system is handy, and pages are rare. Having nonpages duplicated has the same issues as email alerts, and is worse as it tends to be more distracting. You can't filter chat messages away to a folder you ignore like you do with emails.

Annotations and Templates

Alert labels define the identity of the alert, so you can't use them to provide additional information about the alert such as its current value as that can vary from evaluation cycle to evaluation cycle. Instead, you can use *alert annotations*, which are similar to labels and can be used in notifications. However, annotations are not part of an alert's identity, so they cannot be used for grouping and routing in the Alertmanager.

---

4 I am also strongly against any form of email that was not written by hand by a human going to team mailing lists, including from alerts, pull requests, and bug/issue trackers.

5 Invariably among the thousands of spam alerts that everyone ignored there was one alert that foreshadowed the outage. Hindsight is 20/20, but to spot that email you would have had to also investigate the thousands of irrelevant notifications.

The annotations field allows you to provide additional information about an alert, such as a brief description of what is going wrong. In addition, the values of the annotations field are templated using Go's templating system (*https://oreil.ly/x0tjn*). This allows you to format the value of the query to be more readable, or even perform additional PromQL queries to add additional context to alerts.

Prometheus does not send the value of your alerts to the Alertmanager. Because Prometheus allows you to use the full power of PromQL in alerting rules, there is no guarantee that the value of an alert is in any way useful or even meaningful. Labels define an alert rather than a value, and alerts can be more than a simple threshold on a single time series.

For example, you may wish to present the number of instances that are up as a percentage in an annotation. It's not easy to do math in Go's templating system, but you can prepare the value in the alert expression:[6]

```
groups:
  - name: node_rules
    rules:
      - alert: ManyInstancesDown
        for: 5m
        expr: avg without(instance)(up{job="node"}) * 100 < 50
        labels:
          severity: page
        annotations:
          summary: 'Only {{printf "%.2f" $value}}% of instances are up.'
```

Here $value is the value of your alert. It is being passed to the printf function,[7] which formats it nicely. Curly braces indicate template expressions.

In addition to $value, there is $labels with the labels of the alert. For example, $labels.job would return the value of the job label.

You can evaluate queries in annotation templates by using the query function. Usually you will want to then range over the result of the query, which is a for loop:

```
      - alert: ManyInstancesDown
        for: 5m
        expr: avg without(instance)(up{job="node"}) < 0.5
        labels:
          severity: page
        annotations:
          summary: 'More than half of instances are down.'
          description: >
```

---

6 For more advanced cases than this, you can consider using the and operator with the value for templating usage on the lefthand side and the alerting expression on the righthand side.

7 Despite the name, this is actually a sprintf as it returns the output rather than writing it out. This allows you to build up a query that is passed to the query function using printf.

```
Down instances: {{ range query "up{job=\"node\"} == 0" }}
  {{ .Labels.instance }}
{{ end }}
```

The value of the element will be in ., which is a single period or full stop character. So .Labels is the labels of the current sample from the instant vector, and .Labels.instance is the instance label of that sample. .Value contains the value of the sample within the range loop.

 Every alert that results from an alerting rule has its templates evaluated independently on every evaluation cycle. If you had an expensive template for a rule producing hundreds of alerts, it could cause you performance issues.

You can also use annotations with static values, such as links to useful dashboards or documentation:

```
- alert: InstanceDown
  for: 5m
  expr: up{job="prometheus"} == 0
  labels:
    severity: page
  annotations:
    summary: 'Instance {{$labels.instance}} of {{$labels.job}} is down.'
    dashboard: http://some.grafana:3000/dashboard/db/prometheus
```

In a mature system, attempting to provide all possible debug information in an alert would not only be slow and confuse the on call person, but would likely also be of minimal use for anything but the simplest of issues. You should consider alert annotations and notifications primarily as a signpost to point you in the right direction for initial debugging. You can gain far more detailed and up-to-date information in a dashboard than you can in a few lines of an alert notification.

Notification templating (covered in "Notification templates" on page 337) is another layer of templating performed in the Alertmanager. In terms of what to put where, think of notification templating as being an email with several blanks that need to be filled in. Alert templates in Prometheus provide values for those blanks.

For example, you may wish to have a playbook[8] for each of your alerts linked from the notification, and you will probably name the wiki pages after the alerts. You could add a wiki annotation to every alert, but any time you find yourself adding the same annotation to every alerting rule, you should probably be using notification templating in the Alertmanager instead. The Alertmanager already knows the alert's name

---

8 A playbook is a document or set of procedures that outlines the steps to be taken in response to a specific type of incident.

so it can default to `wiki.mycompany/Alertname`, saving you from having to repeat yourself in alerting rules. As with many things in configuration management and monitoring, having consistent conventions across your team and company makes life easier.

 Alerting rule `labels` are also templated in the same fashion as `annotations`, but this is only useful in advanced use cases, and you will almost always have simple static values for `labels`. If you do use templating on `labels`, it is important that the label values do not vary from evaluation cycle to evaluation cycle.

What Are Good Alerts?

In Nagios-style monitoring, it would be typical to alert on potential issues such as high load average, high CPU usage, or a process not running. These are all potential *causes* of problems, but they do not necessarily indicate a problem that requires the urgent intervention by a human that paging the on call person implies.

As systems grow ever more complex and dynamic, having alerts on every possible thing that can go wrong is not tractable. Even if you could manage to do so, the volume of false positives would be so high that you and your team would get burned out and end up missing real problems buried among the noise.

A better approach is to instead alert on *symptoms*. Your users do not care whether your load average is high; they care if their cat videos aren't loading quickly enough. By having alerts on metrics such as latency and failures experienced by users,[9] you will spot problems that really matter, rather than things that maybe might possibly indicate an issue.

For example, nightly cronjobs may cause CPU usage to spike, but with few users at that time of day you probably will have no problems serving them. Conversely, intermittent packet loss can be tricky to alert on directly, but will be fairly clearly exposed by latency metrics. If you have Service-Level Agreements (SLAs) with your users, then those provide good metrics to alert on and good starting points for your thresholds. You should also have alerts to catch resource utilization issues, such as running out of quota or disk space, and alerts to ensure that your monitoring is working.[10]

The ideal to aim for is that every page to the on call person, and every alert ticket filed, requires intelligent human action. If an alert doesn't require intelligence to

---

9 Users don't have to be customers of your company, such as if you are running an internal service within a company.

10 We will demonstrate this in detail in "Meta- and Cross-Monitoring" on page 373.

resolve, then it is a prime candidate for you to automate. As a nontrivial on call incident can take a few hours to resolve, you should aim for less than two incidents per day. For nonurgent alerts going to your ticketing system you don't have to be as strict, but you wouldn't want too many more than you have pages.

If you find yourself responding to pages with "it went away," that is an indication that the alert should not have fired in the first place. You should consider bumping the threshold of the alert to make it less sensitive, or potentially deleting the alert.

For further discussion of how to approach alerting on and managing systems we would recommend reading "My Philsophy on Alerting" (*https://oreil.ly/WYPVf*) by Rob Ewaschuk. Rob also wrote Chapter 6 of *Site Reliability Engineering* (Betsy Beyer et al, eds., O'Reilly), which also has more general advice on how to manage systems.

Configuring Alertmanagers in Prometheus

You configure Prometheus with a list of Alertmanagers to talk to using the same service discovery configuration covered in Chapter 8. For example, to configure a single local Alertmanager, you might have a *prometheus.yml* that looks like:

```
global:
  scrape_interval: 10s
  evaluation_interval: 10s
alerting:
  alertmanagers: ❶
    - static_configs:
        - targets: ['localhost:9093']
rule_files:
 - rules.yml
scrape_configs:
 - job_name: node
   static_configs:
     - targets:
       - localhost:9100
 - job_name: prometheus
   static_configs:
     - targets:
       - localhost:9090
```

❶ This section of the configuration is focused on setting up the discovery of the Alertmanagers.

Here the `alertmanagers` field works similarly to a scrape config, but there is no `job_name` and labels output from relabeling have no impact since there is no notion of target labels when discovering the Alertmanagers to send alerts to. Accordingly, any relabeling will typically only involve `drop` and `keep` actions.

You can have more than one Alertmanager, which will be further covered in "Alertmanager Clustering" on page 372. Prometheus will send all alerts to all the configured Alertmanagers.

The `alerting` field also has `alert_relabel_configs`, which is relabeling, as covered in "Relabeling" on page 149, but applied to alert labels. You can adjust alert labels, or even drop alerts. For example, you may wish to have informational alerts that never make it outside your Prometheus:

```
alerting:
  alertmanagers:
   - static_configs:
       - targets: ['localhost:9093']
  alert_relabel_configs:
   - source_labels: [severity]
     regex: info
     action: drop
```

You could use this to add `env` and `region` labels to all your alerts, saving you hassle elsewhere, but there is a better way to do this using `external_labels`.

External Labels

External labels are labels applied as defaults when your Prometheus talks to other systems, such as the Alertmanager, federation, remote read, and remote write,[11] but not the HTTP query APIs. External labels are the identity of Prometheus, and every single Prometheus in your organization should have unique external labels. `external_labels` is part of the `global` section of *prometheus.yml*:

```
global:
  scrape_interval: 10s
  evaluation_interval: 10s
  external_labels:
    region: eu-west-1
    env: prod
    team: frontend
alerting:
  alertmanagers:
   - static_configs:
       - targets: ['localhost:9093']
```

It is easiest to have labels such as `region` in your `external_labels` as you don't have to apply them to every single target that is scraped, keep them in mind when writing PromQL, or add them to every single alerting rule within a Prometheus. This saves you time and effort, and also makes it easier to share recording and alerting rules across different Prometheus servers as they aren't tied to one environment or even

---

11 Covered in "Going Global with Federation" on page 360 and "Long-Term Storage" on page 363.

to one organization. If a potential external label varies within a Prometheus, then it should probably be a target label instead.

Since external labels are applied after alerting rules are evaluated,[12] they are not available in alert templating. Alerts should not care which of your Prometheus servers they are being evaluated in, so this is OK. The Alertmanager will have access to the external labels just like any other label in its notification templates, and that is the appropriate place to work with them.

External labels are only defaults; if one of your time series already has a label with the same name, then that external label will not apply. Accordingly, we advise not having targets whose label names overlap with your external labels.

Now that you know how to have Prometheus evaluate and fire useful alerts, the next step is to configure the Alertmanager to convert them into notifications, the topic of the next chapter.

---

12 `alert_relabel_configs` happens after `external_labels`.

## CHAPTER 19

Alertmanager

In Chapter 18 you saw how to define alerting rules in Prometheus, which result in alerts being sent to the Alertmanager. It is the responsibility of your Alertmanager to take in all the alerts from all of your Prometheus servers and convert them to notifications such as emails, chat messages, and pages. Chapter 2 gave you a brief introduction to using the Alertmanager, but in this chapter you will learn how to configure and use the full power of it.

Notification Pipeline

The Alertmanager does more for you than blindly convert alerts into notifications on a one-to-one basis. In an ideal world you would receive exactly one notification for each production incident. While this is a stretch, the Alertmanager tries to get you there by providing you with a controllable pipeline for how your alerts are processed as they become notifications. Just as labels are at the core of Prometheus itself, labels are also key to the Alertmanager:

Inhibition

On occasion, even when using symptom-based alerting, you will want to prevent notifications for some alerts if another more severe alert is firing, such as preventing alerts for your service if a datacenter it is in is failing but is also receiving no traffic. This is the role of *inhibition*.

Silencing

If you already know about a problem or are taking a service down for maintenance, there's no point in paging the on call person about it. *Silences* allow you to ignore certain alerts for a while, and are added via the Alertmanager's web interface.

Routing

It is intended that you would run one Alertmanager per organization, but it wouldn't do for all of your notifications to go to one place. Different teams will want their notifications delivered to different places; and even within a team you might want alerts for production and development environments handled differently. The Alertmanager allows you to configure this with a *routing tree*.

Grouping

You now have the production alerts for your team going to a route. Getting an individual notification for each of the machines in a rack[1] that failed would be spammy, so you could have the Alertmanager group alerts and only get one notification per rack, one notification per datacenter, or even one notification globally about the unreachable machines.

Throttling and repetition

You have your group of alerts that are firing due to the rack of machines being down, and the alert for one of the machines on the rack comes in after you have already sent out the notification. If Alertmanager sent a new notification every time a new alert comes in from a group, that would defeat the purpose of grouping. Instead, the Alertmanager will throttle notifications for a given group so you don't get spammed.

In an ideal world all notifications would be handled promptly, but in reality the on call person or other system might let an issue slip through the cracks. The Alertmanager will repeat notifications so that they don't get lost for too long.

Notification

Now that your alerts have been inhibited, silenced, routed, grouped, and throttled, they finally get to the stage of being sent out as notifications through a *receiver*. Notifications are templated, allowing you to customize their content and emphasize the details that matter to you.

Configuration File

As with all the other configurations you have seen, the Alertmanager is configured via a YAML file often called *alertmanager.yml*. As with Prometheus, the configuration file can be reloaded at runtime by sending a SIGHUP or sending an HTTP POST to the */-/reload* endpoint. To detect bad configuration files in advance, you can use the amtool check-config command to check your *alertmanager.yml*.[2]

---

1 In datacenters, machines are typically organized in vertical racks, with each rack usually having its own power setup and a network switch. It is thus not uncommon for an entire rack to disappear at once due to a power or switch issue.

2 amtool can also be used to query alerts and work with silences.

For example, a minimal configuration that sends everything to an email address using a local SMTP server would look like:

```
global:
  smtp_smarthost: 'localhost:25'
  smtp_from: 'yourprometheus@example.org'  ❶

route:
  receiver: example-email

receivers:
 - name: example-email
   email_configs:
     - to: 'youraddress@example.org'  ❷
```

❶ The email address that will be used as the *From* field.

❷ The email address the emails will be sent to.

You must always have at least one route and one receiver. There are various global settings, which are almost all defaults for the various types of receivers. We will now cover the various other parts of the configuration file. You can find a full *alertmanager.yml* combining the examples in this chapter on GitHub (*https://oreil.ly/hQduB*).

Routing Tree

The `route` field specifies the top-level, *fallback*, or *default* route. Routes form a tree, so you can and usually will have multiple routes below that. For example, you could have:

```
route:
  receiver: fallback-pager
  routes:
   - matchers:
       - severity = page
     receiver: team-pager
   - matchers:
       - severity = ticket
     receiver: team-ticket
```

When an alert arrives, it starts at the default route and tries to match against its first *child route*, which is defined in the (possibly empty) `routes` field. If your alert has a label that is exactly `severity="page"`, it matches this route and matching halts, as this route has no children to consider.

If your alert does not have a `severity="page"` label, then the next child route of the default route is checked; in this case, for a `severity="ticket"` label. If this matches your alert, then matching will also halt. Otherwise, since all the child routes have failed to match, matching goes back up the tree and matches the default route. This is known as a *post-order tree transversal*, which is to say that children are checked before their parent, and the first match wins.

Next to the = operator in matchers, there are other operators like !=, =~, and !~ . =~ requires that the given label match the given regular expression, and !~ requires that it does not match the given regular expression. As with almost[3] all other places, regular expressions are fully anchored. For a refresher on regular expressions, see "Regular Expressions" on page 152.

You could use =~ if there were variants in what label values were used for a given purpose, such as if some teams used ticket, others used issue, and others had yet to be convinced that email was possibly not the best place to send notifications:

```
route:
  receiver: fallback-pager
  routes:
  - matchers:
      - severity = page
    receiver: team-pager
  - matchers:
      - severity =~ "(ticket|issue|email)"
    receiver: team-ticket
```

Multiple matchers can be used in the same route, and alerts must satisfy all of the match conditions.

 All alerts must match some route, and the top-level route is the last route checked, so it acts as a fallback that all alerts must match. Thus it is an error for you to use matchers on the default route.

Rarely will it just be one team using an Alertmanager, and different teams will want alerts routed differently. You should have a standard label such as team or service across your organization that distinguishes who owns what alerts. This label will usually but not always come from external_labels, as discussed in "External Labels" on page 323. Using this team-like label you would have a route per team, and then the teams would have their own routing configuration below that:

---

3 The reReplaceAll function in alert and notification templates (*https://oreil.ly/heUJc*) is not anchored, as that would defeat its purpose.

```
route:
  receiver: fallback-pager
  routes:
   # Frontend team.
   - matchers:
       - team = frontend
     receiver: frontend-pager
     routes:
       - matchers:
           - severity = page
         receiver: frontend-pager
       - matchers:
           - severity = ticket
         receiver: frontend-ticket
   # Backend team.
   - matchers:
       - team = backend
     receiver: backend-pager
     routes:
       - matchers:
           - severity = page
           - env = dev
         receiver: backend-ticket
       - matchers:
           - severity = page
         receiver: backend-pager
       - matchers:
           - severity = ticket
         receiver: backend-ticket
```

The frontend team has a simple setup, with pages going to the pager, tickets going to the ticketing system, and any pages with unexpected severity labels going to the pager.

The backend team has customized things a little. Any pages from the development environment will be sent to the backend-ticket receiver, which is to say that they will be downgraded to just tickets rather than pages.[4] In this way you can have alerts from different environments routed differently in the Alertmanager, saving you from having to customize alerting rules per environment. This approach allows you to only have to vary the external_labels in most cases.

---

4 Receiver naming is just a convention, but if your configuration does not result in the backend-ticket receiver creating a ticket, it would be quite misleading.

It can be a little challenging to come to grips with an existing routing tree, particularly if it doesn't follow a standard structure. There is a visual routing tree editor (*https://oreil.ly/KtvK-*) on the Prometheus website that can show you the tree and what routes alerts will follow on it.

Because such a configuration grows as you gain more teams, you may want to write a utility to combine routing tree fragments together from smaller files. YAML is a standard format with readily available unmarshallers and marshallers, so this is not a difficult task.

There is one other setting we should mention in the context of routing—continue. Usually the first matching route wins, but if continue: true is specified, then a match will not halt the process of finding a matching route. Instead, a matching continue route will be matched *and* the process of finding a matching route will continue. In this way an alert can be part of multiple routes. continue is primarily used to log all alerts to another system:

```
route:
  receiver: fallback-pager
  routes:
   # Log all alerts.
   - receiver: log-alerts
     continue: true
   # Frontend team.
   - matchers:
       - team = frontend
     receiver: frontend-pager
```

Once your alert has a route, the grouping, throttling, repetition, and receiver for that route will apply to that alert and all the other alerts that match that route. All settings for child routes are inherited as defaults from their parent route, with the exception of continue.

Grouping

Your alerts have now arrived at their route. By default, the Alertmanager will put all alerts for a route into a single group, meaning you will get one big notification. While this may be OK in some cases, usually you will want your notifications a bit more bite-sized than that.

The group_by field allows you to specify a list of labels to group alerts by; this works in the same way as the by clause that you can use with aggregation operators (discussed in "by" on page 251). Typically you will want to split out your alerts by one or more of alertname, environment, and/or location.

An issue in production is unlikely to be related to an issue in development, and similarly with issues in different datacenters depending on the exact alert. When alerting on symptoms rather than causes, as encouraged by "What Are Good Alerts?" on page 321, it is likely that different alerts indicate different incidents.[5]

To use this in practice, you might end up with a configuration such as:

```
route:
  receiver: fallback-pager
  group_by: [team]
  routes:
   # Frontend team.
   - matchers:
      - team = frontend
     group_by: [region, env]
     receiver: frontend-pager
     routes:
      - matchers:
         - severity = page
        receiver: frontend-pager
      - matchers:
         - severity = ticket
        group_by: [region, env, alertname]
        receiver: frontend-ticket
```

Here the default route has its alerts grouped by the team label, so that any team missing a route can be dealt with individually. The frontend team has chosen to group alerts based on the region and env labels. This group_by will be inherited by their child routes, so all their tickets and pages will also be grouped by region and env.

Generally, it is not a good idea to group by the instance label, since that can get very spammy when there is an issue affecting an entire application. However, if you were alerting on machines being down in order to create tickets to have a human physically inspect them, grouping by instance may make sense depending on the inspection workflow.

---

5 On the other hand, if you are following the RED method, a high failure ratio and high latency can occur together. In practice, one usually happens a good bit before the other, leaving you plenty of time to mitigate the issue or put in a silence.

You can disable grouping alerting in the Alertmanager by setting group_by to [...].[6] However, grouping is a good thing, because it reduces notification spam and allows you to perform more focused incident response. It is far harder to miss a notification about a new incident among a few pages than a hundred pages.[7]

If you want to disable grouping due to your organization already having something that fills the Alertmanager's role, you may be better off not using the Alertmanager and working from the alerts sent by Prometheus instead.

Throttling and repetition

When sending notifications for a group, you don't want to get a new notification every time the set of firing alerts changes as that would be too spammy. On the other hand, neither do you only want to learn about additional alerts that started firing many hours after the fact.

There are two settings you can adjust to control how the Alertmanager throttles notifications for a group: group_wait and group_interval.

If you have a group with no alerts and then a new set of alerts starts firing, it is likely that all these new alerts will not all start firing at exactly the same time. For example, as scrapes are spread across the scrape interval, if a rack of machines fails, you will usually spot some machines as down one interval before the others. It'd be good if you could delay the initial notification for the group a little to see if more alerts are going to come in. This is exactly what group_wait does. By default, the Alertmanager will wait 30 seconds before sending the first notification. You may worry this will delay response to incidents, but keep in mind that if 30 seconds matter, you should be aiming for an automated rather than a human response.

Now that the first notification has been sent for the group, some additional alerts might start firing for your group. When should the Alertmanager send you another notification for the group, now including these new alerts? This is controlled by group_interval, which defaults to 5 minutes. Every group interval after the first notification, a new notification will be sent if there are new firing alerts. If there are no new alerts for a group, you will not receive an additional notification.

Once all alerts stop firing for your group and an interval has passed, the state is reset and group_wait will apply once again. The throttling for each group is independent, so if you were grouping by region, then alerts firing for one region wouldn't make new alerts in another region wait for a group_interval, just a group_wait.

---

6 This is a YAML list composed of a string made of three dots.

7 A hundred pages would be a good-sized pager storm.

Let's take an example, where there are four alerts firing at different times:

```
t=  0  Alert firing {x="foo"}
t= 25  Alert firing {x="bar"}
t= 30  Notification for {x="foo"} and {x="bar"}
t=120  Alert firing {x="baz"}
t=330  Notification for {x="foo"}, {x="bar"} and {x="baz"}
t=400  Alert resolved {x="foo"}
t=700  Alert firing {x="quu"}
t=930  Notification for {x="bar"}, {x="baz"}, {x="quu"}
```

After the first alert the `group_wait` countdown starts, and a second alert comes in while you are waiting. Both these `foo` and `bar` alerts will be in a notification sent 30 seconds in. Now the `group_interval` timer kicks in. In the first interval there is a new `baz` alert, so 300 seconds (one group interval) after the first notification there is a second notification containing all three alerts that are currently firing. At the next interval one alert has been resolved, but there are no new alerts so there is no notification at `t=630`. A fourth alert for `quu` fires, and at the next interval there is a third notification containing all three alerts currently firing.

If an alert fires, resolves, and fires again within a group interval, then it is treated in the same way as if the alert never stopped firing. Similarly if an alert resolves, fires, and resolves again within a group interval, it is the same as if the alert never fired in that interval. This is not something to worry about in practice.

Neither humans nor machines are fully reliable; even if a page got through to the on call person and they acknowledged it, they might forget about the alert if more pressing incidents occur. For ticketing systems, you may have closed off an issue as resolved, but you will want it reopened if the alert is still firing.

For this you can take advantage of the `repeat_interval`, which defaults to 4 hours. If it has been a repeat interval since a notification was sent for a group with firing alerts, a new notification will be sent. That is to say that a notification sent due to the group interval will reset the timer for the repeat interval. A `repeat_interval` shorter than the `group_interval` does not make sense.

If you are getting notifications too often, you probably want to tweak `group_interval` rather than `repeat_interval` because the issue is more likely alerts flapping rather than hitting the (usually rather long) repeat interval.

The defaults for these settings are all generally sane, although you may wish to tweak them a little. For example, even a complex outage tends to be under control within 4 hours, so if an alert is still firing after that long, it is a good bet that either the on call person forgot to put in a silence or forgot about the issue and the repeated notification is unlikely to be spammy. For a ticketing system, once a day is generally frequent enough to create and poke tickets, so you could set `group_interval` and `repeat_interval` to a day. The Alertmanager will retry failed attempts at notification a few times so there's no need to reduce `repeat_interval` for that reason alone. Depending on your setup you might increase `group_wait` and `group_interval` to reduce the number of pages you receive.

All these settings can be provided on a per-route basis, and are inherited as defaults by child routes. An example configuration using these might look like:

```
route:
  receiver: fallback-pager
  group_by: [team]
  routes:
   # Frontend team.
   - matchers:
       - team = frontend
     group_by: [region, env]
     group_interval: 10m
     receiver: frontend-pager
     routes:
      - matchers:
          - severity = page
        receiver: frontend-pager
        group_wait: 1m
      - matchers:
          - severity = ticket
        receiver: frontend-ticket
        group_by: [region, env, alertname]
        group_interval: 1d
        repeat_interval: 1d
```

Receivers

Receivers take your grouped alerts and produce notifications. A receiver contains *notifiers*, which do the actual notifications. As of Alertmanager 0.24.0, the supported notifiers are email, PagerDuty, Pushover, Slack, Opsgenie, VictorOps, WeChat, AWS SNS, Telegram, and the webhook. Just as file SD is a generic mechanism for service discovery, the webhook is the generic notifier that allows you to hook in systems that are not supported out of the box.

The layout of receivers is similar to service discovery within a scrape config. All receivers must have a unique name, and then may contain any number of notifiers. In the simplest cases you will have a single notifier in a receiver:

```
receivers:
 - name: fallback-pager
   pagerduty_configs:
    - service_key: XXXXXXXX
```

PagerDuty is one of the simpler notifiers to get going with, since it only requires a service key to work. All notifiers need to be told where to send the notification, whether that's the name of a chat channel, an email address, or whatever other identifiers a system may use. Most notifiers are for commercial software as a service (SaaS) offerings, and you will need to use their UI and documentation to obtain the various keys, identifiers, URLs, and tokens that are specific to you, and where exactly you want the notification sent to. We are not going to attempt to give full instructions here, because the notifiers and SaaS UIs are constantly changing.

You might also have one receiver going to multiple notifiers, such as having the frontend-pager receiver sending notifications both to your PagerDuty service and your Slack channel:[8]

```
receivers:
 - name: frontend-pager
   pagerduty_configs:
    - service_key: XXXXXXXX
   slack_configs:
    - api_url: https://hooks.slack.com/services/XXXXXXXX
      channel: '#pages'
```

Some of the notifiers have settings that you will want to be the same across all your uses of that notifier, such as the VictorOps API key. You could specify that in each receiver, but the Alertmanager also has a globals section for these so you only need to specify in the case of VictorOps a routing key in the notifier itself:

```
global:
  victorops_api_key: XXXX-XXXX-XXXX-XXXX-XXXXXXXXXXXX

receivers:
 - name: backend-pager
   victorops_configs:
    - routing_key: a_route_name
```

Since each field like victorops_configs is a list, you can send notifications to multiple different notifiers of one type at once, such as sending to multiple Telegram chats:[9]

---

8 PagerDuty also has a Slack integration, which permits acknowledging alerts directly from Slack. This sort of integration is quite handy, and can also cover pages coming from sources other than the Alertmanager that are going to PagerDuty.

9 This is preferable to using continue as it is less fragile, and you don't have to keep multiple routes in sync.

```
receivers:
 - name: backend-pager
   opsgenie_configs:
    - teams: backendTeam    # This is a comma separated list.
   telegram_configs:
    - bot_token: XXX
      chat_id: YYY
    - bot_token: XXX
      chat_id: ZZZ
```

It is also possible for you to specify no receivers at all, which will not result in any notifications:

```
receivers:
 - name: null
```

However, it'd be better where possible for you not to send alerts to the Alertmanager in the first place, rather than spending Alertmanager resources on processing alerts just to throw them away.

The webhook notifier is unique in that it doesn't directly notify an existing paging or messaging system that you might already have in place. Instead, it sends all the information the Alertmanager has about a group of alerts as a JSON HTTP message and allows you to do what you like with it. You could use this to log your alerts, to perform an automated action of some form, or to send a notification via some system that the Alertmanager doesn't support directly. An HTTP endpoint that accepts an HTTP POST from a webhook notification is known as a *webhook receiver*.

 While it's tempting to use webhooks liberally to execute code, it's wise to keep your control loops as small as possible. For example, rather than going from an exporter to Prometheus to the Alertmanager to a webhook receiver to restart a stuck process, keeping it all on one machine with a supervisor such as Supervisord or Monit is a better idea. This will provide a faster response time, and generally be more robust due to fewer moving parts.

The webhook notifier is similar to the others; it takes a URL to which notifications are sent. If you were logging all alerts, you would use continue on the first route, which would go to a webhook:

```
route:
  receiver: fallback-pager
  routes:
   - receiver: log-alerts
     continue: true
   # Rest of routing config goes here.

receivers:
 - name: log-alerts
```

```
webhook_configs:
  - url: http://localhost:1234/log
```

You could use a Python 3 script such as in Example 19-1 to take in these notifications and process the alerts within.

Example 19-1. A simple webhook receiver written in Python 3

```python
import json
from http.server import BaseHTTPRequestHandler
from http.server import HTTPServer

class LogHandler(BaseHTTPRequestHandler):
    def do_POST(self):
        self.send_response(200)
        self.end_headers()
        length = int(self.headers['Content-Length'])
        data = json.loads(self.rfile.read(length).decode('utf-8'))
        for alert in data["alerts"]:
            print(alert)

if __name__ == '__main__':
    httpd = HTTPServer(('', 1234), LogHandler)
    httpd.serve_forever()
```

All HTTP-based receivers have a field called `http_config` which, similar to the settings in a scrape config as discussed in "How to Scrape" on page 162, allows setting a `proxy_url`, HTTP Basic Authentication, TLS settings, and other HTTP-related configuration.

Notification templates

The layouts of messages from the various notifiers are fine to use when starting out, but you will probably want to customize them as your setup matures. All notifiers except the webhook[10] permit templating using the same Go templating system (*https://oreil.ly/pY91X*) as you used for alerting rules in "Annotations and Templates" on page 318. However, the data and functions you have access to are slightly different, as you are dealing with a group of alerts rather than a single alert.

As an example, you might always want the `region` and `env` labels in your Slack notification:

```
receivers:
  - name: frontend-pager
```

---

10 For the webhook it is expected that the webhook receiver was specifically designed to work with the JSON message that is sent, so no templating of the webhook message sent is required. In fact, the JSON message is the exact same data structure that notification templates use under the covers.

```
slack_configs:
  - api_url: https://hooks.slack.com/services/XXXXXXXX
    channel: '#pages'
    title: 'Alerts in {{ .GroupLabels.region }} {{ .GroupLabels.env }}!'
```

This will produce a notification like the one you see in Figure 19-1.

Figure 19-1. A message in Slack with the region and environment

GroupLabels is one of the top-level fields you can access in templating, but there are several others:

GroupLabels

> GroupLabels contains the group labels of the notification, so will be all the labels listed in the group_by for the route that this group came from.

CommonLabels

> CommonLabels is all the labels that are common across all the alerts in your notification. This will always include all the labels in GroupLabels, and also any other labels that happen to be common. This is useful for opportunistically listing similarities in alerts. For example, if you were grouping by region and a rack of machines failed, the alerts for all the down instances might all have a common rack label that you could access in CommonLabels. However, if a single other machine in another rack failed, the rack label would no longer be in your CommonLabels.

CommonAnnotations

> CommonAnnotations is like CommonLabels, but for annotations. This is of very limited use. As your annotations tend to be templated, it is unlikely that there will be any common values. However, if you had a simple string as an annotation, it might show up here.

ExternalURL

> ExternalURL will contain the *external URL* of this Alertmanager, which can make it easier to get to the Alertmanager to create a silence. You can also use it to figure out which of your Alertmanagers sent a notification in a clustered setup. There is more discussion of external URLs in "Networks and Authentication" on page 368.

Status

> Status will be firing if at least one alert in the notification is firing; if all alerts are resolved, it will be resolved. Resolved notifications are covered in "Resolved notifications" on page 343.

Receiver

> The name of the receiver, which is frontend-pager in the preceding example.

GroupKey

> An opaque string with a unique identifier for the group. This is of no use to humans, but it helps ticketing and paging systems tie notifications from a group to previous notifications. This could be useful to prevent opening a new ticket in your ticketing system if there was already one open from the same group.

Alerts

> Alerts is the actual meat of the notification, a list of all the alerts in your notification.

Within each alert in the Alerts list there are also several fields:

Labels

> As you would expect, this contains the labels of your alert.

Annotations

> No prizes for guessing that this contains the annotations of your alert.

Status

> firing if the alert is firing; otherwise, it'll be resolved.

StartsAt

> This is the time the alert started firing as a Go time.Time object. Due to how Prometheus and the alerting protocol work, this is not necessarily when the alert condition was first satisfied. This is of little use in practice.

EndsAt

> This is when the alert will stop or has stopped firing. This is of no use for firing alerts, but will tell you when a resolved alert resolved.

GeneratorURL

> For alerts from Prometheus,[11] this is a link to the alerting rule on the Prometheus web interface, which can be handy for debugging. To us, the real reason this field exists is for a future Alertmanager feature that will allow you to drop alerts

---

11 For other systems it should be a link to whatever is generating the alert.

coming from a particular source, such as if there's a broken Prometheus that you can't shut down sending bad alerts to the Alertmanager.

You can use these fields as you see fit in your templates. For example, you may wish to include all the labels, a link to your wiki, and a link to a dashboard in all of your notifications:

```
receivers:
  - name: frontend-pager
    slack_configs:
      - api_url: https://hooks.slack.com/services/XXXXXXXX
        channel: '#pages'
        title: 'Alerts in {{ .GroupLabels.region }} {{ .GroupLabels.env }}!'
        text: >
          {{ .Alerts | len }} alerts:
          {{ range .Alerts }}
          {{ range .Labels.SortedPairs }}{{ .Name }}={{ .Value }} {{ end }}
          {{ if eq .Annotations.wiki "" -}}
          Wiki: http://wiki.mycompany/{{ .Labels.alertname }}
          {{- else -}}
          Wiki: http://wiki.mycompany/{{ .Annotations.wiki }}
          {{- end }}
          {{ if ne .Annotations.dashboard "" -}}
          Dashboard: {{ .Annotations.dashboard }}&region={{ .Labels.region }}
          {{- end }}

          {{ end }}
```

Let's break this down:

```
{{ .Alerts | len }} alerts:
```

.Alerts is a list, and the built-in len function of Go templates counts how many alerts you have in the list. This is about the most math you can do in Go templates as there are no math operators, so you should use alerting templates in Prometheus, as discussed in "Annotations and Templates" on page 318, to calculate any numbers and render them nicely:

```
{{ range .Alerts }}
{{ range .Labels.SortedPairs }}{{ .Name }}={{ .Value }} {{ end }}
```

This iterates over the alerts and then the sorted labels of each alert.

range in Go templates reuses . as the iterator, so the original . is shadowed or hidden while you are inside the iteration.[12] While you could iterate over the label key value pairs in the usual Go fashion, they will not be in a consistent order. The SortedPairs method of the various label and annotation fields sorts the label names and provides a list that you can iterate over:

---

12 To work around this, you can set a variable such as {{ $dot := . }} and then access $dot.

```
{{ if eq .Annotations.wiki "" -}}
Wiki: http://wiki.mycompany/{{ .Labels.alertname }}
{{- else -}}
Wiki: http://wiki.mycompany/{{ .Annotations.wiki }}
{{- end }}
```

Empty labels are the same as no labels, so this checks if the `wiki` annotation exists. If it does, it is used as the name of the wiki page to link; otherwise, the name of the alert is used. In this way you can have a sensible default that avoids you having to add a `wiki` annotation to every single alerting rule, while still allowing customization if you want to override it for one or two alerts. The {{- and -}} tell Go templates to ignore whitespace before or after the curly braces, allowing you to spread templates across multiple lines for readability without introducing extraneous whitespace in the output:

```
{{ if ne .Annotations.dashboard "" -}}
Dashboard: {{ .Annotations.dashboard }}&region={{ .Labels.region }}
{{- end }}
```

If a `dashboard` annotation is present, it will be added to your notification, and in addition, the region will be added as a URL parameter. If you have a Grafana template variable with this name, you will have it set to point to the right value. As discussed in "External Labels" on page 323, alerting rules do not have access to the external labels that usually contain things such as `region`, so this is how you can add architectural details to your notifications without your alerting rules having to be aware of how your applications are deployed.

The end result of this is a notification like the one shown in Figure 19-2. When using chat-like notifiers and paging systems, it is wise for you to keep notifications brief. This reduces the chances of your computer or mobile phone screen being overcome with lengthy alert details, making it hard to get a basic idea of what is going on. Notifications such as these should get you going on debugging by pointing to a potentially useful dashboard and playbook that have further information, not try to info dump everything that might be useful in the notification itself.

Figure 19-2. A customized Slack message

In addition to templating text fields, the destination of notifications can also be templated. Usually each of your teams has their own part of the routing tree and associated receivers. If another team wanted to send your team alerts, they would set labels accordingly to use your team's routing tree. For cases where you are offering a service, particularly to external customers, having to define a receiver for every potential destination could be a little tedious.[13]

Combining the power of PromQL, labels, and notification templating for alert destinations, you can go so far as to define a per-customer threshold and notification destination in a metric and have the Alertmanager deliver to that destination. The first step is to have alerts that include their destination as a label:

```
groups:
 - name: example
   rules:
    - record: latency_too_high_threshold
      expr: 0.5
      labels:
        email_to: foo@example.com
        owner: foo
    - record: latency_too_high_threshold
      expr: 0.7
      labels:
        email_to: bar@example.com
        owner: bar
    - alert: LatencyTooHigh
```

---

13 Alertmanager configuration is expected to change relatively rarely, as your label structure shouldn't change that often. Alerting rules, on the other hand, tend to have ongoing churn and tweaks.

```
      expr: |
        # Alert based on per-owner thresholds.
          owner:latency:mean5m
        > on (owner) group_left(email_to)
          latency_too_high_threshold
```

Here the different owners have different thresholds coming from a metric, which also provides an email_to label. This is fine for internal customers who can add their own latency_too_high_threshold to your rule file; for external customers you may have an exporter exposing these thresholds and destinations from a database.

Then in the Alertmanager you can set the destination of the notifications based on this email_to label:

```
global:
  smtp_smarthost: 'localhost:25'
  smtp_from: 'youraddress@example.org'

route:
  group_by: [email_to, alertname] ❶
  receiver: customer_email

receivers:
- name: customer_email
  email_configs:
    - to: '{{ .GroupLabels.email_to }}'
      headers:
        subject: 'Alert: {{ .GroupLabels.alertname }}'
```

❶ The group_by must include the email_to label that you are using to specify the destination, because each destination needs its own alert group. The same approach can be used with other notifiers. Note that anyone with access to Prometheus or the Alertmanager will be able to see the destinations since labels are visible to everyone. This may be a concern if some destination fields are potentially sensitive.

Resolved notifications

All notifiers have a send_resolved field, with varying defaults. If it is set to true then in addition to receiving notifications about when alerts fire, your notifications will also include alerts that are no longer firing and are now resolved. The practical effect of this is that when Prometheus informs the Alertmanager that an alert is now resolved,[14] a notifier with send_resolved enabled will include this alert in the next notification, and will even send a notification with only resolved alerts if no other alerts are firing.

---

14 Resolved alerts will have the annotations from the last firing evaluation of that alert.

While it may seem handy to know that an alert is now resolved, we advise quite a bit of caution with this feature as an alert no longer firing does not mean that the original issue is handled. In "What Are Good Alerts?" on page 321 we mentioned that responding to alerts with "it went away" was a sign that the alert should probably not have fired in the first place. Getting a resolved notification may be an indication that a situation is improving, but you as the on call still need to dig into the issue and verify that it is fixed and not likely to come back. Halting your handling of an incident because the alert stopped firing is essentially the same as saying "it went away." Because the Alertmanager works with alerts rather than incidents, it is inappropriate to consider an incident resolved just because the alerts stopped firing.

For example, machine down alerts being resolved might only mean that the machine running Prometheus has now also gone down. So while your outage is getting worse, you are no longer getting alerts about it.[15]

Another issue with resolved notifications is that they can be a bit spammy. If they were enabled for a notifier such as email or Slack, you could be looking at doubling the message volume, thus halving your signal-to-noise ratio. As discussed in "Alerts Need Owners" on page 318, using email for notifications is often problematic, and more noise will not help with that.

If you have a notifier with `send_resolved` enabled, then in notification templating, `.Alerts` can contain a mix of firing and resolved alerts. While you could filter the alerts yourself using the `Status` field of an alert, `.Alert.Firing` will give you a list of just the firing alerts, and `.Alert.Resolved` the resolved alerts.

Inhibitions

Inhibitions are a feature that allows you to treat some alerts as not firing if other alerts are firing. For example, if an entire datacenter was having issues but user traffic had been diverted elsewhere, there's not much point in sending alerts for that datacenter.

Inhibitions currently[16] live at the top level of *alertmanager.yml*. You must specify what alerts to look for, what alerts they will suppress, and which labels must match between the two:

---

15 Alerting approaches to detect this are covered in "Meta- and Cross-Monitoring" on page 373, but the salient point here is that you should be in a place where once an alert starts firing, it will get investigated.

16 They may move to per-route at some point (having them as a global setting increases the chances for an inhibition to accidentally suppress more than was intended).

```
inhibit_rules:
 - source_matchers:
     - severity = page-regionfail
   target_matchers:
     - severity = page
   equal: ['region']
```

Here, if an alert with a `severity` label of `page-regionfail` is firing, it will suppress all your alerts with the same `region` label that have a `severity` label of `page`.[17]

Overlap between the `source_match` and `target_match` should be avoided since it can be tricky to understand and maintain otherwise. Having different `severity` labels is one way to avoid an overlap. If there is overlap, any alerts matching the `source_match` will not be suppressed.

We recommend using this feature sparingly. With symptom-based alerting (as discussed in "What Are Good Alerts?" on page 321) there should be little need for dependency chains between your alerts. Reserve inhibition rules for large-scale issues such as datacenter outages.

Alertmanager Web Interface

As you saw in "Alerting" on page 31, the Alertmanager allows you to view what alerts are currently firing and to group and filter them. Figure 19-3 shows several alerts in an Alertmanager grouped by `alertname`; you can also see all of the alerts' other labels.

---

17 Using `match_re` in your routes makes it easier to have more specific `severity` labels like these, while still handling all pages in one route. If the source alerts are not meant to result in notifications, that would be a good use of a null receiver, as shown in "Receivers" on page 334.

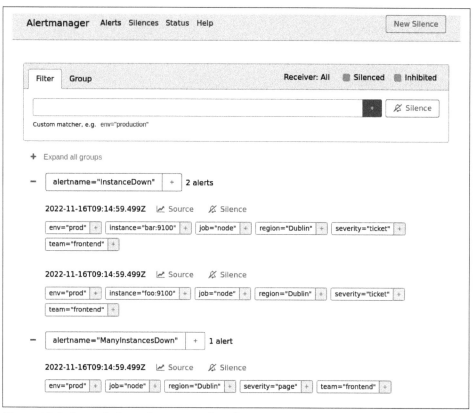

Figure 19-3. Several alerts showing on the Alertmanager status page

From the status page you can click New Silence to create a silence from scratch, or click the Silence link to prepopulate the silence form with the labels of that alert. From there you can tweak the labels you want your silence to have. When working with an existing alert you will usually want to remove some labels to cover more than just that one alert. To help track silences you must also enter your name and a comment for the silence. Finally, you should preview the silence to ensure it is not too broad, as you can see in Figure 19-4, before creating the silence.

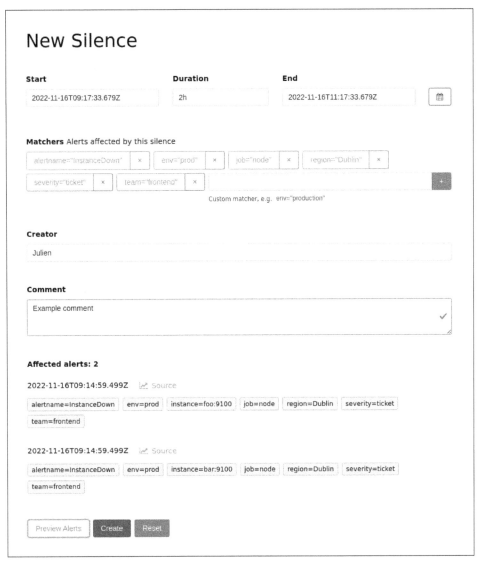

Figure 19-4. Previewing a silence before creating it

If you visit the Silences page, you can see all silences that are currently active, the ones that have yet to apply, and the silences that have expired and no longer apply (as shown in Figure 19-5). From here you can also expire silences that no longer apply and re-create silences that have expired.

Figure 19-5. The Alertmanager Silences page showing the active silences

Silences stop alerts with the given labels from being considered as alerting for the purposes of notification. Silences can be created in advance, if you know that maintenance is going to happen and don't want to pointlessly page the on call person, for example. As the on call, you will also use silences to suppress alerts that you've already known about for a while, so you are not disturbed while investigating. You can think of a silence like the snooze button on an alarm clock. When creating a silence, you have to enter a comment, which you can use to state the reason of the silence, so it is not forgotten or misunderstood.

If you want to stop alerts at a set time every day, you should not do so with silences, rather add a condition to your alerts that the hour function returns the desired value, as shown in "Alerting Rules" on page 312.

Now that you have seen all the key components of Prometheus, it is time to consider how they all fit together at a higher level. In the next chapter you will learn how to plan a deployment of Prometheus.

## PART VI

Deployment

Playing around with Prometheus on your own machine is one thing, deploying it on a real production system is a different kettle of fish.

Chapter 20 covers the built-in server-side security features available to secure your Prometheus server. Chapter 21 looks at the practicalities of running Prometheus in production and how to approach rolling it out.

Server-Side Security

In this chapter, you will learn about security features provided by Prometheus, such as TLS and Basic Authentication.

Security Features Provided by Prometheus

When operating Prometheus, many operators choose to use a reverse proxy to secure its endpoints. Indeed, the Prometheus server APIs are exposed over HTTP, which makes them easy to integrate into any HTTP-capable reverse proxy.

Prometheus itself supports server-side security, making it possible to either directly expose a secured version of Prometheus to the users or secure the traffic between Prometheus and these reverse proxies.

Server-side security as described in this chapter applies to the Prometheus server and most of the official exporters. The same command-line flags and options can be shared between these, so what follows applies to more than just Prometheus.

The options described in this chapter require a dedicated file, whose path can be passed as `--web.config.file`. On each request, the file is read, which means that it is not needed to reload Prometheus or the exporter to apply changes.

Enabling TLS

TLS is widely used in the network area to secure communications between clients and servers. Without going into too much detail, TLS enables the client to validate that the server they connect to is recognized by a known certificate authority (CA), and then encrypt the subsequent traffic. It is also possible to use TLS to authenticate clients by forcing them to also present a valid TLS certificate when connecting to the server.

To enable TLS on a Prometheus instance, you need to start by getting some certificates. In this example, we are using self-signed certificates. However, in real-world deployments, you should use your company's internal CA or public CA like Let's Encrypt, which will be directly recognized by your users.

First, create a self-signed CA with OpenSSL:

```
$ openssl req -new -newkey rsa:2048 -days 365 -nodes -x509 \
    -keyout prometheus.key -out prometheus.crt \
    -subj "/CN=localhost" -addext "subjectAltName = DNS:localhost"
```

This command created two files: *prometheus.key* and *prometheus.crt*.

To enable TLS with the certificate and private key you have just generated, create a *web.yml* file with the content shown in Example 20-1.

Example 20-1. web.yml

```
tls_server_config:
  cert_file: prometheus.crt
  key_file: prometheus.key
```

> You can check the validity of web configuration files with `prom` tool:
>
> ```
> $ ./promtool check web-config web.yml
> web.yml SUCCESS
> ```

Then, you can launch Prometheus with this file, using the following command:

```
$ ./prometheus --web.config.file web.yml
```

You can now access Prometheus with TLS using the following command:

```
$ curl --cacert prometheus.crt https://127.0.0.1:9090/metrics
```

As Prometheus usually scrapes itself, the scrape configuration will also need to be adapted in the main *prometheus.yml*, as in Example 20-2.

Example 20-2. prometheus.yml

```
scrape_configs:
  - job_name: 'prometheus'
    scheme: https
    tls_config:
      ca_file: prometheus.crt
    static_configs:
    - targets: ['localhost:9090']
```

Do not forget to reload the Prometheus configuration after adapting the scrape configuration, if needed:

```
$ killall -HUP prometheus
```

Advanced TLS Options

The TLS configuration of Prometheus offers other settings. In particular, you set client authentication with the settings shown in Example 20-3.

Example 20-3. web.yml

```
tls_server_config:
  client_auth_type: RequireAndVerifyClientCert
  client_ca_file: client_ca.crt
```

Other available settings include:

- `min_version` and `max_version`, which describe the minimum and maximum TLS version negotiated by the server. The versions are named TLS10, TLS11, TLS12, and TLS13, respectively, for TLS 1.0, 1.1, 1.2, and 1.3.

- `cipher_suites`, which describes the cipher suite used by the server. This option does not affect TLS 1.3.

- `prefer_cipher_suites`, which controls whether the server selects the client's most preferred cipher suite, or the server's most preferred cipher suite.

- `curve_preferences`, which lists the elliptic curves that will be used in an ECDHE[1] handshake, in preference order.

These configuration settings allow you to have complete control of the underlying TLS library.

Prometheus comes with secure default for those settings. It is unwise to change them if you don't know what you are doing as you could inadvertently compromise your security.

---

1 Elliptic Curve Diffie-Hellman Ephemeral

Enabling Basic Authentication

Basic Authentication mandates that every request made to a Prometheus server needs to be authenticated by a username and a password. It works by providing a list of users and hashed passwords to Prometheus, then validates every incoming request against that list.

Advanced authorization mechanisms such as restricting which pages a user can see or using other sources of users, such as OAuth or LDAP, are not supported by Prometheus. If you need to use such fine-grained settings, you have to put a reverse proxy in front of Prometheus. Thanks to TLS and Basic Authentication, you could make the reverse proxy authenticate itself on the backend, therefore still securing your Prometheus server while doing appropriate user management on the proxy.

Passwords are not provided in the Prometheus configuration as clear text. They are hashed, which means that if someone gets access to the configuration file, they will not be able to easily find out the password. Bcrypt is the password hash mechanism used by Prometheus.

 Basic Authentication sends the password in clear text in the HTTP headers. To prevent password interception, we highly recommend you use TLS to encrypt the traffic between the client and the server.

To add a user to our Prometheus server and enable Basic Authentication, the first step is to generate the hash for their password. Let's use `htpasswd` for this, but other tools are available as well:

```
$ htpasswd -nBC 10 "" | tr -d ':\n'
New password:
Re-type new password:
$2y$10$LbwE6OVsPc4PqDFaYwvw/uOkMMficVQrQjtY5KT/BGnAKPa0vK45C
```

In this example, the password I have chosen is *demo*.

 `10` is the bcrypt cost. Usually, the cost used should be between 10 and 12, with current computing power. Increasing this number will likely increase the security of the password at the expense of compute resources.

You can now use this password to update your *web.yml* file, as shown in Example 20-4.

Example 20-4. web.yml

```
tls_server_config:
  cert_file: prometheus.crt
  key_file: prometheus.key
basic_auth_users:
  julien: $2y$10$LbwE6OVsPc4PqDFaYwvw/uOkMMficVQrQjtY5KT/BGnAKPa0vK45C
```

You have configured a user *julien* with a password *demo*, in a Prometheus server protected with a TLS certificate. To use the credentials, open *http://127.0.0.1:9090* in your web browser. A prompt should ask for the username and password—enter **julien** and **demo**. You should get access to the web interface of your Prometheus server.

Prometheus itself will need to be configured to scrape itself using Basic Authentication, as in Example 20-5.

Example 20-5. prometheus.yml

```
scrape_configs:
  - job_name: 'prometheus'
    scheme: https
    tls_config:
      ca_file: prometheus.crt
    basic_auth:
      username: julien
      password: demo
    - targets: ['localhost:9090']
```

You can also pass a username using cURL:

```
$ curl --cacert prometheus.crt -u julien:demo https://127.0.0.1:9090/metrics
```

Now that you've learned how to secure your Prometheus server, we'll explore deploying it in a production environment in the upcoming chapter.

## CHAPTER 21

Putting It All Together

In the preceding chapters you learned about all the components in a Prometheus setup: instrumentation, dashboards, service discovery, exporters, PromQL, alerts, and the Alertmanager. In this final chapter you will learn how to bring all of these together and plan a Prometheus deployment and maintain it in the future.

Planning a Rollout

When you are considering a new technology, it's best to start the rollout[1] with something small that doesn't take too much effort, nor prematurely commit you to doing a complete rollout. When starting with Prometheus in an existing system, we recommend you start by running the Node Exporter[2] and Prometheus. You already ran both of these in Chapter 2.

The Node Exporter covers all the machine-level metrics that might be used from other monitoring systems, and then quite a few more, as was covered in Chapter 7. At this stage you will have a wide variety of metrics for little effort, and you should get comfortable with Prometheus, set up some dashboards, and maybe even do some alerting.

Next, we'd suggest looking at what third-party systems you are using and which exporters exist for them and start deploying those. For example, if you have network devices, you can run the SNMP Exporter; if you have JVM-based applications such as Kafka or Cassandra, you would use the JMX Exporter; and if you want blackbox monitoring, you might use the Blackbox Exporter, as covered in Chapter 10. The goal

---

1 A rollout is the process of releasing a new version of a software application or system to users.

2 If you are on Windows, use the Windows Exporter instead of the Node Exporter.

at this stage is to gain metrics about as many different parts of your system as you can with as little effort as possible.

By now you will be comfortable with Prometheus, and will have figured out your approach to aspects such as service discovery, as discussed in Chapter 8. You could have done all the previous steps of the rollout alone. The next step is to start instrumenting your organization's own applications, as covered in Chapter 3, which will likely involve asking other people to also get involved and commit time to monitoring. Being able to demonstrate all of the monitoring and dashboards[3] you have set up so far (which are backed by exporters) will make it quite a bit easier to sell others on using Prometheus; extensively instrumenting all your code as step one would be unlikely to get buy-in.

As before, when adding instrumentation you want to start with metrics that give you the biggest gains. Look for chokepoints in your applications that significant proportions of traffic go through. For example, if you have common HTTP libraries that all of your applications use to communicate with each other and you instrument them with the basic RED metrics, as covered in "Service instrumentation" on page 57, you will get the key performance metrics for large swaths of your online serving systems from just one instrumentation change.

If you have existing instrumentation from another monitoring system, you can deploy integrations such as the StatsD and Graphite Exporters, discussed in Chapter 11, to take advantage of what you already have. Over time you should look to not only transition entirely to Prometheus instrumentation, as covered in Chapter 3, but also to further instrument your applications.

As your usage of Prometheus grows to cover more and more of your monitoring and metrics-monitoring needs, you should start turning down other monitoring systems that are no longer needed. It's not unusual for a company to end up with 10+ different monitoring systems over time, so consolidating where practical is always beneficial.

This plan is a general guideline, which you can and should adapt to your circumstances. For example, if you are a developer you might jump straight to instrumenting your applications. You might even add a client library to your application with no instrumentation yet in order to take advantage of the out-of-the-box metrics such as CPU usage and garbage collection.

---

3 We continue to be amazed by the seductive power of a pretty dashboard, especially over other factors such as if the metrics in the dashboard are in any way useful. Do not underestimate this when trying to convince others to use Prometheus.

Growing Prometheus

Usually you start out with one Prometheus server per datacenter. Prometheus is intended to be run on the same network as what it is monitoring, because this reduces the ways in which things can fail, aligns failure domains, and provides low-latency, high-bandwidth network access to the targets that Prometheus is scraping.[4]

A single Prometheus is quite efficient, so you can likely get away with one Prometheus for an entire datacenter's monitoring needs for longer than you'd think. At some point though, operational overhead, performance, or just social considerations will lead you to start splitting out parts of the Prometheus to separate Prometheus servers. For example, it is common to have separate Prometheus servers for network, infrastructure, and application monitoring. This is known as *vertical sharding* and it is the best way to scale Prometheus.

Longer term, you may have every team run their own Prometheus servers, empowering them to choose what target labels and scrape intervals make sense for them (as discussed in Chapter 8). You could also run the servers for teams as a shared service, but you must be prepared for teams getting overenthusiastic with labels.

A pattern Brian has seen play out many times is that when starting out it is a struggle to convince teams that they should instrument their own code or deploy exporters. At some point though, it'll click, and they will understand the power of labels. Within a short period of time you will likely find that your Prometheus server has performance issues due to metrics with a cardinality that is far beyond what it is reasonable to use in a metrics-based monitoring system (as discussed in "Cardinality" on page 99). If you are running Prometheus as a shared service and the team consuming these metrics is not the one getting paged, it can be difficult to convince them that they need to cut back on cardinality. But if they run their own Prometheus and are the ones getting woken up at 3 a.m., they are likely going to be more realistic about what belongs in a metrics-based monitoring system and what belongs in a logs-based system.

If your team has particularly large systems, they may end up with multiple Prometheus servers per datacenter. An infrastructure team may end up with one Prometheus for Node Exporters, one for reverse proxies, and one for everything else. For ease of management, it is normal to run Prometheus servers inside each of your Kubernetes clusters rather than trying to monitor them from outside.

---

[4] Monitoring across failure domain boundaries, such as across datacenters, is possible but messy as you introduce a whole slew of network-related failure modes. If you have hundreds of tiny datacenters with only a handful of machines each, one Prometheus per region/continent can be an acceptable trade-off.

Where you start and end up on this spectrum of setups will depend on your scale and the culture within your organization. It is our experience that social factors[5] usually result in Prometheus servers being split out before any performance concerns arise.

Going Global with Federation

With a Prometheus per datacenter, how do you perform global aggregations?

Reliability is a key property of a good monitoring system, and a core value of Prometheus. When it comes to graphing and alerting, you want as few moving parts as possible because a simple system is a reliable system. When you want a graph of application latency in a datacenter, you have Grafana talk to the Prometheus in that datacenter that is scraping that application, and similarly for alerting on per-datacenter application latency.

This doesn't quite work for global latency, since each of your datacenter Prometheus servers only has a part of the data. This is where *federation* comes in. Federation allows you to have a global Prometheus that pulls aggregated metrics from your datacenter Prometheus servers, as shown in Figure 21-1.

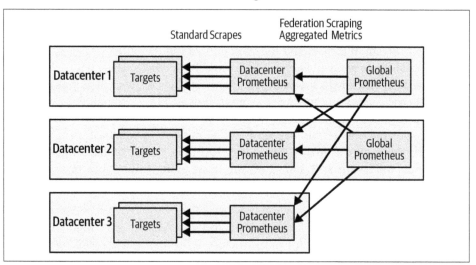

Figure 21-1. Global federation architecture

For example, to pull in all metrics aggregated to the job level, you could have a *prometheus.yml* like:

---

5 For example, it is sane only to have one target label hierarchy within a Prometheus. If a team has a different idea of what a region is than everyone else, they should run their own Prometheus.

```
scrape_configs:
  - job_name: 'federate'
    honor_labels: true
    metrics_path: '/federate'
    params:
      'match[]':
        - '{__name__=~"job:.*"}'
    static_configs:
      - targets:
          - 'prometheus-dublin:9090'
          - 'prometheus-berlin:9090'
          - 'prometheus-new-york:9090'
```

The */federate* HTTP endpoint on Prometheus takes a list of selectors (covered in "Selectors" on page 235) in match[] URL parameters. It will return all matching time series following instant vector selector semantics, including staleness, as discussed in "Instant Vector" on page 237. If you supply multiple match[] parameters, a sample will be returned if it matches any of them. To avoid the aggregated metrics having the instance label of the Prometheus target, honor_labels (which was discussed in "Label Clashes and honor_labels" on page 166) is used here.[6] The external labels of the Prometheus (as discussed in "External Labels" on page 323) are also added to the federated metrics, so you can tell where each time series came from.

 Unfortunately, some users use federation for purposes other than pulling in aggregated metrics. To avoid falling into this trap, you should understand the following:

- Federation is not for copying the content of entire Prometheus servers.

- Federation is not a way to have one Prometheus proxy another Prometheus.

- You should not use federation to pull metrics with an instance label.

Let us explain why you should not use federation beyond its intended use case. First, for reliability you want to have as few moving parts as is practical. Pulling all your metrics over the internet to a global Prometheus from where you can then graph and alert on them means that internet connectivity to another datacenter is now a hard dependency on your per-datacenter monitoring working. In general, you want to align your failure domains, so that graphing and alerting for a datacenter do not depend on another datacenter being operational. That is, as far as is practical you

---

6 The */federate* endpoint automatically includes an empty instance label in its output for any metrics lacking an instance label, in the same way the Pushgateway does, as mentioned in "Pushgateway" on page 76.

want the Prometheus that is scraping a set of targets to also be the one sending alerts for that target. This is particularly important if there is a network outage or partition.

The second issue is scaling. For reliability, each Prometheus is standalone and running on one machine and thus limited by machine size in terms of how much it can handle. Prometheus is quite efficient, so even limited to a single machine, it is quite plausible for you to have a single Prometheus server monitor an entire datacenter. As you add datacenters you just need to turn up a Prometheus in each of them. A global Prometheus pulling in only aggregated metrics will have greatly reduced cardinality data to deal with compared with the datacenter Prometheus servers,[7] and thus will prevent bottlenecks. Conversely, if the global Prometheus was pulling in all metrics from each datacenter Prometheus, the global Prometheus would become the bottleneck and greatly limit your ability to scale. Put another way, for federation to scale you need to use the same approach discussed in "Reducing Cardinality" on page 300 for dashboards.

Thirdly, Prometheus is designed to scrape many thousands of small to medium size targets.[8] By spreading the scrapes over the scrape interval, Prometheus can keep up with the data volumes with even load. If you instead have it scrape a handful of targets with massive numbers of time series, such as massive federation endpoints, this can cause load spikes and it may not even be possible for Prometheus to complete processing of one massive scrape worth of data in time to start the next scrape.

The fourth issue is semantics. By passing all the data through an extra Prometheus, additional race conditions will be introduced. You would see increased artifacts in your graphs, and you would not get the benefit of the staleness handling the semantics.

One objection to this architecture is if all your metrics don't end up in one Prometheus, how will you know which Prometheus contains a given metric? This turns out not to be an issue in practice. As your Prometheus servers will tend to follow your general architecture, it is usually quite obvious which Prometheus monitors which targets and thus which has a specific metric. For example, Node Exporter metrics for Dublin are going to be in the Dublin infrastructure Prometheus. Grafana supports both data source templating and having graphs with metrics from different data sources on them, so this is not an issue for dashboards either.

Usually you will only have a two-level federation hierarchy with datacenter Prometheus servers and globals. The global Prometheus will perform calculations with

---

7 Let's say that you were aggregating up every metric from an application with a hundred instances and a global Prometheus was pulling these aggregated metrics. For the same resources that a datacenter Prometheus uses, the global Prometheus could federate metrics from a hundred datacenters. In reality the global Prometheus can handle far more, as not all metrics would be aggregated.

8 There are no exact numbers, but we would consider 10,000 time series as starting to get large.

PromQL that you cannot do in a lower-level Prometheus, such as how much traffic you are receiving globally.

It is also possible that you will end up with an additional level. For example, it's normal to run a Prometheus inside each Kubernetes cluster you have. If you had multiple Kubernetes clusters in a datacenter, you might federate their aggregated metrics to a per-datacenter Prometheus before then federating them from there to your global Prometheus.

Another use for federation is to pull limited aggregated metrics from another team's Prometheus. It is polite to ask first, and if this becomes a common or more formal thing, the considerations in "Rules for APIs" on page 302 may apply. There is no need to do this just for dashboards though, as Grafana supports using multiple data sources in a dashboard and in a panel.

Long-Term Storage

In "What Is Monitoring?" on page 4 we mentioned that monitoring was alerting, debugging, trending, and plumbing. For most alerting, debugging, and plumbing, days to weeks of data is usually more than enough.[9] But when it comes to trending, such as capacity planning, it's usual for you to want years of data.

One approach to long-term storage is to treat Prometheus like a traditional database and take regular backups that you can restore from in the event of failure. A Prometheus ingesting 10,000 samples per second with a conservative 2 bytes per sample would use a bit under 600 GB of disk space per year, which would fit on a modern machine.

Backups can be taken by sending an HTTP POST to the */api/v1/admin/tsdb/snapshot* endpoint, which will return the name of the snapshot created under Prometheus's storage directory. This uses hard links, so it doesn't consume much additional disk space as the data is stored only once between the snapshot and Prometheus's own database. After you are done with a snapshot, it is best to delete it to avoid using more disk space than is needed. To restore from a snapshot, replace the Prometheus storage directory with the snapshot.

Only a tiny proportion of your metrics will be interesting to you for long-term trending, usually the aggregated metrics. It's usually not worth keeping everything forever, so you can save a lot of storage space by only keeping metrics from a global Prometheus long term[10] or deleting nonaggregated metrics before a certain time.

---

9 Indeed, Brian has heard various different monitoring systems report that around 90% of metrics data is not used after the first 24 hours. The problem, of course, is knowing in advance which 90% you'll never need again.

The */api/v1/admin/tsdb/delete* HTTP endpoint takes selectors in its `match[]` URL parameter[11] and has `start` and `end` parameters to restrict the time range. Data will be deleted from disk at the next compaction. It would be reasonable to delete old data, say, once a month.

For security reasons, both the snapshot and delete APIs require the `--web.enable-admin-api` flag to be passed to Prometheus for them to be enabled.

Another approach is to send your samples from Prometheus to some form of clustered storage system that can use the resources of many machines. *Remote write* sends samples as they are ingested to another system. *Remote read* allows PromQL to transparently use samples from another system, as if they were stored locally within the Prometheus. These are both configured at the top level of *prometheus.yml*:

```
remote_write:
  - url: http://localhost:1234/write
remote_read:
  - url: http://localhost:1234/read
```

Remote write supports relabeling through `write_relabel_configs`, which works similarly to what you saw in "metric_relabel_configs" on page 164. Your main use of this would be to restrict what metrics are sent to the *remote write endpoint*, as you may find yourself limited by cost. From a bandwidth and memory standpoint, you should take care when pulling in large numbers of time series from long time periods via remote read. When using remote write it is important that each Prometheus has unique external labels so that metrics from different Prometheus servers don't clash.

One way to use remote read and write would be to consider Prometheus as a largely ephemeral cache, and the remote storage as the main storage.[12] If Prometheus is restarted with an empty data store, you would rely on remote read for historical graphs. You would also design your alerts to be resilient under such a restart, which is a good idea in any case.

There are many projects that integrate with Prometheus Remote Write. On the open source side, it is worth mentioning CNCF's Thanos, CNCF's Cortex, and Grafana Mimir, which use part of the Prometheus code as a library and use S3-compatible storage as a backend. Those systems are distributed, multitenant, and popular in the Prometheus community.

---

10 As discussed in "Going Global with Federation" on page 360, the global Prometheus will only have aggregated metrics.

11 This works in the same way as the `match[]` URL parameter for federation.

12 Usually a multiweek cache.

When evaluating your options, keep in mind that a load that would be considered light for a single Prometheus server may exceed what another system running across many machines can handle. It is always wise to load test systems based on your own use case rather than relying on headline numbers, as different systems are designed with different data models and access patterns in mind. Simpler solutions can turn out to be both more efficient and easier to operate. Clustered does not automatically mean better.

You should expect clustered storage systems to cost at least five times what the equivalent Prometheus would cost for the same load. This is because most systems will replicate the data three times, plus have to take it in and process all the data. Thus you should be judicious about what metrics you keep only locally and which ones are sent to clustered storage.

Prometheus features an experimental agent mode that can be enabled using the `--enable-feature=agent` flag. When using this mode, Prometheus is optimized for Remote Write scenarios, and data is only stored locally until it is transmitted to the Remote Write. Please be aware that while using agent mode, you will not be able to perform local recording rules or querying the data in Prometheus. This agent mode uses less resources compared to the server mode, making it a more lightweight solution for certain use cases.

Running Prometheus

When it comes to actually running the Prometheus server, you will have to consider hardware, configuration management, and how your network is set up.

Hardware

The first question you will probably ask when it comes to running Prometheus is what hardware Prometheus needs. Prometheus is best run on SSDs, though they are not strictly necessary on smaller setups. Storage space is one of the main resources you need to care about. To estimate how much you'll need, you have to know how much data you will be ingesting. For an existing Prometheus[13] you can run a PromQL query to report the samples ingested per second:

```
rate(prometheus_tsdb_head_samples_appended_total[5m])
```

---

13 For Prometheus 1.x, use the `prometheus_local_storage_ingested_samples_total` metric instead.

While Prometheus can achieve compression of 1.3 bytes per sample in production, when estimating we tend to use 2 bytes per sample to be conservative. The default retention for Prometheus is 15 days, so 100,000 samples per second would be around 240 GB over 15 days. You can increase the retention with the `--storage.tsdb.retention.time` flag, and control where Prometheus stores data with the `--storage.tsdb.path` flag. You can also decide to limit the size of the TSDB with `--storage.tsdb.retention.size`.[14] There is no particular filesystem recommended or required for Prometheus, and many users have had success using network block devices such as Amazon EBS. However NFS, including Amazon EFS, is explicitly not supported by Prometheus because Prometheus expects a POSIX filesystem, and NFS implementations have never really had a reputation for offering exact POSIX semantics. Each Prometheus needs its own storage directory; you cannot share one storage directory across the network.

The next question is how much RAM you will need. The storage in Prometheus 2.x works in blocks that are written out every two hours and subsequently compacted into larger time ranges. The storage engine does no internal caching, rather it uses your kernel's page cache. So you will need enough RAM to hold a block, plus overheads, plus the RAM used during queries. A good starting point is 12 hours worth of sample ingestion, so for 100,000 samples per second that would be around 8 GB.

Prometheus is relatively light on CPU. A quick benchmark on our machine (which has an i7-3770k CPU) shows only 0.25 CPUs being used to ingest 100,000 samples per second. But that is just ingestion—you will want additional CPU power to cover querying and recording rules. Due to CPU spikes from Go's garbage collection, you should always have at least one core more than you think you need.

Network bandwidth is another consideration. Prometheus 2.x can handle ingesting millions of samples per second, which is similar to the one-machine limit of many other similar systems. Prometheus usually uses compression when scraping, so it uses somewhere around 20 bytes of network traffic to transfer a sample. With a million samples per second, that's 160 Mbps of network traffic. That is a good chunk of a gigabit network card, which may be all you have for an entire rack of machines.

Another resource to keep in mind is file descriptors. We could give you the equation and factors, but these days file descriptors are not a scarce resource, so we'd say set your file ulimit to a million and not worry about it.

---

14 The retention size might not take into account blocks being compacted, so it is best to not set it at 100% of your storage capacity. Using size-based retention also means that you don't know how far in the past Prometheus will keep the data as your number of time series grows. In this case, the TSDB metric `prometheus_tsdb_lowest_timestamp` can be handy in alerting rules.

Ulimit changes for file descriptors have an annoying habit of not applying, depending on how exactly you start a service. Prometheus logs the file ulimit at startup, and you can also check the value of `process_max_fds` on */metrics*.

These numbers are just starting points. You should benchmark and verify these against your setup. We would generally recommended leaving room for your Prometheus to double in terms of resource usage to give you time to get new hardware as you grow, and it also gives you a buffer to deal with sudden cardinality increases.

Configuration Management

Prometheus does one thing and does it well—that being metrics-based monitoring. Prometheus does not try to fulfill the role of configuration management, secret management, or service database. To that extent, Prometheus aims to get out of your way and allow you to use standard configuration management approaches, rather than forcing you to learn and work around some Prometheus-specific configuration management contrivance.

If you do not yet have a configuration management tool, we would recommend Ansible for more traditional environments. For Kubernetes, Pulumi (*https://oreil.ly/TwdL-*) looks promising, but there are literally tens of tools in this space.

Just because Prometheus allows for standard approaches does not mean it will automatically work perfectly in your environment. Being generic means avoiding the temptation to cater to platform-specific nuances. It means that if you have a mature setup, Prometheus should be quite easy to deploy. You could view Prometheus as a maturity test for your configuration management, because Prometheus is a standard Unix binary that works in the ways you'd expect. It accepts `SIGTERM`, `SIGHUP`, logs to standard error, and uses simple text files for configuration.[15]

For example, Prometheus rule files (discussed in Chapter 17) can only come from files on disk. If you want to have an API where you can submit rules, there is nothing stopping you from building such a system,[16] and having it output the rule files in standard YAML format. Prometheus does not offer such an API itself, as how, for example, would you ensure Prometheus had rules immediately after a reboot? By only offering files on disk, you will find debugging is simpler since you know exactly what input Prometheus is working from. Those with simpler setups don't have to worry about more intricate configuration management concepts, and those who wish

---

15 Windows users can use HTTP instead of `SIGTERM` and `SIGHUP`, which requires the `--web.enable-lifecycle` flag to be specified.

16 Such a system actually exists, mixtool server (*https://oreil.ly/Dqc2B*), but it is highly experimental.

to do something fancier have an interface that permits them to do whatever they like. Put another way, the cost of more complex and nonstandard setups is borne by those with such setups, not by everyone else.

In simpler setups you can get away with having a static *prometheus.yml*. But as you expand you will need to template it using your configuration management system, at a minimum to specify a different `external_labels` per Prometheus, as Prometheus itself has no templating abilities for configuration files. If you haven't fully progressed to having a configuration management system yet,[17] some runtime environments can provide environment variables to the applications running under them. You could use tools like `sed` or `envsubst`[18] to do rudimentary templating. On the far end of sophistication you have tools like the Prometheus Operator from Prometheus-Community (briefly mentioned in Chapter 9), which will completely manage not only your configuration file but also your Prometheus server running on Kubernetes.

In Chapter 10 we mentioned that exporters should live right beside the application they are exporting metrics from. You should take the same approach with any daemons that provide configuration data for Prometheus, such as if you are using file service discovery (discussed in "File" on page 142). By having such daemons run beside each Prometheus, you will only be affected by the machine running Prometheus having issues, and not other machines that you are relying on to provide key functionality.

If you want to test changes to your Prometheus configuration, you can easily spin up a test Prometheus with the new configuration. Since Prometheus is pull-based, your targets don't have to know or care about what is monitoring them. When doing this it would be wise to remove any Alertmanagers or remote write endpoints from the configuration file.

Networks and Authentication

Prometheus is designed with the idea that it is on the same network as the targets it is monitoring, and can contact them directly over HTTP and request their metrics. This is known as pull-based monitoring, and comes with advantages such as up indicating if a scrape worked, being able to run a test Prometheus without having to configure all your targets to push to it, and more tactical options for handling sudden load increases, as covered in "Managing Performance" on page 374.

---

17 To avoid confusion, systems like Docker, Docker Compose, and Kubernetes are not configuration management systems; they are potential outputs for a configuration management system.

18 Part of the gettext library.

If you have a network setup where there is NAT or a firewall in the way, you should try to run a Prometheus server behind it so that it can directly access the targets. There are also options like PushProx (*https://oreil.ly/nq_fp*), SSH tunnels, or having Prometheus use a proxy via the `proxy_url` configuration field.

 Do not try to use the Pushgateway to work around network architecture, or more generally to try to convert Prometheus to a push-based system.

As was already covered in "Pushgateway" on page 76, the Pushgateway is for service-level batch jobs to push metrics to once just before they exit. It is not designed for application instances to regularly push metrics to, and you should never be pushing metrics that end up with an `instance` label to the Pushgateway. Trying to use the Pushgateway in this fashion will create a bottleneck,[19] the timestamps of the samples will not be correct (which will lead to graph artifacts), and you lose the `up` metric so it's harder to distinguish whether a process has died on purpose or due to a failure. The Pushgateway also has no logic to expire old data, because for service-level batch jobs for which the last run of a cronjob was a month ago doesn't change the validity of the last success time metric that cronjob pushed.

Pull is at the very core of Prometheus; work with it rather than against it.

Prometheus offers some service-side security support, as described in Chapter 20. It is, however, common to secure Prometheus behind a reverse proxy, which enables more flexibility or more functionalities, such as native Let's Encrypt support, which is out of scope for the Prometheus server. That would usually be using a reverse proxy such as Traefik (*https://traefik.io/traefik*), Caddy (*https://caddyserver.com*), nginx (*https://nginx.org*), or httpd (*https://httpd.apache.org*), which offer a wide range of security-related features. You may also want the reverse proxy to block access to the admin and lifecycle endpoints to protect against Cross-Site Request Forgery (XSRF), and use HTTP headers to protect against Cross-Site Scripting (XSS).

When running Prometheus behind a reverse proxy, you should pass Prometheus the URL under which it is available via the `--web.external-url` flag, so that the Prometheus UI and the generator URL in alerts work correctly. If your reverse proxy changes the HTTP path before sending it on to Prometheus, set the `--web.route-prefix` flag to the prefix of the new paths.

---

19 For the same reasons that you want to run a StatsD Exporter per application instance, rather than one per datacenter.

Like Prometheus, the Alertmanager also has `--web.external-url` and `--web.route-prefix` flags.

While Prometheus and the Alertmanager don't support authentication for serving, they do support it for talking to other systems, including alerting, notification, most service discovery mechanisms, remote read, remote write, and scraping, as was covered in "How to Scrape" on page 162.

Planning for Failure

In distributed systems, failure is a fact of life. Prometheus does not take the path of attempting a clustered design to handle machine failures, since such designs are very tricky to get right and turn out to be less reliable than nonclustered solutions more often than you'd expect. Nor does Prometheus attempt to backfill data if a scrape failed. If the scrape failure was due to overload, backfilling when load goes back down a bit could only cause the overload to happen again. It's better when monitoring systems have predictable load and don't exacerbate outages.

Due to the preceding design, if a scrape fails, `up` will be 0 for that scrape, and you will have a gap in your time series. But this is not something you should worry about. You will not care about the vast majority of your samples, gaps included, a week after they are collected (if not sooner). For monitoring, Prometheus takes the stance that it's more important that your monitoring is generally reliable and available, rather than 100% accurate. For metrics-based monitoring, 99.9% accuracy is fine for most purposes. It is more useful for you to know that latency increased by a millisecond than whether that increase was to 101.2 or 101.3 milliseconds `rate` is resilient to the occasional failed scrape, as long as your range is at least four times the scrape interval, as discussed in "rate" on page 289.

When discussing reliability, the first question you should ask is how reliable do you need your monitoring to be? If you are monitoring a system that has a 99.9% SLA, then there's no point spending your time and effort designing and maintaining a monitoring system that will be 99.9999% available. Even if you could build such a system, neither the internet connections that your users use nor the response of the humans who are on call are that reliable.

Taking an example, in Europe it is common to use SMS for paging as it is generally fast, cheap, and reliable. However, for a few hours every year it grinds to a halt when the entire country wishes each other Happy New Year, which makes it at most 99.95% reliable over a year. You can have contingencies in place to handle things like this, but as you try backup paging devices and escalating to the secondary on call, the minutes are ticking away. As mentioned in "for" on page 314, if you have an issue that requires a resolution in under 5 minutes, you should automate it rather than hope your on call engineers will be able to handle it in time.

In this context we'd like to talk about reliable alerting. If a Prometheus dies for some reason, you should have it automatically restart, and disruption should be minimal beyond `for` state resetting (as discussed in "for" on page 314).[20] But if the machine Prometheus is on dies and Prometheus cannot restart, you won't have alerts until you replace it. If you are using a cluster scheduler such as Kubernetes, you can expect this to happen promptly, which may well suffice.[21] If replacement is a more manual process, this probably won't be acceptable.

The good news is that you can easily make alerting more reliable by eliminating the single point of failure (SPOF). If you run two identical Prometheus servers, then as long as one of them is running you will have alerts, and the Alertmanager will automatically deduplicate the alerts because they will have identical labels.

As mentioned in "External Labels" on page 323, every Prometheus should have unique external labels, so to maintain that constraint you can use `alert_relabel_con figs` (as discussed in "Configuring Alertmanagers in Prometheus" on page 322):

```
global:
  external_labels:
    region: dublin1
alerting:
  alertmanagers:
    - static_configs:
        - targets: ['localhost:9093']
  alert_relabel_configs:
    - source_labels: [region]
      regex: (.+)\d+
      target_label: region
```

This will remove the 1 from `dublin1` before sending the alert to the Alertmanager. The second Prometheus would have a `region` label of `dublin2` as an external label.

I've mentioned now a few times that external labels should be unique across all your Prometheus servers. This is so that if you have multiple Prometheus servers in a setup like the preceding one and you are either using remote write or federation from them, the metrics from the different Prometheus servers won't clash. Even in perfect conditions, different Prometheus servers will see slightly different data, which could be misinterpreted as a counter reset, for example. In less optimal conditions, such

---

20 For this reason we recommend you design your critical alerts to be up and running in a fresh Prometheus within an hour, if not sooner.

21 If using network storage such as Amazon EBS, the Prometheus may even continue on with the data of the previous run.

as a network partition, each of your redundant Prometheus servers could see wildly different information.

This brings me to the question of reliability for dashboards, federation, and remote write. There is no general way you can automatically synthesize the "correct" data from the different Prometheus servers, and going via load balancer for Grafana or federation would lead to artifacts. I suggest taking the easy way out and only dashboarding/federating/writing from one of the Prometheus servers, and if it is down, live with the gap. In the rare event that the gap covers a period you care about, you can always look at the data in the other Prometheus by hand.

For global Prometheus servers, as discussed in "Going Global with Federation" on page 360, the trade-offs are a bit different. As global Prometheus servers are monitoring across failure zones, it is plausible that the global server could be down for hours or days if there was, for example, a major power outage in the datacenter. This is fine for the datacenter Prometheus servers since they aren't running, but neither is anything they were going to be monitoring. We recommend that you always run at least two global Prometheus servers in different datacenters and in dashboards making graphs available from all of the global servers. Similarly for remote write.[22] It is the responsibility of the person using the dashboards to interpret the data from the differing sources.

Alertmanager Clustering

You will want to run one centralized Alertmanager setup for your entire organization, so that everyone has one place to look at alerts and silences, and you get the maximum benefits from alert grouping. Unless you have a small setup, you can take advantage of the Alertmanager's clustering feature, whose architecture is shown in Figure 21-2.

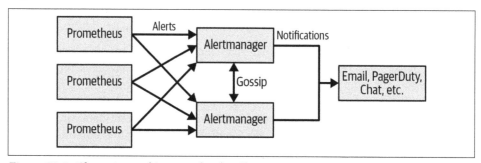

Figure 21-2. Clustering architecture for the Alertmanager

---

22 Global Prometheus servers are at the top of the federation hierarchy, so nothing generally federates from them.

The Alertmanager uses HashiCorp's memberlist (*https://oreil.ly/fbRs_*)[23] to gossip information about notifications and silences.[24] This is not a consensus-based design, so there is no need to have an odd number of Alertmanagers. This is what is known as an AP, or Availability and Partition-tolerant, design, so as long as your Prometheus can talk to at least one Alertmanager that can successfully send notifications, your notifications will get through. When there are rare issues such as network partitions, you may get duplicate notifications, but that's better than not getting notifications at all.

For the clustering to work, every Prometheus must send its alerts to every Alertmanager. How it works is that the Alertmanagers order themselves. The first Alertmanager sends notifications normally, and if successful, gossips that the notification was sent. The second Alertmanager has a small delay before sending notifications. If it doesn't get the gossip that the first Alertmanager sent the notification, then it will send the notification. The third Alertmanager will have a slightly longer delay and so on. The Alertmanagers should all have identical *alertmanager.yml* files, but the worst that should happen if they don't is that duplicate notifications will be sent.

To get it running with Alertmanager version 0.24.0 on two machines called foo and bar, you would start the Alertmanager as follows:

```
# On the machine foo
alertmanager --cluster.peer bar:9094

# On the machine bar
alertmanager --cluster.peer foo:9094
```

The easiest way for you to test if clustering is working is to create a silence on one Alertmanager and see if it appears on the other Alertmanager. There will also be a list of all members of the cluster on the Alertmanager's Status page.

Meta- and Cross-Monitoring

Thus far we have covered monitoring many different types of systems, but among those we have not covered monitoring your monitoring system. It is fairly standard to have each of your Prometheus servers scrape itself, but that doesn't help you when that Prometheus is having issues. How you monitor your monitoring is known as *metamonitoring*.

The general approach to metamonitoring for you to take is to have one Prometheus per datacenter that monitors all of the other Prometheus servers in that datacenter. This doesn't have to be a Prometheus server dedicated to this purpose as Prometheus

---

23 Prior to 0.15.0, the Alertmanager used the Weaveworks Mesh library.

24 Aside from gossiping, the Alertmanager also stores data on local disk, so even in a nonclustered setup you won't lose state by restarting the Alertmanager.

is pretty cheap to monitor, and even if you have a setup where each team is entirely responsible for running their own Prometheus servers, it is still wise to offer metamonitoring as a central shared service.

A global Prometheus can then scrape all of your per-datacenter metamonitoring Prometheus servers, likely both for */metrics* and federating aggregated metrics about all of the Prometheus servers in your organization.

This still leaves the question of how you should monitor the global Prometheus servers. *Cross-monitoring* is metamonitoring where Prometheus servers monitor each other, rather than the usual metamonitoring hierarchy where Prometheus servers at the same "level" monitor each other. For example, you will usually have two global Prometheus servers scrape each other's */metrics* and alert if the other Prometheus is down. You could also have the datacenter Prometheus servers alerting on the global Prometheus servers.[25]

Even with all this meta- and cross-monitoring, you are still depending on Prometheus to monitor Prometheus. In the absolute worst case, a bug could take out all of your Prometheus servers at the same time, so it would be wise to have alerting that can catch that. One approach would be an end-to-end alerting test. An always firing alert would continuously fire a notification via your paging provider, which feeds into a dead man's switch. The dead man's switch would then page you[26] if it doesn't receive a notification for too long a period. This would test your Prometheus, Alertmanager, network, and paging provider.

When designing your metamonitoring, don't forget to scrape other monitoring-related components, such as the Alertmanager and the */metrics* of Blackbox/SNMP-style exporters.

Managing Performance

Unless you have a particularly small and unchanging setup, running into performance issues is more of a when than an if. As discussed in "Cardinality" on page 99 and elsewhere, high cardinality metrics are likely to be the primary cause of the performance problems you encounter.

You may also encounter recording rules and dashboards using overly expensive queries, such as those with range vectors over long durations, as mentioned in

---

25 With all these alerts ready to fire when a global Prometheus goes down, you should to ensure that they all have the same labels and get automatically deduplicated at the Alertmanager. An explicit alert label of `datacenter: global` (or whatever you use as a datacenter label) to prevent the datacenter Prometheus's datacenter external label applying is one approach you could take.

26 Preferably not solely via your usual paging provider, since that could be what has failed.

"Histogram" on page 233. You can use the Rules status page, as you saw in Figure 17-1, to find expensive recording rules.[27]

Detecting a Problem

Prometheus exposes a variety of metrics about its own performance, so you don't just have to rely on noticing that your dashboards have gotten sluggish or are timing out. While metrics can and do change names and meanings from version to version, it is unusual for a metric to go away completely.

`prometheus_rule_group_iterations_missed_total` can indicate that some rule groups are taking too long to evaluate. Comparing `prometheus_rule_group_last_duration_seconds` against `prometheus_rule_group_interval_seconds` can tell you which group is at fault and if it is a recent change in behavior.

`prometheus_notifications_dropped_total` indicates issues talking to the Alertmanager, and if `prometheus_notifications_queue_length` is approaching `prometheus_notifications_queue_capacity`, you may start losing alerts.

Each service discovery mechanism tends to have a metric such as `prometheus_sd_file_read_errors_total` and `prometheus_sd_ec2_refresh_failures_total` indicating problems. You should keep an eye on the counters for the SD mechanisms you use.

`prometheus_rule_evaluation_failures_total`, `prometheus_tsdb_compactions_failed_total`, and `prometheus_tsdb_wal_corruptions_total` indicate that something has gone wrong in the storage layer. In the worst case you can always stop Prometheus, delete[28] the storage directory, and start it back up again.

Finding Expensive Metrics and Targets

As was mentioned in "by" on page 251, you can use queries such as:

```
topk(10, count by(__name__)({__name__=~".+"}))
```

to find metrics with high cardinality. You could also aggregate by `job` to find which applications are responsible for the most time series. But these are potentially very expensive queries as they touch every time series and accordingly should be used with caution.

In addition to up, Prometheus adds three other samples for every target scrape. `scrape_samples_scraped` is the number of samples that were on the */metrics*. As this is a single time series per target, it is much cheaper to work with than the

---

27 By looking at the duration, for example.

28 Or rename, to back up existing data.

previous PromQL expression. `scrape_samples_post_metric_relabeling` is similar, but it excludes samples that were dropped by `metric_relabel_configs`.

The final special sample added is `scrape_duration_seconds`, which is how long that scrape took. This can be useful to check if timeouts are occurring if it is reaching the timeout value, or as an indication that a target is getting overloaded.

Hashmod

If your Prometheus is so overloaded by data from scrapes that you cannot run queries, there is a way to scrape a subset of your targets. There is another relabel action called `hashmod` that calculates the hash of a label and takes its modulus. Combined with the `drop` relabel action, you could use this to scrape an arbitrary 10% of your targets:

```
scrape_configs:
 - job_name: my_job
   # Service discovery etc. goes here.
   relabel_configs:
    - source_labels: [__address__]
      modulus:       10
      target_label:  __tmp_hash
      action:        hashmod
    - source_labels: [__tmp_hash]
      regex:         0
      action:        keep
```

With only 10% of the targets to scrape, if you can spin up a test Prometheus, you should now be able to find out which metric is to blame. If only some targets are causing the problem, you can change which 10% of targets to scrape by changing the `regex` to 1, 2, and so on up to 9.

Reducing Load

Once you have identified expensive metrics, you have a few options. The first thing to do is try to fix the metric in the source code to reduce its cardinality.

While you're waiting for that to happen, you have several tactical options. The first is to drop the metric at ingestion time using `metric_relabel_configs`:

```
scrape_configs:
 - job_name: some_application
   static_configs:
    - targets:
      - localhost:1234
   metric_relabel_configs:
    - source_labels: [__name__]
      regex: expensive_metric_name
      action: drop
```

This still transfers the metric over the network and parses it, but it's still cheaper than ingesting it into the storage layer.[29]

If particular applications are being problematic you can also drop those targets with relabeling.

The final option is to increase the `scrape_interval` and `evaluation_interval` for the Prometheus. This can buy you some breathing room, but keep in mind that it's not practical to increase these beyond 2 minutes. Changing the scrape interval may also break some PromQL expressions that depend on it having a specific value.

There is one other option in the scrape config that can be of use to you called `sample_limit`. If the number of samples after `metric_relabel_configs`[30] is higher than `sample_limit`, then the scrape will fail and the samples will not be ingested. This is disabled by default but can act as an emergency relief valve in the event that one of your targets blows up in cardinality, such as by adding a metric with a customer identifier as a label, for example. This is not a setting to micromanage or to attempt to build some form of quota system on top of; if you are going to use it, choose a single generous value that will rarely need bumping.

We advise having enough buffer room in your Prometheus to be able to handle a moderate spurt in cardinality and targets.

Horizontal Sharding

If you are running into scaling challenges due to `instance` cardinality rather than instrumentation label cardinality, there is a way to horizontally shard Prometheus using the `hashmod` relabel action you saw in "Hashmod" on page 376. This is an approach that is only typically needed if you have many thousands of targets of a single type of application, as vertical sharding is a far simpler way to scale Prometheus (as discussed in "Growing Prometheus" on page 359).

The approach to horizontal sharding is to have a master Prometheus and several scraping Prometheus servers. Your scraping Prometheus servers each scrape a subset of the targets:

```
global:
  external_labels:
    env: prod
    scraper: 2
scrape_configs:
```

---

29 The Java and Python clients support fetching specific time series using URL parameters such as */metrics?metric[]=process_cpu_seconds_total*. This may not always work for custom collectors, but it can save a lot of resources on both sides of the scrape if there are only a small number of specific metrics you want.

30 Which is to say, the value of `scrape_samples_post_metric_relabeling`.

```
  - job_name: my_job
    # Service discovery etc. goes here.
    relabel_configs:
     - source_labels: [__address__]
       modulus:       4
       target_label:  __tmp_hash
       action:        hashmod
     - source_labels: [__tmp_hash]
       regex:         2 # This is the 3rd scraper.
       action:        keep
```

Here you can see there are four scrapers from the modulus setting. Each scraper should have a unique external label, plus the external labels of the master Prometheus. The master Prometheus can then use the remote read endpoint of Prometheus itself to transparently pull in data from the scrapers:

```
global:
  external_labels:
    env: prod
remote_read:
 - url: http://scraper0:9090/api/v1/read
   read_recent: true
 - url: http://scraper1:9090/api/v1/read
   read_recent: true
 - url: http://scraper2:9090/api/v1/read
   read_recent: true
 - url: http://scraper3:9090/api/v1/read
   read_recent: true
```

Remote read has an optimization where it will try not to read in data it should already have locally, which makes sense if it is being used with remote write to work with a long-term storage system. read_recent: true disables this. Due to the external labels, the metrics from each scraper will have a scraper label matching where they came from.

All the same caveats as with federation, covered in "Going Global with Federation" on page 360, apply here. This is not a way to have one Prometheus that can let you transparently access all of your Prometheus servers. In fact, it would actually be a great way to take out all of your monitoring simultaneously through a single expensive query. When using this it is best to aggregate what you can inside the scrapers (following "Reducing Cardinality" on page 300), to reduce the amount of data that the master needs to pull in from the scrapers.

You should be generous with the number of scrapers and aim to only have to increase every few years. When you do increase it, you should at least double the number of scrapers to avoid having to increase the number again soon.

Managing Change

Over time you will find that you need to change the structure of your target labels due to changes in the architecture of your systems. Which applications will host the metrics used for capacity planning will change over time as your applications split and merge as a natural part of development. Metrics will appear and disappear from release to release.

You have the option of using `metric_relabel_configs` to rename metrics and cram the new hierarchy into your existing target labels. But over time you would find that these tweaks and hacks accumulate and ultimately cause more confusion than you may have been trying to prevent by trying to keep things the same.

We would advise accepting that changes like this are a natural part of the evolution of your system, and as with gaps due to failed scrapes, you usually find that you don't care much about the old names after the fact.

Long-term processes such as capacity planning, on the other hand, do care about history. At the least you should note the names of the metrics over time and possibly consider using the approach in "Rules for APIs" on page 302 in your global Prometheus if the changes are a bit too frequent to manage by hand.

In this chapter you learned how to approach a Prometheus deployment, and in what order to add Prometheus monitoring to your system, how to architect and run Prometheus, and how to handle performance problems when they arise.

Getting Help

Even after reading everything up to this point, you may have questions that are not covered here. There are a number of places you can ask questions. The Community Page of the Prometheus website (*https://oreil.ly/lqZT8*) lists the official communication method of the Prometheus projects, such as the prometheus-users (*https://oreil.ly/CTPNp*) mailing list, which is also available for user questions. There are also unofficial venues for questions, including the Prometheus tag on StackOverflow (*https://oreil.ly/MGxtQ*), the #prometheus channel on the CNCF Slack (*https://slack.cncf.io*), and the PrometheusMonitoring subreddit (*https://oreil.ly/nDPxu*). Finally, there are several companies and individuals offering commercial support listed on the Support & Training (*https://oreil.ly/XEg_F*) page, including Brian's company, Robust Perception (*https://oreil.ly/X9OYd*), and Julien's company, O11y (*https://o11y.eu*).

We hope you have found this and all of the preceding chapters useful and that Prometheus will help to make your life easier through metrics-based monitoring.

Index

Symbols

!= (negative equality matcher), 236
!~ (negative regular expression matcher), 236
() (parentheses), using to change order of evaluation, 276
.* prefixing/suffixing regular expressions, 236
; (semicolon) separator in source_labels, 151
= (equality matcher), 236
== operator, 33
=~ (regular expression matcher), 236
@ (at) modifier, 242, 257
^ (exponent) operator, 280
| (pipe symbol), alternation operator, 151

A

abs function, 279
absent function, 287
absent_over_time function, 287
__address__ labels, 157
    relabeling, 158
agent mode, 365
agents (Consul), 146, 188
aggregation, 93
    basics of in PromQL, 229-235
        counter, 231
        gauge, 229-231
        summary, 232
    functions for aggregation over time,
        295-296, 302
    level of in recording rule names, 305
    preaggregating every application metric, 303
    using in recording rules, 301
aggregation operators, 249-259
    avg, 254
    count, 253
    count_values, 258
    group, 255
    grouping, 249-252
    max and min, 256
    quantile, 257
    stddev, 255
    stdvar, 256
    sum, 252
    topk and bottomk, 256
alert field, 312
Alert status page, 314
alerting, 5, 31-38, 311
    choosing alert thresholds, 314
    how to approach, further information on,
        322
    missing job and, 287
    predict_linear function for resource limit
        alerts, 294
    preservation of job and instance labels for,
        250
    reliable, 371
alerting field, 323
alerting rules, 16, 32, 312-322
    annotations and templates, 318-321
    for field, 314
    good alerts, 321
    labels for, 316-318
Alertmanager, 16, 325-348
    clustering, 372
    configuration file, 326-345
        inhibitions, 344
        minimal configuration example, 327
        receivers, 334-344

routing tree, 327-334
  configuring, 35, 322-324
    external labels, 323
  downloading and installing, 35
  notification pipeline, 325
  Prometheus and Alertmanager architecture, 311
  starting, 36
  telling Prometheus which one, 34
  web interface, 345-348
alertmanagers field, 322
alertname labels, 313
alerts, 4
  defining multiple alerts with different thresholds and labels, 317
  firing alert on Alerts page, 35
  good alerts, 321
  owners for, 317, 328
Alerts list, 339
ALERTS metric, 313
ALERTS_FOR_STATE metric, 313
alert_relabel_configs, 323, 371
aliasing, 113
aligned data, 247
Amazon EC2 (see EC2)
and operator, 274, 313, 319
annotations (alert), 318-321
Ansible, 139, 367
  using its templating to create targets for Node Exporter, 141
APIs, 242
  (see also HTTP API)
  rules for, 302
application logs, 10
applications, metric names coming from, 63
architecture of Prometheus, 11-17
arithmetic mean, 254
arithmetic operators, 261-263, 267
  summary of, 262
at (@) modifier, 242, 257
atan2 operator, 263
authentication, 370
  enabling Basic Authentication, 354
  in HTTP SD, 145
  for Kubernetes API servers scrapes, 178
  options in scrape config, 162
authorization, 162, 175, 354
average load, 132
averages

attempt to average averages, 254, 307
calculating average event size using histograms, 235
calculating with summary, 232
avg operator, 254
avg without expression, 127, 230
avg_over_time, 95, 239, 295, 295
  range vectors as input, 277

B

backend-ticket receiver, 329
base units, 25, 61
  quantiles and percentiles, 53
  seconds as base unit for time, 49
Basic Authentication, enabling, 354
basic_auth, 162
batch jobs, 58, 76
  alerting on not succeeding recently, 314
  idempotency for, 58
  recording when Cassandra backups completed, 135
  service-level, Pushgateway metrics cache for, 76
bcrypt cost, 354
billing, 18, 160
binary operators, 261-276
  operator precedence, 275
  vector matching, 265-275
    many-to-many and logical operators, 271-275
    many-to-one and group_left, 268-271
    one-to-one, 266
  working with scalars, 261-265
    arithmetic operators, 261-263
    comparison operators, 263-265
    trigonometric operator atan2, 263
Blackbox exporters, 194-208, 211
  catching filed scrapes or failed probes, 316
  default registry and, 222
  DNS name resolution, 196
  DNS probes, 204-205
  downloading and running, 194
  HTTP probes, 201-204
  ICMP probes, 195-199
  Prometheus configuration, 205
  TCP probes, 199-201
bool modifier, 264
  using to compare scalars, 265
boolean values, 95

---

bottomk operator, 256, 257
bridges, 79
buckets (in histograms), 53, 60, 233
    cumulative histograms, 54
    dropping to reduce cardinality, 165
    using rate before sum on, 253
by clause, 251
    count by, 254
    group by, 255
    sum by, 94
    versus without clause, 251

C

caches, 9, 11, 60
    memory usage of, 48
    metrics for cache overall and cache misses,
      59
    tracking size or number of files in, 50
cAdvisor, 169-172
    container CPU metrics, 170
    container labels, 171
    container memory metrics, 171
    embedded in Kubelet, 176
callbacks, 50
cardinality, 99
    performance problems with, 359
    reducing with recording rules, 300, 304
case, changing for label values, 160
Cassandra, 135
ca_file, 175
ceil function, 281
certificate authority, 175
    self-signed, creating using OpenSSL, 352
certificates, TLS, 352
cgroups
    hierarchy of, 171
    metrics about (see cAdvisor)
change of base function, 280
change, managing, 379
changes function, 293
characters (in metric names), 60
Chebyshev's inequality, 255
check config (promtool), 298
check metrics, 83
check rules, 298
check-config (amtool), 326
Chef, 139
child metrics, 90, 91-93
    of node_hwmon_sensor_label, 270

child routes, 327
chokepoints in your applications, 358
clamp function, 281
clamp_max function, 281
clamp_min function, 281
client libraries, 3, 12, 41, 219
    exposition in (see exposition)
    fetching time series using URL parameters,
      377
    metrics related to runtime, 62
    official versus unofficial, 12
    registration of metrics with, 44
Cloud Native Computing Foundation (CNCF),
    3, 172, 364
Cloudwatch Exporter, 226
cluster labels, 250
clustered storage system, 17, 364
clustering, 15
clustering (Alertmanager), 372
Collect method, 220
collectd, 209
--collector.diskstats.device-exclude flag, 128
--collector.textfie.directory flag, 135
CollectorRegistry.collect, 79
CollectorRegistry.metricFamilySamples, 79
collectors, 126
    (see also Node Exporter)
    custom, 13, 95, 219-224
      labels for metrics, 223
compaction duration, time series database, 233
comparison operators, 263-265, 267
    bool modifier and, 264
configuration
    asking Prometheus to reload, 298
    checking with promtool check rules, 298
configuration files, use of YAML, 21
configuration management, 367
configuration management systems, 139
connection refused error, 32
console templates, 104
ConstMetrics, 13
Consul, 139, 141
    keeping only Consul services with prod tag,
      161
    monitoring Consul, 147
    production tags for production services, 152
    service discovery, 146
      using replace to relabel team label, 157
    writing Consul Telemetry exporter, 215-219

consul_up, 220
container orchestrators, 172
    (see also Kubernetes)
containers, 169-172
    cAdvisor, 169-172
    CPU metrics, 170
    labels, 171
    memory usage metrics, 171
context deadline exceeded error, 32
context of events, 8
context switches, 131
continue setting (routing), 330, 336
continuous profiling, 8
count, 98, 100
    about, 253
    by clause, 252
    count by, 132, 254
    counting unique label values, 253
    dividing by sum, 232
    histogram metric, 235
    using count_values with, 259
    using rate before sum on, 253
counters, 26, 43-47, 289-292
    aggregating, 231
    attempting to increase by negative number, 47
    Consul, 216
    container CPU metrics, 170
    counting exceptions, 45
    counting size, 47
    increase function, 291
    irate function, 291
    multiprocess mode and, 70
    Node Exporter diskstat metrics, 128
    processing in custom collector, 221
    rate function, 289
    resets function, 292
    text exposition format for, 81
    unit testing in Python, 56
    using rate before sum with, 253
CounterValue, 220
count_over_time, 295
count_values operator, 258
    use with count, 259
cpu collector, 126
cpu labels, 126
CPUs
    calculating 90th percentile of system mode CPU usage, 257

counting number in each machine, 253
    metric for container CPUs, 170
    PDUs and, 140
    requirements for Prometheus, 366
CPython, 68
credentials_file, 163, 175, 178
cronjobs, 134, 145
    causing CPU usage to spike, 321
    outputting to textfile collector, 136
cross-monitoring, 374
cube root, 280
cumulative histograms, 54
cURL utility, 71
custom collectors (see collectors)
custom registries, 44, 68, 77

D
dashboard annotation, 341
dashboards, 15, 103, 358
    (see also Grafana)
    avoiding wall of graphs, 109
    creating using Grafana template variables, 118
    with graph and Stat panels in Grafana, 113
    making faster, 300
    new Grafana dashboard, 107
    Promdash and console templates, 104
    with Stat panels and Table panel, 116
data sources, 106
date functions, 284
days, 240
days_in_month function, 284
day_of_month, 284
day_of_week function, 284
day_of_year function, 284
debug logs, 10
    scrape errors on, 32
debugging, 5
dec method, 48
default namespace, 180
default registry, 65
    (see also registry)
default route, 327
    error to use matchers on, 328
DefaultExports.initialize, 73
degrees and radians, converting between, 282
delete_from_gateway, 77
delta function, 294
dependencies

Java servlet client library, 75
simpleclient in Java, 73
deploying Prometheus, 357-379
   federation, 360-363
   getting help, 379
   growing Prometheus, 359
   long-term storage, 363-365
   managing change, 379
   managing performance, 374-378
      detecting a problem, 375
      finding expensive targets and metrics, 375
      hashmod relabel action, 376
      horizontal sharding, 377
      reducing load, 376
   planning a rollout, 357-358
   planning for a failure, 370-372
      Alertmanager clustering, 372
      meta- and cross-monitoring, 373
   running Prometheus, 365-370
      configuration management, 367
      hardware, 365-367
      networks and authentication, 368-370, 368
deriv function, 241, 293
   using instead of delta, 294
Desc type, 219, 223
Describe method, 219
destination (notifications), 342
   setting based on email_to label, 343
device labels, 127, 129, 229, 249
   recording rules and, 303
   removing using sum without, 231
df command, 127
disk I/O, 27, 125, 128, 129
diskstats collector, 128
distributed tracing, 9
DNS
   kube-dns, 182
   name resolution used by Prometheus and Blackbox exporters, 196
   probing with Blackbox exporter, 204-205
Docker
   container labels, 171
   id labels from, 170
   installing Grafana with, 104
   running cAdvisor with, 169
   running Node Exporter within, 126
dotted string notation, 213

DOWN state, alerting on, 32
drop (relabel action), 151, 164, 376
Dropwizard metrics, 211
   counters, 216
durations
   instrumenting, not excluding failures, 58
   metrics on, 57
      probe_duration_seconds, 196
   not adding metric for duration of every function, 60
   in Prometheus as used in PromQL, 240

E
eBPF (enhanced Berkeley Packet Filters), 8
EC2 (Elastic Compute Cloud), 139, 148-148, 161
   relabeling tags using labelmap action, 159
   team tags, 152
Elasticsearch, 80
email alerts, 35, 327
email_to labels, 343
end, 245, 247
end function, 242
endpoints (Kubernetes), 174, 177
endpointslice service discovery, 177, 182
enums, 94
env labels, 250, 317, 331
   in Slack, 337
epsilon, 264
equality matcher (=), 236
escaping characters in exposition format, 82
evaluation_interval, 299, 377
   changing to an hour, reasons not to, 304
events, 7
   counters tracking, 26
exceptions, counting, 45
exp function, 254, 280
exponent operator (^), 280
exporters, 3, 13, 187-208, 368
   Blackbox, 194-208
   cAdvisor, 169-172
   considering in Prometheus rollout, 357
   Consul, 187-189
   Consul Exporter, 147
   Consul metrics exporter written in Python 3, 222
   default ports, 190
   default registry and, 222
   exposing timestamps, staleness and, 238

Grok, 191-194
  guideline for, 187
  kube-state-metrics, 184
  MySQLd, 189-191
  Node Exporter (see Node Exporter)
  other monitoring systems, 209, 214
  Prometheus configuration for Blackbox
      probe URL parameters, 205
  SaaS monitoring systems, 210
  server-side security, 351
  writing, 215-226
      Consul Telemetry, 215-219
      custom collectors, 219-224
      guidelines for, 224
exposition, 65-86
  from batch jobs using Pushgateway, 76-79
  custom collector, 222
  from Go client libraries, 71
  from Java client libraries, 72-76
  from Python client libraries, 66-71
      parsers, 80
  using bridges, 79
exposition formats
  OpenMetrics, 83-86
      labels, 85
      metric types, 84
      timestamps, 85
  parsers in Python client libraries, 80
  Prometheus text format, 80-83
      escaping characters in, 82
      labels, 82
      metric types, 81
      timestamps, 82
      using promtool check metrics, 83
  supported by Prometheus, 65
expression browser, 15, 21
  range vector in Console tab, 239
  using, 23-27
external labels, 323, 364
  unique, for every Prometheus, 371
external_labels, 154, 317, 328

F
failures
  metrics for total and failures, 59
  planning for, 370-372
      Alertmanager clustering, 372
      meta- and cross-monitoring, 373
fallback (or default) route, 327

FDsNearLimit alert, 317
federation, 301, 378
  global Prometheus servers, 372
  going global with, 360-363
file descriptors, 366
file service discovery (file SD), 139, 142-145
files field, 298
filesystem collector, 127
filesystems, 366
  node_filesystem_size_bytes metric, 229
  returning total filesystem size on each
      machine, 253
file_sd_configs, 143, 298
filtering, 263
  avoiding in recording rule expressions, 312
  bool modifier and, 264
firing alerts, 313, 314, 317
five-minute rate, 290
float64, 222
floating-point math
  comparisons with NaN, 256
  dividing by zero, resulting in NaN, 46
floating-point numbers
  64-bit, use by Prometheus, 47
  using equality comparisons with, 264
for field, 314, 317
fork syscalls, 131
formats
  Prometheus text format and OpenMetrics, 4
      (see also exposition formats)
  third-party software exposing metrics in
      non-Prometheus format, 3
frequency histograms, 258
frontend-pager receiver, 335
fstype labels, 127, 229, 249
fully anchored regular expressions, 150, 236
functions, 277-296
  aggregation over time, 295-296
  changing gauges, 293-295
      changes function, 293
      delta function, 294
      deriv function, 293
      holt_winters function, 295
      predict_linear function, 294
  changing type
      scalar, 278
      vector, 277
  composing range vector functions, 302
  counter, 289-292

increase function, 291
irate function, 291
rate function, 289
resets function, 292
histogram_quantile, 288
label_join, 286
label_replace, 286
math, 279-283
    abs, 279
    ceil and floor, 281
    clamp, clamp_max, and clamp_min, 281
    exp, 280
    ln, log2, and log10, 279
    round, 281
    sgn, 282
    sqrt, 280
    trigonometric functions, 282
missing series, absent and
    absent_over_time, 287
sorting with sort and sort_desc, 288
time and date, 283-285
    days_in_month, 284
    day_of_month, 284
    day_of_week, 284
    day_of_year, 284
    hour function, 284
    minute function, 284
    month function, 284
    time function, 283
    year function, 284

G

gaps
    between data points you have and bound-
        aries of the range., 231
    due to failed scrapes, 370, 379
    in exception ratio graph for no requests, 46
Gather method, 79
GaugeHistograms, 84
gauges, 26, 47-50
    aggregating, 229-231
    changing, functions for, 293-295
        changes function, 293
        delta function, 294
        deriv function, 293
        holt_winters function, 295
        predict_linear function, 294
    Consul, 216
    multiprocess_mode configuration, 69

needed by histogram_quantile, 289
processing in custom collector, 221
text exposition format for, 81
timestamp in text exposition format, 83
used as enum, custom collector for, 94
using callbacks, 50
GaugeValue, 220
geometric mean, 254
get_sample_value function, 56
global Prometheus servers, 372
global section (prometheus.yml), 323
globs, use in filenames, 143
Go
    client library metrics for, 62
    collectors written in, 219
    custom collectors written in, 13
    exposition from client libraries, 71
    RE2 regular expression engine, 152
    Registry.Gather, 79
    running Consul Telemetry exporter, 218
    templating language, 104
    templating system, 319
    WithLabelValues, 88
    writing exporters in, 215
Grafana, 15, 103-121, 363
    aligned data, 247
    dashboards and panels, 107-109
        avoiding wall of graphs, 109
    data source, 106
    installing, 104-106
    reporting_enabled setting, 104
    Stat panel, 113-114
    State timeline panel, 117
    Table panel, 115
    template variables, 118
    Time series panel, 109-113
    time shifting panel to different time range,
        241
Graphite, 6, 209
    bridge, 79
    dotted string notation, 213
Graphite Exporter, 358
graphs
    graph editor in Grafana, 109
    limiting number on a dashboard, 109
Grok Exporter, 191-194
    configuring for scraping by Prometheus,
        193
    defining where to expose its metrics, 193

grok.yml to parse logfile and produce metrics, 191
  metrics produced by, 192
  use of patterns based on regular expressions, 192
group operator, 255
grouping, 249-252
  of alerts in Alertmanager, 326, 330
    disabling, 332
  by clause, 251
  without clause, 250
grouping keys, 79
groups, 78
  alerting rules in, 312
  problem with rule groups, 375
  repeating notifications for, 332
  in rule files, 298, 300
  throttling notifications for, 332
group_by, 330, 343
group_interval, 332
  tweaking, 333
group_left, 97, 131, 268-271, 272
group_right, 271
group_wait, 332
growing Prometheus, 359
guests, CPU usage by, 127
Gunicorn, 68-71

H

handler labels, aggregating away, 232
hardware, 365-367
hashmod relabel action, 376, 377
health checks, standardizing across services, 200
health monitoring, HTTP SD, 145
Helm, use to create components from Prometheus ecosystem, 185
HELP (metrics), 81, 84, 136
help, sources of, 379
histograms, 52-56, 100, 233-235
  buckets, 53, 60
    using rate before sum on, 253
  cumulative, 54
  dropping buckets to reduce cardinality, 165
  frequency histogram, 258
  HTTP request latency from Grok Exporter, 192
  text exposition format for, 81
histogram_quantile function, 53, 81, 233, 258

about, 288
holt_winters function, 295
Home Dashboard (Grafana), 105
honor_labels (scrape config), 166
horizontal sharding, 377
host labels, 153
hour function, 275, 284
hours, 240
HTTP
  exposition to Prometheus over, 65
  probing with Blackbox exporter, 201-204
  receivers based on, 337
HTTP API, 242-247
  aligned data, 247
  query or query endpoint, 242-245
  query range endpoint or query_range, 245-247
HTTP Basic Authentication, 162
HTTP Bearer Token Authentication, 162
HTTP requests, 9
  exposition format in response to, 13
  logging latency for, using Grok Exporter, 192
  metrics on, 11
  metrics on broken out by path, 87
  rejected, 32
HTTP server in Python (example), 41
HTTP service discovery (HTTP SD), 139, 145
HttpServer class, 73
HttpServlet class, 74
http_config field, 337
http_requests_total, 242
http_response_size_bytes, 232
http_response_size_bytes_count, 232
http_response_size_bytes_sum, 232
http_sd_configs, 145
hwmon collector, 130

I

I/O, disk, 27, 128, 129
IAM user (Amazon), 148
ICMP probing, 195-199
  extra privileges required for, 195
  failed probe from IPv6 target URL parameter, 197
  icmp module, 197
  pinging localhost, 195
  probing google.com with debug=true ending URL, 197

id labels, 170
idempotency for batch jobs, 58
idle time per second per CPU, 127
ignoring clause, 266
    use with and operator, 275
    use with or operator, 272
    using with group_left, 271
image labels, 171
imports, 44
inc method, 48
increase function, 231, 291
InfluxDB, 209, 211
info metrics, 84, 96
    joining to another metric, 97
ingress, 183
inhibitions, 325, 344
instance labels, 23, 132, 250
    grouping alerts and, 331
    including in sum without, 94
    on clause with, 270
    in recording rule output, 304
    relabeling, 158
    removing using sum without, 230, 231
    service-level batch jobs and, 76
InstanceDown alert, 35
    viewing in Alertmanager, 37
instant rate (see irate function)
instant vector selector, 235, 237
instant vectors, 243, 245
    binary operators applied to, 261
    empty, input to aggregation operator, 252
    empty, returned by binary operator, 266
    gauge-changing functions returning, 293
    matching (see vector matching)
    quantile working across in aggregation
        group, 258
    return by PromQL functions, 277
    {} 0, 261
instrumentation, 41-63, 65, 358
    counters, 43
        counting exceptions, 45
        counting size, 47
    deciding how much to instrument, 59
    deciding what to instrument, 57
        library instrumentation, 59
        service instrumentation, 57
    direct, use by info metric, 97
    example Python program exposing Prome-
        theus metrics, 41

feeding data into non-Prometheus library,
    79
gauges, 47-50
Go program demonstrating, 71
histograms, 52-56
for languages running on JVM, 72
naming metrics, 60-63
Python batch job and pushing its metrics to
    Pushgateway, 77
summary, 50
unit testing, 56
instrumentation labels, 88-93
    child, 91-93
    clashes with target labels, honor_labels and,
        166
    device, fstype, and mountpoint, 249
    metric, 90
    metrics without, working with, 273
    mode, 253
    multiple labels for a metric, 90
iptables command, 134
IPv4, 199
IPv6, 197
irate function, 231, 291

J
Java
    client library, 377
        integration with Dropwizard, 211
    CollectorRegistry.metricFamilySamples, 79
    exposition in client libraries, 72-76
        HttpServer class, 73
        servlet, 74
    JMX (Java Management eXtensions), 210
    labels method, 88
jinja2 templating (Ansible), 141
JMX (Java Management eXtensions), 210
    Dropwizard exposing metrics via, 211
job labels, 24, 78, 144, 250
    k8apiserver, 178
    kubelet, 175
    Kubernetes service names, 180
    relabeling, 158, 163
job:process_cpu_seconds:rate5m, 300
jobs
    duplicate, 163
    getting average response size across all
        instances, 233
job_name, 142

JSON, 143, 215
    use by HTTP SD endpoints, 145
JVM (Java Virtual Machine), 72

K

keep (relabel action), 150, 164
kill -HUP command, 298
kube-dns, 182
Kubelet, 174
Kubernetes, 139, 172-185
    configuration management, 367
    kube-state-metrics, 184
    Prometheus deployment in, alternatives,
        185
    running Prometheus in, 172-174
    service discovery, 174-183
        endpointslice, 177
        ingress, 183
        node, 174
        pod, 182
        service role, 177
kubernetes service, 177
kubernetes_sd_configs, 176

L

labeldrop (relabel action), 165, 171
labelkeep (relabel action), 165, 171
labelmap (relabel action), 159
labels, 4, 87-101, 286, 359
    about, 87
    aggregating, 231
    aggregating with, 93
    alert, 316-318, 319, 321
    for Alertmanager, 325
    changes in, other monitoring system
        exporters, 214
    clashes in and honor_labels, 166
    container, 171
    counting unique label values, 253
    for custom collector metrics, 223
    displaying label values in Grafana, 114
    exposition format, escaping characters in
        values, 82
    Graphite bridge, 79
    grouping key for metrics from push to
        Pushgateway, 78
    instrumentation, 88-93
    instrumentation and target, 88
    limiting by, using selectors, 235

metric names and, 62
naming, 89
not using recording rules to fix bad labels,
    304
in OpenMetrics format, 85
patterns in, 94-98
    breaking changes and labels, 98
    enum, 94
    info, 96
in Prometheus text exposition format, 82
provided for targets by static config, 142
recording rules undoing benefits of, 303
relabeling and, 14
removing any you don't know about with by
    clause, 252
set by Consul, 221
specifying in labels field of rule file, 299
specifying to keep using by clause, 251
target labels, 140
use in exporters, gotchas, 225
when to use, 98-101
labels method, 88, 91
label_join function, 286
label_replace function, 286
last_over_time, 296
latency
    calculating average latency, 56
    latency SLAs and quantiles, 55
    logging for HTTP requests using Grok
        Exporter, 192
    tracking for Hello World program (exam-
        ple), 51
latency_too_high_threshold, 343
le labels, 81, 165, 233
least-squares regression, 293
left-associative (operators), 276
level (recording rule names), 305
libraries
    instrumentation, 59, 65
    in metric names, 62
Linux
    metrics on offer, 125
    profiling of kernel events, 8
lists
    list comprehensions, 54
    produced by service discovery, relabeling,
        161
ln function, 254, 279
load, reducing, 376

loadavg collector, 132
log10 function, 279
log2 function, 279
logging, 9
    categories of, 10
    converting logs to metrics using Grok
        Exporter, 191
logging systems, 10
logical operators, 271-275
    and, 274
    or, 271
    unless, 273
Long Term Support (LTS) releases, 20
long-term storage, 17, 363-365
lowercase (relabel action), 160
LTS (see long-term storage)
LTS (Long Term Support) releases, 20

M
machine roles approach, 96
Management Information Base (MIBs), 210
many-to-many vector matching, 271-275
many-to-one vector matching, 268-271
ManyInstancesDown alert, 312
matchers, 235, 328
    error to use on default route, 328
match_re, 345
math functions, 279-283
    abs, 279
    ceil and floor, 281
    clamp, clamp_max, and clamp_min, 281
    exp, 280
    ln, log2, and log10, 279
    round, 281
    sgn, 282
    sqrt, 280
    trigonometric functions, 282
matrix (see range vector selector)
max, 256
    using with gauges, 230
max_over_time, 240, 295, 302
mean, 254
meminfo collector, 130
memory
    container metrics for, 171
    memory usage graph in Grafana, 110
    results of process_resident_memory_bytes,
        25

usage by Prometheus and Node Exporter,
    30
metadata
    labels for Docker containers, 171
    mapping to targets using relabeling, 149
    node service discovery in Kubernetes, 176
    provided by service discovery, 140
    target discovered by EC2 SD, 148
    viewing for target labels in file SD, 144
metamonitoring, 373
method labels, 93
    removing using sum without, 94
metric (recording rule names), 305
metric family, 90
metrics, 10
    alerts on, 321
    automatic registration with client library, 44
    configuring types to collect with Node
        Exporter, 126
    Consul, 215
    from Consul Exporter, 188
    container, 170
        CPU, 170
    converting logs to with Grok Exporter, 191
    definitions of, 44
    details handled by client libraries, 13
    from exporters, 125
    exposed by Node Exporter, 27, 126
    exposition to Prometheus, 65
    finding expensive metrics, 375
    from Grok Exporter, 192, 193
    from Java client libraries, 73
    from kube-state-metrics, 184
    limits on Prometheus' handling of, 59
    machine-level from other monitoring sys-
        tems, 357
    /metrics page of Prometheus, 23
    /metrics path, 67
    from MySQLd Exporter, 190
    naming, 60-63, 307
    not using recording rules to fix metric
        names, 304
    problems from too much cardinality, 359
    produced by Blackbox probes, 196
    Pushgateway showing from Python batch
        job, 78
    relabeling, 164
    for simple HTTP server in Python (exam-
        ple), 41

suffixes, 49

total and failures, not success and failures, 59

types in OpenMetrics format, 84

types in Prometheus text format, 81

use of in monitoring systems, 303

metrics (pod port), 182

metrics.Samples, 221

MetricsServlet class, 74

metrics_app, 66

metrics_path, 162, 176

metric_relabel_configs, 164, 286, 376

versus relabel_configs, 164

MIBs (Management Information Base), 210

milliseconds, 240

min, 256

Minikube, 177

minute function, 284

minutes, 240

min_over_time, 295

missing series, 287

mmap utility, 70

mode labels, 126, 267, 268

counting without, 253

modulo operator (%), 262

modulus setting, 378

monitoring, 4-11

about, 4

brief history of, 6

categories of, 7

cross-monitoring, 374

metamonitoring, 373

monitoring systems (other), 209-214

about, 209-211

existing instrumentation from, 358

having parsers for Prometheus text format, 80

InfluxDB, 211

Prometheus integration with, 211

StatsD, 212-214

month function, 284

mounted filesystems, metrics on, 127

mountpoint labels, 127, 229, 249

mtime, 137

multiple labels for a metric, 90

multiplication, 1 as identity element for, 272

multiprocess deployments, 214

multiprocess mode with Gunicorn, 68-71

MultiProcessCollector, 68

multiprocess_mode configuration (gauges), 69

MustNewConstMetric function, 13, 220, 221

specifying label values in, 223

MustRegister function, 72

MySQLd Exporter, 189-191

configuring for scraping by Prometheus, 190

downloading and running, 189

metrics from, 190

N

Nagios, 6

Nagios Remote Program Execution (NRPE), 211

name (metrics), 61

name labels, 171, 236

namespace labels, 176

naming labels, 89

naming recording rules, 304-308

NaN (not a number), 46, 272

input to avg operator, 254

return by max and min, 256

sorting and, 288

Native Histograms (experimental feature), 55

natural logarithm, 279

negative equality matcher (!=), 236

negative regular expression matcher (!~), 236

NetBox, 139

netdev collector, 129

network bandwidth, 366

networks, 368-370

New dashboard (Grafana), 111

NewCounter, 72

NewDesc, 219

nice mode, 127

Node Exporter, 27-31, 125-137, 357

configuring Prometheus to monitor, 28

cpu collector, 126

diskstats collector, 128

downloading and installing, 28

filesystem collector, 127

hwmon collector, 130

loadavg collector, 132

meminfo collector, 130

netdev collector, 129

node_filesystem_size_bytes metric, 229

OS collector, 132

pressure collector, 133

running with Consul, 147

running within Docker, 126
stat collector, 131
textfile collector, 134-137
uname collector, 132
version 1.4.0 with 5.18.0 Linux kernel, metrics from, 126
node service discovery, 174
nodename label, 132
node_boot_time_seconds, 131
node_cpu_guest_seconds_total, 127
node_cpu_seconds_total, 126
node_disk_io_time_seconds_total, 129
node_filesystem prefix (metrics), 127
node_filesystem_avail_bytes versus node_filesystem_free_bytes, 128
node_filesystem_files, 128
node_filesystem_files_free, 128
node_filesystem_size_bytes, 249
   aggregation of, 251
node_hwmon prefix (metrics), 130
node_hwmon_sensor_label, 131, 270
   using or operator to substitute missing time series, 272
node_hwmon_temp_celsius, 131
node_intr_total, 131
node_memory_Buffers_bytes, 130
node_memory_Cached_bytes, 130
node_memory_MemAvailable, 130
node_memory_MemFree_bytes, 130
node_memory_MemTotal_bytes, 130
node_network prefix (metrics), 129
node_network_receive_bytes_total, 129
node_network_transmit_bytes_total, 129
node_os_info, 132
node_os_version, 132
node_uname_info, 132
notifications, 311, 326
   Alertmanager notification pipeline, 325
   resolved, 343
   sending only at certain times for an alert, 313
   templating, 320, 337-343
notifiers, 334-336, 337
NRPE Exporter, 211
Nyquist-Shannon sampling theorem, 113

O

OAuth2, 162
observe method, 51

offline-serving systems, 58
offset, 241
on clause, 267, 270, 313
   use with and operator, 275
one-to-one vector matching, 266
online-serving systems, 57
OpenMetrics, 4, 83-86
   metric suffixes, 49
   metric types, 84
   support for format by Python client library, 71
   timestamps, 83, 85
OpenTelemetry (OTel), 7
operational monitoring of computer systems, 5
operations (recording rule names), 305
or operator, 271
OS collector, 132
OTel (OpenTelemetry), 7
outliers, detecting, 255
over_time functions, 302, 315

P

pager storm, 332
PagerDuty notifier, 335
parsers, 80
passwords, 354
path labels, 87, 192
   aggregating away, 93
paths
   HTTP requests broken out by, 87
   options in scrape config, 162
patterns (regular expressions), 152
   use by Grok Exporter, 191
PDUs (Power Distribution Units), 140
pending alerts, 313, 314
percentiles, 53
   median, 25th, and 75th, 257
performance
   aggregate cAdvisor metrics, issue with, 170
   importance for client libraries, 70
   managing, 374-378
      detecting a problem, 375
      finding expensive targets and metrics, 375
      hashmod relabel action, 376
      horizontal sharding, 377
      reducing load, 376
Perl, 214
pgw (see Pushgateway)

PHP, 214
pid (process ID), 298
planning a rollout, 357-358
playbook for alerts, 320
plumbing, 5
pods (Kubernetes), 177
    backing all Kubernetes services except API
        servers, scraping, 179
    service discovery, 182
pod_name labels, 176
population standard deviation, 255
ports, exporter default, 190
POST method (HTTP), 298
post-order tree transversal, 328
Power Distribution Units (PDUs), 140
precedence (operator), 275
predict_linear function, 294
present_over_time, 296
Pressure Stall Information (PSI), 133
ProbeFailing alert, 316
probe_ip_protocol, 197
probe_success, 196
process ID (pid), 298
process library, 62
processes
    blocked or running, metrics on, 131
    long-lived and multithreaded in Prome-
        theus, 214
    moving from checks on individual processes
        to service health as a whole, 7
    multiprocess with Gunicorn, 68-71
process_cpu_seconds_total, 235
process_resident_memory_bytes, 24, 30
    in Grafana graph editor, 110
    graph of in expression browser), 26
process_start_time_seconds, 293
production tags (Consul), 152
profiling, 8
promauto, 72
Prometheus
    about, 3
    architecture, 11-17
    use cases not suited for, 17
Prometheus Community Kubernetes Helm
    Charts, 185
Prometheus Operator project, 185
Prometheus vCloud Director SD, 139
prometheus.Collector interface, 219
prometheus.MustNewConstMetric, 220

prometheus_build_info, 269
prometheus_multiproc_dir environment vari-
    able, 69, 71
prometheus_sd_http_failures_total, 145
promhttp.Handler, 71
PromQL, 4
    about, 229
    aggregation basics, 229-235
        counter, 231
        gauge, 229-231
        histogram, 233-235
        summary, 232
    aggregation operators, 249-259
        avg, 254
        count, 253
        count_values, 258
        group, 255
        grouping, 249-252
        min and max, 256
        quantile, 257
        stddev and stdvar, 255
        sum, 252
        topk and bottomk, 256
    alerting rule, expression for, 33
    binary operators, 261-276
        operator precedence, 275
        vector matching, 265-275
        working with scalars, 261-265
    functions, 277-296
        aggregation over time, 295-296
        changing type, 277
        counters, 289-292
        histogram_quantile, 288
        label, 286
        math functions, 279-283
        missing series, absent and
            absent_over_time, 287
        sorting with sort and sort_desc, 288
        time and date, 283-285
    HTTP API, 242-247
        aligned data, 247
        query, 242-245
        query_range, 245-247
    recording rules, 297-308
        naming, 304-308
        using, 297-300
        when to use, 300-304
    selectors, 235-242
        at (@) modifier, 242

matchers, 235
offset, 241
range vector, 238
subqueries, 240
promtool
check metrics, 83
check rules, 298
proxy_url, 162
pull, 369
push, 369
pushadd_to_gateway, 77
Pushgateway, 76-79
improper use of, 369
target labels, 88
push_to_gateway, 77
Python
application using label for counter metric,
88
client libraries in Python 3, 41
client library, 377
Consul metrics exporter written in, 222
exposition from batch jobs using Pushgateway, 77
exposition in client libraries, 66-71
multiprocess with Gunicorn, 68-71
Twisted, 67
WSGI, 66
exposition using Graphite bridge, 79
unit testing a counter in, 56
python_info expression, 42, 96

Q
quantile operator, 257
quantiles, 52, 233
calculating with histograms, 233
latency SLAs and, 55
limitations of, 55
and percentiles, 53
quantile_over_time, 258, 295
quartiles (1st and 3rd), 257
query, 242-245, 285, 319
query endpoint, 242
query range endpoint, 245
(see also query_range)
query_range, 245-247, 285, 300
gotcha when using with topk and bottomk,
257
using time function with, 283

R
race conditions, 314, 362
radians and degrees, converting between, 282
RAM, 366
range loop, 319
range vector selector, 238
range vectors, 240
composing range vector functions, 302
functions and, 277
gauge-changing functions taking, 293
in recording rules, 301
use with query endpoint, 244
use with query_result, 245
rate function, 26, 30, 44, 51, 113, 231, 232, 234
about, 289
increase function and, 291
irate function and, 292
not using with a counter, 253
offset and, 241
use with range vectors, 238
using at (@) modifier with, 242
using before sum with counters, 253
using first for buckets exposed by histogram
metric type, 289
using to determine if resources are overloaded, 134
using with max_over_time, 240
using with sum, 302
rate, errors, and duration (RED method), 57
ratio, calculating for exceptions, 46
RE2 engine for regular expressions, 152
read_recent: true, 378
receivers, 326
backend-ticket, 329
configuring, 334-344
notification templates, 337-343
resolved notifications, 343
record field, 312
recording rules, 16, 297-308, 312
detecting bad rules with promtool check
rules, 298
naming, 304-308
level, metric, and operations, 305
using, 297-300
when to use, 300-304
composing range vector functions, 302
how not to use recording rules, 303
reducing cardinality, 300
rules for APIs, 302

RED method (rate, errors, duration), 57
refresh interval menu (Grafana), 111
region labels, 317, 323, 331
    in Slack, 337
registry, 44, 65
    custom collector registered with default registry, 222
    custom registry for multiprocess exposition with Gunicorn, 68
    custom registry for Python client library, 77
    metrics pushed to Graphite using a bridge, 79
    registration with Go client library, 72
Registry.Gather, 79
regression, 293
regular expression matcher (=~), 236
regular expressions
    expect regex failing in TCP probe, 200
    matchers, 235, 328
    patterns based on, use by Grok Exporter, 192
    quick primer on, 152
    RE2 engine for, 152
    use in replace relabel action, 154
    using to match targets in relabeling, 150
relabeling, 14, 149-162, 322
    alert_relabel_configs, 323
    automatic deduplication with, 158
    choosing what to scrape, 150-153
    hashmod action, 376
    labeldrop and labelkeep actions, 165
    metrics, using metric_relabel_configs, 164
    providing URL parameters for Blackbox exporters in, 205
    support by remote write, 364
    using to add labels from Kubernetes service or pod metadata, 181
    using to override scrape config settings, 163
    using to specify target labels, 153-162
        changing case, 160
        job, instance, and __address__, 158
        labelmap action, 159
        lists, 161
        replace action, 154
relabel_configs, 151
    for Kubernetes API server scrapes, 178
    versus metric_relabel_configs, 164
reliability, 370
remote read, 364, 378

remote write, 364
remote write endpoint, 364
rename system call, 136, 145
repeat_interval, 333
repetition of notifications, 326, 332
replace (relabel action), 154
reporting_enabled setting, 104
request logs, 10
resets function, 292
resident set size (RSS), 171
resolved notifications, 343
resource pressure for CPU, memory, and I/O, 133
restarts, 292
resultType
    matrix, 244
    scalar, 244
    vector, 243
reverse proxy, 354
    running Prometheus behind, 369
root user, 128
round function, 281
routes field, 327
routing, 326
routing tree, 326
    configuring for Alertmanager, 327-334
        grouping, 330
        throttling and repetition, 332
    visual editor for, 330
RSS (resident set size), 171
rule files, 297, 367
    example, 298
Rules status page (Prometheus), 299
rule_files field, 298
running Prometheus, 19-23, 365
    (see also deploying Prometheus)
    configuration, 21
    expression browser, 21
    requirements, 19

S

SaaS (software as a service) monitoring systems, 210
sample standard deviation, 255
sample_limit, 377
sampling
    fundamental limitation of, 113
    not catching every possible change, 293
    for tracing, 9

scalar function, 278
scalars, 244
    conversion to instant vector, 245
    working with, 261-265
        arithmetic operators, 261-263
        comparison operators, 263-265
        trigonometric operator atan2, 263
scaling Prometheus, 359, 362
scheme (scrape config), 162, 175
scrape errors, 32
scraper labels, 378
scrape_configs, 142
    adapting for TLS, 352
    for cgroup scraping with cAdvisor, 170
    for Kubernetes API servers, 177
    Prometheus scraping Consul Exporter, 188
    showing several available options, 162
scrape_interval, 163, 299, 377
scrape_samples_post_metric_relabeling, 377
scrape_timeout, 163
scraping, 14, 23, 362
    catching failed scrapes in Blackbox exporter, 316
    choosing which targets to scrape in relabeling, 150-153
    configuring Prometheus to scrape itself using Basic Authentication, 355
    in custom exporters, 226
    how to scrape, 162-167
        label clashes and honor_labels, 166
        labeldrop and labelkeep, 165
        metric_relabel_configs, 164
    Kubelet embedded cAdvisor, 176
    Prometheus scraping MySQLd Exporter, 190
    prometheus.yml to scrape Grok Exporter, 193
    prometheus.yml to scrape InfluxDB Exporter, 212
    scraping Prometheus servers, 377
    scraping subset of targets, 376
SD (see service discovery)
seconds, 240
sectors, 129
selectors, 235-242
    at (@) modifier, 242
    matchers, 235
    offset modifier, 241
    range vector, 238

subqueries, 240
send_resolved field, 343
sensor labels, 131, 270, 272
sensors command, 130
server-side security, 351, 369
    advanced TLS options, 353
    enabling Basic Authentication, 354
    enabling TLS, 351-353
    security features from Prometheus, 351
service discovery, 4, 14, 139-167
    how to scrape, 162-167
        label clashes and honor_labels, 166
        metric_relabel_configs, 164
    Kubernetes, 174-183
    mechanisms, 140-148
        Consul, 146
        EC2, 148-148
        file SD, 142-145
        HTTP SD, 145
        static, 141
        top-down versus bottom-up, 141
    problems in, 375
    relabeling, 149-162
        choosing what to scrape, 150-153
        using for target labels, 153-162
service labels, 317
services
    administering, manual approach to, 6
    instrumentation, 57
    service role in Kubernetes, 177
servlets, 74
set method, 48
sets, 95
set_function method, 50
severity labels, 316, 327, 345
sgn function, 282
shard labels, 79
SIGHUP signal, 298, 367
SIGTERM signal, 367
silences, 325
silencing alerts, 325
simple linear regression, 293
simpleclient (Java), 72
single point of failure (SPOF), 371
size, counting, 47
Slack
    customized message, 341
    message with region and environment, 338
    PagerDuty integration with, 335

slack_configs, region and env labels in, 337
SMART metrics, 134
smartctl command, 134
smoothing factor, 295
SMPT, 35
snake case for metric names, 61
SNMP, 210
SNMP-style exporters, 194, 210, 211
    (see also Blackbox exporters)
    default registry and, 222
software as a service (SaaS) monitoring sys-
    tems, 210
sort function, 288
sort_desc function, 288
    using by clause, 251
source_labels, 150
source_match, 345
sqrt function, 280
SSH, 199
ssh_banner module, 200
stability guarantees, Prometheus versions, 20
stale markers, 237
staleness, 237
    range vectors and, 239
    for resolved alerts, 313
stalled metrics, 134
standard deviation, 255
    (see also stddev)
standard variance, 256
    (see also stdvar)
start, 247
start function, 242
start time, 245
start_http_server, 66
stat collector, 131
Stat panel, 113-114
State timeline panel, 117
StateSets, 84
statfs system call, 127
static config service discovery, 141
static typing (PromQL), 277
static_configs, 142, 287
StatsD, 210, 212-214
StatsD Exporter, 358
stddev, 255
stddev_over_time, 295
stdvar, 256
stdvar_over_time, 295
step, 245, 247

maximum number for query_range, 247
storage, 15
    long-term, 17, 363-365
storage layer, problem in, 375
string type, 261
subqueries, 240, 302
suffixes (metrics), 49, 61
sum, 98, 100, 254
    about, 252
    by clause, 94, 251
        using empty by or omitting by, 252
    using in counter aggregation, 231
    using in histogram of aggregates, 234
    using rate before, 302
    using with gauges, 229
    using with summary, 232
    without clause, 93, 95, 250
summary, 50
    aggregating, 232
    example in Prometheus text exposition for-
        mat, 82
    metrics.Sample, 221
    text exposition format for, 81
    using rate before sum on, 253
sum_over_time, 295
symptoms, alerting on, 321, 331, 345
systemd, 170

T

table exceptions, 99
Table panel, 115
target labels, 88, 140, 153-162
    clashes in and honor_labels, 166
    hierarchy of, 154
    instance target label, 132
    job and instance, 250
    metadata for, in file SD, 144
    using relabeling to specify
        case, 160
        job, instance, and __address__, 158
        labelmap action, 159
        lists, 161
        replace action, 154
    variances in, 250
targets
    creating in static config service discovery,
        141
    discovered by EC2, 148
    for each individual application instance, 152

finding expensive targets, 375
in HTTP service discovery, 145
mapping from metadata using relabeling, 149
provided by Consul service discovery, 146
scraping subset of, 376
spotting metric missing from target using unless, 274
Targets page, 22
scrape errors on, 32
showing Prometheus and Node Exporter, 29
target_match, 345
TCP probing, 199-201
checking if local SSH server is listening on port 22, 199
ssh_banner module, 200
tcp_connect module, 200
tcp_connect_tls, 200
tcpdump, 8
team labels, 144, 317
EC2 instances, 152
removing using replace relabel action, 156
using defaults to remove succinctly, 157
using replace relabel action with, 154
teams
alerts grouped by, 331
routing alerts and notifications to, 328
templating
alerts, 318-321
Go templating language, 104
of notifications by Alertmanager, 337-343
template variables in Grafana, 118
using Ansible jinja2 to create targets for Node Exporter, 141
text format (Prometheus), 4, 80
(see also exposition formats)
parsers for, 80
textfile collector, 134-137
timestamps, 137
using, 135
thread and worker pools, instrumentation, 59
throttling notifications, 326, 332
time, 49, 61
context manager and function decorator, 52
durations in Prometheus as used in PromQL, 240
precision in Prometheus, 52
time controls in Grafana, 111
time URL parameter, 243

tracking latency, 51
time and date functions, 283-285
time function, 283
time series, 90
finding how many have same name, 251
number of, or cardinality, 99
total of rest of metric, avoiding, 98
Time series panel, 109-113
time controls, 111
timers, 216
timestamp function, 285
timestamps
aligning with start time and step, 246
exporters exposing, staleness and, 238
InfluxDB and, 212
in OpenMetrics format, 85
in Prometheus text exposition format, 82
returned by instant vector selector, 237
textfile collector and, 137
Unix, use of @ modifier with, 242
TLS, 354
advanced options, 353
enabling, 351-353
tcp probe connecting via, 200
TLS certificates, 175
TLS client authentication, 162
TLS/SSL certificate expiring, 201
tls_config, 176
tls_server_config, 353
__tmp prefix for labels, 162
topk operator, 242, 256
tracing, 9
transaction logs, 10
trend factor, 295
trending, 5
trigonometric functions, 282
trigonometric operators, 263
Twisted, 67
TYPE (metrics), 81, 84
types
changing, 277
static typing in PromQL, 277

U
uberagent, 125
uname collector, 132
unary operators, 261
UNIT metadata (metrics), 84
unit tests for instrumentation, 56

units
    base units in Prometheus, 49
    in metric names, 50, 61
    quantiles and percentiles, 53
Unix
    epoch, 82, 85
    filesystems, 128
    Note Exporter exposing metrics on, 27
    time, 49
unless operator, 273
untyped (metric type), 81
UntypedValue, 220
up, 23, 29, 32, 270
    added by Prometheus after each scrape, 273
    adding version label from python_info to
        all, 97
    consul_up, 188
    displaying up metrics in Grafana State time-
        line panel, 117
    failed scrapes and, 316
uppercase (relabel action), 160
URL parameters (scrape config), 162
USE method (utilization, saturation, and
    errors), 58
user mode, 127
UTC (Coordinated Universal Time), 284
UTF-8 encoding, 82
    label values, 89

V

vector function, 278
vector matching, 265-275
    many-to-many and logical operators,
        271-275
    many-to-one and group_left, 268-271
    one-to-one, 266
vectors, 235
    (see also instant vector selector)

version labels, 97, 270
versions of Prometheus, 20
vertical sharding, 359, 377
Vim, 15

W

waiting metrics, 134
wall of graphs, avoiding, 109
web configuration files, 352
    launching Prometheus with, 352
web interface (Alertmanager), 345
Web Server Gateway Interface (WSGI), 66
--web.enable-lifecycle flag, 298, 367
--web.external-url flag, 369
--web.route-prefix flag, 369
webhook notifier, 334, 336, 337
webhook receiver, 336
    written in Python 3, 337
weeks, 240
Windows Exporter, 125
WithLabelValues, 88
without clause, 250
    avg without, 254, 312
    by clause versus, 251
    count without, 253
    quantile without, 257
    sum without, 93, 250
worker pools, instrumentation, 59
write_relabel_configs, 364
writing exporters (see exporters)
WSGI (Web Server Gateway Interface), 66

Y

YAML, 21, 143
    multiline strings in, 300
year function, 278, 284
years, 240

Ingram Content Group UK Ltd.
Milton Keynes UK
UKHW030025070423
419775UK00004B/12